Wittgenstein and Psychology

Wittgenstein made use of his insights into the nature and powers of language to search out the source of conceptual confusions in the foundations of mathematics and in philosophy of psychology. Once he has established the use account of language, his *Philosophical Investigations* opens out into an extensive coverage of psychological phenomena and the concepts with which we identify and manage them.

In this book Harré and Tissaw display Wittgenstein's analysis of the 'grammar' of the most important of these concepts in a systematic and accessible way. Previous studies of the psychological aspects of Wittgenstein's writings, admirable as exegeses of his thought, have paid little attention to the relevant psychology. Here, the 'adjacent' theories and empirical investigations from mainstream psychology have been described in sufficient detail to show how Wittgenstein's work impinges on psychology as it has actually been practised. In using this book, philosophers will be able to get a sense of the relevance of Wittgenstein's philosophical psychology to the development of psychology as a science. Psychologists will be able to see how to use Wittgenstein's insights to enrich and discipline their attempts to gain an understanding of human thinking, feeling, acting and perceiving, the domain of psychology as science.

The book includes an historical overview of the sources of Wittgenstein's philosophy in the Vienna of the last years of Austro-Hungary, as well as a brief presentation of the main themes of his *Tractatus Logico-Philosophicus* as it anticipated computational models of cognition. Student use is emphasized with frequent summaries and self-test questionnaires.

Wittgenstein and Psychology

A Practical Guide

Rom Harré

Linacre College, Oxford, Georgetown and American Universities

Michael A. Tissaw

SUNY, Potsdam, New York, USA

Routledge
Taylor & Francis Group

LONDON AND NEW YORK

First published 2005 by Ashgate Publishing

Reissued 2018 by Routledge
2 Park Square, Milton Park, Abingdon, Oxon OX14 4RN
605 Third Avenue, New York, NY 10017

First issued in paperback 2021

Routledge is an imprint of the Taylor & Francis Group, an informa business

© Rom Harré and Michael A. Tissaw, 2005

Rom Harré and Michael A. Tissaw have asserted their moral right under the Copyright, Designs and Patents Act, 1988, to be identified as the authors of this volume.

Typeset in Times New Roman by Manton Typesetters, Louth, Lincolnshire, UK.

A Library of Congress record exists under LC control number: 2004021054

Notice:
Product or corporate names may be trademarks or registered trademarks, and are used only for identification and explanation without intent to infringe.

Publisher's Note
The publisher has gone to great lengths to ensure the quality of this reprint but points out that some imperfections in the original copies may be apparent.

Disclaimer
The publisher has made every effort to trace copyright holders and welcomes correspondence from those they have been unable to contact.

ISBN 13: 978-0-815-39904-9 (hbk)
ISBN 13: 978-1-351-14300-4 (ebk)
ISBN 13: 978-1-138-35862-1 (pbk)

DOI: 10.4324/9781351143004

Contents

Preface

There is no question that scientific research has contributed substantially to our understanding of human psychology. That there should be such a discipline is of the greatest importance. Yet a satisfactory, coherent and uncontentious understanding of human thinking, acting, feeling and perceiving continues to elude the practitioners of 'scientific psychology' and the inadequacy of what has been achieved is evident in the comparatively rare occurrences in which the 'findings' of academic scientific research are put to use by psychiatrists, educationalists and other practical people. Diagnoses of the failure to establish a coherent and progressive psychology along the lines of the natural sciences have focused on the many ways that the nature of human psychology, as a domain of phenomena, precludes any simple transfer of methods from the natural sciences. How, then, should a systematic psychological discipline be (re)created? This is surely as much a question for philosophers as it is for psychologists.

An important preliminary to a richer psychology, as well as an essential part of the philosophy of mind, is the process of becoming sensitive to some of the many kinds of intellectual illusion that bedevil attempts to understand how human beings think and feel, and why they say and do the things they say and do. Wittgenstein is an unrivalled guide through the labyrinth of misleading pictures and intellectual illusions to which we all are prone, particularly when we try to think clearly about the topics that comprise the field of psychology.

Wittgenstein's two major works, the *Tractatus Logico-Philosophicus* (1921) and *Philosophical Investigations* (1953), are not psychology texts *per se*. However, a good grasp of the doctrines of the *Tractatus* helps one to appreciate the sources and limitations of attempts to develop a computational psychology, inspired by Alan Turing's (1950) brain-to-computer analogy. Wittgenstein eventually abandoned the logicism of the *Tractatus* in favor of a new kind of investigation into the illusions and errors endemic to the study of mind. He believed we could trace many of these illusions and errors to misunderstandings of the language we ordinarily employ to manage our lives. Philosophers in particular are prone to errors that have their origins in misunderstandings of language, and none more so than those who reflect on the topics comprising the subject matter of psychology. Psychologists too are not immune from philosophical errors. So much is evident in past and current psychological theorizing and research. A study of Wittgenstein's writings can help to guard against these errors. Our exposition of Wittgenstein's insights as essential preliminaries to a scientific psychology is intended both as a textbook for courses in the philosophy of mind, as well as for the growing number of courses in which psychology students are introduced to the writings of Wittgenstein. Though he wrote extensively on topics relevant to the philosophy of mind and the foundations of psychology, for practical reasons we have confined ourselves to the *Philosophical Investigations* as a course reader.

Wittgenstein's writings are notoriously difficult to read and often are misunderstood. The value of a course on 'Wittgenstein and Psychology' depends on the ease with which a good understanding of some important topics can be reached by an undergraduate class. Our aim in this project has been to achieve clarity and simplicity of exposition without sacrificing too much in the way of depth. Our text owes a good deal to the experiences we have both had in several years of teaching Wittgenstein at SUNY Binghamton and Potsdam, and Georgetown and American Universities. We thank our students for their many helpful suggestions. Our friend at Georgetown University, Ali Moghaddam, has given invaluable assistance in critically reading drafts of several difficult chapters.

Rom Harré
Michael A. Tissaw
Oxford, Washington, DC, and Potsdam, NY, October 2003

Introduction

As a way of briefly conveying the purposes and limitations of this book, it is important to position it within the wider context of Wittgenstein scholarship. Our primary purpose is to encourage discussion and use of Wittgenstein's ideas in psychology (and perhaps other of the social and behavioral sciences) while at the same time presenting a flavor of his writings more or less in keeping with the 'spirit' of his life-work. But this is made problematic by legitimate concerns expressed about the past and present state of Wittgenstein scholarship. The most common and pressing of these is that Wittgenstein's 'broken text' or 'aphoristic' style of exposition encourages interpreters of his writings to take individual remarks (and even parts of remarks) out of their wider context for dubious purposes. David Stern (1996), for example, points out that by making eclectic use of selected passages outside the context of wider, sustained arguments, Wittgenstein's 'real views' can be used 'to provide support for almost any view one looks for. This often leads to interpretations that provide their authors with an opportunity to find their own preconceptions at work in Wittgenstein's philosophy' (pp. 444–5). What, then, does this say about the prospect of our offering a 'sufficient' or 'accurate' account of Wittgenstein in a book of this sort?

Our answer is that this book is conceived and constructed in light of a lengthy evolution in thinking and experience about how to teach Wittgenstein to undergraduate students over the course of a single semester. We quote individual remarks and even sections of remarks throughout, and we present remarks from wider arguments by Wittgenstein in an order quite different from how they are presented, say, in the *Investigations*. Also, we occasionally mix remarks from two or more works. This is simply 'our way' of presenting Wittgenstein's ideas to students in a way that reveals the applicability of his insights to topics in psychology. This is, as we have called it, a 'practical guide.' Certain patterns in the overall thrust of Wittgenstein's *Investigations* emerge, however gradually, as 'the course' goes on. But we emphasize that understanding Wittgenstein is a daunting undertaking and is, in our view, a life-long project.

From Part Two, this book should be read in concert with a reading of the *Investigations*, matched with sections specified in chapter titles. The remarks by Wittgenstein we have chosen for exposition and comment have been taken almost exclusively from that text. (Enthusiasts will, no doubt, wish to consult the *Remarks of the Foundations of Psychology*, but that text would be unmanageable as a class reader.) For those reading this book independently – and for motivated students – we suggest consultation with the excellent exegetical guides by Baker and Hacker (1980, 1985) and Hacker (1993a, 1993b, 1996).

Several features have been included in this book to aid understanding and retention of material, including a selection of 'Topics introduced' at the beginning of each chapter, suggestions for 'Further reading' at the end of each chapter, and 'Learning point' summaries within chapters. Also, there are 'Self-tests' at the end of each of the three parts and a glossary of important 'Wittgensteinian' terms.

In Part One, Chapter 1, we introduce the idea that, to a significant extent, psychology has been and is mired in conceptual problems that militate against its full development as a science. Wittgenstein's studies of the ways we use psychological concepts may serve to resolve at least some of these difficulties. But to understand the writings of Wittgenstein it is necessary to have some idea of his life and the influences that bore upon him. It was in the Vienna of his youth that he acquired some of the leading ideas that stayed with him through many turns and shifts of his subsequent thought. Chapter 2 provides a sketch of his life and describes the work of some of the people in Wittgenstein's Vienna who influenced him, in particular Karl Kraus. We discuss other influences as well, including Wittgenstein's teacher at Cambridge, Bertrand Russell, and especially the physicists Heinrich Hertz and Ludwig Boltzmann, whose views were integral to shaping the *Tractatus*.

In Chapter 3 we summarize the main themes of the *Tractatus* while suggesting how, in both direct and indirect ways, the idea of constructing computational models of cognition – subsequent to the technical success of artificial intelligence research – owes a great deal to the themes that occupied Wittgenstein's early thought. By this point we will have learned, to a limited extent, why Wittgenstein's enthusiasm for a 'perfect language,' so to speak, in the tradition of logical positivism, was undermined. But his genius is nowhere more manifest than in his repudiation of the formal themes of his great logical edifice, the *Tractatus*. We believe the transition from his earlier to his later philosophy is of great significance for psychology, and we take up his new insights in Part Two, 'Insights.'

Chapter 4 provides an account of Wittgenstein's 'later' views on meaning in the initial sections of the *Investigations* and expands on applications of these to developmental psychology. Students of psychology and psychologists interested in human development should be aware that, although we do not provide a chapter specifically devoted to conceptual issues in developmental psychology, the implications of Wittgenstein's ideas for developmental theory and research are discussed at several points throughout the final two-thirds of this book. More extensive applications of Wittgenstein's thinking to developmental psychology are provided by Erneling (1993) and in Chapman and Dixon (1987).

Chapter 5, on skills and abilities, expands upon a number of themes encountered in subsequent chapters that bear on contemporary perspectives in psychology. Among these are challenges to accounts of skills and abilities that depend primarily on reference to cognitive states and processes (mentalism) and/or implicitly or explicitly stated 'causes.' As discussed, both of these forms of account fall victim to what we call 'explanatory regresses.' The chapter ends with a summary of

Wittgenstein's lengthy and detailed remarks on the cognitive skill of reading, which serves to reinforce the pitfalls of mentalist and causal accounts of cognitive skills and abilities.

Conclusions we can draw from Wittgenstein's remarks on rules and rule-following, presented in Chapter 6, are of the utmost importance for psychologists, particularly those who believe, roughly, that human mental life is governed by internal rules laid out, in some form, within the recesses of the mind/brain. Again, Wittgenstein's analysis of rules that guide (or constitute?) human normative action poses serious challenges to causal, mentalistic and computationalist perspectives. A major goal of this chapter is to conceptualize human normative action in such a way that we can speak sensibly about natural regularities and training, contingencies, causes and standards of correctness. Certain bases for normative action certainly will have cross-cultural implications.

Having encountered Wittgenstein's views on meaning, skills and abilities, and rule-following, we will be ready to address his later philosophical method in Chapter 7. At first blush, nothing could seem more remote from scientific psychology than a discussion of 'philosophical method.' But in fact understanding the method itself – its whys, 'hows' and wherefores – paves the way for realizing its potential as a prophylaxis against conceptual confusion in scientific psychological theorizing and research. Also, gaining some insight on Wittgenstein's method will prove beneficial in following the various lines of argument in the six chapters comprising Part Three.

Part Three is entitled 'Applications' for two reasons. First, its chapters are geared more directly toward conveying Wittgenstein's overall approach to psychological concepts largely in light of his analysis of meaning from the opening remarks of the *Investigations*. Second, Wittgenstein's analyses are applied more directly to theoretical perspectives and research in psychology. This is especially the case in Chapters 8 (on thinking and understanding), 10 (on anticipating and remembering), 12 (on the emotions), and 13 (on color and perception concepts). Of course in all of the chapters of Part Three we continue to encounter already established themes, such as the temptation to explain various forms of experience and thought on causes and 'inner' physiological processes. However, at various points in these chapters we see Wittgenstein making fine distinctions in word use toward exposing conceptual confusions that hinder research and theorizing in many branches of psychology.

Part One
ORIGINS

Contemporary psychology: its problems and needs

> The confusion and barrenness of psychology is not to be
> explained by calling it a 'young science'; its state is not
> comparable with that of physics, for instance, in its beginnings
> ... For in psychology there are experimental methods and
> *conceptual confusion* ... The existence of experimental method
> makes us think we have the means of solving the problems
> which trouble us; though problem and method passing one
> another by.
>
> Wittgenstein, *Philosophical Investigations* II, xiv, p. 232

Topics introduced: the nature of philosophy; causal concepts; the nature of science as classifying and explaining; needs of a scientific psychology; positivism; empiricism; ontology; Cartesianism; behaviorism; cognitivism; causal and normative explanations; discursive and cultural psychology

As indicated in our Preface, this book is based on the need, still very much alive, for psychology to find a plausible and coherent paradigm within which to conduct and interpret research. To whom shall we turn for enlightenment? We believe that invaluable insights can be found in the philosophy of psychology, and, in particular, the writings of Ludwig Wittgenstein. Before we undertake our exposition of the relevant topics, we need to clarify, in preliminary fashion, what we mean by 'philosophy' in this context. At later points – particularly in Chapter 7 – we will examine carefully Wittgenstein's conception of philosophy and the nature of philosophical problems.

'Philosophy'

Every human practice depends on certain taken-for-granted principles and presumptions as to the material and social contexts in which it occurs. Furthermore, these practices and our understanding of them presuppose the ability to use a system (or systems) of concepts. Philosophy, in our sense, has much to do with the critical study of such presuppositions. While it often may be that philosophers can do little more than catalogue what has been taken for granted in the sciences and other human endeavors (e.g. jurisprudence), often bringing to light presuppositions can lead to criticism and even rejection of some central principles taken for granted by a community. This has been particularly true of attempts to develop a science of human thinking, feeling, acting and perceiving – the purported domains of scientific psychology. We will find much that will help us in the project of setting scientific psychology on a sound footing through a critical review of its presuppositions in the writings of Wittgenstein.

In addition to taken-for-granted principles, every human practice depends on two main kinds of presuppositions. First, there are *matters of fact* that, rightly or wrongly, we take for granted. Philosophers can help us to recognize these, but of course the critical assessment of such presuppositions calls for scientific appraisal when appropriate. Second, there are *matters of meaning*. What do we presuppose about the meanings and interrelations of concepts we are using in some inquiry? These may be put to work in identifying and classifying phenomena, or in putting together explanations of why things are as they seem to be. The revealing and critical assessment of conceptual presuppositions is the work of philosophy. That is one of its tasks.

Here is an example of each kind of presupposition, taken from the natural sciences. As scientists, paleontologists make all sorts of inferences about the nature of animals and plants, some of which have been preserved as fossils. In order to make these inferences, paleontologists must presuppose that the processes described by the laws of nature have, as a matter of fact, remained the same for eons – for example, since before the Jurassic era to the present day. In applying the Darwinian theory of natural selection to explain the fossil record, paleontologists presuppose that these creatures came into being by causal processes involving chemical reactions and physical regularities more or less as they are seen today.

For conceptual presuppositions we need look no further than the implications of the word 'evolution.' Darwin was careful to point out that the usual implication of 'improvement,' in accordance with some enduring standard, was not to be included as part of his theory of natural selection. At most we could say that the members of a later population were better adapted to life in a certain environment than the population it succeeded. The development of organic beings had no long-term goal. Which presupposition should we choose – improvement or adaptation? That is not a scientific question.

The same considerations obtain in the case of other human practices, such as making moral judgments. Many moral judgments depend on the presupposition that all people and many animals can be killed and that many display signs of fear and pain. That is a matter of fact, in the sense that we can investigate the contexts in which humans and/or animals display fear or pain. However, in making decisions as to what persons should do in specific contexts, what do we man by 'acting for the best'? Philosophers have argued about the meaning of moral goodness. Is it a matter of doing one's duty, or is it a matter of trying to assess what would bring about the greatest happiness of the greatest number of people? No scientific study of human beings could ever settle a question of this sort. Answering the question is a matter for philosophical discussion and debate.

Our study program will be directed toward learning how to bring out and critically assess the factual and conceptual presuppositions of the science of psychology, or, rather, one should say the various attempts that have been made to create such a science.

Why Wittgenstein?

Many philosophers have expressed interest in the foundations of psychology, at least since the time of Aristotle at around 385 BC. We are turning to the writings of Wittgenstein because in the twentieth century a new way of looking at human psychology came to the fore. A number of psychologists, anthropologists, communication theorists and so on pointed out the enormous importance that language plays in human life, not least as the main tool with which human beings think and coordinate their actions. Of course, it is not the only tool. Language is one among a variety of systems of objects-with-meanings, or symbols, that we put to use. For example, there are flags, models, pictures, gestures and so on that play a role in our lives because of how we use them and what we take them *to mean*.

What do we presuppose in making use of meaningful symbols with which to think and act? Wittgenstein was a leading figure in developing two very different accounts of what symbols mean, and consequently of what the basis of thinking might be. Roughly, his first attempt was based on the presupposition that all words, except those expressing grammatical structure, are names. So what a word means is the object it signifies. His development of this idea had implications for accounts of cognition as a kind of computation. Later in life he lost faith in this project almost completely. Why? One reason is that he realized the presupposition which underlay it – that all words are names – was mistaken. Adopting this 'false picture' distorted his and others' understanding of language and therefore of cognition in general. He returned to the task of exploring the foundations of psychology by considering very different presuppositions about language and meaning – namely, that words are tools for accomplishing all sorts of tasks. This insight has developed into an account of cognition-as-discourse.

In the course of his later studies he developed a method for identifying the kinds of mistakes about words and their meanings that lead people – including the early Wittgenstein – astray. He thought that philosophers, psychologists and mathematicians were particularly prone to fall into linguistic traps. He likened them to flies trapped in a fly-bottle. These very intelligent people, with their good intentions, buzz around hopelessly inside the bottle, never finding their way out of its opening. Wittgenstein hoped his method would 'shew the fly the way out of the fly-bottle.' In essence, his method consists in making very careful studies of the way key words are actually used and identifying the false comparisons that led to mistakes. He characterized his method as 'a surview' of relevant language. We will learn how to do this for ourselves by following some of his more important studies.

The outcome of some of these inquiries into the uses of words has helped resolve puzzles and problems that have stood in the way of fruitful development in psychology. For example, behaviorism still exercises an influence on the thought of psychologists. By following Wittgenstein's work on how we come to be able to understand what other people tell us about their private feelings, their pains and itches, we come to see that there is nothing scientifically wrong with asking people how and what they feel and incorporating the subjective states of others as data in psychological research. Behaviorism was based, in part, on mistakes about language. It is important to add that these mistakes and the eventual 'downfall' of behaviorism as a dominant paradigm in psychology have never precluded that certain behavioral principles and methods, applied in certain contexts, would not be useful.

The most important aspect of Wittgenstein's psychologically oriented studies is his emphasis on the general mistake of using causal concepts in describing and explaining psychological phenomena. Improper use of causal concepts occurs at two levels. At one level it is a mistake, for example, to think of a person's plans as causing the behavior realized from those plans. Rules do not cause rule-following behavior. Rather, the active person is the causal agent who *uses* plans and rules in the management of behavior, be it public action or private thought. At another level, it is a mistake to follow the pattern of the natural sciences and invent hypotheses of unobservable mental mechanisms that intervene between the relevant aspects of the situations in which a person thinks, feels, or acts. When we describe a person using words to work out who or what to blame for something, we do all that there is to be done. There is no further role for mental concepts in explaining the subsequent judgment that person makes by hypothesizing a hidden cognitive function. This is the 'mentalism' that Wittgenstein is concerned to combat at every stage of his later philosophical investigations of psychological concepts.

Learning point: philosophy and science

1. *What is philosophy?*

    (a) It involves the bringing out and critical study of *presuppositions* of human practices.
    (b) Every human practice depends on two kinds of presupposition
        (i)   Factual: facts and laws are assumed in carrying out the practice. We ask whether the factual presuppositions are true or false, well or poorly supported.
        (ii) Conceptual: we fix the meanings of concepts used in practice. We ask what the relevant concepts mean in practice, whether these meanings are coherent, and whether they are consistent with one another.

2. *The work of philosophers is the critical study of conceptual presuppositions*

    (a) Philosophy of natural science
        (i)   Factual: we presuppose the 'uniformity of nature' (that the laws of nature are the same at all times and places).
        (ii) Conceptual: we could presuppose, for example, that 'evolution' means 'improvement according to a universal standard' or 'better adapted to a particular local environment.' Experiments cannot be used to choose between these alternatives.

(b)   *Moral philosophy*
   (i)   Factual: we presuppose that all people and some animals can suffer pain.
   (ii) Conceptual: we presuppose, for example, that 'good' means 'dutiful.' Someone else might argue that 'good' means 'the greatest happiness of the greatest number.'

In studying philosophy of psychology we will be concerned with the *conceptual presuppositions* of the project of trying to set up a 'scientific' psychology.

3.   *What does Wittgenstein contribute to our attempts to understand human activities?*
   His thought and writings pertain to – and even may be viewed as integral to – the development of *two* major paradigms currently in use in psychology.

   (a)   The first is cognitive psychology as a development of *logic*, a position he rejected later on grounds that it involved a naïve idea of language.
   (b)   The second is discursive psychology, or the study of the *management of meanings* according to local rules. This perspective is connected with his later philosophy.
   (c)   Importantly, he developed a *method* for bringing to light fallacies and errors that come from misunderstandings of how language works, to which psychologists, mathematicians and philosophers are particularly prone.
   (d)   Taking all of this together, he provided insight as to the origins (in language use) of long-standing philosophical problems that have troubled psychology throughout the course of its history, modern or otherwise.
   (e)   In our view, Wittgenstein's most important contribution to psychology as a science was his demolition, case by case, of the mentalism that led to hypotheses of redundant mental mechanisms.

Characteristics of science and the search for a scientific psychology

What is needed for any discipline to emulate the established sciences such as physics and biology? To answer this question we must turn to some observations from the philosophy of natural science to summarize a few components that are part of any mature scientific practice. Our very brief set of observations focuses on the effort to systematically classify and explain phenomena, including the construction of explanatory models. Then we turn to the question of whether psychology could be cloned from the natural sciences.

Systems for classifying and explaining phenomena

There must be a system for classifying the concepts of a natural science, and the system should be 'true' to the nature of the phenomena to which those concepts are applied. This demand calls for an analysis of the nature of the phenomena and for the refining the concepts with which to build a suitable taxonomy. So, for example, until the distinction between elements and compounds was well understood, there was no stable chemical taxonomy grounded in the phenomena studied by would-be chemists. Now we have the periodic table of the elements and a systematic use of the terminology for describing and classifying compounds. According to this system, sodium and chlorine are distinct elements, and the simplest compound containing them is 'sodium chloride.'

In similar fashion, constructing a scientific psychology requires a powerful way of classifying psychological phenomena. This no simple task, and because psychology is a discipline of competing theoretical perspectives, there have been and continue to be competing classifications of psychological phenomena. Moreover, every classification system in psychology involves numerous presuppositions that need to be examined.

On the other hand, there must be a system of well-grounded ways of developing a conceptual system (or systems) for describing the real or hypothetical processes by which the relevant phenomena are brought into existence, work, interact and so on. In other words, we need to explain. So chemists presuppose that differences in material substances are due to the types of atoms involved and how they are arranged in molecules. Chemical change is explained as the rearrangement of atoms into new patterns. However, we cannot directly perceive the molecular structures of even such simple substances as common salt.

Chemistry and other of the natural sciences have solved this problem through the construction of models. Most students have witnessed a physical science teacher construct models of this sort. If we cannot observe 'the real thing,' we make or imagine something analogous. But how do we know we are not imagining and constructing something nonsensical or implausible? Of course, we base our model-making on something we know. Again, Charles Darwin imagined a process of 'natural selection' that could have produced the variety of plants and animals we have today as well as the fossil forms we find in the earth. He drew on his knowledge of the way new breeds of animals and new plant forms are produced by stock-breeders and gardeners by selecting the breeding stock and plants with characteristics he desired. Darwin used this knowledge to create his model of the real process of development that occurs in the natural world.

For a psychology modeled on the established natural sciences, we need to develop ways of making models of unobservable processes, both cognitive and neurological. (Models of more overt processes, such as social interaction, are also possible.) But since human psychology is enormously complex, many questions must be answered before models of unobservable psychological processes are constructed. Is thinking like calculating, or is it more like having a conversation? Which of these (or other) possibilities will make the best source for models of cognition? Perhaps we will need to make use of both. Also, when should we interpret a model *literally* as a representation of a real, but hidden, reality?

Could psychology be cloned from the natural sciences?

Now let us turn to a slightly more complete overview of possible difficulties inherent in taking the format and methods of the natural sciences as the basis of a scientific psychology.

First, establishing a vocabulary for precise descriptions of the relevant phenomena follows a well-founded pattern in the natural sciences. We may start with the vernacular, ordinary ways of describing what goes on in our domain of interest. For example, we have a group of words such as 'hot,' 'warm,' 'cold,' 'chilly' and so on to describe temperatures. Over the last three centuries scientists have transformed this vocabulary into a technical form, with new concepts such as 'degrees Celsius,' 'relative humidity' and 'wind chill.' The meanings of these expressions are quite precise and have analogues in formal equations. Does it make good scientific sense to set about the same sort of transformation for psychological vocabularies?

Our studies of Wittgenstein's later writings will call any such move into serious question. For example, in English there is a very large and finely differentiated vocabulary for describing and expressing emotions. Other languages have emotion vocabularies that may not translate perfectly into English. Indeed, in some cases there are no English equivalents. Would we gain or lose in scientific precision by attempting to create a universal technical vocabulary?

Second, typically, explanations in the natural sciences involve citing causes, or necessary and sufficient conditions for phenomena to come into being. But the matter is never left at that. The question of *how* a cause produces an effect is central to the research programs of the natural sciences. How are earthquakes produced? Alfred Wegener (1912), drawing on the analogy of ice floes grinding against each other in the spring thaw, proposed a 'hidden mechanism' amounting to the movements of tectonic plates. Does it make sense for psychologists to adopt the same explanatory method? Those answering in the affirmative might propose 'hidden cognitive processes' or 'emotions of which one is not aware.' Others might question the invention of what amounts to a 'mind behind the mind.'

When it comes to 'ontological' considerations of this sort, Wittgenstein, in his later writings, emphasizes the extent to which explanations of many human behaviors necessitate reference to rules and conventions, in so simple a case as why Americans and French drive on the right and British and Japanese drive on the left. Furthermore, he uncovers problems with inventing mental states and processes of which we are not aware to explain those of which we are conscious. Here again we are referring to his battle against 'mentalism.' People actively use the rules and conventions of their cultures to achieve their goals, and indeed to set those very goals themselves. Conscious rule-following soon settles down to action out of habit. It is a fatal error to project a hypothetical and hidden version of active rule following behind the habits that we form. Psychological habits *mimic* causal processes, but they have their origins in the activity of human agents.

The influence of philosophy: positivism and its legacy

There are other myth-making influences on psychology as well as mistakes about the meanings of key words and expressions. At the beginning of the twentieth century, when psychology was just beginning to set itself up as a science on the model of the natural sciences for the third time, for a range of historical reasons physical scientists embraced the philosophical doctrine of 'positivism.' This proved disastrous in the natural sciences and was soon abandoned. However, it lingered in psychology and its influence is not difficult to detect even today. Though our project is to bring Wittgenstein's insights to bear on the re-making of psychology, it will be helpful to rid ourselves of the idea that, in order to be a science, a discipline must follow the dictates of positivism.

Positivism was both a cluster of philosophical claims about the scope and possibilities of obtaining knowledge and an attitude toward the place of human beings in the world. Positivists, since the inauguration of this point of view in modern times by Auguste Comte (1835), have argued for the restriction of claims to knowledge to *what can be observed*. We can directly experience earthquakes, but we cannot directly observe the movements of tectonic plates, which allegedly cause earthquakes. According to the positivist interpretation of science, the hypothesis of the existence and relative motions of tectonic plates can, at best, be a psychological help to thinking about the correlations of observable geological phenomena. Modern geology clearly is non-positivistic, since it is based on a firm belief in the existence of these subterranean entities and in the reality of their slow and inexorable movements.

Though psychologists know very well that correlation is not causation, nevertheless there is an easily documented and systematic neglect of the question of how statistically significant phenomena are *actually* related. Psychologists widely presume that causal explanations should involve the exploration of relevant causal mechanisms only to a limited extent – if at all. Surely this is due largely to the aforementioned complexities of psychological phenomena that make the prospect of exhaustive explanations in terms of causal mechanisms daunting indeed. But any physicist or chemist would be astounded by the very notion of, at best, a limited exploration of the causal mechanisms lying behind a particular phenomenon. Undergraduate students of psychology are aware of many cases of scientific research that simply correlate behaviors, attitudes and so on, with no exhaustive explanation as to the precise causal mechanisms behind what is of interest. Now compare this with physical chemists, who believe that a potential difference causes metal to be deposited on the cathode of an apparatus set up for electrolysis. They believe, with good reason, that there is a causal mechanism behind this deposit: the transport of ions through the solution under the influence of the potential gradient between cathode and anode. Can the explanation of psychological phenomena be so precise and exhaustive?

The positivist attitude can be summed up as follows: believe in less than you could for fear that you might believe more than you should.

If we apply this aphorism to psychology we create a very simple *empiricism*. Empiricism is the philosophical point of view according to which our claims to knowledge may go no further than what we can observe with our senses, what we can see, touch, hear, taste and smell. All that can be observed of a person's thinking, feeling, planning and so on is what that person does overtly. When this simple empiricism is put into practice based on the basic tenets of positivism, we have a scientific psychology whose investigative practices and explanations do not move beyond what is shown overtly. This returns us to the question of how psychological concepts are classified, organized and used by scientific psychologists. How do they relate to the same and similar concepts used by persons going about their business in everyday life? Well, for the psychologist enamored with positivism, classifying these phenomena in terms of their meanings in local cultures is not an option *because the meanings of behaviors are no more observable than the alleged cognitive processes by which they are managed.*

The foregoing leads directly to another consideration: the empiricist *ontology* of modern psychology. In philosophy, ontology is concerned with being, or 'what is.' The ontology of a science defines the kinds of 'things' that are presumed to exist in a given domain of inquiry. So, for example, the ontology of astronomy consists of galaxies, stars, planets, comets and other heavenly bodies. Philosophers often try to set out explicitly the range and nature of the things presumed to be the subject matter of a science or some other human practice. But laypersons also are able at least partially to account for the ontologies of their own specific practices. The ontology of baseball includes the players, the bat, the ball, the diamond, the bases, home plate and so on. But what should be included as part of the ontology of psychology? As interpreted positivistically, it can cover only what an investigator can observe with his or her senses. Interestingly, while John B. Watson (1919, 1925) insisted that only publicly observable behavior should find a place in psychology, B.F. Skinner (1974) allowed for a science of experiences known alone to the person who has them. In this sense, Watson's behaviorism was positivistic and Skinner's was not.

The legacy of positivism in psychology is a methodology that eschews the meanings of what people say and do, use and wear. The 'what it means for them' has no place. This positivist methodology is, for the most part, satisfied with statistical analyses of 'data' described in a technical vocabulary, often divorced from its origins in the vernacular. Very few psychologists would call themselves 'positivists.' But this does not stop them from conducting their research and providing explanations of psychological phenomena as if they were.

This leads not only to the falsification of the phenomena of human thought, action and feeling, but to shallow and fallacious explanatory efforts. Establishing a statistical correlation at better than the 0.05 level *explains* nothing in any scientifically relevant sense.

Psychology needs a vastly expanded ontology and, at the same time, a richer and more plausible mode of explanation than that which is currently encouraged and practiced by many academic psychologists, influenced directly and more often indirectly by the legacy of a long-outdated philosophical standpoint.

A new era in the search for a scientific psychology
A new era in psychology has already arrived in many places, influenced to a considerable extent by the critical insights offered by Wittgenstein and others who have drawn encouragement and inspiration from his writings. It is evident in much 'cutting-edge' research, particularly in such disciplines as discursive psychology (Billig, 1987) and cultural psychology (Cole, 1996). Unfortunately, the underlying

rationale of the new paradigm has not been absorbed or even acknowledged by the majority of academic psychologists, particularly in the United States. Courses introducing the work of Wittgenstein to psychologists may serve to redress the current situation, to the long-lasting benefit of the project of creating a truly scientific psychology. To appreciate the role that Wittgenstein's investigations can play we must first get very clear about what it is that contemporary psychology needs in order to establish itself as a science. At the same time we must also get very clear about the shortfalls in many areas of recent psychology relative to this desirable end. We can approach this question by examining the presuppositions of some famous attempts at constructing a scientific psychology. Below is a brief résumé of three important attempts to set up the study of human thought, feeling, action and perception as a science. We will bring out and highlight the most contentious root presupposition underlying each.

Paradigms for a scientific psychology – old and new

While it is reasonable to regard scientific psychology as still in its youth, the systematic study of human thoughts, feelings, actions and modes of perception is a very old project. For example, one of the greatest 'pre-scientific' practitioners of psychology, Aristotle, lived and worked in the fourth century BC. Granted, Aristotle's investigations into human psychology were not scientific by today's standards. But they were systematic. Over the last five hundred years numerous attempts have been made to create a satisfactory paradigm for a science of human mental life, but each has met with only very limited success. The failures have been the result, for the most part, of building the project on faulty foundations, on unsatisfactory presuppositions. Some of these can be found, in one form or other, implicitly or explicitly, in more recent and contemporary theorizing and research. Below we review just one of the former (pre-scientific) and two of the later (scientific) projects, whose presuppositions are still very much alive. Our primary focus will be on their presuppositions.

Cartesianism

According to this famous perspective, each person is a doublet, composed of two substances. (There is a dual ontology.) Somehow a material body is associated with an immaterial mind. Psychology was to be a science of the immaterial stuff of mind, paralleling physics in general style and method. So the science of the material stuff of the body would serve as a model for the science of the immaterial stuff of the mind. We need two basic sciences because the attributes of material stuff, such as mass and motion, are quite different from the attributes of mental stuff, such as meanings. We call this paradigm 'Cartesian' because it had its most explicit formulation in the writings of René Descartes in the seventeenth century.

Presupposition: Since human beings display two very distinct kinds of attributes, mental and material, there must be two distinct substances to which members of each group are assigned.

Here is an example of a research project conducted within the framework of the Cartesian paradigm by Descartes himself. In order to show that the mind-as-mental-substance is quite unlike the body-as-material-substance, Descartes set out to show that the mind is neither extended in space nor divisible into parts. Primarily as a result of thought-experiment, he declared that the essence of matter is extension, while the essence of mind is thought, which has no extension.

Having established to his own satisfaction that the mind has no parts nor is it extended, Descartes offered a comprehensive typology for the operations of the mind. Note well that this is not a typology of the *parts* of the mind. There are none, according to Descartes. However, when we come to study Descartes's psychology in detail we find that he draws on hypotheses concerning the material realm of 'animal spirits' and on hypotheses concerning the mental realm of the 'soul' equally freely.

After having taken into consideration all the functions that belong to the body alone, it is easy to understand that there remains nothing in us that we should attribute to our soul but our thoughts, which are principally of two genera – the first, namely, are the actions of the soul; the other are its passions. The actions include all volitions because we find by experience that they come directly from our soul and seem to depend only on it. On the other hand, all the sorts of cases of perfection or knowledge to be found in us generally can be called its passions, because it is often not our soul that makes them such as they are and because it always receives them from things that are presented by them (Descartes, 1649/1958, Article 17).

There are two subtypes of volitions, those that terminate in the soul (such as willing oneself to believe in God) and those that terminate in the body (such as willing oneself to get up in the morning). Then there are two types of the passions of the soul, having to do with our *perceptions*. There are those caused by the soul itself, for example, perceiving an act of volition, such as being aware of trying to do something. Then there are those caused by the body, such as feelings of pain. The psychological treatise that contains Descartes's most detailed development of his dualism is devoted to the passions, with a few brief mentions of volitions or actions of the soul.

Behaviorism
Psychology is the study of statistical correlations between observable stimuli and observable responses established by conditioning of various kinds (Watson, 1925).

Presupposition: Subjective experience cannot be a topic for *scientific* psychology.

Here is an example of a research project conducted with the framework of behaviorism, conducted not by Watson, but Edward Thorndike, who in some ways can be regarded as the leading exponent of behaviorism. It is notable that the pattern of research that grew up in the wake of theoretical behaviorism favored research on animals. It was assumed that the human case differed only in the complexity and variety of the conditioned responses. For example, Thorndike's (1911) 'law of effect,' which held that the quality of the effect of an action determines how readily it will be performed, was cheerfully projected from animal studies to human behavior.

The experiment by Thorndike we have in mind is his famous 'puzzle-box' experiment. A very hungry cat is placed in a puzzle box equipped with a simple escape mechanism: a wire loop that opened the door to the box when pulled. At first the cat struggled and thrashed about, finally hitting on the escape trick by accident. Once outside it was given some food. The procedure was repeated many times. Each time the cat's struggles were more and more curtailed until in the end it simply pulled on the loop and emerged from the box. Did the animal come to 'understand' the problem? Not according to Thorndike. The result of the experiment was to demonstrate 'the wearing smooth of a path in the brain, not the decision of a rational consciousness' (Thorndike, 1911).

The attempt to bring human psychology under this conception of behaviorism ran into trouble in a very simple way. The Russian psychologist Volkova conditioned a boy to salivate (reminiscent of Pavlov's dogs) on hearing the word 'good,' but not to salivate when hearing 'bad.' But then the boy was found to salivate on hearing the sentence 'The Soviet Army is victorious.' Clearly a concept is intermediate between the stimulus and the response. How should we construe this? Should we introduce the idea of an unconscious *mental representation* to serve as the intermediary? To adopt that way of explaining Volkova's results would amount to stepping straight back into Cartesianism. This was just the sort of step that led, toward the mid-twentieth century, to cognitivism.

Cognitivism

There are cognitive (mental) processes of which we are unaware that explain those of which we aware.

Presupposition: Behind cognitive practices there are unobserved mental processes.

Behaviorism did not fall because psychologists took notice of the profound philosophical arguments against it. A precipitating cause and incentive towards the development of cognitive psychology was the early work of Jerome Bruner on the role of cognitive factors in perception and in responses to perceptual stimuli. His experiments suggested that there must be prior cognitive schemas that are involved in perception, put to use in cognitive processes of which we are unaware.

Bruner's first experiment involved exploring the interaction between perceptual recognition and the valuation of what is to be perceived (Bruner and Goodman, 1947). School children from Boston were asked to manually adjust a patch of light to match US coins of penny, nickel, dime, quarter and half-dollar denominations. Half of the children were from affluent parts of Boston and half were from the city's slums. The results showed, first, that the more valuable the coin, the more participants overestimated its size. Second, the poorer children overestimated the size of the more valuable coins to a greater extent than did the affluent children. Evidently, the difference in value of the coins played a role in the perceptual process at work behind perception of their size. Thus, in this case, perception was not a matter of retinal image alone.

In another experiment, Bruner carried the research into non-conscious cognitive processes much further (Bruner and Postman, 1947). Each participant was briefly presented with a word from a list of pre-selected words according to the relative speed of associative reactions: quick, slow, or average. The participants had to say as quickly as possible which word had been shown. In general, the time taken to recognize a word was related to the time to offer an association. Interestingly, when the words were threatening in some way and had slow associative reactions, they were either recognized more swiftly than average, or more slowly.

How could this be possible? It must be because the meaning of the word had been *grasped* and categorized as emotionally significant or neutral before it was *consciously perceived*. If it had been categorized only after it had been perceived, then there should have been no difference in the time it took to recognize similar words, whatever the emotional load.

Perception of something *as something* is not just a response to a stimulus. It is the upshot of a cognitive process, the precise nature of which Bruner could only guess. That there is such a process and that it is cognitive – that is, employing knowledge according to rules and conventions – is a hypothesis. In these experiments we have two different kinds of cultural knowledge being deployed. There is knowledge of the *value* of coins and there is knowledge of the *meanings* of words.

The tenets and presuppositions of behaviorism clearly are inadequate for explaining the results of these experiments. But do they show that the tenets and presuppositions of cognitivism are sufficient? Why should we suppose that there is anything mental *behind* a skill that involves mental work? Bruner presupposed that his 'schemata' must refer to something analogous to the molecular processes 'behind' observable chemical reactions, to hidden cognitive processes of which the person is not aware.

In our view, informed by Wittgenstein, each and every one of the presuppositions behind these projects for a scientific psychology is mistaken. Each one is the result of confusions about the meanings of key words. We want to suggest that by clarifying the meanings of such terms as 'thinking,' 'remembering,' 'seeing,' 'reading' and so on, we will be able to avoid the traps set for us by the very language that we must use to make the first steps toward any viable project of a scientific psychology. In the course of the chapters to come we will show how attention to meanings will break the spell of language, the spell that led well-intentioned and very clever people to make these unfortunate mistakes.

The source of a deeper and more realistic scientific psychology

Rarely are fundamental questions considered with the care they deserve. For example, are psychological phenomena primarily interpersonal, having only a secondary and derived existence as 'attributes' of individuals? What similarities and differences should we draw on by which one domain of life can throw light on another? We believe there are profound and important lessons concerning the problems of developing a classification system for cognitive and affective phenomena. And we believe instructive examples of classification problems and their solutions can be found in Wittgenstein's later writings.

We need to be ready to cope with the possibility that there are both causal and normative processes evident in the genesis of human thought and feeling. Causality requires that there be some representation of a plausible causal mechanism by which causes engender their usual effects, *ceteris paribus*. It is evident in the writings of Wittgenstein that normative explanations require reference to local rules and customs in which the prevailing standards of correctness – so central to psychological functioning in both the cognitive and affective domains – can be expressed. We think also that, in the domain of psychological phenomena, normative explanations far outweigh causal explanations in both number and force. Wittgenstein's later writings contain many and deep reflections on the nature and use of rules, the ground of normative explanations, both in the conduct of life and in the explanations of it.

These gains from Wittgenstein's work are not all we can profitably derive from it. His positive contributions are almost always part of a program for resolving seemingly intractable problems and confusions of thought. Wittgenstein believed that much trouble comes from unreflective use of unsuitable grammatical models in making sense of our words, models that seem so natural that they bewitch our intellects. For example, our tendency to use nouns in describing psychological phenomena promotes an easy slippage into an implicit belief in immaterial psychological entities. This makes the attainment of a clear view of the nature of such psychological phenomena as the display of, for example, emotion, very difficult. Anger takes on the character of a state rather than an activity. Self-esteem seems to play the role of an inner feature of a person's character by reference to which one explains the sorts of beliefs and opinions someone exhibits. Explanations in terms of tendencies are displaced by references to mental states. In these and many other cases, there is an unexamined grammatical model leading us astray. Nouns refer to things, so we think. If there do not seem to be material or behavioral referents for a certain noun, say 'intelligence,' then we are tempted to suppose that there must be an *immaterial* referent!

An alternative pattern for a scientific psychology

Causal and normative explanations

Commonsense explanations of what people do typically invoke projects, great and small. 'Why is she weeding the cabbage patch?' 'She wants to get a good crop of cabbages.' This simple example includes an explicit reference to the end or aim of her activities, and an implicit presupposition that she knows how to achieve it. Compare this with the following: 'Why is she sneezing?' 'She has inhaled some grass pollen.' Here we make an explicit reference to a causal condition necessary for the effect to occur, and an implicit reference to a complex physiological mechanism activated by the pollen grains.

In the cabbage patch example, we presuppose that the person is an active and intelligent agent, managing her activities according to the principles and rules of proper behavior. In the sneezing example, we presuppose that the person is a passive mechanism reacting automatically to an environmental condition.

A person dining at the Victorian Restaurant in Montrose, Pennsylvania, is seen to order a helping of Tin Roof Fudge Pie (TRFP) when there is also fruit salad and low-fat yogurt available for dessert. Everyone knows that TRFP is the most delicious sweet ever devised. Should we offer a causal explanation in terms of low blood sugar, or Pavlovian conditioning bringing about an automatic response to the presentation of TRFP as a stimulus object? Or should we offer an *agentive* explanation, invoking such concepts as the gourmet's rule of life, that one should order what one believes to be the most delicious item on the menu? This custom might be at war with the person's project to curb the expansion of the waistline. As an acceptable explanation we might say their greed got the better of them.

There is nothing particularly 'scientific' about opting for a physiological rather than a normative explanation. Both satisfy the requirements for an explanation to be scientific. We have given a tight description of the phenomenon and of the conditions under which it occurs, according to a well-established classification system, coupled with a plausible model of the process that brought it about.

So far our survey of the needs of psychology as a science has yielded two main requirements. First, psychological phenomena should be *described* by the use of terminology that involves meanings. Second, causal *explanations* of what people do must be supplemented and often displaced in favor of normative accounts, in which we refer to a person's knowledge of principles, norms, conventions and customs.

To achieve a genuinely scientific account of the phenomena we call 'psychological,' we need to understand what it is for something to be meaningful, and we need to understand the nature, scope and conditions of application of rules in the explanation of how those phenomena come to be and to exhibit the sequential patterns that they do.

Ordinary language in the classification of psychological phenomena

How do we know what states and processes to pick out as *psychological phenomena* from the rich tapestry of the world as we know it? In other words, what should be our ontology? Psychologists, like everyone else, already possess a powerful and comprehensive classificatory system finely adjusted to exactly this purpose in their mastery of their mother tongues. In most cases, we are quite adept at knowing when someone is sad, angry, or happy. We are able to distinguish between feeling ill and feeling tired. We are skilled in reasoning and the art of persuasion. We know how to act modestly and to defer to those who have prior rights to something. And so on. In learning our mother tongues as part of a mastery of the practices of our cultures, we acquire the skills to manage everyday life in our tribe. Very rarely do we stop to reflect on *how* we do these things and what *tools and devices* we employ in doing them.

Asking 'how' and 'what' questions is the beginning of psychology. However, we must never lose sight of the fact that the topics are *defined* by the language-in-use among the people who live their lives in a certain way. It makes no sense whatever for a psychologist to announce that he or she has discovered that what we had hitherto picked out as 'anger' is really something else. That does not mean that psychologists cannot refine the concept, disclosing more varieties in its scope than those that are recognized in the vernacular. Nor does it mean that they cannot bring to light cases in which people were calling something 'anger' when they ought to be calling it 'chagrin' and so on. The point is that the meaning of the basic psychological words of our ordinary vocabularies cannot be overturned, nor can the situations in which we learned to use them be declared to be something else.

To put this in another idiom, psychological concepts are always and necessarily defined 'top down.' A state of the brain revealed by a PET scan can only be identified as relevant to the recognition of the differences between two ways of printing a word (font recognition) if the person being studied has told the investigator what he or she can and cannot distinguish. A flush of noradrenaline in the bloodstream is relevant to excitement and aggression only if we can recognize by ordinary day-to-day criteria that the person from whom we have taken a blood sample is excited and aggressive. Just as the distinction between solid, liquid and gas is deeply embedded in the physical sciences, however refined the characterization of 'phases' becomes, so the root distinctions among psychological phenomena are deeply embedded in whatever further developments take place in response to research programs of various sorts.

It follows directly that the psychological competencies and abilities that any individual has are the product of the transformation of native endowments through the acquisition of cultural-specific ways of thinking, feeling and acting. This, we believe, comes about largely through the learning of a mother tongue, and the customs and practices that go along with it. Here again we encounter the priority of a study of local languages as cognitive tools in any attempts to generalize research findings from tribe to tribe, or from era to era, or to introduce 'technical' vocabularies into the means by which psychological phenomena are classified and explained.

Managing meanings

Two new branches of psychology have appeared in recent years in response to the realization that psychological phenomena are patterns of meanings, managed by people in the performance of tasks and in attempts to bring all sorts of projects to fruition.

Discursive psychology has emerged as the confluence of a number of independent streams of work, beginning in the 1970s outside the established mainstream of positivistically inspired psychology. There is now a large and growing literature in this area. Discursive psychology is based on the twin principles that the core psychological phenomena are the meanings of symbolic systems in daily use for the performance of all sorts of tasks and the rules that express standards and conventions of correct and proper performances.

From this point of view psychological phenomena include facial expressions, costumes and uniforms, household artifacts, words and other written and spoken symbols, models and pictures, and so on. The objects in any and all of these categories are effective not by reason of their physical form and composition, but by reason of what they mean to those who are putting them to use or recognizing their significance and responding to them as meaningful. Neither the uses nor the responses are best construed as the effects of causes. Instead of a search for causal mechanisms, discursive psychologists try to formulate catalogues of explicit and implicit rules, expressing the norms according to which symbolic activity is carried on.

Cultural psychology developed from the realization that attempts to construe the emotions, the patterns of reasoning, the social conventions and so on of people in cultures remote from our own led to serious misunderstandings of meanings and misconstruals of intentions, at the very least. Even the export of a methodology established in the psychology departments of American universities to manage research in other parts of the world turned out to be a mistake, concealing rather than revealing the psychological phenomena and cognitive processes of the 'Others' (Cole, 1996). The focus of cultural psychology is on diversity, at the same time looking within that diversity for any common themes that might be generalizable to other peoples at other times (Wierzbicka, 1992).

Wittgenstein's insights into the role of psychological concepts, in the forms of life of the cultures of and derived from Western Europe, provide part of the groundwork for the analytical methodologies of both discursive and cultural psychology. His attempts to bring out complex patterns of interrelated meanings and the subtle way that rules and conventions entered into the management of meanings drove him to develop a way of revealing explicitly what we, the users of symbolic systems, know implicitly. Though his purposes were mainly those of a philosopher intent on revealing the deep fallacies in certain important and influential philosophical theses presupposed by psychologists and others, we can 'hi-jack' the method and many of its results to help in the task of developing a truly scientific psychology.

Learning point: psychology as a science

1. *What is needed for a science?*

   (a) A system of concepts for *classifying* phenomena.
   (b) A system of concepts and models for *explaining* phenomena.

2. *Can we use the natural sciences as models for the human sciences?*

   (a) There are problems with transforming vernacular vocabularies into technical terminology in psychological research programs.
   (b) The natural science practice of inventing hidden mechanisms to explain observable phenomena runs into difficulties in several branches of psychology.

3. *Three attempts at a scientific psychology*

   (a) *Cartesianism:* Psychology is the study of the immaterial mind in a way parallel to physics, the scientific study of matter.
        Presupposition: Because there are two kinds of human attributes there must be two distinct kinds of substances. Illustrated by Descartes's account of thinking.
   (b) *Behaviorism:* A scientific psychology must be confined to discov-

ering the statistical relations between external stimuli and external responses of the human organism.

Presupposition: The reports that people give of their private thoughts and feelings are not legitimate data for psychology.

(c)   *Cognitivism*: Psychology is the study of the hidden mental mechanisms that explain overt and observable cognitive and affective phenomena.

Presupposition: There are unobserved cognitive processes that accompany thinking, feeling and so on, which are the real topic of psychology. Illustrated by Bruner's experiments on schemata.

In each case we will come to see that among the presuppositions of these paradigms of psychological science there are mistakes about meaning that profoundly affect how we interpret the results of research based on one or other of them.

4.   *The causal and the normative format*
Causal explanations of human behavior invoke environmental conditions that activate causal mechanisms, with respect to which people are passive. Normative explanations invoke meanings and rules, conventions and so on used by active people in carrying through everyday projects. Scientific psychology requires both modes of explanation.

5.   *Ordinary language and classification*
Whatever development may come about in the vocabulary for classifying psychological phenomena, the links to local vernaculars must be maintained.

Further reading

Burr, V. (2003), *Social Constructionism*. Milton Keynes: Open University Press.

Coulter, J. (1979), *The Social Construction of Mind*. London and Basingstoke: Macmillan.

Gillies, D. (1993), *Philosophy of Science in the Twentieth Century: Four central themes*. Oxford: Blackwell.

Moghaddam, F. (2004), *Great Ideas in Psychology*. New York: Worth.

2 Wittgenstein's life and Viennese cultural background

> Tell them I've had a wonderful life.
> Wittgenstein on his death bed, 28 April 1951

> I don't believe I have ever *invented* a line of thinking, I have
> always taken one over from someone else. I have simply
> straightaway seized on it with enthusiasm for my work of
> clarification. That is how Boltzmann, Hertz, Schopenhauer,
> Frege, Russell, Kraus, Loos, Weininger, Spengler, Sraffa have
> influenced me.
> Wittgenstein, *Culture and Value*, p. 19

Topics introduced: Wittgenstein's family background and education; Cambridge and Bertrand Russell; military service; *Tractatus Logico-Philosophicus*, departure from and return to philosophy; 'Sraffa's gesture'; Karl Kraus, Viennese expressionism and parallels with Wittgenstein; nonsense; Arnold Schönberg's musicology; the influence of German philosophy of physics (Heinrich Hertz and Ludwig Boltzmann); picture theory of meaning; simple objects; phase space

Wittgenstein's life

The life and times of Ludwig Wittgenstein have been the subject of several admirable biographies. In our view, foremost among these is Ray Monk's (1990) rich and accessible study. It would provide an excellent accompaniment to the philosophical developments we will be describing in this and following chapters. Only a rough and ready account of Wittgenstein's life is needed for our purposes.

Ludwig Josef Johann Wittgenstein was born in Vienna on 26 April 1889 as the youngest in a family of eight precocious children. Karl, his father, was a leading industrialist and one of the wealthiest men in Austria. Although certain of his forebears were Jewish, Karl was Protestant. Leopoldine, Ludwig's mother, was Catholic and he was brought up in the Catholic tradition.

Ludwig was educated at home until he was fourteen. His formative education included not only instruction from tutors, but also visits to the family home by notable musicians and composers such as Brahms and Mahler. From 1903 to 1906 he attended the technically oriented Realschule at Linz where he was, at best, an average student. For a short time there, during the 1904–05 school year, he had Adolph Hitler as a classmate. Next he attended the Technische Hochschule in Charlottenburg, Berlin, to study science and mathematics as preliminaries to becoming an engineer. Then, from fall 1908 through spring 1911, he undertook aeronautical engineering studies and conducted research on aircraft propeller design at Manchester University, England. He was registered to continue at Manchester the next fall, but for some time his thoughts had been directed toward the philosophy of mathematics and logic. So he sought advice from the philosopher of logic Gottlob Frege, who seems to have suggested that Ludwig study logic under Bertrand Russell at Cambridge. Beginning in 1912, the result was an intense and often emotional struggle over the nature of logic, in the course of which Wittgenstein came to realize how unsatisfactory were the views of his erstwhile mentor.

Even at this point in his life Wittgenstein yearned for solitude to develop his ideas. So in 1913, in his mid-twenties, he abruptly decided to isolate himself in Norway to write on logic unhindered by the distractions of university life. After his father had been struck down by cancer, Wittgenstein used a small portion of his considerable inheritance to construct a hut on the side of a fjord, about a mile from the nearest village. (Most of his remaining inheritance was donated to needy artists and writers of the Austro-Hungarian Empire and then later given to his siblings.) But, as happened often in later life, loneliness drove him back to Cambridge from his retreat in Norway – that is, until the First World War broke out in 1914.

Thinking the dangers of battle would test his character, Wittgenstein volunteered for service in the Austro-Hungarian Army. He served admirably, particularly in his service at an observation post for an artillery unit on the Russian Front. He was cited more than once for bravery and promoted to Lieutenant. Through his diary notes and letters it is evident that Wittgenstein's approach to military service was symptomatic of a lifelong concern with ethical principles and religious experiences as they impinged on the conduct of everyday life. And his duties as a soldier did not keep him from continuing to work on logic. By the time Wittgenstein was transferred to the Italian Front and eventually held prisoner for ten months in Italy toward the end of the war, he had finished the first and only book on philosophy he would publish in his lifetime. *Tractatus Logico-Philosophicus* (Logico-Philosophical Treatise) appeared first in the German periodical *Annalen der Naturphilosophie* in 1921 and by the next year it was translated into English with an introduction by Russell.

Later in this chapter and in the chapter that follows we will encounter relevant aspects of the *Tractatus* in more detail. For the time being we may think of it as a philosophical treatise aimed at showing that a language organized according to the principles of logic, and in which meanings are established by pointing to exemplars, would be so transparent that it would equip philosophers with all they needed to avoid or solve all the problems of philosophy. Being outside the range of this perfect language, the important things in life – personal relationships, religion, art, music and so on – could only be expressed in action.

Believing that he had brought the struggle with philosophical problems to an end, only a morally acceptable life of service was left open to him. So after working for a brief period as a monastery gardener's assistant, Wittgenstein received training as an educator to teach children in rural Austrian villages (Trattenbach, Puchberg and Otterthal) during the years 1920 to 1926. His stint as an elementary school teacher ended, however, with protests from parents about his draconian discipline.

It is no exaggeration to say he was 'run out of town.' So in 1926 he returned to Vienna to assist in the construction of a house for one of his sisters. Not long thereafter he began an intimate relationship with a woman that lasted until sometime in 1931. This is significant to the extent that, after the affair, all of his intimate relationships were with men.

During Wittgenstein's stay in rural Austria, the *Tractatus* became the subject of a great deal of discussion among philosophers and intellectuals in and around Vienna and at Cambridge. He was becoming famous among philosophers. In 1923 Frank Ramsey, a promising young undergraduate mathematics student at Cambridge, began to correspond with and visit Wittgenstein. Although Ramsey had immense respect for Wittgenstein's genius, he was critical of certain views expressed in the *Tractatus*. These criticisms, along with Wittgenstein's own misgivings about the book, would contribute to his eventual return to philosophy. Through the latter half of the 1920s Wittgenstein was beginning to see that 'philosophy-as-logic' fell far short of a catchall solution to the kinds of problems that concerned him. His increasing distance from some central tenets of the *Tractatus* did not go unnoticed by members of the Vienna Circle, a group of philosophers whose meetings he occasionally attended beginning in 1927.

We should mention another event that contributed to Wittgenstein's doubts about the *Tractatus* during his 'transition.' In 1929, the same year he returned to Cambridge, Wittgenstein had a conversation with the Italian economist Piero Sraffa concerning the Tractarian doctrine that propositions and what they describe must have the same 'logical form.' Sraffa, who disagreed, made the Neopolitan gesture of brushing the back of his fingers on one hand upward and across the under-part of his chin, then saying, 'What is the logical form of *that*?' As we will see in more detail in the next chapter, one of the central assumptions made by Wittgenstein in the *Tractatus* is that true and meaningful propositions, which are 'pictures' of reality, are composed of words that stand in one-to-one correspondence with what they refer to in the world. The logical forms of propositions, he thought, correspond to the logical forms of the things in the world to which they refer. Perhaps it occurred to Wittgenstein that Sraffa's gesture, which was meaningful (something like, 'what nonsense!'), was neither true nor false. Although it was directed at Wittgenstein, the gesture did not refer to anything in the world. It had no 'logical form' but it had a use and was meaningful. This event may have set Wittgenstein to thinking that he had yet to address adequately the kinds of meaningful communication exemplified by Sraffa's gesture.

Now forty years old and back at Cambridge, Wittgenstein's first order of significant business was to earn his doctorate, which he did by discussing his 'thesis,' the *Tractatus*, with his examiners Russell and G.E. Moore. (Russell noted on the occasion: 'I have never known anything so absurd in my life.') But Wittgenstein had already begun to develop a radically new approach to philosophy and language. It would take years to develop his new philosophical tool – a method for surveying *actual uses* of language in key areas of thought and action. This idea came, in part, from his realization that the main medium of cognition is not the formal algebra of logic. It is language, the principal tool for living a human life. At the same time, unless its workings are properly understood, that very language is full of pitfalls and temptations to error, through various kinds of misunderstandings of how language is actually used.

For the remainder of his life Wittgenstein wrote assiduously, mostly in short remarks which he revised and rearranged obsessively. None of these remarks was published in his lifetime, though versions of collected remarks were circulated widely. His lectures were famous, not only for their content, but for the manner in which they were delivered. After apparently agonizing struggles with his own thoughts, Wittgenstein would engage in discussions with various members of his class.

During the Second World War, after working as a hospital porter, he joined a research unit studying 'wound shock.' Though he returned to Cambridge in 1945, he continued to find academic life oppressive and repeatedly sought refuge in remote places, including the southern coast of Wales, the far west of Ireland and his retreat in Norway. But he never neglected work on his manuscripts.

In 1950, after visiting the United States to stay with his student and friend, Norman Malcolm, in Ithaca, NY, Wittgenstein was diagnosed with prostate cancer. He had suffered bouts of severe illness for some time. He died in Cambridge on 29 April 1951, at the home of his doctor.

Learning point: Wittgenstein's life

1. *Birth, family and childhood education*

    (a) Born in 1889 in Vienna as the youngest of eight children in a wealthy aristocratic family.
    (b) His mother was Catholic and his father, a successful industrialist, was Protestant. Viennese high culture strongly evident in his home life. Regular visitors included Brahms, Mahler and other distinguished persons of the day.
    (c) Educated at home by tutors until he was fourteen. He continued with a predominantly scientific/technical education in Linz (where he was a contemporary of Adolph Hitler) and then in Berlin.

2. *From engineering to philosophy, war years and* Tractatus Logico-Philosophicus

    (a) From fall 1908 through spring 1911, he undertook aeronautical engineering studies at Manchester University, England. During these years he became interested in philosophy of mathematics and philosophical logic.
    (b) He consulted Gottlob Frege, who suggested logical studies under Bertrand Russell at Cambridge. Wittgenstein began studies under Russell in 1912. Eventually, he became disenchanted with Russell's conception of logic.
    (c) He served with distinction in the Austrian army during the First World War while continuing to work on logic. He maintained a

concern with the personal struggle for moral integrity and how to live a good life.

(d) He was held prisoner in Italy at the close of the war. The *Tractatus* was finished and published in its first German edition in 1921. Its first English edition, with an introduction by Russell, was published in 1922.

(e) Convinced that the *Tractatus* had provided philosophers with what is needed to avoid or solve all philosophical problems, he gave up logic and philosophy to work as a country school teacher.

3. *Disenchantment and return*

(a) During the 1920s he gradually lost faith in his work in logic as the final solution to all problems, scientific and moral.

(b) In 1929 he returned to Cambridge to begin anew his work on language and philosophy. He earned his doctorate that year, at age 40. 'Sraffa's gesture' contributed to his new conception of philosophy.

4. *The transformation of his project*

(a) He rejected the Tractarian conception of language-as-calculus as, while being fit for science, is not fit for moral and religious expression. The main medium of cognition is not a kind of calculus, but language use itself as the principal tool for human living.

(b) He set about surveying actual uses of language in key areas of thought and action.

(c) In both phases of his work he tried to show how mistakes about language led people astray, not only in philosophy, but also in psychology and in mathematics.

5. *Later life*

(a) He continued to escape academic life by staying in remote areas in Wales, Ireland, and Norway. Meantime, he continued to write extensively.

(b) He was diagnosed with prostate cancer after a trip to the United States in 1950. He died in Cambridge on 29 April 1951.

Viennese influences

The stylistic characteristics and doctrinal aims of Wittgenstein's philosophical writings did not emerge from strictly 'philosophical' considerations. This becomes clear only if we read Wittgenstein in light of his Viennese upbringing. Due to the

manifold complexities of accounting for the influences on his personal and intellectual life, we will consider only those influences pertinent to his style of expression
and the doctrinal aspects of his philosophical method. This will facilitate understanding of those aspects of his philosophical method most relevant to the task of
identifying philosophical problems and conceptual errors that plague philosophy
and other disciplines classified as social and behavioral sciences, in particular
scientific psychology. Apart from considerations on scientific psychology, we owe
much of this 'angle' on understanding Wittgenstein to Janik and Toulmin (1973).

Surely the most important of Wittgenstein's Viennese influences were the writings of Karl Kraus (1874–1936). He was a man who exerted so much influence on
Wittgenstein that it is fair to say the central message of the *Tractatus* is 'a Krausian
message.' 'Wittgenstein's life [was] a Krausian life' (Janik and Toulmin, 1973, p.
202). To show the extent to which Wittgenstein is properly regarded as a Krausian
man and philosopher, we will begin with a sketch of the background, aims and
characteristics of Kraus's work, informed by Bodine (1981, 1989) and others. This
will be followed by a brief account of Wittgenstein's familiarity with and lifelong
respect for Kraus. Then, after establishing which aspects of Wittgenstein's early
philosophy have clear origins in Kraus's work, we will follow some changes in
Wittgenstein's thinking after the *Tractatus* to underscore those aspects of the book
that are attributable to the influence of Kraus. In closing this chapter we will
discuss other important influences, specifically the composer and musicologist
Arnold Schönberg and the German physicists Hertz and Boltzmann.

Wittgenstein as a Krausian man

Expressionism

Like his counterparts in art, architecture and music – the painter Oscar Kokoschka,
the architect Adolf Loos, and the composer and musicologist Arnold Schönberg –
Kraus was a prominent figure in the Viennese movement for 'truthful literary and
artistic expression' that we now know as 'Austrian Expressionism.' This movement
came into its own during the first two decades of the twentieth century as a
response to the historical eclecticism and taste for excessive ornamentation of
Austrian Impressionism (Bodine, 1981, p. 42). Expressionists sought more 'truthful' expression in two ways. First, they stripped ornamentation from their various
artistic and literary creations, including architecture, and second, when it came to
social perception, they strove to 'tell it like it is' (Bodine, 1989, p. 144). This 'new
mode of expression' was, for example, reflected in the structure and materials of
Adolf Loos's buildings. Absent the ornamentation that might otherwise conceal the
functions of structure and material, the structural and materialistic functions of
Loos's buildings were left open to view. The same may be said of Kraus the literary
expressionist. His literary productions are marked by an absence of flowery language that would otherwise detract from their presentation of the truth.

The underlying impetus for Kraus's work was his conviction that Viennese
culture was corrupt and lacked *integrity*. Nowhere was the glare of corrupt Vienna
more blinding than in the popular cultural essay (or *feuilleton*) that appeared in the
newspapers of the day, which distorted the news by mingling fact and opinion in a

form of language 'laden with adverbs and especially adjectives; so much so, that the objective situation was lost in the shuffle' (Janik and Toulmin, 1973, p. 79). Accordingly, Kraus not only took it upon himself to expose corruption and restore integrity and truth to the people of Vienna, but insisted that artists and writers wage an all-out assault on moral and aesthetic corruption by carrying out a more truthful critique of their own area of human experience. For Kraus, the prerequisite for any such critique was the artist or writer's 'creative separation' of the sphere of *values* from the sphere of *facts*. Throughout his career he 'identified absolutely the aesthetic form and the moral content of a literary work, seeing its moral and aesthetic worth as reflected in its language' (Janik and Toulmin, 1973, p. 89).

Kraus put his own stamp on Austrian Expressionism in his popular fortnightly published journal *Die Fackel* ('The Torch,' first published in 1899), wherein he evaluated and attacked the misuse of language by abstracting examples of everyday discourse from their original settings to display their 'real' content. One methodological aim of Kraus's critique of language, or '*Sprachkritik*,' was to demonstrate the *polysemous meaning* or multiplicity of meanings of a given word or words by displaying the many possible aspects of the description or exposition of a situation. With his gift for word play, simile and satire – not to mention his knowledge of current events – Kraus was especially adept at exposing the truth content (or lack thereof) of a given literary or artistic production. Kraus's *Sprachkritik* was not simply the byproduct of a talented writer with certain ideological aims, like many of the *feuilletonists* he criticized. His work was based on a theory of how the powers of human reason and conceptualization combine through personal development and are ultimately expressed in language to reflect reality.

Theoretical elements of Kraus's Sprachkritik
Behind Kraus's evaluation of the words and deeds of his contemporaries is a connection between reason or the power of mental association (*Geist*) and feelings, natural drives and the power of the imagination or non-verbal conceptualization (*Phantasie*). For Kraus, human fulfillment comes about through the 'natural' development and interplay of *Geist* and *Phantasie* in the process of growing up (Bodine, 1989, p. 149). When a child first projects meaning upon encountered linguistic expressions, there is an original interaction between *Geist* and *Phantasie* and there continues to be cooperative and coordinate development of the two powers as more linguistic expressions are encountered and language is learned. Ultimately, *Geist* is involved primarily with the various levels of linguistic form and in mentally associating the forms in a particular language with their respective conceptualizations. As Bodine (ibid.) explains,

> Geist thus deals with the language system, the 'langue,' and sets appropriate forms together in the basic formal unit of language, the 'Satz' (sentence and proposition). The individual conceptualizations of reality are brought forth by the faculty of 'Phantasie.' Thus in language use, 'Geist' deals primarily with linguistic form, 'Phantasie' with meaning ...

Two other key Krausian terms are *Wort* (word or linguistic form) and *Wesen* (the individual's conceptualization). But *Wort* and *Wesen* do not benefit from an original automatic association like reason (*Geist*) and the power of imagination or non-verbal conceptualization (*Phantasie*) at an early point in one's youth (*Ursprung*). Rather, the association between word and conceptualization must be pursued diligently. Finally, there is *Zweifel*, or doubt, expressed when one strives to achieve

> the closest possible association between form and concept, which will likely vary with each repeated usage. Doubting or calling into question the work of 'Geist' and of 'Phantasie' … evokes greater individual human development (thus approximating one's 'Ursprung' or original employment of 'Geist' and 'Phantasie'), but doubting also accomplishes in each respective usage the closest possible mental association between 'Wort und Wesen,' form and concept.
>
> (Bodine, 1989, p. 150)

Kraus employed all of these theoretical elements to evaluate the words of his contemporaries. First, he exercised doubt (*Zweifel*) by questioning the reasoning (*Geist*) and conceptualization (*Phantasie*) behind a linguistic expression. He checked reasoning by looking at the linguistic form (*Wort*) of the expression to determine the extent to which it was properly generated. Then he made the more important check on conceptualization by looking at the expression through reference to its context, background, possible motivations behind its production, and how it compared with reality. Having considered all these factors and believing that he had a 'truthful' view of what the actual state of affairs in question was, Kraus thought himself able to determine whether the expression was conceptualized to the fullest, whether it was forthright and whether it was socially or ethically valid. In sum, Kraus's critique of spoken and written language amounted to a kind of verification procedure whereby the truth content of an expression was compared with reality. If the conceptualization of an expression did not reflect the real state of affairs in the world, the reasoning behind the expression was deemed faulty (see Bodine, 1989, pp. 150–52).

Wittgenstein's familiarity with and lifelong respect for Kraus

We know that Wittgenstein's sister Margarete was an enthusiastic reader of *Die Fackel* and it is doubtless through her that Wittgenstein, during his mid-teens, first became familiar with the overall spirit of Kraus's publication (see Monk, 1990, pp. 15–17). Later, in 1914, Wittgenstein would have copies of *Die Fackel* sent to him during his stay in Norway and would follow Kraus's indirect advice in giving away a substantial share of his inheritance. Later still, Wittgenstein would consider presenting Kraus with a copy of the *Tractatus* with the hope that it would meet with Kraus's approval.

So Wittgenstein not only respected and admired Kraus's work and ideals, but also apparently agreed with Kraus's overall views on language – at least during his Tractarian period. But this brings up some questions. There are considerable differences between Wittgenstein's early and later philosophies. So what do we make of the continuity in Wittgenstein's respect for Kraus as reflected in the quote from *Culture and Value* that heads this chapter, a passage written in 1931? What aspects (if any) of Kraus's life-work survived Wittgenstein's Tractarian period and are given voice in his later philosophical method, the characteristics of which we will address in Chapter 7? The overwhelming evidence provided by philosophical and biographical accounts of Wittgenstein's personal and intellectual development shows this question to be premature. Kraus's influence on Wittgenstein runs deeper than that which emerges through doctrinal and stylistic characteristics of Wittgenstein's philosophical writings alone. Evidently, both Kraus and Wittgenstein recognized that their conceptualizations of and concerns with language were different from those of most of their contemporaries. To identify the 'deeper' ways in which Kraus influenced Wittgenstein we must understand Kraus's world conceptualization as taken up by Wittgenstein and displayed through further revelations about the latter's *personality*. Only then will we be in a position to address the ways in which those aspects of Kraus's world conceptualization are expressed in both Wittgenstein's early and later philosophies.

A matter of style: Wittgenstein's 'Krausian' personality

We mentioned earlier that, beginning in 1927, Wittgenstein occasionally attended meetings of the Vienna Circle. At one point he was asked by the Circle's leader, Moritz Schlick, to speak on the *Tractatus*. Wittgenstein agreed, but on the occasion members of the Circle were surprised to see their speaker turn his back on them to read aloud poems by Rabinadrath Tagore! What could be the meaning of this? The best guess is that Wittgenstein thought the Circle had completely misunderstood the central point of the *Tractatus*, which was ethical, not logical. So perhaps reading poetry might direct the Circle's attention to its ethical message. But why not take a more direct approach and just tell the Circle that they had misunderstood his book? Why not just instruct them on the book's central message? In this way and in others Wittgenstein was a difficult man. He has been described as having a character of 'high seriousness and integrity, which carried with them a fierce hatred of pretence, affectation, slickness, mere cleverness, and superficiality of any sort' (Pitcher, 1964, pp. 11–12). This character was displayed in just about every dimension of Wittgenstein's life, such as his refusal to wear a beard or a necktie, his austerely furnished rooms, and his refusal to sit at the Cambridge 'high table.'

What accounts for these characteristics of Wittgenstein's personality? The answer lies in his Expressionist ideals – his Krausian nature. For Wittgenstein was one among a generation of alienated Viennese intellectuals disgusted by the ostentation, obsession with etiquette, and high-minded bourgeois superfluities of their own culture. To these young Krausian/Expressionist 'rebels,' the beards, mustaches, sideburns, dress and mannerisms of eminent Viennese doctors, businessmen and academicians were bodily manifestations of the gaudy ornamentation found on, around and inside their mansions. They were the expressions of a pretentious society that lacked integrity. Thus, men like Kraus and Wittgenstein sought to symbolize and achieve their own integrity by rejecting facial hair and all other bourgeois superfluities (see Janik and Toulmin, 1973, p. 203). The Krausian Wittgenstein sought to uphold integrity of expression through a hawkish attention to the use of words – his own and that of others. Throughout his life Wittgenstein displayed 'Kraus's habit of taking his opponent at his word and reading from a single ill-judged sentence a whole moral character' (McGuinness, 1988, p. 37).

Wittgenstein as a Krausian philosopher

Stylistic and doctrinal parallels

Commentators on the *Tractatus* have noted that the book's style of presentation makes it one of the most difficult philosophical classics to understand. Its extreme condensation forces readers to attend to every word. Its inexplicit conceptual scheme makes it difficult indeed to grasp various steps in the argument and to discern its direction. Therefore it has been suggested that, more than anything else, the matter of style is of the greatest importance for understanding the *Tractatus* (Schulte, 1992, p. 40). To be sure, without knowledge of the author's cultural background anyone picking up the book for the first time will be struck by its absence of section titles or chapters that indicate topics to be addressed. There is also its complex numbering scheme by which the book's pithy remarks are organized and presented. In a footnote to the book's first remark, Wittgenstein explains that the decimal numbers assigned to individual remarks indicate the relative logical importance of the propositions.

Like other Viennese intellectuals, Wittgenstein was familiar with the eighteenth-century theoretical physicist and natural philosopher Lichtenberg, who helped popularize the aphoristic style of philosophizing. Combine this style with the Expressionist aim of achieving more truthful expression through less ornamentation and Kraus's facts/values separation, and the result is a book that serves as a platform for Krausian and Expressionist ideals in philosophy. The style of writing and argument taken up by Wittgenstein in the *Tractatus* is not based on mere stylistic preference. The style both *demonstrates* and *serves* the overall (Krausian) message. But is it the case that the central message of the *Tractatus* and its style of presentation are the *only* reasons Wittgenstein considered sending Kraus a copy of the book? The conceptual scheme of the book shows the answer to this question to be 'no.'

Concerns of the Tractatus: *mapping a conceptual scheme*

To compare directly Kraus's conception of language with that of the *Tractatus* we follow Peterson (1990) in mapping the conceptual scheme of the book using Wittgenstein's own metaphor of logic (or language) 'mirroring' the world, an image Wittgenstein himself used both in his wartime *Notebooks* (Wittgenstein, 1979, p. 39) and in the *Tractatus* (e.g. §5.511). Although Peterson (1990) divides the conceptual scheme of the *Tractatus* into two threefold divisions that constitute the mirror of language, we think it more helpful to envision one mirror divided into three separate sections.

The first section comprises representational language that reflects the world of facts. So the *Tractatus* begins with remarks about the factual world and moves on to consider representational language. The second section comprises non-representational language. Although this mirror might be regarded as reflecting *discourse* about the syntactic features of language as part of the factual world, the middle parts of the *Tractatus* argue that various aspects of that discourse are, in fact, *part* of the mirror of language. The third section comprises what Wittgenstein labels *nonsense*, which deals with the 'ineffable' or 'mystical' but which ultimately *can-*

not be reflected in the mirror of language. To Wittgenstein, 'nonsense' does not mean foolish, absurd, or not useful. It more closely resembles 'meaningless.' Our representational system, as Wittgenstein argues toward the end of the *Tractatus*, cannot describe the 'mystical' (or ineffable) domain of what is real (see Peterson, 1990, pp. 4–5). Roughly, if we use the language of the first mirror to explain the ineffable, we slide into nonsense.

To summarize, Wittgenstein begins the *Tractatus* by showing that our representational system (language or logic) has as its target the real world or the world of 'facts.' Language consists of names in relation which are not part of its target – the real world (first mirror). In using language to talk about these syntactic relations and necessities, we are not representing facts in the real world and are thus using language in a non-representational way (second mirror). And finally, the language that comprises the first mirror of language cannot describe the mystical, religious or aesthetic aspects of reality (third mirror).

The foregoing shows how, in the *Tractatus*, from beginning to end, Wittgenstein places emphasis on each succeeding mirror of language. Combining what we know about the book's conceptual scheme with what we know about its central message, a comparison can be made between the overall concerns and intentions of the *Tractatus* with Kraus's conception of language. In addition, the components of Wittgenstein's mirrors (representational language, non-representational language, nonsense) and what they reflect respectively (the world of facts, the syntactic conventions, the mystical) can be compared with the theoretical components of Kraus's conception of language. These are reason or the power of mental association (*Geist*), feelings, natural drives and the power of the imagination or non-verbal conceptualization (*Phantasie*), word or linguistic form (*Wort*), and conceptualization (*Wesen*). There follows the natural development and cooperative engagement of *Geist* and *Phantasie* during an individual's youth (*Ursprung*) with the expression of doubt (*Zweifel*).

Summary of the Krausian parallels and Wittgenstein's early philosophy

There are four parallels between Kraus and Wittgenstein's *Tractatus*. The first is a general concern with the relationship between language and the world, manifest in Kraus's '*Sprachkritik*' and referred to in Wittgenstein's pronouncement that 'All philosophy is a "critique of language" (though not in Mauthner's sense)' (Wittgenstein, 1921/1961, §4.0031). The reference to Fritz Mauthner in this remark is intended to show that 'the type of language critique being carried out that served as a model for Wittgenstein was Kraus' (not Fritz Mauthner's, skeptical one)' (Bodine, 1989, p. 153). Wittgenstein's principal debt to Mauthner consists in the view that language is not a 'thing,' but an activity. In any case, all three sections of the Tractarian mirror assign language–world relationships or, perhaps better put, describe *possible* language–world relationships. Like Kraus, Wittgenstein tries to establish a close isomorphic relationship between the form of language and the form of the world. For Wittgenstein, the world as reflected by representational language is the world of facts; for Kraus, utterances are compared with states of affairs in the world.

Second, both men attempt to establish a *truth relationship* between language and the world. Kraus's '*Sprachkritik*' aims to find out whether or not the linguistic form

(*Wort*) of an utterance, along with its conceptualization (*Wesen*), truthfully reflect the events or states of affairs to which they refer. Now recall that Kraus called upon those of his ilk to engage in a critique similar to his own area of human experience. With respect to the relation between language and reality, Wittgenstein did so in philosophy with his own form of '*Sprachkritik*,' grounding the logical form of language in reality. 'What any picture, or whatever form, must have in common with reality, in order to be able to depict it – in any way at all, is logical form, i.e. the form of reality' (Wittgenstein, 1921/1961, §2.18). Indeed, the connection between language (or thought) and reality is the main theme of the *Tractatus* and the book's principal thesis is that sentences, or their mental counterparts, are 'pictures' of facts. This thesis – the so-called 'picture theory of meaning' – holds that

(1) the relation between the elementary components of a sentence (or picture) corresponds to the objects or situations in the world it depicts and
(2) the structure of the sentence (configurations of its names) is the same as the structure of the situation depicted in the factual world.

Despite the influence of philosophy of physics, to which we will turn below, the impetus for Wittgenstein finding such a view attractive in the first place is surely owed to Kraus. For it was Kraus who personified the concern over the relation between states of affairs in the world, linguistic expressions about the world, and conceptions of the world behind those expressions, and sought to establish *the* truthful relationship between all of these factors.

A third parallel between the two men's conceptualizations of language is the effort to give sentences and signs *sense* by thinking through their content. As noted earlier, Kraus's critique of language often aims to show that the utterances of speakers reflect a certain amount of ignorance as to their own hidden motivations and interests, in addition to the social realities that have implications for the sense of those utterances. As a social critic, Kraus thought it his duty to shed light on those hidden motivations, interests and social realities for the greater interests of society. As a philosopher and for the greater interests of philosophy, Wittgenstein sought to shed light on those kinds of language that do and do not have sense. For Wittgenstein, representational sentences have sense, while non-representational language – statements about syntax – do not concern the world, lack sense and 'say nothing' (Wittgenstein, 1921/1961, §6.11).

The final parallel between Kraus and Wittgenstein's early conception of language cuts to the very heart of the central message of the *Tractatus*: the distinction between the realm of facts and the realm of values. Kraus preferred to think of values as being demonstrated in actions, rather than being developed through rational deliberation. This resembles the Tractarian distinction between *saying* and *showing*. 'What *can* be shown, *cannot* be said' (Wittgenstein, 1921/1961, §4.1212) and 'What we cannot speak about we must pass over in silence' (§7). In the Preface to the *Tractatus* Wittgenstein says: 'The whole sense of the book might be summed up in the following words: what can be said at all can be said clearly, and what we cannot talk about we must pass over in silence' (Wittgenstein, 1921/1961, p. 3).

What remains to be pointed out is that there are some notable *differences* between Kraus and Wittgenstein regarding their concerns about the relation between language and the world. After all, Wittgenstein's philosophical analysis of language goes far beyond that of Kraus. The most obvious of these differences is that Kraus did not rigorously elaborate on the difference between representational and non-representational language and did not propose, as Wittgenstein did, that language about syntax is part of the mirror of non-representational language and not part of the world of facts. By the same token, nowhere in the *Tractatus* was Wittgenstein specifically concerned with the development of the powers of reason (*Geist*) and non-verbal conceptualization (*Phantasie*) at a particular point in one's youth (*Ursprung*). Nor did he elaborate on or formalize Kraus's methodological aim of demonstrating the polysemous meaning of a word or words in order to show that their meanings have been restricted to serve a particular agenda or way of looking at the world. As we will see in later chapters, Kraus's concern with polysemous meaning and *Ursprung* is to be found in many of Wittgenstein's later philosophical remarks, most notably §244 of *Philosophical Investigations*, where he suggests that natural expressions of pain during infancy are *replaced* by linguistic expressions through training.

Other influences

Arnold Schönberg and the limits of music

In search for a delimitation of what is meaningful, Wittgenstein rejected the idea that the boundary that separates the meaningful and meaningless is like a boundary between the territories of two nations, though he did not express it in quite this image. Outside the realm of the meaningful there is nothing at all! The scope of meaningful language is determined from within, by the rules for the construction of meaningful propositions.

Where did Wittgenstein get this idea? It has been suggested by Janik and Toulmin (1973) that he might have come across a similar conception in the musicology of Arnold Schönberg. Debates on the topic then current in Vienna would surely have been very familiar to Wittgenstein's mother as a keen musician and one much involved in the musical life of the city. Should a musical composition inspired by a poem be subject to criticism as to whether it faithfully portrays the topic and manner of the poem? Or should the musical quality of the composition be paramount?

In his discussion of these matters, Schönberg (1950, p. 2) makes it quite clear that there is no necessity about the portrayal. The meaning of music, he says, 'is perverted if one tries to recognize events and feelings in music, as if they *must* be there.' The presence or absence of these effects and intimations is irrelevant to musical quality. But why is this?

The meaning of music is a consequence of the rules of composition. Musical rules of composition have meaning only relative to the principles of order of some epoch. In commenting on the appearance of the 12-tone method of composition,

Schönberg compares the older style with the music he himself initiated. 'Formerly the use of the fundamental harmony had been theoretically regulated by the recognition of the effects of root progressions,' based on the tonic with its associated harmonic progressions, and the system of major and minor scales derived from it. Innovation is first intuitive. 'Nevertheless, the desire for conscious control of the new means and forms will arise in every artist's mind; and he will wish to know *consciously* the laws and rules which govern the forms which he has conceived "as in a dream"' (Schönberg, 1950, p. 106).

What counts as music is determined by the laws and rules of composition which intuitively or consciously are used by the composer. It is not difficult to draw a parallel with logic and the limitations of meaningful language.

German philosophy of physics

We have emphasized Kraus's influence on the *Tractatus* in terms of its critique of language and overall message. But in certain respects the philosophy of physics of Helmholtz, Hertz and Boltzmann constituted equally significant influences on Wittgenstein's early thinking. It is important to emphasize the deep differences that separated the interpretations of physics proposed by the German philosopher–scientists in the tradition of Helmholtz and the phenomenalist turn taken by Mach (1886/1959), echoed by the Vienna Circle. Mach held that the laws of physics were simply mnemonics for the reproduction of items from a vast catalogue of sensory correlations. That is to say, objects were nothing more than persisting groupings of elements, qualities when considered with respect to each other, and sensations when considered with respect to the person who experiences them.

Unlike their positivistically inclined successors, the older generation of physicists held to a qualified realism, in that physics was concerned with systems of simple or elementary masses that we know must exist from certain conditions on the meaningfulness of formulae expressing physical laws. There was no requirement that these elementary masses be presented to human beings perceptually. For Hertz and Boltzmann, the world represented in the laws of physics extended far beyond the bounds of human sensory capacities. These ideas were, we believe, the sources of what seems most original and arresting in the *Tractatus*. In the next chapter we will pick up and explain the picture theory of meaning, the doctrine of simple objects and the truth-tables as iconic displays of the domain of possibility. In this chapter we will set out the aspects of the Geman interpretation of physics that we believe were more or less directly translated into the logical principles of Wittgenstein's *Tractatus*.

The picture theory of meaning as offered by Hertz
Hertz's *Principles of Mechanics* begins with a statement of the picture theory:

> We form for ourselves images or symbols of external objects; and the form which we give them is such that the necessary consequences of the images in thought are always the images of the necessary consequents in nature of the things pictured. In order that this requirement may be satisfied, there must be a certain conformity between nature and our thought.
>
> (Hertz, 1899/1956, p. 1)

The standard translation renders the German word '*Bild*' as 'image' or 'symbol.' However, the formal isomorphism or conformity between *Bild* and the 'things pictured' suggests that 'picture' would be a translation more faithful to Hertz's intention.

Hertz lays down criteria for the acceptability of physicists' pictures. They must be permissible, that is in conformity with the laws of thought (logic). But they must also be *correct*. Hertz defines this relation indirectly as follows: 'We shall denote as incorrect any permissible images, if their essential relations contradict the relations of external things' (Hertz, 1899/1956, p. 2). Images can be ranked to the degree to which they represent the essential relations of the objects in question.

Wittgenstein, as a young man who frequently quoted Hertz's well-known claim that there are problems which cannot be solved, but will simply cease to trouble us when we have a clear grasp of the forms of the propositions with which we represent the world, and have devised an appropriate symbolism to picture the world, surely would have found Hertz's version of the picture theory attractive.

The necessary enrichment of ontologies

The connection between the picture theory and truth and the principle that there must be simple objects is brought out not only by Hertz, but also by Boltzmann. He points out that the development of theories considered as pictures requires 'hypothetical features added to experience, which are fashioned, as always, by transferring the laws we have observed in finite bodies to fictitious elements of our own making' (Boltzmann, 1899/1974, p. 226). That is, the catalogue of elementary objects of the world is necessitated not by experience, but by the forms of the laws themselves. 'Differential equations', says Boltzmann, 'require, just as atomism does, an initial idea of a large number of numerical values and points in the manifold of numbers' (ibid., p. 227). A mathematical function can be thought of extensionally as a pattern of correlations among sets of numbers. Some such set corresponds to the numerical results of systematic experimentation. This is how a law can be a picture. If laws are pictures, the world must have a similar degree of multiplicity as the elements of the picture. For Boltzmann, imperceptible atoms are the elementary objects of the world, known through the isomorphism with the structure and elements of the picture. That the basic elements are simple entails that their behavior cannot be explained by citing their compositions. This point is emphasized by Boltzmann in the following passage:

> When I say that mechanical pictures might be able to illuminate such obscurities, I do not mean by this that the position and motion of material points in space is something whose simplest elements are completely explicable. On the contrary, to explain the ultimate elements of our cognition is altogether impossible; for to explain is to reduce to something better known and simpler, and therefore that to which everything is reduced must forever remain inexplicable.
>
> (Boltzmann, 1899/1974, p. 257)

Hertz believed that mechanics could account for all motions and hence for all material processes and phenomena using only three properties: mass, space and time, that is, mass and motion. The troubling concepts of 'force' and 'energy,' according to Hertz, are not required. In order for the laws of nature, built out of symbols for mass and motion alone, to have a definite meaning, another hypothesis is needed. In addition to the perceptible masses that can be studied by observation and experiment, the universe must contain hidden masses, related to one another by fixed (necessary) relations. The realization that such elementary objects must exist is not the result of *analysis* of the meanings of laws, nor does any empirical research program establish it. It follows from the requirement that the laws of nature be capable of meaningfulness within the context of the worldview of physics. That is, the laws of nature should have a determinate interpretation. The isomorphism must be complete so that the law should be a picture, in that the multiplicity of the world must exactly match the multiplicity of the picture, as Boltzmann described it.

Hertz's way of introducing the ultimate simple objects runs as follows:

> If we try to understand the motions of bodies around us, and to refer them to simple and clear rules, paying attention only to what can be directly observed, our attempt will, in general, fail ... We become convinced that the manifold of the actual universe must be greater than the manifold of the universe which is directly revealed to us by our senses. If we wish to obtain an image of the universe which shall be well-rounded, complete, and conformable to law, we have to presuppose, behind the things which we see, other, invisible things – to imagine confederates concealed beyond the limits of our senses.

> (Hertz, 1899/1956, p. 25)

Interestingly, Helmholtz, while expressing general approval of Hertz's project, criticized it for the absence of any examples of simple objects. Wittgenstein's *Tractatus* was criticized on the same score. Of course Hertz could no more give examples of his simple objects than could Wittgenstein. They are not known by means of empirical research. They are not arrived at by conceptual analysis. We know that they must exist by virtue of the requirements that must be met if the *meaning* of the laws of physics should be determinate.

Here is how this would work for a well-known law in physics: the general gas law of Boyle and Gay-Lussac:

$$PV = RT$$

where P, V and T are properties of confined samples of gas.

We know that the law is true since it pictures the behavior of real gases, via the correspondence between a set of numbers that represents the above function (R is a constant) and the set of numbers generated by experimenting. It is also obvious that neither P, nor V, nor T is an elementary name denoting a simple object. How then can the general gas law have a determinate meaning? According to Hertz, we add sufficient elementary masses to our conception of the world until we have a complete match between the law and the world. So the term P must be a conjunction of terms p_1, p_2 ... p_n which are elementary names, referring to simple objects, namely instances of momentum, mv. And so for the other variables: the molecular equation is $pv = 1/3nmc^2$, which can be seen as isomorphic with the general gas law.

What we wish to emphasize is that the picture theory of the meaning of propositions and the doctrine of elementary objects come 'as a package.' That pictures have a determinate sense is intimated to us by the fact that we can understand and use them in highly refined ways. That they do have such a sense requires that the projection relation between the law as a structure and the world as a structure is actually achieved, though not through acts of human perception. It is achieved overall in the way one part of the world, the sentences of some language, are isomorphic with the world in general.

Boltzmann and phase space

Physics would collapse into Machian catalogues of facts if all reference to possibilities were excluded. As Boltzmann and Hertz emphasize, the propositions of physics are differential equations, the domains of which are manifolds of numbers, representing possibilities which might or might not be realized by the development of real systems, represented by particular sets of values of the parameters that define their possible states. Physics, too, handles this routinely by the construction of phase spaces to represent all possible states of a system, as represented by a certain set of variables.

The algebraic formulation of laws suggests a systematic distinction between what might have happened in the past and what might happen in the future from what has and will happen. Laws of motion in mechanics, for example, represent the totality of possible motions. That they have solutions for particular conditions allows a physicist to make predictions of what will happen in specific circumstances and explain what has happened in specific circumstances in the past. There is a systematic and ontologically highly significant difference between the domain of laws as algebraic functions and the domain of their solutions for motions that have occurred or will actually occur. The law of motion, $s = \frac{1}{2} at^2$, represents all possible cases of free fall from rest in all possible uniform gravitational fields. Setting a to 9.8 m/second fixes a certain trajectory through space near the surface of the earth. Solving the equation for $t = 2$ seconds gives us a value of $s = 19.6$ meters, a point in that trajectory. We have arrived at a description of an actual motion, say of this particular cannon ball dropped from the Tower of Pisa on this particular day in 1624. We can think in Cartesian terms of the variables s and t as represented by perpendicular axes to form a two dimensional space of all possible motions, that is, changes of position with the elapse of time. Choosing different gravitational constants picks out specific trajectories of free fall on different planets.

The notion of a 'phase space' is simply a generalization of this basic idea. In classical physics there is a general geometrical representation in which the rectangular axes of a three-dimensional 'space' represent the entropy, the energy and the volume of a material system. This 'space' represents all possible states of the material world in which systems of this sort are embedded. Each state of such a system is represented as a point, that is a particular value of the x and p variables. The trajectory of these points represents the history of a particular system.

Boltzmann shared with Hertz a concern with freeing science from metaphysics by reflecting on the nature of science and, like Hertz, 'sharply distinguished between its empirical and a priori elements ... [linking] the latter to the nature of representation' (Glock, 1996, p. 341). But Boltzmann counted Hertz's use of hidden masses in motion as constitutive of those very metaphysical speculations that were to be avoided in mechanics. Thus the two men disagreed as to what a mathematical picture of reality should consist in.

> For Boltzmann, a physical picture was quite literally a visualizable image of reality, something [Boltzmann] could picture in his mind that had both physical content and form. Boltzmann had to be able to see physical reality in his mind's eye. This is one reason why he rejected Hertz's use of hidden masses in motion as one of the principles of mechanics. For Boltzmann, physically visualizable representations come first, followed by mathematical formalism.
>
> (Wilson, 1989, pp. 254–5)

Instead of producing mathematical pictures, the independent elements of which would include metaphysical hidden masses that lend determinacy to the pictures, Boltzmann opted to treat the independent properties of a physical system as defining separate coordinates in a multidimensional system. The points of such a system constitute the 'ensemble of possible states.' In the *Tractatus* Wittgenstein did much the same with respect to the syntactic mirror of language, mapping out the possible meaningful combinations of propositions (i.e. possible states of affairs in the world) through his truth-table logic. The 'ensemble of possible states' in the world postulated by Boltzmann (1899/1974) is thus extended to the 'logical space' of possible relations of propositions to states of affairs in the world by Wittgenstein in his truth-table logic.

The full significance of these influences will become clear when we encounter Wittgenstein's *Tractatus* in the next chapter.

Learning point: cultural and scientific influences on Wittgenstein

1. *Karl Kraus's 'Critique of Language'*

    (a) This gave Wittgenstein the idea that only scientifically anchored language was honest. All other uses of words were open to self-deception and hypocrisy.
    (b) Expressing values should not be confused with stating facts. Values are shown in style of writing and in the course of a life.
    (c) It was possible to shape one's own life along the same lines of authenticity and honesty as a Krausian man.

2. *Arnold Schönberg's musicology*

    (a) Schönberg argued that the only way to distinguish music from non-music was to attend to the rules of composition. 'Music' is defined from within.
    (b) This principle may have given Wittgenstein the idea of defining any human practice (e.g. language) 'from within' by reference to its rules of construction, in particular the domain of language.

3. *German philosophy of physics*

    (a) From *Heinrich Hertz* Wittgenstein seems to have taken
        (i)   the idea of a proposition as a 'picture' of a fact and
        (ii) the need to postulate a realm of unobservable simple objects
            to ensure the intelligibility of meaningful propositions.
    (b) From *Ludwig Boltzmann* Wittgenstein may have adopted and adapted
        the other basic ideas of the *Tractatus*: a logical space of possible
        states of affairs, expressed in truth-tables.

Further reading

Bartley, W.W. (1985). *Wittgenstein*, 2nd edn. LaSalle, IL: Open Court.

Bodine, J.F. (1981), Paradigms of truthful literary and artistic expressivity. Karl Kraus and Vienna at the turn of the century. *The Germanic Review*, *56*(2), 41–50.

Bodine, J.F. (1989), Karl Kraus, Ludwig Wittgenstein and poststructural paradigms of textual understanding. *Modern Austrian Literature*, *22*(3/4), 143–85.

Janik, A. and Toulmin, S. (1973), *Wittgenstein's Vienna*. New York: Simon & Schuster.

Malcolm, N. (1958). *Wittgenstein: A memoir with a biographical sketch by G.H. von Wright*. London: Oxford University Press.

McGuinness, B. (1982), *Wittgenstein and his Times*. Oxford: Blackwell.

Monk, R. (1990). *Wittgenstein: The duty of genius*. New York: Penguin Books.

3 The *Tractatus* and its connection with cognitive science

> Psychology is no more closely related to philosophy than any
> other natural science ... Does not my study of sign-language
> correspond to the study of thought-processes, which
> philosophers used to consider so essential to the philosophy of
> logic? Only in most cases they got entangled in unessential
> psychological investigations, and with my method too there is an
> analogous risk.
>
> Wittgenstein, *Tractatus Logico-Philosophicus*, 4.1121

Topics introduced: particulars and universals; facts, propositions; the picture theory of meaning; elementary objects and elementary names; ostension; isomorphism; showing; sense; logical form; what can be said; logical space and truth-tables; tautology; positivism; verifiability criterion; behaviorism and methodological behaviorism; operational definition; eliminative materialism; cognitive psychology and cognitive science; the computational model and artificial intelligence; Turing test

Why should the *Tractatus* be of any interest to psychologists? Wittgenstein's basic insight early in his philosophical career was that there are two kinds of language and thought: scientific and ethical–religious. These can be termed in other ways. For example, we like to call scientific language 'fact-stating language' or 'fact-stating discourse.' Thinking scientifically might be called 'scientific thinking.' Also, ethical–religious language can be characterized as 'language pertaining to values' and ethical–religious thought as 'values-thinking.' Scientific thinking is expressed in fact-stating discourse, while values-thinking is expressed, to put it simply, in ways of life. We have seen that the insight to divide language and thinking along these lines almost certainly came from Karl Kraus. His critique of language brought out the radical difference between stating facts and expressing values. Even today, ordinary people and scientists alike have a strong tendency to conflate these two forms of discourse.

The second insight that underlies the *Tractatus* may have come from Arnold Schönberg, whose musicological writings were mentioned in Chapter 2. Schönberg argued that the domain of 'what is music' can only be determined 'from within.' Music is just that which is created according to certain rules of composition. In similar fashion, Wittgenstein set out to determine the domain of scientific language by laying out the rules for making statements that would be both meaningful and factual. Uses of language that do not conform to these rules, he thought, would not be factually meaningful. Wittgenstein held that statements pertaining to values and commitment to a way of life – ethical and religious statements, including statements expressing 'ineffable' experiences – have nothing in common with factual statements (or what he termed 'propositions'). Such statements and expressions cannot be used to describe anything.

If language is the primary means for thinking and expressing thought, then there are two quite different kinds of thinking. Scientific thinking involves the use of words whose meanings are fixed by objects and events in our world. Values-thinking is largely a matter of acting with integrity and honesty. One's ethical and religious commitments, experiences and so on cannot be described using scientific language. However, they can be *shown* in how one lives. Thus, to reveal the nature of values, Wittgenstein believed he had to give a thorough and final account of scientific discourse, bounded from within (Schönberg) by the rules and principles of the construction of factual propositions. The important matters of life, pertaining to values, lay outside this domain and so beyond the reach of factual, scientific language.

So what does the *Tractatus* have to do with psychology? Well, it is the first widely known and comprehensive attempt to construct a wholly formal representation of the main medium of cognition – namely language – and to provide a computational scheme for passing from one formal representation to another – that is, from language to cognition and from cognition to language. We emphasize that it was not Wittgenstein's plan to develop a comprehensive cognitive psychology. His purposes were much more grandiose! He wanted to develop a final account of all legitimate forms of discursive thought as expressed using language. One of his aims in the *Tractatus* was to eliminate all philosophical problems that have their origins in confusions about the way language works. (In this sense, his 'early' and 'later' philosophies are strikingly similar.) Another was to demonstrate the scope of scientific language and its limits. All that was important in human life lay outside those limits and so was 'unsayable.'

Unbeknownst to the great majority of psychologists today, directly and indirectly, the *Tractatus* has had a profound influence on the origins of cognitive psychology as a science concerned with constructing formal models of cognitive processes. In order to bring out this influence and its implications, we set out here some of the leading ideas of the Tractarian treatment of language. We believe that the formal treatment of language in the *Tractatus* was intended as a generalization of the formal treatment of physics by some of Wittgenstein's 'heroes,' in particular Hertz and Boltzmann, to the whole domain of language as an instrument of thought. In reading what follows, one should bear in mind the sketches of the ideas of Hertz and Boltzmann in the previous chapter.

The basic ideas of the *Tractatus*

The *Tractatus* begins with remarks about the world of facts and moves on to consider the nature of the language that would be ideally adapted to the representation of facts. To keep psychologists in the picture, as it were, as we go through our account of the *Tractatus* we may think of psychologists constructing and using models to picture psychological processes. People do things. Psychologists take note of how people do things. They construct models that seem to correspond to how people do things. Then they 'test' their models under experimental conditions. Wittgenstein's proposal for an ideal language for science can be thought of as a general prescription of how such processes should be described.

What are propositions? Wittgenstein's 'picture theory' of meaning

One of the age-old problems in philosophy is posed by the contrast between (1) individual and particular objects (such as houses and people), each unique in its own way, and (2) general or shared properties, such as being made of stone like some houses, or walking on two legs like billions of other human beings. Unlike many philosophers, from Plato to Bertrand Russell, who puzzled about how particulars could be fused with what was general or universal, Wittgenstein begins the *Tractatus* with the thesis that everything in the world is already given in the form of a 'fact' – that is, as an object with properties which it shares with other things.

1   The world is all that is the case.

1.1   The world is the totality of facts, not of things.

Given this bold beginning, Wittgenstein must show how facts are created out of things without invoking any mysterious universals, like 'stoniness' or 'bipedality,' in which individuals are supposed to partake or exemplify. Language comes to us, to those who use it and understand it, as *propositions*. Propositions express facts. The meaning of any proposition must fit with the fact it is used to express. But how is it possible to see the fit between a proposition and a fact? To answer this question, Wittgenstein proposed what became known as the 'picture theory of meaning.'

Propositions are *pictures* of facts and pictures show the isomorphism, the common structure, shared by propositions and the states of affairs that correspond to them in the world. The picture theory aims to show how language 'touches' reality. There must a match between the basic constituents of the world (elementary or 'atomic' facts composed of objects and their configurations) and representational language (elementary sentences that are composed of names and their configurations). The names in an elementary sentence are the elements of the picture and the configuration of those names is the structure of the picture. In order for the picture to be a 'truthful' representation of the world, its elements and their configuration must be isomorphic with the situation in the world of facts the picture depicts (see Peterson, 1990, p. 18). That is, picture and situation must have the same structure. To understand how 'The dog gnawed the bone' can be a word-picture of a dog gnawing a bone we must detail further Wittgenstein's account of the nature of facts and propositions.

According to the picture theory, facts and propositions are patterned groups of entities – thing-like beings. In the ultimate analysis, facts are patterned groups of elementary objects and propositions are patterned groups of elementary names. For the uninitiated, the ideas of 'elementary object' and 'elementary name' will be somewhat difficult to grasp. But this is perfectly understandable because, like Hertz, Wittgenstein himself was unable to give a specific example of an elementary object. Like many other terms introduced in the *Tractatus*, the precise meanings of 'elementary object' and 'elementary name' are still debated by Wittgenstein scholars. But for present purposes, we can think of elementary objects – alternatively, 'simple objects' or 'simples' – as ultimate constituents of reality. As for elementary names, Max Black's (1964) description of 'simple sign' is serviceable. He compares Wittgenstein's 'names' with 'the linguists' "morphemes," the smallest units of meaning in the sentence' (Black, 1964, p. 108). We can think of hanging elementary names, the smallest units of meaning, on to elementary objects, the smallest units of reality or 'thing-ness.'

Back to propositions. *A proposition is true if it matches a corresponding fact.* For every elementary object in the fact there must be an elementary name in the proposition, and the arrangement of the names in the proposition must match the arrangement of the factual objects. Here are a few relevant remarks from the *Tractatus*:

2.1   We picture facts to ourselves.

2.15   The fact that the elements of a picture are related to one another in a determinate way represents that things are related to one another in the same way ...

2.223   In order to tell whether a picture is true or false, we must compare it with reality.

This account of truth (and falsity in mismatch) also gives us an account of meaning. Any such account must keep separate the question of how a proposition has a meaning from the question of whether it is true or false.

3.202   The simple signs employed in propositions are called names.

3.203   A name means an object. The object is its meaning ...

Peterson (1990) has a wonderful way of summarizing how meaning arises from this relationship between a name and an object: 'When names and objects correspond, and the structures are the same, the semantic spark jumps the gap, and meaning is born' (p. 32). The phrase 'and the structures are the same' marks our entry into the domain of *logical syntax*. In addition to elementary names, a proposition displays a certain arrangement of names, expressed by words for relations, such as 'and,' 'or,' 'on' and so on. *These words do not name anything.* Rather, they *display the structure* of the proposition to which the structure of the relevant fact must correspond. An atomic fact is the simplest arrangement of which a cluster of elementary objects is capable. Elementary objects can be fitted together only in certain ways.

3.21   To the configuration of objects in a situation corresponds the configuration of simple signs in the propositional sign.

That Wittgenstein holds a special place for logical syntax means *not all words are names.* Generally, the words we use to express propositions do not display the 'real meaning' of what is said or thought. The statements of ordinary discourse are in need of analysis. The process of analysis is no more but no less than displaying *the ordered structure of names that is the proposition*. A word is meaningful because there is an object it signifies. That is, in fact-stating discourse, *meaning is object signified*. Presumably we learn new words by having our attention drawn to the objects they signify, that is, by ostension or the pointing out of the relevant referent. A mother with a child points to a dog: 'Look, honey, *that's* a dog!'

To clarify these ideas, we should consider the advantage of this picture metaphor. Why not just say, for example, that specific names 'match' or 'correspond to' specific objects or configurations of objects in the world? Wittgenstein's preference for the picture metaphor has to do with his belief that language cannot *describe* the isomorphism between an elementary sentence and elementary fact (Peterson, 1990, pp. 25–6). This is a very important point that illuminates the picture theory as a metaphorical and methodological device. If we say a name in an elementary sentence 'matches' an object, we must go on to explain what that matching consists in – an extra step that is *external* to the elementary sentence, its names and their configurations, the object or objects depicted by it, and their configurations. Any attempt to describe through language what an elementary sentence (or even a name) has in common with reality would take us to another level of analysis. We would need to have a representation of the state of affairs and a representation for the proposition that is structurally isomorphic to it, so that these representations could be brought together into a higher-order proposition which had the same structure as the relation between the original proposition and the fact pictured. Wittgenstein realized that this higher level of analysis was redundant, since one could just gesture to an example of a proposition matching a fact and so *show* what the relation must be. Instead of *describing* the relationship between sentences and factual states of affairs, Wittgenstein constructs pictures to *show* that relationship (see Peterson, 1990, p. 25).

It is already apparent, we hope, that at a very basic level the method of picturing in the *Tractatus* carries on the Krausian project of distinguishing the fact-stating language of science from the expression of moral commitments in a person's way of life. But whereas Kraus compared the *conceptualization* of an utterance with what he believed to be the 'real' state of affairs in the world it depicts in order to determine its social and ethical validity, Wittgenstein proposes to compare the *structure* of sentences with the structure of reality in order to verify the truth of sentences. Notice that, at least when it comes to discerning the truth of an utterance, the *Tractatus* eliminates 'the psychological' (or 'conceptualization,' as Kraus put it). No wonder it is difficult to find a thinking individual in the *Tractatus*.

What we have thus far is the presentation of a philosophical method intended to equip philosophers once and for all with a way of analyzing the truth-value of their propositions. Since ethical propositions have no factual content, moral commitments can only be discerned in what people do, not in what they say. Finch (1995) characterizes Wittgenstein's method in the *Tractatus* as a philosophical 'method of abstraction,' which 'refers to the gradual spread into one field of mathematics after another and then into logic of algebraic methods ... which substitutes contentless or meaningless signs ... for natural numbers, geometrical curves and shapes, trigonometric functions, functions of the calculus, and finally the propositional functions in logic' (p. 150). The *Tractatus* may be seen as that point in the history of philosophy where the method of abstraction reaches its zenith.

The doctrine of 'showing'

We have seen that propositions consist of *names* and their arrangement (or structure) and that facts consist of *things* and their arrangement or structure. But there is a fundamental difference between what must be shown and 'what can be said.'

> 4.022   A proposition *shows* its sense.
> A proposition *shows* how things stand *if* it is true. And it *says that* they so stand.

To understand this point we must go back to the account of meaning as object signified. Suppose you try to explain to someone what the word 'dog' means. You might try something like: '"dog" means dog' or 'a "dog" means canine – you know, an animal that barks, has four legs, a tail, and long ears.' But in order for the person to whom we are speaking to *understand* descriptions of this sort, they must already know – at least to some degree – what 'dog' means! How do we escape from this circle of words? You have to direct their attention to a thing, a doggy thing, and then they will know what the word 'dog' means. So you opt for *showing* them a picture of a dog, or you point to a dog on the street (ostension).

The same holds for the truth of a proposition. How can I know whether a certain sentence is true? What would have to be the case about the sentence and the fact for the sentence to be true? The sentence consists of words in a certain relational structure and the fact consists of objects in a certain relational structure. What relationship would have to hold between the structures for the sentence to be true of the fact? They must be seen to match. The structure of the sentence and the structure of the fact have to be the same. But because of the 'circle of words' mentioned above, this match cannot be said. *It must be shown.*

If, as Wittgenstein thought, you could break down sentences into elementary names and their structural arrangements, and if you could break down the world into elementary objects and their structural arrangements, it would be very easy to see whether a sentence were true or false. Just compare the structures 'Dog bites man' and 'Man bites dog' with the state of affairs depicted by these possible newspaper headlines. The word 'bites' is a complex linguistic sign. It denotes an action and so is one of the attributes of the dog or the man. It also serves to link the biting dog and the bitten man to a specific relationship. In its structural significance, 'bites' expresses the direction, or *sense*, of the relation between a biting being and a bitten being. 'Sense' has been used in mathematics to denote this kind of directionality. 'Dog bites man' and 'Man bites dog' differ in sense in the way that 50 miles per hour up Wisconsin Avenue and 50 miles per hour down Wisconsin Avenue are motions at the same speed, but differ in direction (or sense).

Like Bertrand Russell, Wittgenstein thought that the study of relations between names in propositions and between elementary and complex propositions – that is, *logical form* – constituted the domain of logic. But Wittgenstein had a new and different idea of where such forms were to be located:

5.61   Logic pervades the world: the limits of the world are also its limits ...

This remark means the structure of all the meaningful sentences one can make about the world must match the structure of the states of affairs they picture. If the structure of true propositions, as arrangements of elementary propositions, must match the structure of the world, surely the structure of the world – as it can be expressed in the perfect language of science – must also be the structure of logic. Ingenious! But logic does not fix the nature of the world. It fixes the shape of *what we can say* about the world.

We have mentioned previously at several points that Wittgenstein's analysis purported to show that values cannot be captured by fact-stating language. What are the elementary objects that populate these realms of human thought and endeavor? There are the virtuous acts of the saint, but where is the 'virtue'? There are the daubs of color on the canvas, but where is the artistic merit? There are the confessions, prayings and so on that we see in church. But where is the Holy Spirit? The 'where is ... ?' question is to be seen in the Tractarian frame as inviting a 'look and see' response. Virtue, artistic merit and the Holy Spirit can only be shown, gestured at in what people *do*. 'Forgiveness of sins' is not the *name* of a divine act. Similarly, I draw your attention to Rembrandt's *Night Watch*. But I can only gesture at the painting: 'See the look on his face and quality of light!' There is no specific bit of the painting to which such an expression refers.

Making language computable: logical space and the significance of truth-tables

To understand how this highly refined and recondite account of language has to do with the origins of computational functions in cognitive science, we need to go further into Wittgenstein's treatment of the domain of logic. 'The dog bit the man' is a meaningful sentence because 'biting dog' and 'bitten man' are names and the asymmetrical relationship between the biter and the bitten can be shown. However, there are two situations. In one, the actual state of affairs matches the proposition; in the other it does not. The proposition is true in the first situation and false in the second. Any proposition has two possible truth-values, 'true' or 'false.'

Elementary propositions can be combined by the use of logical conjunctions to describe more complex states of affairs. The propositions 'The roses are blooming' (p) and 'The delphiniums are blooming' (q) can be linked by 'and' to create a detailed verbal picture of a garden. The conjoint proposition 'The roses are blooming and the delphiniums are blooming' could express four possible facts. The array of such facts is the logical space of the proposition. (Remember 'phase space'?)

Thus it was that Wittgenstein made use of truth-tables: to display logical spaces. Here is the truth-table for the logical space of the complex proposition about the garden.

p true	q true	p and q true
p true	q false	p and q false
p false	q true	p and q false
p false	q false	p and q false

Here we have a pictorial presentation of the 'space' of possible states of affairs comprehended in the sentence form 'p and q.' This table displays the meaning of the logical sign 'and' (&) as a structural device for creating all possible arrangements of the two propositions represented by 'p' and 'q.' Each of these could picture a state of affairs, depending on the arrangement of elementary propositions ('p' and 'q') in each and the sense; that is, how they are arranged with respect to the relational structure that bonds them into elementary propositions (e.g. 'p and q'). Imagine this in terms of the elementary names 'dog' and 'man' and the relation 'bites,' with which 'p' is created. Then we can add 'kicks,' with which 'q' is created. So in line 1 we would have 'Dog bites man' (p true), 'Man kicks dog' (q true) and thus 'Dog bites man and man kicks dog' (p and q true). Lines 2 and 3 show that 'p and q' is false if *either* the dog does not bite the man or the man does not kick the dog. And finally, line 4 shows that 'p and q' is false if *neither* the dog bites the man nor the man kicks the dog. This was Wittgenstein's point in developing truth-tables. The possible states of affairs with respect to the dog biting the man and the man kicking the dog are accounted for, or shown, entirely.

A logical space is a little bit like a seismograph. The roll of paper represents all possible markings an earthquake might register. The marks made by the seismograph's stylus during an earthquake represent some actual earthquake. The seismograph is set up in such as way as to capture the marks of all possible earthquakes.

Of course, before the *Tractatus* several basic relations like '&,' the meanings of which could be expressed in terms of patterns in a logical space of truth and falsity, had already been identified by logicians – for example, 'not,' 'either ... or ... ,' 'if ... then ... ,' 'not both ... and ... ' and so on. Wittgenstein's project was to show that in so far as language is employed for fact-stating alone, then a few such relations among simple propositions would suffice to express *everything that could be said*. In sum, the whole of the logical space of descriptions of material reality was thereby covered.

Let us illustrate the power of these few 'truth-functions' with some further examples. The logical space of 'The cat is on the mat' consists in its being true when there is a cat on the mat and false otherwise, expressed as:

A (The cat is on the mat)	B (The cat is not on the mat)
p true	not-p false
p false	not-p true

If the cat is on the mat, saying it is not is false (line 1). If the cat is not on the mat, saying it is not is true (line 2).

Now here is another example that is a bit more complex. The logical space of the US Presidential election of 2000 is expressed in the proposition 'Either George W. Bush wins or Al Gore wins.' (This discounts such maverick candidates as Ralph Nader, who have no chance to win.) Here is the logical space of the proposition:

A (Bush wins)	B (Gore wins)	A or B
p true	q true	p or q false
p true	q false	p or q true
p false	q true	p or q true
p false	q false	p or q false

Both candidates cannot win, so line 1 is false. Either candidate can win, so lines 2 and 3 are true. And finally, both candidates cannot lose, so line 4 is false.

Now suppose the proposition had been 'Either George W. Bush swims or Al Gore swims.' (A warm November day in Florida.) This 'either ... or ... ' is different since it includes the cases where they both go swimming. Thus, the logical space of this (inclusive) 'or' looks like this:

A (Bush swims)	B (Gore swims)	A or B
p true	q true	p or q true
p true	q false	p or q true
p false	q true	p or q true
p false	q false	p or q false

It is possible for Bush and Gore to swim (line 1), just as it is possible that one or the other may swim and not swim (lines 2 and 3). But it would not be the case that either Bush or Gore swims if neither went swimming (line 4). If the proposition is 'Will you have Tin Roof Fudge Pie or Bavarian Cheese Cake or fresh fruit salad?' we could work out the possibilities including that which is expressed by 'I'll have some of each!' And so on. However complex the truth-function might be, using such a table we can display the logical space – or the possibilities – it covers.

To indicate where we are going with this, let us imagine a person reading a news story about Bush and Gore on the campaign trail, visiting swimming pools in respective Florida districts where they need to pick up votes. The news story suggests that the public perceives each candidate as 'too stuffy and not willing to mingle with the common folk.' So, by coincidence, both Bush and Gore chose to visit swimming pools to foster a different impression. Depending on what each candidate actually did, we would have a story recounting and discussing the implications of either both candidates swimming, neither candidate swimming, or only one candidate swimming. The foregoing Bush–Gore truth-table showed the logical space of these possibilities. We can look upon truth-tables as showing *the logical space of our language*, in this case language referring to candidates on the campaign trail one fine day in Florida. Here we have language referring to actions – states of affairs brought about by actions. It is an easy step to extend this idea to *thoughts* behind actions that bring about states of affairs.

A glance at the truth-table for '&' suggests the possibility of an arithmetical interpretation of it:

A	B	A & B
p true	q true	p & q true
p true	q false	p & q false
p false	q true	p or q false
p false	q false	p or q false

Now entering into the realm of computing the possibilities in terms of binary coding, one could create a very similar-looking table by interpreting '&' to mean 'multiply,' 'true' to mean '1' and 'false' to mean '0':

$p = 1$	$q = 1$	$p \times q = 1$
$p = 1$	$q = 0$	$p \times q = 0$
$p = 0$	$q = 1$	$p \times q = 0$
$p = 0$	$q = 0$	$p \times q = 0$

The logical space of a given proposition – its possibilities – is computed in accordance with modern binary coding procedures. In this fashion – albeit with programs designed to make the computationalist's job far easier – a great many psychological processes can be modeled via the computer.

Suppose that the roses are blooming but the delphiniums are not. This state of affairs is represented in line 2 of the above table. Suppose further that the gardener knows each fact singly. We could represent the cognitive process by which the gardener arrived at the conclusion that the joint proposition was false, as a computation, that is the application of a 'mechanical' or rule-bound procedure to the binary symbols, 0 and 1, in the relevant line of the table.

We can see that the *Tractatus* presents a powerful and elegant account of a language appropriate to describing facts, its possibilities, its varieties and its limits. Wittgenstein's views on language in the *Tractatus* transform directly into foundations for cognitive science if we accept as our working hypothesis that language is the main instrument of thought. Though Wittgenstein did not intend his truth-tables to be algorithms for calculating the truth-value of a complex proposition from the truth-values of its components, it was clear that they did have this possibility. The example of such a computation above gives the gist of the idea. Instead of having to guess what the results of some piece of thinking are, we could express them in the language of the *Tractatus* and then calculate the outcome by constructing a truth-table. It is an easy step to the hypothesis that this way of arriving at the end product of a cognitive process, say deducing a conclusion from premises, is also the way that human beings carry out the same task cognitively. To a significant extent, cognitive science is just the application of a generalized version of the logic of the *Tractatus* to all that could be thought and said. But we must remember that the computational model, as it is first dimly seen in Wittgenstein's *Tractatus*, is applicable only to scientific and factual cognition.

Tautologies

By a 'tautology' is meant a truth-functional proposition, the truth-table of which is 'true' in every line. For example:

p or not-p

If p is true we have 'T or F' which, according to the truth-table for 'or,' is T. If we have p is false we have 'F or T' which, according to the truth-table for 'or,' is also T. So in the whole of the logical space of 'p or not-p' the proposition is true. Similarly, throughout the logical space of 'p *and* not-p' the proposition is false. There are no situations which have the same structure as this proposition.

What, then, could possibly be the role of tautologies? Wittgenstein's insight, which ramifies throughout his work, is that these propositions have a special role. They express the rules for use of the logical symbols with which complex propositions are constructed. Thus the tautology 'p or not-p' expresses a rule for the correct use of 'not.' Later, Wittgenstein generalized this insight to ordinary language. Thus the proposition 'This cloth is either white or black' expresses one of the rules for the use of the color words 'white' and 'black,' namely that 'white' and 'black' cannot be properly used for the same surface at the same time, that is unless the surface has *separate* black and white patches.

Back to the three mirrors: summarizing the Tractatus

Wittgenstein finds that people are using language in *two* domains. There is the domain of science in which language is used to describe the material world, and there is the domain of philosophy, addressing problems such as the nature of mind, the grounds for ethical judgments and so on. Philosophy also seems to be about something. But what? The topics for philosophy can be further divided into two subdomains: logic and ethics (the latter including aesthetics and other considerations on values). Logic is concerned with the correct way to use language, while ethics is concerned in general with the best way to live. Apropos of the uses of language, this two-step analysis yields *three* domains: (1) language as description of matters of fact, (2) language as expressing the rules of correct reasoning, and (3) language as the expression of attitudes and commitments (values). What view does he come to apropos of the uses of language in the three domains?

Wittgenstein's study of descriptive (or representational) language led to the thesis that the form of a proposition pictures the structure of facts. The form-creating words of syntax do not refer to anything, but are used to display the structure of a fact by displaying the isomorphic structure of the proposition true of it. Such propositions are meaningful because they contain elementary names.

In science, propositions – which are also facts or objects arranged in certain ways – depict facts. In logic, propositions do not depict logical facts, but are ways of showing or depicting logical forms which are presented in truth-tables. These (logical) propositions are senseless, since they do not consist of names in relation. Propositions that are the result of attempts to describe anything else, such as the

Divine Being, the Ultimate Good and so on, are strictly 'nonsense,' since there is nothing to which a person can point in order to give meaning to the names that make them up. That is, 'metaphysical propositions' do not consist of names in relation. Nor do their forms depict anything. We introduced the notion of 'nonsense' in Chapter 2. But now we can think of it a bit differently. By 'nonsense' Wittgenstein really means that metaphysical propositions are, in a way, like tautologies (always true) and contradictions (always false), in that they do not represent anything or have any sense. They cannot be assessed as true or false. Hence the notorious final remark of the *Tractatus*, proposition 7: 'What we cannot speak about we must pass over in silence.'

Therefore, in the first domain, *natural science,* language has meaning and pictures things. Propositions in this domain have 'sense'; they can be true or false. In domain two, *logic,* language has no meaning. That is, it does not refer to objects outside itself, but nevertheless pictures or shows forms of thought. Therefore, propositions in this realm do not have 'sense' because 'true or false' judgments do not apply to them. In the third domain, *values* (or ethics), language pictures nothing and is not meaningful in terms of fact-stating discourse. Therefore, propositions in this domain are nonsense. They neither picture nor do they show anything.

Learning point: the basic ideas of the *Tractatus*

1. *Themes and the project*

   (a) Philosophers, psychologists, mathematicians and theologians especially are prone to philosophical errors that result from misinterpreting words by false analogies. Ordinary persons on the street also are prone to these kinds of mistakes, for example, thinking it is a 'matter of fact' that someone is virtuous, or that some work of art is beautiful.

   (b) Wittgenstein's project is to construct a perfect language, the use of which would make impossible these kinds of errors. At the same time, this language would make it clear that no factual statements could be made about morality, art and religion.

2. *Some vocabulary of the* Tractatus

   (a) A *fact* is a cluster of objects, and an atomic fact is a cluster of simple objects. We do not know what the simple objects are, only that they must exist; so all our examples are of complex objects which can be used to illustrate how simple objects behave.

   (b) *Objects* can go together only in certain ways, depending on their inherent characteristics. For example, if Tom and Jerry are simple objects, then there are two facts. In the cases of 'Tom chases Jerry' and 'Jerry chases Tom,' only one of these can hold to be 'true' of a given moment.

(c)   The *world* consists of all the facts, possible and actual, that can be put together out of simple objects.

(d)   A *name* has a meaning by association with an object and its meaning is the object denoted. So simple names mean simple objects. Also, names are themselves objects.

(e)   A *proposition* is an arrangement of names and a proposition is true when the arrangement of names is the same as the arrangement of objects in the fact it describes. Otherwise, a proposition is false.

(f)   The arrangement of names in propositions and propositions in more complex propositions are *logical forms*.

(g)   The arrangements of names in a proposition is its *meaning*, but the fact that consists of the objects it names can have the opposite sense. Therefore, a proposition's structure may or may not match a fact that actually obtains. Thus 'Tom chases Jerry' is true if $T \rightarrow J$, but false if the fact has an opposite sense (i.e. $J \rightarrow T$).

3.   *The truth-tables*

(a)   By setting out all possible truth-value combinations for a schematic proposition of any given logical form, one can map out the logical space of all possible meaningful propositions – a kind of general phase space.

(b)   The same technique can be used to 'compute' the truth-value of a complex proposition and to display the character of tautologies and self-contradictions.

4.   *Tautologies*

(a)   It is evident from its truth-table that a tautology is true in all circumstances, while a self-contradiction is true in none. The latter has no applications and so is strictly meaningless.

(b)   The role of tautologies is to express the rules of the grammar of a perfect language. Self-contradictions are not false, but nonsense.

(c)   'Nothing can be red and green all over at once' is a tautology. It does not describe a super-fact, but fixes the relational meanings of the words 'red' and 'green.' The apparent statement 'This is red and green all over at once' has no application in any circumstances. Tautologies, then, fix the boundaries of meaningful language from within.

5.   *The three mirrors: summarizing the* Tractatus

(a)   The kind of language imagined by Wittgenstein can describe only that which can be pictured by a proposition, isomorphic with a state of affairs among material objects.

> (b)   That which cannot be so pictured can either be shown or displayed
>   in language (logic), or must lie outside the language of science and
>   logic.
> (c)   Thus our experiences of ethics, religion and art cannot be described
>   in the Tractarian language at all. Words in these domains can be
>   used only expressively.

The *Tractatus,* scientific psychology and cognitive science

The philosophical doctrines of positivism, advocated by the philosophers of the
Vienna Circle during the 1920s and 1930s, included two basic principles drawn
largely from Wittgenstein's *Tractatus* that were significant for psychology (particularly in the United States). The first, stated by Rudolf Carnap (1932/1959), is that
'the meaning of a statement lies in the method of its verification' (p. 76). Gillies
(1993) explains the thinking that led to Carnap's famous statement of the verifiability criterion in terms of the Vienna Circle's interpretation of the *Tractatus* as
defending the thesis that all meaningful propositions are truth-functions of simple
observation statements. It follows that any meaningful proposition is either a logical contradiction or a logically valid statement. It further follows that if a meaningful
proposition is true, this can be verified by observation. The meaningful proposition
(P, say) is, by the central premise of the theory, a truth-function of simple observation statements. We can determine by observation the truth-values of these simple
observation statements, and in this way verify that P is true (Gillies, 1993, p. 171).
Since a proposition can be verified (or falsified) only by observing a state of affairs
it is purported to describe, the verifiability criterion is similar to Wittgenstein's
account of the relation between simple names and elementary objects, together
with the picture theory of meaning.

The second basic principle of positivism has to do with Wittgenstein's distinction between fact-stating discourse and value-expressing discourse described
earlier. The verifiability criterion excludes from fact-stating discourse all propositions purported to be about unobservables, such as God, moral values and
mystical experiences. This is evident in the following set of propositions from the
Tractatus:

6.42   So too it is impossible for there to be propositions of ethics.
        Propositions can express nothing that is higher.

6.421   It is clear that ethics cannot be put into words.
        Ethics is transcendental.
        (Ethics and aesthetics are one and the same.)

The 'nothing that is higher' in 6.42 and 'transcendental' in 6.421 indicate clearly
that Wittgenstein positioned ethics 'above' science. Also, his claim that 'ethics and
aesthetics are one and the same' amounts to a grammatical bonding of the two,
separate from the grammar of propositions in science. In other words, in these two
remarks 'Wittgenstein is trying to set the ethical off from the sphere of rational

discourse, because be believes that [the ethical] is more properly located in the sphere of the poetic' (Janik and Toulmin, 1973, p. 193).

What is interesting about all of this is that although the *Tractatus* may be seen as bolstering the positivistic atmosphere surrounding behaviorism in psychology during the 1920s and 1930s, behaviorists took a rather different stance on value-expressing discourse. Ethical talk was just the expression of personal preferences. Thus, to the behaviorists, value-experience (such as religious, magical, or mystical experience) was anything but 'higher.'

Another consequence of the positivism of the behaviorist paradigm in psychology was a prohibition on statements which appeared to refer to entities, properties and processes that could not be observed publicly. A famous example of this is John B. Watson's (1925) claim that 'belief in the existence of consciousness' (as representative of cognition) 'goes back to the ancient days of superstition and magic' (p. 2). Consciousness, above all other psychological phenomena, is a private state known by observation only to he or she who is awake and paying attention!

The Tractatus, *behaviorism and beyond*

Carnap's (1932) statement of the verifiability criterion coincided with the appearance of E.C. Tolman's (1932) *Purposive Behavior in Animals and Men*, in which he proposes a 'molar' conception of behavior as an alternative to Watson's 'molecular' conception. Despite drawing this distinction, Tolman acknowledged that the unifying principle behind all 'brands' of behaviorism was that *the domain of scientific psychology must be confined to observable behavior and the observable conditions under which it occurs*. This principle can be interpreted in terms of behaviorism's ontology and investigative methods. The behaviorist ontology – or what is worthy of study as a verifiably existing 'something' – simply is overt behavior. The method is methodological behaviorism. A description of methodological behaviorism from a contemporary research methods textbook calls to mind Tolman's (1932) assertion that mental processes are 'deducible from behavior' and forges a methodological and explanatory link worth pointing out between the *Tractatus*-inspired Vienna Circle, behaviorism and contemporary cognitive psychology:

> Most contemporary psychologists subscribe to methodological behaviorism, a philosophical stance evolving from Watson's beliefs. Methodological behaviorism suggests that psychologists should study overt and observable behaviors as the primary focus of their research. Psychologists use observable behaviors to make inferences about the emotional, cognitive, and other mental processes that occur within a person.
>
> (Pittenger, 2003, p. 11)

Bearing in mind the tight link demanded by the positivists between being observable and being meaningful, it is clear that methodological behaviorism is not the same as behaviorism as a general psychological stance. On strict positivist–behaviorist principles, words which seem to refer to mental processes of any kind are meaningless, and can have no place in science. But, as indicated in the above passage by Pittenger (2003), psychologists interested in scientifically investigating cognitive processes rely on observation of observable behaviors. In this sense they are no less committed to methodological behaviorism than are their behaviorist counterparts.

In so far as the doctrines of meaning and of the exclusively logical ordering of scientific propositions can be found at the heart of the *Tractatus*, the relation between Tractarian philosophy and behaviorism is clear. Being concerned primarily with overt behavior and its measurement (given certain controlled conditions), behaviorists during and subsequent to the days of the Vienna Circle saw the only legitimate relation between stimuli and responses as statistical correlations between the one and the other. In a word (and roughly), the meaning of psychological concepts can only be the environmental stimuli and consequential behavior to which they refer. Everything worth measuring and explaining scientifically is open to view and the meaning of 'responses to noxious stimuli,' for example, lies in the methods used to verify the relevant stimulus–response phenomena. Thus there is a strong connection between behaviorism and the verifiability criterion. Methodological behaviorism is a means by which the verifiability criterion can be met. So clearly, behaviorism as a scientific practice is rooted firmly in the sort of positivism advocated by the *Tractatus*-inspired Vienna Circle.

We are not suggesting that Watson, Tolman, or B.F. Skinner for that matter, were apprized of the Vienna Circle's interpretation of the *Tractatus* and so deliberately set about realizing its principles in a new kind of psychology. After all, Watson (1919) put his initial stamp on behaviorism before the *Tractatus* was published. Rather, the influence of the *Tractatus*, later to Wittgenstein's disgust, powerfully supported the positivistic atmosphere of the time. Behaviorism was one among many ways that positivism has manifested itself in science and scientific psychology. What remains is to explore further the link, hinted at above, between the *Tractatus* and cognitivism. But in so doing, we will go well beyond methodological behaviorism and the prohibition on the use of theoretical concepts that refer to unobservable states of affairs.

We should make a few further points before proceeding. Behaviorism lost its dominant position in psychology in the United States during the 1950s and 1960s in large part because its proponents dogmatically insisted that mental states and processes could not be investigated scientifically. Yet behaviorism's *scientific* standing remains intact to this day. There is no question that behaviorists worked out experimental methods marked by parsimony, objectivity, careful measurement and control, replication and so on – all characteristics of scientific practice. In addition, behaviorists' ability to control the behavior of animals was impressive, as were their applications of behavioristic principles in the clinic. These are but a few of behaviorism's achievements. The 'fall' of behaviorism had more to do with the criticism that it could only tell 'part of the story.' As Gardner (1985) puts it, 'too much of consequence in human behavior was denied by the behaviorist approach' (p. 110).

But there is something more insidious in the restrictions behaviorists leveled on 'what can be studied scientifically.' To be specific, behaviorism *restricted the grammar of psychology* and regarded entire neighborhoods in the 'city of language,' to borrow a phrase from Ackerman (1988), as illegitimate for the purposes of science. (Note again the contrast with the *Tractatus*, which held that value-expressive discourse is not illegitimate, but 'higher' than scientific discourse.) Here we have a different form of 'control' in the context of science: *conceptual control*. Undergraduates attending courses on research methods in psychology learn that operational definitions basically tell others: 'If you want to replicate my research, do precisely what I did, namely *this*.' Students are taught to construct operational definitions to ensure clarity of the meanings of variables and replication of experimental and other forms of research. Now some operational definitions – for example, 'reward' defined as a specific kind of food pellet – are not problematic. But others – such as 'surprise' or 'anger' – potentially are *very* problematic.

It is significant that the idea of the operational definition, imported into psychology from physics (from which it has long since departed), continues to be plagued by a host of seemingly intractable problems. One of the most important of these stems from the idea that operational definitions restrict (or, as we have put it, 'control') the meanings of psychological concepts, which vary across uses in everyday contexts. Since psychological phenomena are made meaningful by the uses of vernacular language, 'operational definitions' often lead away from the very topic they were intended to elucidate. For example, it is very difficult to see how the distinction between recollecting something and recognizing something could be defined operationally.

Another problem is raised by the assumption that the results of psychological experiments can be generalized to people everywhere and always as an extreme form of external validity. How can the results of an experiment (or set of experiments), which employ quite specific meanings of key psychological concepts, be *generalized* to humans in everyday contexts, where meanings of those concepts can be – and probably are – culturally and contextually variable? In one way or other, we will have much more to say on this in coming chapters as we explore Wittgenstein's post-Tractarian approach to language. So we are suggesting that many of the difficulties with attempts to create a coherent scientific psychology come from misuses and misunderstandings of language. These problems are on equal standing with problems that come from misunderstandings of the methods of the natural sciences in looking for models of science for psychology.

The Tractatus *and cognitive science*

Remember that, according to the *Tractatus*, all the important matters of life, love, loyalty, reverence for God or Nature and so on are outside the realm of fact-stating language. These aspects of human experience can be neither described nor shown using fact-stating language. We have already quoted Wittgenstein's famous remark that closes the *Tractatus*: 'What we cannot speak about we must pass over in silence.' (Presumably it is no coincidence that this remark bears the number '7'.) Essentially, he is saying: Do not try to speak in either the scientific true/false way or the logical, showing way, about the most important things in human experience. A person can 'feel it,' express 'it' as a feeling, but cannot say anything about it as if it were factual. Only that part of nature and language that we can comprehend in a fact-stating discourse is inside the boundaries of what can be expressed in propositions. Outside it lies everything that is 'important.' Thus it was that Wittgenstein, at the age of thirty-two, believing himself to have demonstrated the barrenness of logically ordered thought, decided that the best thing to do with the rest of his life was to be a gardener in a monastery, or failing that, a school teacher in rural Austria.

If Wittgenstein is correct, then it appears that what we have labeled variously as 'values-thinking' or 'value-expressive discourse' lies outside the boundaries of any possible scientific, fact-stating psychology. Were he alive and living in the US during the latter part of the twentieth century, Wittgenstein would have scoffed at popular attempts on the part of certain religious groups to support their beliefs through science! But is this borne out in the course of cognitive psychology and cognitive science? We think so. By the looks of it, in contemporary cognitive science language pertaining to values is either conspicuously absent or 'translated' into the verbiage of science. A notorious example of the latter is the neuroscientist Paul Churchland's (1981) assertion that with increased knowledge of neurophysiology, neurophysiological terms might be substituted for everyday 'common-sense' concepts. Here is his description of his 'eliminative materialism':

> Eliminative materialism is the thesis that our common-sense conception of psychological phenomena constitutes a radically false theory, a theory so fundamentally defective that both the principles and the ontology of that theory will eventually be displaced, rather than smoothly reduced, by completed neuroscience.
>
> (Churchland, 1981, p. 67)

Consider the word 'belief.' Eliminative materialism proposes that 'belief' actually refers to material processes of the brain that can be invoked to explain some cognitive performance of belief. Ultimately, in the name of psychological science modeled on the 'hard' sciences (e.g. physics), the folk-psychological concept belief will be replaced by its more informed cousin. So too with concepts such as 'faith,' 'beauty' and 'love.' Inevitably, brain states and processes will be found to be 'at the bottom' of these ineffable experiences and the terms so used would be translated into a neuroscientific language, as if the words used to express these feelings were inadequate – even 'defective.' It is tempting to note an air of arrogance in this proposal. But really, the point is that, according to the *Tractatus*, the real problem lies in thinking that science can explain the mysteries of the most significant aspects of human experience with fact-stating discourse. There is more to human mental and social life than just that which can be studied by an analogue of the methods of physics. In this sense, it is ironic that Wittgenstein's *Tractatus* still is viewed as pre-eminent in the logical positivist literature.

Assumptions of cognitive science

As the successor to behaviorism, cognitive psychology is based on two fundamental ideas, the first of which we pointed out in connection with eliminative materialism: there are unobservable cognitive processes at work behind cognitive performances, achievements, and so on (e.g. remembering, calculating, reading, recognizing a face) and we may invoke these unobservable processes to explain cognitive phenomena. For example, some of Jerome Bruner's experiments published before the 'cognitive revolution' in psychology later were interpreted through the lens of cognitivism. In one such study, Bruner and Postman (1949) briefly flashed playing cards in front of their experimental participants, but the colors of the cards were of another suit than would ordinarily be expected (e.g. black hearts, red clubs). Nevertheless, the participants reported seeing the cards in the colors of their original suit. To explain this phenomenon, Bruner invoked unobservable cognitive processes of 'comparison' with 'pre-existing schemata.' He and many others have used this style of explanation in their studies of a wide variety of cognitive processes.

The second fundamental idea of cognitive psychology is that cognitive processes can be *modeled* by developing abstract, formal (computable) 'representations' of cognitive processes. The idea is that 'behind' skilled activities, for example, there is a process of comparison with a pre-existing standard, so that the activity ceases when the standard has been met. But what is meant by the proposal that cognitive processes can be represented by formal, *computable* representations? It simply means that we can represent the initial situation – the information (or *data*) for the exercise of a cognitive skill – numerically, and we have rules of computation. These would be computable functions representing cognitive processes, allowing us to calculate the outcome of the thought process as a form of purely mechanical operation in a computing machine.

So the invocation of unobservable cognitive processes in order to explain human psychological abilities, which together with the modeling of those processes in terms of abstract, formal representations, are the two primary hallmarks of cognitive psychology. The term 'cognitive science' tends to be used when the functions of the brain are tied in with cognition by a dual interpretation of a formal model. On the one hand, there is a representation of the rules for performing the task and on the other there are the neural processes by which someone performs a task. The methodological validity of using dual interpretations is an issue outside the scope of this text. Many cognitive scientists hold out hope that one day their models will be 'seen at work,' so to speak, in the brain. This would amount to seeing the modeled processes at work. For the time being all we have is performance. In what follows, we will be discussing primarily cognitive science as a branch of cognitive psychology.

Brains, computers and meaning

As a branch of cognitive science, computational modeling was initiated in large part by Alan Turing's (1950) intuition that computing machines can exhibit some of the same thinking behavior as living organisms. A process such as making an inference or classifying something into its appropriate category can be represented through calculations. The outcome of the calculations represents the outcome of cognitive process modeled by the calculations. Here, in rough outline, is Turing's famous 'Turing test.' He asks us to imagine a computing machine and a person in two separate locations. In a third location is a computer terminal of sorts, where questions from an interlocutor can be posed to the computing machine and person via a kind of rudimentary network. (The questions would be posed and answered similarly to a modern-day computer 'chat' or instant messaging.) In a nutshell, Turing proposed that if a machine could pass his test, it would be impossible to say for sure which answers came from the machine and which answers came from the person. Turing thought this proved that computers can think. Just as the computer is acting like the human, it is thinking. And just as the person is acting like the computer, he or she is computing.

Despite its limitations, this idea tied in very nicely with the extraordinary advances in computing machines, again made possible largely by Turing's insights.

Turing's analogy between the brain and computing machine can be represented as follows:

brain : thinking : computing machine : computing

Basically, this means that a brain when thinking is like a computer when computing. This simple formula is still a guiding principle – at least implicitly – behind much research in cognitive science. As far as the outcomes of computational processes in a machine can be interpreted as being very much like the outcome of human thought, then the brain, the human cognitive tool, must be very much like the computational tool, the computer.

Originally the basic idea that all cognitive processes can be represented by computable functions was very simple in outline. Yet it has proven extraordinarily difficult to establish models that account fully for the vicissitudes of specific cognitive phenomena in humans. There are several reasons for this, but we are concerned primarily with the computational account of *meaning* on grounds that it ties in remarkably well with Wittgenstein's account of meaning in the *Tractatus*, which he eventually rejected. If we are to understand the extent to which the computational account of meaning needs considerable revision – or if it should not be abandoned altogether – we need to ask whether it repeats mistakes of the *Tractatus*.

Quite a number of writers on Wittgenstein have made connections between perspectives associated with what we term the 'computational model' of cognition (e.g. cognitive science and artificial intelligence) and the *Tractatus*, all the while identifying similar pitfalls of both. Winograd and Flores (1986) argue that the account of meaning typified by artificial intelligence (hereafter AI) is virtually identical with Wittgenstein's Tractarian account of meaning, exhibited in what we (following Peterson, 1990) have termed the mirror of representational language. Both the *Tractatus* and the AI model of cognition present a 'rationalist account of meaning' by which language is seen 'as a system of symbols that are composed into patterns that stand for things in the world' (Winograd and Flores, 1986, p. 17), with the meanings of those patterns being 'built up systematically from smaller elements, each with its own determinate meaning' (p. 64). Fodor's (1975) influential and controversial 'language of thought' doctrine is one case among many. It shares with the *Tractatus* the assumption that 'meaning is a compositional function out of atomic meaning particles' (McDonough, 1989, p. 14). Another angle on these similarities is provided by Johnson (1997). He argues that the accuracy of computer models of cognitive processes rests on the assumption that there is a one-to-one correspondence between coded elements in a computer program and the objects, events, states of affairs and so on they represent.

Unifying these criticisms of the computational model is the assertion that, in setting up a one-to-one correspondence between symbols and what they stand for – even if the symbols represent 'instructions' – this approach to modeling human cognition is exposed to Wittgenstein's post-Tractarian attack on the 'Augustinian picture' of language, which we will address in the next chapter. McDonough's (1989) criticism of the model on the grounds that it presents a mechanistic theory of meaning will be especially pertinent to Chapter 6, where we encounter rules and rule-following. If you punch in rules for computation, the 'actions' of a computational device are laid out in such a way that they cannot be performed otherwise. The device is a causal mechanism. This is not the way rules operate in Wittgenstein's post-Tractarian philosophy. The *basic idea* behind Wittgenstein's use of truth-tables was integral to the development of binary computer coding and subsequent attempts at computational modeling of cognitive processes. So much was apparent in our prior demonstration of how truth-table symbols can be converted easily into binary coding. But again, Wittgenstein's use of truth-tables in the *Tractatus* presupposes that the non-syntactic elements in any truth-table stand in a one-to-one correspondence with things in the world. The aforementioned Augustinian picture of language finds expression in truth-tables.

Losing faith

In the 1920s Wittgenstein began to lose faith in the doctrines of the *Tractatus* on at least three grounds – each of which has implications for cognitive psychology, cognitive science and the computational model of cognition. First, there are many uses of words in everyday contexts and in the sciences and putative sciences (e.g. psychology) that give rise to philosophical problems. These problems do not emerge because words refer to things and processes beyond the bounds of observation, but because of the multiplicity of meanings of almost all words of any significance. Most important words are 'polysemous.' We run into trouble whenever we privilege one meaning of a word over all others and insist that this is what such a word 'really means.' More often than not, this legislation of meaning is implicit in how words are used in a discipline. At other times, public arguments break out over the 'real meaning' of a word or expression.

Second, the principle that only those words with direct real-world referents can be meaningful also troubled Wittgenstein. His account of extra-scientific language as only expressive seemed to leave even such words as the numerals outside the boundaries of meaningfulness, even in the strict positivistic sense of the *Tractatus*. Surely the word 'five' is a word of everyday significance. But to what object does it refer? The associated rigidity of the logical conception of 'form' began to appear obstructive. Wittgenstein's friend Sraffa made this perfectly clear with his gesture while asking: 'What is the logical form of *that*?'

Finally, the principle of meaning that linked simple names to elementary objects one to one and independently of one another seemed to fail for some very obvious fragments of our vocabulary. For instance, color words are part of a system according to the principle of determinates under a determinable. This principle simply means that the words under the determinable 'color' are linked by the logical rule that the truth of the assertion of one of some object, say 'blue chair,' entails the falsity of assertions of all the other determinates, such as 'green,' 'yellow,' and so on, to that chair at that time. It is either a blue chair or a green chair.

Taken together, these were among the considerations that took Wittgenstein back to philosophy to begin his task of clarification all over again. It is to the nature and results of this new task, applied to issues in psychology, that we attend to from here forward.

Learning point: the *Tractatus* and psychology

1. *Themes and the project:* The *Tractatus* directly influenced philosophers towards positivism and, indirectly, psychologists towards behaviorism.

    (a) *Positivism:* As a source for positivism, the doctrine of meaning as object signified was transformed into the principle that the meaning of a statement was its method of verification, and that value statements expressed personal preferences.
    (b) *Behaviorism:* Scientific psychology is the study of the public conditions of observable behavior and the correlations between stimuli and responses.
    (c) Behaviorism and positivism fitted one another perfectly, in that positivism expressed the presuppositions of behaviorism. This was made explicit in the adoption of 'operational definitions' for psychological concepts. In 'eliminative materialism' the positivistic attitude is extended to a restriction of all psychological concepts to the vocabulary of neuroscience.

2. *Cognitive psychology and the computational model:* Based on the use of hypothetical cognitive processes to explain phenomena which were underdetermined by the environmental conditions. These processes can be modeled using computing machines and through other means (e.g. flow-charts).

    (a) The development of truth-table logic is implicated in development of the idea of computational representations of cognitive processes.
    (b) Turing's analogy: brain is to thinking as computer is to computing.
    (c) Turing test: If one could not tell from their responses whether one was interacting with a person or a computer, then the person was operating like the computer and the computer was thinking.

3. *Why Wittgenstein lost faith in the* Tractatus

    (a) Real words are *polysemous.* That is, they have multiple uses and meanings in various contexts.
    (b) There were meaningful symbols that did not have observable referents, such as gestures, numbers and so on.
    (c) Many simple attribute words form systems, so are not logically independent; for example the color words. (*Determinates under a determinable.*)

Further reading

Coulter, J. (1983), *Rethinking Cognitive Theory*. New York: St Martin's Press.

Peterson, D. (1990), *Wittgenstein's early philosophy: Three sides of the mirror*. Toronto: University of Toronto Press.

Winograd, T. and Flores, F. (1986), *Understanding Computers and Cognition: A foundation for design*. Norwood, NJ: Ablex.

SELF-TEST: PART ONE

- On what kinds of presupposition does every human practice depend?
- On what sort of presuppositions are the sciences specifically built?
- What are the main components of a science?
- Why do we question whether psychology can be cloned from the natural sciences?
- What picture of the human being underlies Cartesianism?
- What are the main presuppositions of behaviorism and cognitivism?
- Compare causal with normative explanations of human thought, feeling and action.
- What role do we say ordinary language should play in psychology?
- What do we mean by 'managing meanings'?
- What were the main features of Wittgenstein's education?
- Why did Wittgenstein leave philosophy after writing the *Tractatus*?
- What considerations brought Wittgenstein back to philosophy?
- What might Wittgenstein have learned from 'Sraffa's gesture'?
- What are the main themes of the work of Karl Kraus?
- What makes Wittgenstein a 'Krausian man'?
- How are facts distinguished from values?
- What was the main theme of the musicology of Schönberg?
- What did Wittgenstein get from Hertz and Boltzmann?
- What are the main concerns of the *Tractatus* as captured by the 'mirror' metaphor?
- Describe what can and cannot be accomplished with fact-stating language.
- What is 'ostension' and how does it link up with fact-stating language?
- What, according to Wittgenstein, is a proposition?
- What was the 'picture theory' supposed to explain?
- What is the difference between 'showing' and 'saying'?
- What was the point of setting out truth-tables? How do they relate to 'phase space'?
- What do tautologies and contradictions show?
- What does the final remark of the *Tractatus* mean?
- Connect the *Tractatus*, positivism, the verifiability criterion and behaviorism.
- What is the relationship between the operational definition and 'conceptual control'?
- Connect the *Tractatus* with cognitive science.
- What is 'eliminative materialism' and why is it an implausible thesis?
- What was Turing's analogy and what was his 'test' meant to show?
- For what reasons did Wittgenstein 'lose faith' in the *Tractatus*?

Part Two
INSIGHTS

4 The meaning of meaning: from naming to using
Philosophical Investigations §§1-43

> It is interesting to compare the multiplicity of the tools in language and of the ways they are used, the multiplicity of kinds of word and sentence, with what logicians have said about the structure of language. (Including the author of the *Tractatus Logico-Philosophicus*.)
>
> Wittgenstein, *Philosophical Investigations*, §23

Topics introduced: 'Augustinian picture' of language; denotational theory of meaning; stage-setting; ambiguity of exemplars; Wittgenstein's interlocutor; block/slab game; toolbox analogy of language; form and function of words; linguistic essences and family resemblance; language-games; performatives; meaning-as-use; request formats; habituation studies; the concept of imitation

The fundamental insight on which much of Wittgenstein's treatment of psychology depends is that language is the most important tool or instrument that human beings use in order to think. We do have other cognitive tools such as images, feelings, non-verbal symbols, models, drawings and so on. But by and large, language is of utmost importance because it is the most powerful and subtle of our cognitive tools. That is why Wittgenstein's studies of the way that language can lead us into illusions and mistakes, particularly in psychology and mathematics, are so important. As we will see, his studies often may be termed 'negative' in the sense that they show us where we tend to go awry and when and why we need to be vigilant. But they are positive as well. In the course of displaying the treacherous margins of proper discourse he explored some of our most useful psychological concepts in their various forms of use. We have seen that the language tool was given a rather narrow scope in the *Tractatus*. As a Krausian, recognition of this fundamental flaw must have tormented Wittgenstein deeply, providing strong impetus to explore the richness and complexity of the uses and functions that language actually has in human ways of living.

Let us review a number of key ideas from the *Tractatus* that we will see stand in stark contrast to the view expressed in the selection from the opening remarks of the *Investigations* that heads this chapter. Wittgenstein's new account is, for the most part, driven by a conscious rejection of much that he had put forward in the *Tractatus*. From our point of view, the two most important features of his formalistic approach to the nature and limits of language and with which he became deeply dissatisfied were (1) the assimilation of grammar to logic and (2) the restriction of meaning to whatever a sign is used to denote.

These features of the 'perfect language' were linked. The only things that 'could be said' were factual and so under the constraints of truth and falsity. The rules for the management of propositions, in as far as they were true or false, were governed by logic. Concerning all else one must be silent. The penalty for trying to capture the rest of human affairs in language was, from the point of view of the constraints on fact-stating discourse, nonsense. (Again, 'nonsense' is a technical term.) Insisting that grammar and logic should coincide leads to a very narrow conception of cognition.

The first forty or so paragraphs of the *Investigations* develop a far more powerful account of language than that of the *Tractatus*. Wittgenstein realized, in a manner of speaking, that we need to 'open up' grammar and logic. The critical revisions of his earlier philosophy parallel much of what one learns in a cognitive science course as one realizes that computational models of cognition are not adequate as representations of complex cognitive processes. We need to open up grammar beyond the limits of logic. In so doing, we open up concepts of meaning beyond that of objects signified. All this must be done if we are going to get anywhere near capturing what it is like to be a human being using language for the multitudinous purposes of everyday life.

One of the great virtues of Wittgenstein's work is the richness and variety of examples with which he illuminates our many ways of communicating – with language and by other means. In the previous chapter we mentioned that Wittgenstein eventually came to regard his early philosophy as having been under the spell of what is referred to as the 'Augustinian picture' of language. Wittgenstein's form of analysis in the *Tractatus* was based, in part, on his belief that sentences are combinations of names and that words stand for objects. The *Investigations* begins with an exposition of the old picture of language drawn from St Augustine. Let us begin by elaborating the Augustinian picture more thoroughly before following Wittgenstein as he turns to a contrasting view of language in the latter part of the first section of the *Investigations* and in subsequent remarks.

The critique of meaning as object designated by a sign

Philosophical Investigations (PI) begins with a lengthy quote from Book I, §8 of St Augustine's *Confessions*, where Augustine describes how he learned to use words as an infant. By his analysis, this must have involved four factors. First, Augustine says that when his elders named an object and accordingly moved toward it, he 'grasped' the thing to which their utterances and movements were directed. Second, he says the intentions of his elders were shown through their bodily movements, expressions on their faces, the 'play of their eyes' and tone of voice that the infant Augustine *already recognized* as expressions of such states of mind as 'seeking, having, rejecting, or avoiding something.' Third, Augustine claims he gradually learned to understand the objects to which his elders' words referred through repeatedly hearing their words used in well-formed sentences. And finally, a further step in Augustine's language apprenticeship was to train his own mouth 'to form these signs' in order to 'express my own desires.'

To Wittgenstein, the 'particular picture of the essence of human language' presented by Augustine is based on the related ideas that 'the individual words in language name objects' and that 'sentences are combinations of names' (PI §1). So here we have Wittgenstein's specific acknowledgment of the two primary assumptions about language that constitute the Augustinian picture of language. These are more or less identical with his views on representational language in the *Tractatus*: *words name objects and sentences are combinations of names*. And it is in these two ideas that Wittgenstein finds 'the roots of the following idea: Every word has a meaning. This meaning is correlated with the word. It is the object for which the word stands' (PI §1). This sounds very much like the denotational theory of meaning, which holds that what a word means is that to which it refers, or names. Further, Wittgenstein observes that Augustine 'does not speak of there being any difference between kinds of word.' It seems that Augustine had in mind primarily words like 'table,' 'chair,' 'bread' and the names of people, and secondarily 'the names of certain actions and properties.' The remaining kinds of word (e.g. connectives like 'and' and 'but,' and what we may call 'location' words 'here' and 'now') were 'something that will take care of itself' (PI §1). So the Augustinian picture of language appears to be primarily concerned with nouns and only secondarily, if at all, with other kinds of word. It bears repeating that taken together, these assumptions constitute Wittgenstein's own account of representational language in the first third of the *Tractatus*. Here is a summary of the five elements of the Augustinian picture of language as introduced by Augustine and quoted by Wittgenstein in PI §1:

(1) Words name objects.
(2) Sentences are combinations of names.
(3) Every significant word has a meaning.
(4) Meaning, correlated with a word, is the object for which a word stands.
(5) There is primary concern with nouns and property-words are secondary.

But there is a good deal more to the Augustinian picture of language than what Wittgenstein observes in the first half of PI §1. McGinn (1997) has argued convincingly that 'further themes' of the Augustinian picture emerge if we turn back from Book I, §8 of Augustine's *Confessions* to §6 of that same work. Wittgenstein was well acquainted with the writings of St Augustine and he takes up these meaning-related themes gradually as the *Investigations* proceed. In *Confessions* §6, Augustine says that as an infant he gradually began to realize 'where I was and to want to make my wishes known to others, who might satisfy them.' But he could not make these wishes known 'because my wishes were inside me, while other people were outside, and they had no faculty which could penetrate my mind.' Thus the infant Augustine reverted to '[tossing] my arms and legs about and [making] noises, hoping that such few signs as I could make would show my meaning, though they were quite unlike what they were meant to mime.'

McGinn (1997, p. 38) sums up her expanded version of the Augustinian picture of language in terms of the following four elements. First, Augustine '[tends] to think of the human subject in terms of a private essence or mind – in which there are wishes, thoughts, desires, etc. – and as a physical interface with the outside world.' Second, this private essence or mind 'is conceived *as somehow already fully human* [emphasis added], but as lacking the capacity to communicate with others' in that it 'already possesses its own internal articulations into particular thoughts and wishes, which cannot yet be expressed.' Third, 'the primary purpose of language is to communicate thoughts and wishes that are initially locked within the private sphere.' And fourth, the private essence is seen as making 'the essential link between word and the object which is its meaning, and understanding is conceived as the mind's making the appropriate connection between a sound and the object it signifies.' Here is a summary of these four further themes of the Augustinian picture of language added to our previous five that, according to McGinn (1997), Wittgenstein addresses as the *Investigations* proceeds.

(6)   The human subject is an interface between its own private essence and the world.
(7)   The private essence has internal articulations that cannot yet be expressed, thus making it somehow already 'communicatively human.'
(8)   At least initially, the primary purpose of language is to communicate thoughts and/or wishes locked in the private essence.
(9)   The private essence links words and objects to attain meaning. Understanding consists in connecting sounds and the objects they signify.

There are good reasons for accepting McGinn's (1997) claim that these four elements should be added to those specified by Wittgenstein as constituting Augustine's views on language-learning and we will see that, in fact, they are gradually taken up in the course of the *Investigations*. But there is an important and subtle difference between our first (1 through 5) and second (6 through 9) set of Augustinian themes. Notice that, whereas the first set is primarily concerned with word- and sentence-meaning, the second set is concerned largely with communicating and understanding meaningful thoughts. Clearly, the meanings of words are communicated to the infant Augustine, so the communication of thoughts and their understanding must be assumed by the first set of themes. This is why we need to jump ahead in PI to §31. This remark introduces an idea that is essential to any account of meaning and understanding.

The importance of stage-setting

It is notable that in exposing the weaknesses of the Augustinian view that word-meaning is established by correlating words with objects by pointing to an object and saying its name, Wittgenstein suggests that establishing the meaning (use) of a piece in chess is part of the process of learning the game. The statement 'This is the king' constitutes a definition of that piece 'only if the learner already "knows what a piece in a game is". That is, if he has already played other games, or has watched other people playing "and understood" – *and similar things*' (PI §31). There must be some kind of *stage-setting* for definitions such as 'This is the king' to contribute to a learner's understanding of the game of chess. (Recall what we said, in Chapter 3, about teaching someone the meaning of 'dog.')

To illustrate this important notion of stage-setting further, suppose a hundred or so people have gathered in a large room in Virginia, USA, for a Republican fund-raising event. The Republicans have pulled out all the stops for this event, inviting numerous prominent representatives of their political party. One of these is Oliver North, an American military officer made famous for having been found guilty of supplying Nicaraguan 'freedom fighters' with arms to fight the Sandinista government under the Reagan administration in the 1980s. Colonel North just happens to be standing along the north wall of the room. Now two attendees of this event are having a conversation and one asks, 'Where's North?' The other looks around and finally points toward Oliver North and says, 'That's North!' What is the meaning of this response? Does it mean, 'That's Oliver North' or 'North is in that direction'? It depends on the stage-setting. If the two attendees had been making efforts to identify the more famous Republicans among them, the meaning is quite clear. On the other hand, if they had been discussing the approximate direction of Washington, DC from their location and only one of them knew DC was approximately north of Virginia, we have another meaning.

Distinguishing between the meanings of a single action that might adequately answer two different queries depends on the queries and subsequent action or actions being surrounded by the proper stage-setting. To return to Wittgenstein's 'this is the king' example, such a definition would make little or no sense to a person who was unfamiliar with the notion of 'game.' We emphasize, however, that *it would be a mistake simply to identify stage-setting with context*. Stage-setting is *one* form of context that makes meaning and understanding possible.

We have already observed that Augustine's picture of language-learning and understanding rests on the assumption that one's mind makes a connection between a sound (e.g. 'king') and the object it signifies. But that is not all. According to Augustine, one's mind has a basic or original language all its own. It must some-how translate its own internal articulations into the articulations of others that refer to public objects signified by those others. In PI §32, Wittgenstein imagines someone visiting a strange country, sometimes learning some of the words of the language of its inhabitants from ostensive definitions they have given him. On occasion this traveler will have to guess the meanings of these definitions and sometimes will guess these meanings correctly, sometimes not. This, says Wittgenstein, is similar to how 'Augustine describes the learning of human language as if the child came into a strange country and did not understand the language of that country; that is, as if [the child] already had a language, only not this one.' Wittgenstein adds that Augustine presents a picture of language-learning 'as if the child could already *think*, only not yet speak. And "think" would here mean something like "talk to itself"' (PI §32). Here we have all of McGinn's (1997) additional elements, save the one numbered 9 in our scheme – the view that understanding consists in one making an appropriate connection between a sound and object signified.

Context, ostension and the 'situatedness' of meanings

Quite apart from all the different uses we make of words and other signs in managing our everyday lives, ostension – or the meaning-fixing procedure on which the *Tractatus* and the works of many other philosophers has been based – has inherent difficulties of its own. We do indeed learn some words as the names of things, but can this be achieved determinatively by pointing to exemplars?

The ambiguity of exemplars and context

In investigating this issue Wittgenstein uses a technique he employs in several discussions of meaning, asking how such-and-such a word could be learned. He shows that on some accounts of learning the meaning of a word, the word could be learned by ostension. According to the 'all words are names' thesis, one would have to learn words by ostension, or pointing to an exemplar (e.g. 'dog'). But ostension is always, to some degree, ambiguous. As learners we do not know which of the many aspects of an exemplar we are supposed to attend to. Suppose that a teacher tries to teach someone the meaning of 'two' by displaying two nuts in the palm of his or her hand (PI §28). Think of the many different aspects of this demonstration a learner might attend to unless it had been made clear in advance that it was the *number of nuts* to which they were to attend!

Pointing to something does not necessarily help us to grasp the full meaning or significance of a word. Consider the word 'gun.' A policeman teaches this word to his son not only by showing him his pistol, but also by explaining its use to deter violence and to safeguard the public. Now suppose a felon robs the policeman of this very gun and teaches his son what 'gun' means. But of course the same material thing attracts a very different significance in this latter circumstance. Context makes a huge difference to what happens cognitively when you point to something and say a word. (Of course this relates to the chess example at PI §31.)

Here is another example. There are a great many different things one might be doing in attending to the color of some object, even when it has been made clear that the word in use is intended to mean the color and not the shape of the object in question. There is nothing in any of these procedures that can fix the meaning of a sign in perpetuity and without some possibility of ambiguity. Developmental psychologists of language are well aware of this problem in the learning of word-meaning.

The many kinds of meaning: 'five red apples'

The foregoing will assist novice readers of PI in their understanding of Wittgenstein's first illustrative examples of meaning-in-use. About midway through PI §1, just as we have been introduced to the Augustinian picture of language, he imagines sending someone shopping for apples with a slip marked 'five red apples.' Wittgenstein's purpose in presenting us with this fable is clear in one respect. He wants to explore the extent to which the basic elements of the Augustinian picture he has just described could account for the success of this foray to market. If words stand for things in the world, what is the shopkeeper to make of 'five,' 'red' and 'apples'? What is he to make of the words combined as a *request* for five red apples? Being a word that names an object, 'apples' presents no difficulty at all. The shopkeeper simply opens a drawer marked 'Apples.' With 'red,' the shopkeeper employs a somewhat different procedure, using a table of color samples and finding the color red, labeled with the word 'red.' For 'five,' the shopkeeper says 'one' and takes an apple, 'two' and takes another, and so on up to five – on each occasion choosing an apple of the proper color, by matching it to the sample next to the name 'red' in the color chart.

It is at this point that we are confronted, for the first time in the *Investigations*, with Wittgenstein's interlocutor. (Many key paragraphs in this and other of Wittgenstein's later writings are presented in the form of dialogues.) While Wittgenstein's interlocutor has been variously described as the voice of the philosopher Frege, or Wittgenstein's old mentor Bertrand Russell, our suggestion is to think of the interlocutor as the voice of one who is more often than not under the spell of the Augustinian picture of language. Given his Augustinian tendencies, the interlocutor's query makes sense in light of the shopkeeper's success following the request for five red apples, in particular with respect to 'what he is to do with the word "five"?' For if words name objects, to which object does 'five' refer? Indeed, how could the meaning of 'five' ever be learned by the shopkeeper if, as the Augustinian picture implies, the shopkeeper's private mind could only learn the meaning of 'five' by linking its sound with (for lack of a better term) a five-object? There simply is no object to which 'five' refers! 'Five' is neither the name of a sample of quintuplicity, nor the name of a particular quintuple, or even an abstract 'fiveness' exemplified in each quintuple. This is why Wittgenstein, toward the end of PI §1, insists that for the shopkeeper the meaning of 'five' was never in question. We only witnessed the shopkeeper's actions in relation to his being presented with a slip of paper marked 'five red apples.' That he brings out the proper number of apples shows us clearly that he knows the meaning of 'five.' In other words, to this extent he has mastered a procedure.

What is the significance of the shopkeeper's ability here for our general question about meaning? Obviously it is that the Augustinian picture of language, which holds (in part) that words stand for objects, cannot account for his understanding the meaning of a word that does not stand for an object! So has Wittgenstein discovered a new kind of word? Since Plato, philosophers have supposed that since words like 'five' do not have representations in the world, they must be represented somehow, somewhere, in an alternative realm of sorts – in this case, a Platonic realm of symbols. No, Wittgenstein has not discovered a new kind of word. He has only shown us that *the meaning of words that do not denote objects can only be realized in the context of human activities*. This is an extraordinarily important idea that has wide-ranging implications for psychology. But what of words that denote objects? Does their status remain as before, as in the *Tractatus*? In remarks subsequent to PI §1, Wittgenstein proceeds to answer these questions in the negative. Even the meanings of nouns are not simply based only on observation of the objects they signify. For example if I hold up my hand to teach you the Spanish word 'dado,' you might think it means the English word 'hand.' But it means 'finger.' In the case of someone trying to teach the meaning of 'two' by showing the learner two nuts, how does the learner know, from this experience alone, that the word 'two' does not mean 'nut'? Only if a place has already been prepared for where this word is to go in the language of the learner can the learner grasp the correct semantic import of the display.

The diversity of uses: language as a toolbox and words as tools

In PI §2 Wittgenstein tries to imagine a world in which the Augustinian account of meaning would be adequate. A builder and his assistant are at work using several kinds of building materials including blocks, slabs, beams and pillars. There are only four words in the language of this imaginary world: 'block,' 'slab,' 'beam' and 'pillar.' When the builder calls out 'block,' his assistant brings a block. However, reflection on the necessities of the uses of language in this simple world soon brings out a further inadequacy of the Augustinian account. The assistant has not only to be trained to identify the items in the yard, but also to bring them when the builder says the word. The word 'block' is not just a description, but also an order of sorts. Describing is one use for the word and ordering is another, related use.

The forms of signs do not determine their uses
Wittgenstein continues to reflect on the builders in PI §11. There he takes the intuition of §2 further, asking us to think of words as if they were tools in a toolbox. Tools are created to fulfill certain functions. Some tools look very different from others. A hammer looks as different from a saw as a nail differs from a ruler. But then again, a nail may look quite similar to a screw and a screwdriver may look like a chisel. We should not allow similarity in form to dominate our understanding of such tools. If we know their *uses* we will consider even these similar-looking tools to be rather different. This is even more the case with words, whether they be spoken or in print. As Wittgenstein points out, 'what confuses us is the uniform appearance of words when we hear them spoken or meet them in script and print. For their *application* is not presented to us so clearly. Especially when we are doing philosophy!' (PI §11).

As we will see in more detail when encountering Wittgenstein's later philosophical method in Chapter 7, Wittgenstein attributes the longevity of certain philosophical problems to habits of thought and language use. His method, being directed toward breaking philosophers of these habits, turns our attention from the misleading uniformity of words in our language to their not-so-uniform use. Psychologists are just as inclined as philosophers to fall into this trap because philosophical problems permeate their ways of thinking about and investigating psychological phenomena. By treating a word as if it has only one or two uses, we are likely to run into trouble.

Carrying the metaphor further in PI §12, Wittgenstein points out that words are like the handles we see in a locomotive cabin. They look 'more or less alike,' but their functions are very different. (Think also of the many switches in the cockpit of a commercial airliner and consider the implications of a pilot mistaking their functions!) Here is another, perhaps more familiar, example. In Anglo-American homes we often enough hear the parent-to-child expression, 'Why don't you eat your spinach?' Having eaten all the meatloaf and waiting for her ice cream, a three-year-old resentfully sits at the dinner table. There before her, on the edge of her plate, is a mound of green spinach. She responds to her father's query by saying 'I don't like it!' Now, will her father regard this response as a 'correct' reply? Certainly not. In most circumstances, though the expression seems to have the form of a question, it functions more like an order. Meanings (uses) of the same sign are manifold and how each one should be taken depends on context. 'Get me the book,' 'I am booking you,' 'I want to book a flight' and so on. It might appear that nothing of great significance hangs on this example of context-sensitive meanings. But what about the use of a word like 'response' in psychology? How might its uses in varieties of ordinary context muddle our understanding of what it means 'to respond' when 'response' is defined for use in experimental psychology?

Let us briefly address a possible objection that might be raised at this point. Wittgenstein is presenting us with a tool analogy for language. But is it not the case that tools have quite specific uses and does this not contradict his insistence that we look to the possible wide-ranging uses of words? Well, hammers are manufactured and used principally for pounding nails. But a hammer also can be used as part of an artist's installation, to prop open a window or keep a door open, as a nutcracker, a murder weapon, a counter-weight, to hold open a map in a strong wind, to break a lock, or as a gift. By using our imaginations and heeding the principle of polysemous meaning, we now see the diversity of possible uses of a hammer. How does this demonstration relate to our theoretical and empirical practices in psychology? Think of the degree to which our uses of psychological concepts (e.g., 'attention') are quite specific in each experimental context, and yet how much of the gamut of ordinary uses can be smuggled into our thinking in the context of psychological research. Does the use of the word 'attention,' as related to the concept of ADHD (attention deficit hyperactivity disorder), bear much resemblance to any of its uses in common parlance? In some ways yes. But in other ways no.

There are no linguistic essences: family resemblance and word classes

Philosophers and linguists no longer believe that every word has an 'essential' meaning; a common meaning that lies behind all the various ways each word is used. Instead, the notion of a semantic field or, as Wittgenstein calls it, a pattern of *family resemblances*, can be used to express how words have multiple meanings (see for example PI §67). In PI §66 Wittgenstein offers the word 'game' as an example of a word with no single essential meaning, but as having a pattern of uses that are related by similarities and differences. It is a cardinal mistake to try to find an essential meaning, to invent one because one believes there must be such a thing, and then to import it into every situation in which the word is used. The mistake of searching for essences is ubiquitous in human ways of thinking.

What sorts of words are there? In PI §17 Wittgenstein asks whether there is just one way of putting words into groups. In the language of the builders in PI §8, in which there are only the words 'block,' 'slab,' 'pillar' and 'beam,' the letters of the alphabet a, b, c, d could be used instead. One might think that there is an obvious way of grouping them. However, PI §17 suggests that all sorts of grouping are possible. There is no one, definite way. Because we have been to school we are accustomed to group words as nouns and adjectives. One can group words in other ways very easily: for example, abstract versus concrete, or Teutonic versus Latinate, long versus short, and so on.

Language-games

PI §§7 and 23 are very important remarks that introduce readers to one of Wittgenstein's few technical terms: 'language-game.' It is true that scholars have debated the precise meaning of this term. But for our purposes the term has a dual meaning. First, it is a methodological tool for Wittgenstein. Second, we may think of language-games as practical activities where words are used as an essential part of the procedure. Here are some examples: playing baseball, having dinner in a restaurant, giving orders and obeying them, betting, conducting a murder trial, doing a chemical experiment and so on. (The latter should bring to mind the notion of 'language-games of science.') We should keep in mind the contrast between this way of thinking of language as a tool for accomplishing a huge range of tasks, on one hand, and the old theory of language that reigned at least since the time of Augustine, on the other hand. In §23 Wittgenstein asks us to compare the multiplicity of the ways words are used and the multiplicity of kinds of word in a single sentence with what logicians have said about the nature of language, including the author of the *Tractatus Logico-Philosophicus*.

If we take words as the main instruments of cognition, then our entrance into cognitive psychology is going to take a rather different direction from the current experimental paradigm, which had its origins in behaviorism. Studying language-in-use is going to lead us to include things like guessing a riddle, translating, asking for something, praying and so on. Praying is a bit like asking for something, but not exactly. In PI §27 Wittgenstein lists some of the many everyday exclamations in which words play various roles. Let us think about why you might use the cry 'Water!' Staggering through the desert, you came to a hut and you cry 'Water!' Alternatively, on being entertained by somebody, they produce the only drink in the house out of the tap. But you were expecting whisky. You exclaim 'Water!' in surprise. And so on. We will see that, in the context of philosophical and psychological inquiry, it is a worthwhile exercise to run through a list of possible uses this way, imagining as many different circumstances as possible in which a word or linguistic expression might be used.

The lists of language-games and word uses presented in PI §§23 and 27 respectively point to a more significant intuition as to what people use words to accomplish, an intuition Wittgenstein shares with J.L. Austin (1975). According to Austin, in many cases words are the means by which certain social acts are brought about. He called utterances with which social acts and actions are accomplished 'performatives.' In saying 'I sentence you to life' a judge performs a legal act. The sentence is not a description of anything. There are several examples of performatives in PI §23 (not to mention at many points in the *Investigations*). For example, in PI §23 we have the performatives of 'Giving orders, and obeying them … asking, thanking, cursing, greeting, praying.' We could add many more. Wittgenstein teaches us that none of the words listed in PI §27 is the name of an object. For example, 'Ow!' 'Help' and 'Fine,' as offered in response to a greeting, do not name anything. None of the verbal tasks implicit in either of these lists is solely and primarily a description of something. This point will be of great importance in subsequent chapters when we discuss how moods, emotions, bodily feelings and so on, are expressed and understood.

Opening up the variety of word use in the management of our lives gives us a sound footing in our understanding of language. Since language is the main tool of cognition among humans, exploring the roles of words widens the scope of cognitive research in general.

The grand conclusion of the analysis and further implications for psychology

In PI §43 Wittgenstein's critique of the Augustinian picture thus far is summed up as follows: 'For a *large* class of cases – though not for all – in which we employ the word "meaning" it can be defined thus: the meaning of a word is its use in the language. And the *meaning* of a name is sometimes explained by pointing to its *bearer.*'

Most of the time when we ask about meanings, we are really asking about uses. The meaning of a word is usually not some object of which the word is the name. In a great many cases word meaning can be made clear by looking at real people using the word in real (and imagined) circumstances. New uses are influenced in subtle ways by old uses. Often we are tempted to settle on a single model for the use of a word when we reflect on what it means. That model may be covertly influencing what we mean by the word. We must make no assumptions about linguistic essences, but look and see how words are *actually used*. In this way we can trace out fields of family resemblance.

We have moved from presupposing that the meaning of a word is the object it signifies to the idea of meaning as the word's use in specific human practices.

In applying Wittgenstein's later philosophy to modern psychology, must we share his rejection of the Augustinian picture of language in all its guises? The argument so far strongly suggests that our misunderstandings of the way words and other symbolic devices acquire meaning is likely to lead us into philosophical conundrums in philosophy and psychology. The behaviorist approach to determining the proper scope for a scientific discipline can be thought of as having the Augustinian picture at its root, in that behaviorists demanded an observational basis for meaning – the so-called operational definitions of psychological concepts. Still, it may not always be the case that it is the Augustinian picture that lies at the root of our philosophical problems in psychology. (And we have yet to see precisely what distinguishes a philosophical problem from other sorts of problems, such as 'empirical problems.') In addition to the malign influence of the idea that the meaning of a word is the object it denotes, the idea that for every word there is a linguistic essence, something that it means in all circumstances, is equally potent in leading philosophers and psychologists into confusions of thought. The second key idea from Wittgenstein's later philosophy is that of the field of family resemblances. Taking just one use of a word as its established meaning can lead us to serious mistakes in the interpretation of observations in the research context.

To illustrate Wittgenstein's insight that linguistic practices are acquired in the course of language-games, and not as the result of acts of ostension, we turn now to

Bruner's (1983a) study of the activities within which young children acquire the skill of making verbal requests. Subsequently, we will take a brief look at the study of 'infant cognition' to illustrate the importance of sensitivity to fields of family resemblances and the mistake of presuming a linguistic essence or common meaning for all the uses of an expression. In the Bruner study, we will be looking at how human beings under investigation by a psychologist acquire the meanings of certain words. These ways of acquiring word-meaning run contrary to the Augustinian picture. In the infant cognition example we will be looking at how *psychologists* misuse the language they use to report and interpret the results of their studies, slipping into assuming a common meaning for the whole field of uses of some key words.

Bruner's request formats

On many occasions when infants are learning a word, or an expression, they are not acquiring its meaning by following the act of the teacher pointing to something. The teacher and the infant jointly engage in a language-game of sorts, or complex activity in which a natural reaction is transformed into a linguistic skill.

The ability to express what one wants would seem to be a necessary condition for acquiring the skill of expressing what one means to do. Jerome Bruner's (1983a) work on 'request formats' has opened the way to a more comprehensive understanding of the acquisition of the expression of thoughts about the future. His research reveals how at least one component of the skill of expressing intentions might arise as a public language-game, the game of request formats.

How do infants learn to ask for or demand something they do not have? How do they express, in this simple case, a thought about the future? Bruner distinguishes three main types of requests: (1) for an object, (2) to share a role relationship such as playing some game and (3) for supportive action (or help in achieving some goal).

Usually, a very young infant's cries are interpreted by care-givers as expressions of 'physical' wants and needs. At about six months a mother 'begins interpreting the child's cries as due to more psychological "causes"' (Bruner, 1983a, p. 92) to which the child begins to respond appropriately. Note that Bruner intends his use of the word 'cause' as a metaphor for a thought form not yet sufficiently clearly experienced to be called an 'intention' or 'want.' 'So long as the mother can provide an interpretation of an appropriate referent from the context, the child adapts his cries to [the conditions the mother imposes, such as] waiting for uptake' (Bruner, 1983a, p. 92). At about eight months an additional step toward the development of a format for deliberate requests appears. Infants reach for something and make sounds and facial expressions while doing so. According to Bruner (1983a), this has to do entirely

> with the child's first 'requestive referential' manoeuver; an extension *towards* a desired object … At first, this reach is as if 'real'; it is effortful, the body inclined with the reach, and the child makes 'effortful' noises when opening and closing his [or her] extended hand. In a few months this reach becomes stylized and conventional. The reach is now open-handed, noneffortful, and its accompanying vocalization … becomes distinctive. It is, in effect, an 'ostensive reach' that seems to be intended to indicate an object of desire.
>
> (p. 93)

A child throws a ball on the floor. A care-giver picks it up and returns it to the child, who throws it again. As this game progresses the child begins to reach for the ball, stretching and grunting as it does so. Further along the line of development the child finds that the stretching of the hand towards the ball has the desired effect. Finally, just making the appropriate noise alone achieves success. The next step in this progression is an example of the substitution of a word for a natural expression, as the 'effort sounds were ... replaced by stylized request calls' (Bruner, 1983a, p. 95). By the end of the second year the child has substituted words such as 'More mouse' and 'Richard cake' for stylized request calls.

In short, at one point in the course of development an infant naturally reaches out for something just out of its grasp. The mother, for example, will see the direction of the child's stretching and pass it the ball. Very soon thereafter the child uses the reaching motion as a gesture, expressing the thought later formulated in language as 'I want ... ' The grunting noises that the child makes as it stretches are gradually substituted for the natural expression. Bruner's studies show very clearly just how this language-game is the origin of the skilled linguistic practice of asking for things. Each culture elaborates the primitive request format with norms of politeness and all the rest of the paraphernalia that goes into civilized life. We will be reminded of Bruner's request formats when we encounter Wittgenstein's own take on how children learn to use words as substitutions for natural expressions of pain and other bodily feelings at PI §244.

The use of cognitive concepts in studies on infants and neonates
Our example of presuming a common meaning when words are used in ways that display only family resemblances is the well-known 'habituation' method used in developmental research for many years. The basic idea is that we may come to know what prelinguistic children are thinking by habituating them to a stimulus. Successful habituation involves repeatedly presenting a stimulus (e.g. a tone) until the infant's attention appears to be reduced. Then we might present the same stimulus in an altered form (e.g. a tone of noticeably higher pitch) and the infant displays renewed interest in the stimulus. This is 'dishabituation.' Developmental psychologists have used expressions such as 'paying less attention,' 'becoming bored,' 'noticed,' 'recognized' and so on to describe the course of infants' habituation and dishabituation.

The issue we want to bring out has to do with whether 'becoming bored,' 'notice,' 'recognize' and so on are *meaningful* as used in the context of infant cognition in the same sense as when they are used for describing cognitive activities, events and processes among adults. The developmental psychologist might say: 'Of course not!' But our point is much more subtle. Could that very psychologist have learned these and other similar linguistic expressions by witnessing an instructor pointing to examples of people knowing or recognizing something? What would these 'pointings' be examples of? They could not be examples of the experiences of noticing something and recognizing what sort of thing that is. If that had indeed been the case, then our psychologist could legitimately apply them to an infant based on what s/he has seen the infant do. However – and here is the paradox – the use of these words (e.g. 'notices') by developmental psychologists seems to affirm that infants are capable of the cognitive activities for which the words stand in ordinary language among competent speakers. But for such words to have a cognitive dimension to their meanings they could not have been learned by ostension alone! The full-fledged language-games of 'noticing' are activities carried on by those with a linguistic repertoire more advanced than an eight-week-old infant.

This is not to say that care-givers are mistaken when they attribute 'noticing' to their prelinguistic infant. Nor are we saying that informative research using the habituation paradigm has not been and cannot be undertaken. We are simply pointing out two things. First, do we not say that the family pet notices things? But certainly human adults are capable of noticing in far more complex ways than dogs or cats! In habituation research, words such as 'noticing' seem to be applied to prelinguistic infants as if there is little or no difference between noticing as an infant, noticing as a human adult, and noticing as a dog. Our second point is that, without recognizing the immediately foregoing, psychologists have no impetus whatever to qualify their observations and conclusions in the context of scientific research. This is a source of continuing frustration for the Wittgenstein-informed psychologist, as important subtleties of meaning are ignored and important questions are not posed.

A striking example of the pitfalls that await even the most distinguished researchers is the use of the word 'imitation' by Meltzoff and Moore (e.g. 1983) to describe the remarkable results of many studies on neonatal responses to adult facial expressions. These researchers (and many others) claim that newborns will (1) respond to the pursed lips of an adult by pursing their own lips, (2) stick out their tongues when an adult in their line of sight sticks out their tongue, and (3) open their mouths in response to mouth-opening on the part of an adult. We have no reason to doubt the 'empirical results' of these famous experiments which, by the way, are summarized in many introductory psychology textbooks. Our 'issue' is conceptual. A detailed description of the research methods is not necessary here, other than to say that these studies have been performed under controlled laboratory conditions that involve the researcher (or researchers) making facial expressions in the newborns' line of sight. Should we be satisfied with the description of the responses, described above, as 'imitation'? We think not. A Wittgenstein-informed analysis of the concept of imitation as used by these researchers, pitted against the possibilities of use of the concept in contexts outside the laboratory, shows, in part, the following:

(1)   Imitation is not *responsive alone*, as it is with newborns. (Older children and adults can *purposively* imitate the facial expressions of others when the others are not present. Or they can decide to do so at some other time.) This leads to the second point.

(2)   The 'object of imitation' *need not be present and seen* in many contexts of imitation.

(3)   As indicated in 1 above, imitation *can be purposively withheld*, while with newborns it cannot be so withheld. (That is, when a newborn does not imitate, s/he simply is counted as not having imitated.)

(4)   There are normative constraints on what counts as 'imitation.' (Imitation, as in the case of the comedian who tries to imitate a celebrity, can be done well or poorly.)

(5)   Imitation often expresses values. (One risks getting sent to the Principal's office for imitating one's teacher in school.)

In sum, the concept of imitation is far more complex than portrayed by researchers studying neonates. They seem to see no problem in applying the concept to neonates as if it had more or less the same meaning when applied to adults. We have yet to see an article of any kind that explores these complexities in such a way that qualifications can be made with respect to the meaning of 'neonatal imitation' versus the full range of 'imitation' as it can be applied in a field of family resemblance.

Learning point: enriching and correcting the understanding of meaning

1.   *Against generalizing 'meaning-as-object-signified'*

   (a)   The opening remarks of PI constitute an effort to dismantle the Augustinian picture of language. After characterizing this faulty picture, Wittgenstein turns to showing that individual words can have meanings of many kinds.
   (b)   'Stage-setting' is an important idea that helps to put Wittgenstein's efforts in context. The example of 'this is the king' (PI §31) shows that the learning of a definition of that piece in chess depends already on the learner knowing about other games.
   (c)   Thus learning by ostension alone is impossible. We must establish a place in the language (for example in some language-game) in order to disambiguate pointing (PI §§28 and 33).
   (d)   In PI §1 ('five red apples'), meaning is an instance of a type or match to a sample or part of a procedure. In PI §2 (the block/slab game), meaning is a social act. For example, the word 'slab' is used both to describe and to command. In PI §23 there is a great variety of linguistically performed social acts, or performatives. In PI §27 we have exclamations.
   (e)   Form does not determine function. We must study the uses of words in practices, that is, in language-games (PI §§7 and 23), or activities in which words play an essential role. This insight carries with it the important toolbox analogy for language.

2.   *There are no linguistic essences*

   (a)   There are no final forms of expressions to be discovered.
   (b)   The same word has many uses, forming a field of family resemblances. This idea is introduced at PI §67, but demonstrated in

numerous prior remarks (for example, Wittgenstein's famous 'game' example at PI §66). It is a serious mistake to suppose that there *must* be an essential, but covert, 'common meaning' to all uses of a word.

3. *Conclusion*

(a) We must abandon the idea that meaning is *object designated* and instead think of *meaning as use in a practice*, including the practice of designating objects (PI §43).
(b) The importance of thinking in terms of language-games is illustrated by Bruner's research into request formats.
(c) The importance of thinking in terms of fields of family resemblance in the context of psychological research is illustrated by research into infant cognition. 'Habituation' and 'neonatal imitation' are cases in point.

Further reading

Baker, G.P. and Hacker, P.M.S. (1980), *Wittgenstein: Understanding and meaning. An analytical commentary on the Philosophical Investigations* (Vol. 1). Oxford: Blackwell. (In particular pp. 20–32.)

Chapman, M. and Dixon, R.A. (eds) (1987), *Meaning and the Growth of Understanding: Wittgenstein's significance for developmental psychology*. Heidelberg: Springer-Verlag.

Erneling, C.E. (1993), *Understanding Language Acquisition: The framework of learning*. Albany, NY: State University of New York Press.

Glock, H.-G. (1996), *A Wittgenstein Dictionary*. Oxford: Blackwell. (Specifically pp. 236–8 and 376–81.)

5 Skills and abilities

Philosophical Investigations §§156-78

> By thus restricting himself to data in and for itself, as the subject
> matter of the philosopher's exclusive attention, [Wittgenstein]
> necessarily turns away from many interesting and significant
> questions about the mental reality ... that might be illuminated
> by use of his descriptive material not merely as data but as
> evidence. In both cases, we find a restriction of attention to
> behavior, a studied refusal to examine and elaborate the mental
> structures that underlie observed performance.
>
> Noam Chomsky (1969), p. 28, on Wittgenstein's remarks on
> 'reading'

> [Chomsky] apparently sees no conceptual difficulties in claiming
> that it is an intelligible hypothesis to propose a mental state as
> criterial to the proper avowal and ascription of 'reading'.
>
> Jeff Coulter (1979), p. 73, on Chomsky on Wittgenstein on
> 'reading'

Topics introduced: skills and abilities; powers; competent use; mentalism; causality and causal accounts of human activities; homogeneous and heterogeneous explanation regresses; essentialism; the concept of reading, mechanism and mechanistic and mentalist criteria for reading; *modus tollens*; word sign to speech sound; phenomenological differences; context of investigation; the threshold fallacy

To use a sign correctly and effectively a person must have the relevant ability. Obviously using a sign, as a kind of linguistic action, is linked with 'ability' as a psychological concept. There are other concepts closely related to 'ability,' such as 'skill,' 'competence,' 'capacity' and so on. In this chapter we will concentrate on 'ability' and 'skill' as key concepts for a psychology based upon the 'use' principle outlined in the previous chapter. Generally, an ability or skill can be exercised more or less competently in relation to what an actor may want or need to achieve. The concept of an 'ability' is applicable where there is a recognized task or project and the need to accomplish it effectively.

In Chapter 1, during our discussion of what it takes for a practice to be a scientific practice, we mentioned the importance of constructing a catalogue and associated taxonomy for the field of phenomena relevant to that science. Now, in anticipating the direction of Wittgenstein's analysis of the practice of using signs for all sorts of tasks (including thinking and managing the social world), we might suspect that the relevant field of phenomena will be tied closely to skills and abilities. Our first task will be to set out some of the characteristics of psychological phenomena as the exercise of abilities, rather than as responses to external or internal contingencies. How does one *know how* to use a sign, accomplish a task and so on? Wittgenstein looks at several different proposals for explaining what it is to have an ability. As will be the case throughout remaining chapters on other topics, our exposition of Wittgenstein's investigation into skills and abilities will make use of a selection of appropriate remarks not necessarily in proximity within the *Investigations*. Also, quite a number of the remarks we use as examples stand outside the range of remarks specified in our chapter title (§§156–78).

'Having an ability'

It is important to distinguish between skills and abilities, on one hand, and powers on the other hand. An ability, say to use words, is what *some living being* (e.g. a human) can do. Abilities are connected with concepts like learning and proficiency. A power is what some *stuff* can do. A boulder rolling down a hillside has the power to topple a small tree. But the boulder never learned to knock down trees with proficiency. Animals and human beings also have what we might term natural powers or natural abilities. Examples of these would be the sucking and rooting reflexes in newborn humans. But we need to be cautious about classifying such abilities as 'natural abilities.' For obvious reasons, natural abilities in humans are different from powers as we have described them.

We can follow the natural science model and explain phenomena in terms of the physical powers of material things and substances. Take the chemical phenomenon of 'acidity.' It is manifested in all sorts of ways, such as the taste of lemon juice, the etching of copper by hydrochloric acid, and so on. However, in whatever circumstances it is manifested, acidity is explained *scientifically* in one way: by the citation of the presence of unobservable positively charged hydrogen ions. We can characterize this sort of explanation as an effort to find the *foundation* for a power. A single foundation is identifiable in all cases of acidity.

If we follow Wittgenstein and abandon the idea that meanings are objects signified, we must ascribe to human beings the skills and abilities related to using signs. We turn to a 'use' account that is rather different from the natural science account. The question remains as to whether the use account will result in our finding a uniform and universal foundation for the ability to use this or that sign, word, or instrument. Such foundations have been proposed by linguists and psycholinguists. Wittgenstein examines many cases in which one might be tempted to follow the pattern of natural science explanations. In each case, he demonstrates that this would be a mistake.

The basic point to keep in mind throughout this discussion is quite simple: *we do not have to investigate a person's state of mind or the configuration of their brain to know whether they have or lack an ability.* 'Can you ride a horse?' 'Yes!' 'Okay, then ride that horse over there. Her name is Lucky.' We do not undertake an empirical investigation into the mental states or brain of Lucky's would-be rider in order to see if they can, in fact, ride a horse. It is true that, in principle, a research program might be devised to find a neurophysiological foundation for horse-riding. But we have to ask ourselves what import such research might have for everyday exhibitions of skills and abilities. Will not the deciding factor always be *that* the person can ride a horse? Still, this does not rule out the possibility that abilities might be kept in the mind and put into action on appropriate occasions. In considering skills and abilities, Wittgenstein's focus is the ability to use words in meaningful ways. But the results of his investigation can be generalized to any number of other skills and abilities.

Having a picture in mind as a foundation for an ability

Isn't the meaning of a word something in the mind, a mental accompaniment that occurs to us when we hear the word or see the sign? Perhaps we consult the accompanying image in order to use a sign correctly. This image might take the form of a proposition, setting out an interpretation or a definition for the word or sign in question. Or this image might be a mental picture. Reference to it while encountering a word might explain how we can perform tasks displaying the ability to use a sign.

Wittgenstein considers several ways in which having an ability to use a sign, especially a word, might be explained as having a picture in mind of how to use it. In PI §73 he discusses the possibility of understanding shape and color words by making use of an imagined sample. First he mentions a color table, with words written under each color sample in the table. If one looks at a color sample and sees under it 'red,' then one might come to understand the definition of red. 'One is now inclined to extend the comparison: to have understood the definition means to have in one's mind an idea of the thing defined, and that is a sample or picture ... .' So now the definition of the color sample has moved from the table into the mind in the form of a mental picture.

Among other matters, in PI §73 Wittgenstein introduces an extremely important principle. Suppose I am successful at understanding the definition of 'red' by the above procedure. I could not have done so without having understood how to use the color table. So I have, in fact, understood and carried out two procedures. This means that my competent use of 'red' has been established by competent use of something else (the color table). In this sense, competent use depends on competent use.

Why does Wittgenstein bring up the example of a color table? The answer is that we often try to explain memories, dreams, instructions and so on in terms of mental pictures. A color table is located outside my body. I would think of a mental picture of the table, of course, as being located inside my body – or maybe even as being *part* of my body if I think of my mental picture as being grounded in neural processes. There are quite a number of possible explanations as to what a mental picture 'is.' But in any case, we are encountering a theme that reappears throughout the *Investigations*. It is our own habit of drawing a sharp distinction between the 'inner' and 'outer.' Wittgenstein's post-*Tractatus* analyses of the 'grammar' of psychological concepts often blurs this boundary. (His later conception of 'grammar' will be discussed in Chapters 6 and 7.)

Now I am shown a collection of leaves and, with the aid of instruction, 'I get an idea of the shape of a leaf, a picture of it in my mind' (PI §73). What is the relationship between my mind-picture of a leaf and the leaves I have been shown? Have I formed a mental picture of a leaf in such a way that my mind-leaf has the shape of 'what is common to all shapes of leaf'? What might such a mental image look like? Furthermore, what about the color of my mind-leaf? Wittgenstein asks: Is the green shade of my mind-leaf 'the sample of what is common to all shades of green'?

We are presented with a case where the ability to use the words 'leaf' and 'green' is grounded in the formation and use of a mental picture. Note that we can continue discussing this ability without the mental picture at all, opting to ground the ability in use of the color table or collection of actual leaves. It does not matter. But our focus is on the mental picture.

The first objection to the mental picture thesis concerns its generality. Since the mental picture of the leaf must be of a *particular* leaf or shade of green it cannot be a representation of what is common to all the cases in which we would want to use the words 'leaf' or 'green.' It must be *understood* as a 'schema,' says Wittgenstein. Then he adds that in order to understand the image or picture as a schema, one must know 'the way the samples are used.' By now we know why he makes this qualification. Even if we allow that use of the words 'leaf' and 'green' is grounded in use of a mental picture, we are going nowhere in linking the mental picture with the ability to use it. In other words, we get nowhere on the question of how to use a mental picture (or word) by stepping back into the mind. A picture of a leaf – whether it be a mental picture or actual photo – will help us only if we already know how to use it. I know how to use the word 'leaf.' I base this ability on using a mental picture of a leaf. Then I must explain how I know how to use the picture of the leaf to use the word 'leaf.' This opens up a regress. It necessitates an investigation into *understanding* because I must understand that *this* mental picture is a picture of a leaf, that it is not just a picture of a particular leaf but that it is, in fact, my leaf-schema, and so on. Explaining one ability by another leads us nowhere, and so one ability never could serve as the *foundation* of an ability.

Wittgenstein insists that such regresses are to be ended by realizing that the last ability in the chain has been acquired by training or by an inherited feature of the brain or nervous system. Whether it is a habit or a natural ability passed on through the genes, it is not based on any further, deeper, or hidden *psychological* level. 'This is simply what I do,' he remarks apropos of a similar case at PI §217.

To be clear, the full regress might go as follows: we explain the foundation of 'use' by investigating 'understanding,' then we explain understanding through reference to something behind understanding, and then something behind that, and so on. The very idea that we will expose 'the bottom' of this mystery in some cognitive or physiological process or state is a prejudice. We can say that the workings of words pertaining to skills and abilities lead us nowhere if we are committed (by prejudice) to find an explanation of skills and abilities via inner states and processes standing behind them.

Another objection to explaining an ability by rooting its foundation in a cognitive state or process is raised in PI §139. 'When someone says the word 'cube' to me, for example, I know what it means. But can the whole *use* of the word come before my mind, when I *understand* it in this way?' Of course not. That would take quite a bit of thought, and even then one might suspect that the possible uses of 'cube' might not be exhausted. What Wittgenstein is getting at here is that any cognitive state of knowing – if there is such a state – cannot consist in picturing something, as if we were to '*grasp it in a flash.*' Suppose a complete picture of uses of 'cube' does come before one's mind when another person utters 'cube.' How can this help as an explanation of knowing what 'cube' means? Wittgenstein asks: 'In what sense can this picture fit or fail to fit a use of the word "cube"?' Here we need to emphasize '*a* use.' Such a picture could be used to fit *any* use of the word! So what is the significance of explaining this single use of the cube picture? Furthermore, in PI §140 Wittgenstein points out that if we think that the cube picture *forced* a certain way of using it on us, then 'only the one case and no other occurred to us.'

It seems that any mentalist account of the meaning of skills and abilities must fall to the same general objection. We will use the term 'mentalist' (or 'mentalis- tic') at many points in chapters to follow. In so doing, we are keeping with the general description of 'mentalism' as any doctrine that insists upon the reality of inner states and processes of 'mind.' In many cases, mentalists explain the various forms of cognition in terms of such processes. Also, they are known to ground mental processes in material brain states and processes. In order for something in the mind (or brain) to be a foundation for a skill, we must know how that something is to be used. So we have not explained the use of the word or sign by referring to inner states and processes that underlie it. We have only set the 'use' account one step back. In effect, to know the use of something is an *ability concept*, not a concept descriptive of some state or process of mind.

Having an interpretation in mind as the foundation for a linguistic ability

> 'I take "Moses" to mean the man, if there was such a man, who led the Israelites out of Egypt, whatever he was called then and whatever he did or may not have done besides.' – But similar doubts to those about 'Moses' are possible about the words of this explanation [that is, what they mean] (what are you calling 'Egypt', whom the 'Israelites' etc.?). Nor would these questions come to an end when we got down to words like 'red,' 'dark,' 'sweet'.
>
> (PI §87)

Wittgenstein's interlocutor immediately retorts that if an explanation of Moses, like that given above, is shown not to be 'complete' or 'final,' then he can never understand who Moses was. Such an explanation is not an explanation at all. We can bring up doubts about the adequacy of so many words. Isn't there a way to have a final explanation that leads to final understanding? To this Wittgenstein responds: 'As though an explanation as it were hung in the air unless supported by another one' (PI §87). The way out of the interlocutor's conundrum is to see that *what it is to know* how to use a word or to have a non-verbal skill is displayed in a practice, and not in propositionally expressible knowledge of a set of instructions. It is to know how to do something, as opposed to knowing *that* something is the case.

A similar point is emphasized in PI §19, which is a further elaboration of the 'block/slab' game of §2. Suppose it was said that 'Slab!' is only a shortened form of the sentence 'Bring me a slab.' Later in the paragraph Wittgenstein remarks: 'But when I call "slab!", then what I want is, *that he should bring a slab!* – Certainly, but does wanting this consist in thinking in some form or other a different sentence from the one you utter?' Evidently not, for the same reason that pictures in the mind cannot be the foundations for skills, even if they can be interpreted as a display of what acting skillfully would look like.

The contrast with causal accounts of human activities

Is there one uniform way in which the possession of an ability can be explained that is the same for everyone who has the ability? The implausibility of this proposal leads to the proposal that the study of abilities in general must end in a simple assertion that the person in question can do whatever it is they are able to perform. An ability is not a special state of mind. An ability is displayed in a public performance, and one demonstrates that one has an ability by successfully performing a task that requires it. Moreover, using an ability to carry out a task is framed in terms of 'means and ends,' not in terms of causes and effects. Throughout Wittgenstein's discussion of skills and abilities there is an implicit contrast with causal explanations of the activities needed to accomplish a task. We should keep this contrast in mind. Briefly explicated, the concept of 'causality' has three components:

(1) To say that one event causes another is to say that there is a regular correlation between events of the type of the cause, and events of the type of the effect.
(2) The relation of causality is always asymmetrical, running from cause to effect.
(3) The relation of causality is naturally necessary. If the cause occurs, the effect must follow, unless something interferes. Hence, we always state causal laws *ceteris paribus*, meaning that a causal law will hold everything else being equal. The 'necessity' is a reflection of the presumption that a causal mechanism *must* exist, linking cause and effect productively.

There are many kinds of explanation other than causal explanations. In everyday explanations the exercise of a skill is usually framed in a means–end format. A person has some project in mind and attempts to bring it to a successful conclusion by the exercise of the relevant skill. The temptation to try to set up causal explanations of skilled performances leads to the omission of the agency of the performers, the projects in which they are engaged, and the standards according to which their performances are or could be assessed as well or poorly accomplished.

Homogeneous and heterogeneous explanation regresses

Psychologists may well be reluctant to accept Wittgenstein's way of ending explanatory regresses for the skills and abilities that loom so large in psychology. Surely, one might say, there must be something about the person who can ride a bicycle that is different from one who cannot. 'After training in bike riding, clarinet playing, French verb uses, and so on, the learner's brain has acquired a new structure.' Of course, it would be foolish to deny such a thing. To see where Wittgenstein's insight leads us we need to distinguish between two different kinds of explanatory regresses.

Homogeneous explanation regresses use the same concept over and over again. So in the case of abilities, abilities in one sort of task are explained by reference to abilities in another sort of task, mastery of which is relevant to the first ability. The explanation of an ability to use color words by reference to an ability to use mental pictures as samples would be such a regress. A homogeneous regress in psychology and other human domains terminates in something like a habit, acquired skill, or natural ability. Such regresses are *closed*. What if we do not admit that the regress ends in a habit, skill, or natural ability? The likelihood is that we will carry on the regress until we find a convenient point at which to end it. Our explanation, therefore, will be both wrong-headed and incomplete.

Heterogeneous explanation regresses reach this point, but then shift from one conceptual system to another. A homogeneous regress that terminates in a habit may be followed by a new explanatory level in which a quite different set of concepts is employed, say those pertaining to neural nets and parallel distributed processing. But here *psychological concepts are not being employed*, in part because we have taken the causal turn and human agency is no longer in the picture. There may be several ways in which a homogeneously terminated psychological regress can be transformed into a heterogeneous regress. For example, the same skill, according to performance criteria, may be grounded in different brain systems in different people, and there is some evidence that in the fine grain this is so. On the other hand, as frequently happens, the second phase of the regress may lead off into the sociological or historical origins of a practice.

As we have said, in psychology homogeneous regresses terminate in a habit, acquired skill, or natural ability. Nothing more could be said with the aid of psychological concepts alone. Wittgenstein is not proposing to do psychology 'in a new key,' but to provide us with the concepts with which to do it. A consistent criticism of his is that while psychologists have their experimental methods, they are conceptually confused. They are particularly prone to essentialism, thinking that there must be something in common to every situation in which we make use of a word, particularly words that seem to specify something psychological. They are also inclined to use the concept of 'causality' inappropriately.

To illustrate fully the study of abilities and skills, we will follow Wittgenstein's investigation of a skill at which most people the world over have at least some rudimentary mastery, namely reading aloud from a text. Among other things, the ability to read is to know how to use a word as a guide to speaking. The exercise of the skill can range from barely acceptable to fully competent, even masterful. But in any case, norms always are involved.

Learning point: the character of explanations via skills and ability

1. *Wittgenstein's critical analysis of 'mentalist' accounts*

    (a) We distinguish between skills and abilities, on one hand, and powers on the other hand. The former are related to such concepts as learning and proficiency. The latter are not.

(b) We might follow the natural science model of explanation and postulate material dispositions being the foundation of an ability to do something. This is connected with the postulation of mental states as explanations of abilities.

(c) We might refer to pictures in the mind as the foundation of the ability to use words. This explanation of abilities regresses to more abilities.

(d) Interpretations expressed in propositions need to be understood. This is likely to lead to another ability regress.

2. *Using abilities and skills concepts*

(a) It requires the presumption that the agent is actively engaged.

(b) It uses a means–end schema rather than cause–effect.

(c) It presupposes standards of adequate accomplishment.

3. *Types of regress (or common explanation formats)*

(a) *Homogeneous*: The same leading concept is used throughout the levels. For example, the ability to perform an action is explained by ability to use a mental picture. Such regresses terminate in 'habits,' acquired skills, or natural abilities.

(b) *Heterogeneous*: After the 'habit' concept halts the regress, we change the leading concepts (e.g. to neuroscience, history, sociology and so on.). In making this latter move, we run the risk of taking the causal turn where human agency is no longer in the picture.

Application of the ability analysis in psychology: the case of reading

In the *Investigations* Wittgenstein devotes 22 remarks on the topic of reading as a skilled cognitive performance (§§156–78). The remarks not only extend his attack on mentalism, but target mechanism. Mechanistic explanations of human skills and abilities reject reference to purposes, aims and desires. In other words, they are a kind of causal explanation in which we find no reference to agency.

Besides guiding readers through the remarks on reading, we hope our lengthy exposition will illustrate the thoroughness of Wittgenstein's approach, his depth of insight, ability to address alternative viewpoints, and, to some extent, the workings of his method. We do not think a summary of recent empirical research on reading is necessary as a comparison. It is more important to generalize, however minimally, his investigation and its results to the idea of any empirical investigation into a cognitive skill. That could be reading, but it also might be calculating, remembering, recognizing and so forth.

Before proceeding we need to comment on why we have included the quote by Noam Chomsky at the beginning of this chapter. To our knowledge, Chomsky's

(1969) chapter is the only point in his productive and influential career where he made a substantial effort to address Wittgenstein's writings. It is true that Chomsky's critical study focuses on an immature version of Wittgenstein's remarks on reading toward the end of the first section of the *Brown Book* (Wittgenstein, 1958, pp. 119–25). But that does not matter. As the quote shows, Chomsky (1969) accuses Wittgenstein of shirking interesting empirical questions, restricting his attention to behavior, and refusing 'to examine and elaborate the mental structures that underlie observed performance' (p. 28). But he misses the point(s) of Wittgenstein's remarks by a mile! And we already know one reason for this. When it comes to explaining the cognitive skill of reading, Chomsky is in a regress. He is oriented toward finding a 'mental structure' behind a cognitive and normative skill. This is but one example of how even the best and brightest misunderstand Wittgenstein – and for the very reasons established by Wittgenstein at many points in the *Investigations*. It is one thing to make the effort to understand and then disagree with Wittgenstein. It is quite another to make little or no effort to understand, then to disagree! But of course Wittgenstein is hardly alone in this regard as a major intellectual figure.

What constitutes the ability to read aloud?

Wittgenstein says he will not count 'understanding' of what is read as part of the kind of reading he is using as his example of a performance skill. Rather, he is concerned with reading as the 'activity of rendering out loud what is written or printed; and also of writing from dictation, writing out something printed, playing from a score, and so on' (PI §156). The kind of person Wittgenstein has in mind 'has received at school or at home one of the kinds of education usual among us, and in the course of it has learned to read his native language. Later he reads books, letters, newspapers, and other things' (PI §156).

The first of four themes introduced by Wittgenstein is the distinction between and emphasis on subjective or 'inner' experiences while one is reading and the 'outer' performances or exercises of the skill at reading or a display of the lack of it, or a simulation of having the ability in question. There is a variety of ways a reader can engage a printed text. For example, one who passes his eye along the printed words of a text may say the words aloud or to himself. He may 'take in' the shapes of words as wholes, may read syllable by syllable or letter by letter and may be said to have read a sentence if he has neither spoken it aloud nor to himself, but is later able to repeat the sentence verbatim (or nearly so). Or, he may read aloud and correctly without attending to what he is reading and thus, on request, be unable to give an adequate account of what he has read. Wittgenstein contrasts these subjective accompaniments of skilled reading with that of a beginning reader or pupil, who may read words by laboriously spelling them out or may guess how to read them from context or perhaps by already knowing what the text is about.

To introduce the second theme, Wittgenstein suggests that if we concentrate on the case of the pupil, if 'we ask ourselves what *reading* consists in, we shall be inclined to say: it is a special conscious activity of the mind' (PI §156). It seems the pupil lacks it.

The third theme is introduced immediately thereafter. We may also be inclined to say that the pupil alone knows if he is really reading. He will have privileged access to his way of using the written text as a guide that we can only tap into, for example, by testing his comprehension of the text. Wittgenstein admits that a pupil who is pretending to read may also have privileged access to his own *lack* of understanding. However, we would be inclined to think that in these cases 'to read' and 'reading' would be applied differently when referring to the beginner and to the skilled reader.

The fourth theme follows from these reflections. If, upon 'reading' the same word, a pretender and skilled reader say the same thing, we would be inclined to think – with knowledge of their skill levels in reading – that what goes on in their minds *must be different.* That is, we would be inclined to think 'two different [*psychological or neural*] mechanisms [are] at work here. And what goes on in them must distinguish reading from not reading. – But these mechanisms are only hypotheses, models designed to explain, to sum up, what you observe' (PI §156).

Wittgenstein has laid out a range of likely alternatives as candidates for the necessary and sufficient conditions for picking out genuine cases of someone reading, that is, for the prevailing use of the word 'reading' and related words. These include inclinations to think that reading involves both inner accompaniments and outer performances. This is supplemented further by the idea that readers have privileged access to their own experience of what they are doing when reading.

Two forms of explanation have been suggested to account for the inabilities of the pupil and abilities of the skilled reader. The first – that reading is a special conscious activity of the mind – is mentalistic, and the second – that reading behavior is based on an inner mechanism of the unconscious mind or even the brain – bears some of the hallmarks of mechanism. Despite their differences, these two perspectives regard either a special conscious activity of the mind or brain mechanisms and/or states as mediating 'between the operative facts (the letters) and the rule-guided action (reading)' (Baker and Hacker, 1980, p. 591).

Mechanist criteria for reading

Wittgenstein (PI §157) first turns to the mechanistic account through employment of a hypothetical language-game. He conducts a thought-experiment, just as a physicist would to test a concept. The situation is similar to that of the skilled reader and pupil, except we are asked to imagine human beings (or some other kind of creature) being used as reading-machines, trained and used for the purpose of reading aloud, with or without understanding. An untrained pupil is shown a written word and sometimes utters sounds, some of which are judged by the trainer to be more or less in line with how the word should be pronounced. Suppose the word this person reads correctly on occasion is 'psychology.' A second trainer comes upon the scene when the pupil utters 'psychology' more or less correctly. So the second trainer says the pupil 'is reading.' Now the first trainer disagrees and informs the second trainer that the pupil still often makes mistakes and has yet to become a full-fledged reader. With time and practice, fewer errors are made until finally the trainer counts the pupil as having the ability to read. Now, asks

Wittgenstein, what do we make of the first word that was read correctly (in our example, 'psychology')? 'Is the teacher to say: "I was wrong, and he *did* read it" – or: "He only began really to read later on"? – When did he begin to read? Which was the first word that he *read*?' (PI §157).

Wittgenstein says such a question makes no sense unless we arbitrarily define how many words must be correctly read in succession in order for the first word of that group to count as the first word that was 'really read.' Alternatively, we might use 'reading' to stand for a particular 'experience of transition from marks to spoken sounds, then it certainly makes sense to speak of the *first* word that he really read' (PI §157). In this case, the pupil would only have to express the *feeling* that he had read in order to be counted by the trainer as having read.

Neither arbitrary definition of how many words must be read correctly or the reader having a certain feeling will provide adequate criteria for acquisition of reading competence. Here as elsewhere, Wittgenstein emphasizes the spectrum of cases between 'can read' and 'cannot read.' The concept of reading is applied

> quite independent of that of a mental or other mechanism. – Nor can the teacher here say of the pupil: 'Perhaps he was already reading when he said that word'. For there is no doubt about what he did. – The change when the pupil began to read was a change in his *behaviour*; and it makes no sense here to speak of 'a first word in his new state'.
>
> (PI §157)

Wittgenstein contrasts both of these possibilities with a non-living reading-machine, designed to make certain sounds when being 'fed' certain written words, much as a player piano produces notes as the serrated drum or disc rotates. Given that the machine is constructed properly and is in good working order, it would make sense to say the first word it 'read' was when it had been properly connected up and set in motion.

Wittgenstein concludes that a living person who is reading, even when making no special effort to understand, will be said to have read when he or she reacts to written signs in certain ways. That is, we do not make this judgment on the basis of the existence of some inner state, but on performance. Why is he so sure of this conclusion? It is based on the thesis that neurophysiological states and/or processes have nothing to with the application of the word 'reading' to the living reader's behavior when he or she shows evidence of being able to read. To repeat a point from earlier in this chapter, our ability to assess the reader's skill does not require, and never has required, an examination of his or her brain states and processes. Nor has it been based on an extensive interview concerning such subjective matters as the thoughts and feelings a person is experiencing when reading. The argument that eliminates the usefulness of a 'brain-state' criterion is deep and important, and in no way is it intended to destroy the assumption that something must be occurring in a person's brain when they read.

We can see now that Wittgenstein has arrived at this conclusion by a standard logical move known as *modus tollens*. ('If *p* then *q*. It is not the case that *q*. Therefore it is not the case that *p*.') How would I know what unconscious processes or brain mechanisms were to be examined as relevant to the skill of reading? I would have to be already able to identify when someone was reading from consistent performance, before I could 'look in' to his or her inner states to find which were correlated with the correct performance of the task. If we are to describe someone as reading based on an examination of the brain and nervous system (*p*), then we must be able to identify specific neurophysiological states and/or processes as evidentiary criteria for reading (*q*). However, no such alleged states or processes can be identified independently of the prior identification of reading as a performance (not *q*). Hence the claim that neurophysiological states and/or processes can be used as criteria for saying that reading *has occurred* is false (not *p*).

Wittgenstein realizes the mechanist is likely to respond by insisting that increased knowledge of the brain and new investigative techniques might enable us to witness neuronal connections that are established during the training of people to read various texts. In that case, the mechanist would say the person is able to read a word because the necessary neuronal connection has been made. To address this possibility Wittgenstein asks, 'That it is so is presumably a priori – or is it only probable? And how probable is it? … But if it is a priori, that means that it is a form of account which is very convincing to us' (PI §158).

The point expressed in this paragraph is similar to what we have seen in PI §157. The psychologist who claims that future discoveries of neural states and processes will be likely to contribute to a neurological account of reading might presume that, in the future, we will be able to know whether someone is 'really reading' independently of performance. (We imagine a psychologist of the future looking at a collection of brain scans and being asked, 'Now which of these people were really reading?') Of course this achievement would open the door for future *empirical* discoveries to transform the *conceptual* structure of the concept of reading. It is not just because Wittgenstein is investigating *conditions* for the application of the verb 'to read' in the here and now that the psychologist's appeal to future discoveries misses the mark. For what is going on in someone's brain when they read has not had and will not have any bearing on the application of the verb as it is *ordinarily used* by people to express their ability to read or by people describing the behavior of others as reading behavior. That such and such a mechanism has been activated can be discovered only if we can already pick out instances of reading. We must already have criteria, independent of brain states and processes, to do so.

Mentalist criteria for reading

Wittgenstein now turns to the mentalist's view on the matter. Believing that reading is a special conscious activity of the mind and relying on introspection, the mentalist will say something like the following: 'A man surely knows whether he is reading or only pretending to read!' (PI §159). Note that as Wittgenstein puts it, the mentalist is not only counting the conscious act of reading as a criterion for being able to read, but tacitly invoking a theme we have already encountered in the Augustinian picture of language: the theme of privileged access to understanding. In response, Wittgenstein introduces a language-game in which 'A' wants 'B' to believe he (A) can read a Cyrillic script. A's scheme is to learn a Russian sentence by rote and, perhaps with B peering over his shoulder, looking at the printed sentence while voicing what has been memorized. Clearly, A knows he is not reading and that his performance for B is a sham. But, says Wittgenstein, A does not experience some of the 'many more or less characteristic sensations in reading a printed sentence' (such as sensations of hesitation, looking closer at the words, misreading and so on), but instead is likely to experience characteristic sensations of reciting something he has learned by heart and perhaps even 'a set of sensations characteristic of cheating' (PI §159). Here Wittgenstein acknowledges the mentalist's assertion that there is a sense in which we may know ourselves to be reading. However, B's criteria for saying that A is or is not actually reading are quite independent of A's experiences of his alleged conscious reading. For example, suspecting something is amiss, B may test A with another randomly selected sentence in Cyrillic.

Wittgenstein's objection to the idea that experiences accompanying reading (or pretend reading) are criterial for having the ability is based on illustrations that show the experiences are neither necessary nor sufficient for identifying genuine reading.

The study so far shows that the concept 'reading' is used for a *family of practices* in which written or printed words somehow guide a speaker in correctly and fluently rendering them vocally. There seems to be no single experiential criterion for settling the question of whether someone is really reading. Any attempt to use neurophysiological criteria falls foul of the basic principle that we can only pick out which neural processes are relevant if we already have ways of recognizing when someone is really reading. The range of the phenomena is now settled, but how are the skilled performances to be explained?

Learning point: what would a study of the psychology of reading require?

1. *The range of phenomena* under study is determined by the range of uses of the word 'reading,' since we use this word to pick out the phenomena.
    In PI §156 the range of uses of 'reading' and the range of accompanying patterns of attention is set out. This displays a field of family resemblances (no essence). (PI §160, a remark we have passed over, explores a spectrum of cases from reciting to reading.)

2. *Beginners and experts*

    (a) Comparing the beginner to the expert reader, we note mental phenomena (e.g. 'feelings of accomplishment') characteristic of the beginner. This tempts us to look for others for the skilled reader.
    (b) But the same 'feeling' may accompany skilled and beginning reading.
    (c) *Temptation*: There must be unconscious or unfelt brain processes distinguishing the expert and the beginner. See below.

3. *Mentalist and mechanist accounts*

(a) Two test questions probe the issue of whether there is a common mentalistic core for reading as a phenomenon or whether there is a common neurophysiological core.
    (i)   What was the first word someone 'read'? The answer will be indeterminate for people, but determinate for a machine (PI §157).
    (ii) When is someone 'really reading'? The 'reading-machine' example suggests there must be a characteristic brain process.
(b) Such processes can be picked out only from independently identified performances.
    (i)   Top-down investigations, for instance PET scan techniques, depend on the ability to identify reading independently of the results of the scan.
    (ii) Even in the case where someone is really reading (that is, reading an unfamiliar text correctly), in PI §160 Wittgenstein points out that the skilled reader could have the same feeling as someone who pretends to read.

4. *Conclusion*
Reading is a practice characterized by using written or printed signs as guides to vocal performances. The conscious accompaniments of the process are indeterminate, and the physiological mechanisms involved are irrelevant to identifying skillful reading.

From sign to spoken word

The next phase of Wittgenstein's study of the way the concept of 'reading' is used opens up another general dimension to our ways of understanding psychological phenomena. How are rules, conventions, habits, instructions and so on related to people's skilled performances?

Is 'deriving' the essence of reading?

If neither neurophysiological processes nor states, mental events, nor accompanying experiences count as necessary and sufficient criteria for application of the word 'reading,' what does? Perhaps we need a definition of reading that will capture one or more of the essential features of the activity that must obtain in all cases of reading. While any number of possibilities are available to us here, Wittgenstein (PI §162) suggests we may define as reading any case in which an individual *derives* a reproduction from the original – be it an original text from which one reads or copies, a dictation from which one writes, a score from which one plays a melody on a musical instrument, and so on.

Wittgenstein asks us to consider two language-games. First, we teach someone how to pronounce each letter of the Cyrillic alphabet and present him with a passage printed with letters from that alphabet. We then give him a rule, such as 'pronounce every letter from left to right, pausing a bit between each group of letters.' In this case, the person may be said to read what has been put before him if he derives the sound of each word in accordance with our rule. There are obvious faults with this language-game. If we teach someone how to pronounce the letter 't' he or she will probably be unable to properly derive the pronunciation of a word such as 'think.' Nevertheless, we may suppose that in most cases the pupil's teacher will be able to understand the pupil's utterances, albeit with some difficulty.

In the second language-game a person is presented with a table of letters, with one column of printed letters and another beside it with their cursive renditions. The rule here is to use the table of printed letters to convert a printed text into a cursive text. However, the rule does not specify whether the cursive letters in the table should be derived from printed letters *on the same row*. Having done as we asked, the person will be said to have 'derived' a cursive script from the printed words by following some convention of correlation.

In both of these language-games rules are followed to read aloud or copy a text. But, asks Wittgenstein, why do we say that in either of these cases our pupils have 'derived' the spoken from the printed or the cursive from the printed? In the first case, 'do we know anything more than that we taught him how each letter should be pronounced, and that he then read the words out loud?' (PI §162). The suggestion is that in both language-games we do not know what 'deriving' consists in; how the rules we have given 'enter into' the activity of reading, or what exactly shows us the rules have been followed. This is to say that we have not captured the *essence* of deriving, although our pupils certainly may be said to have derived the spoken from the written and the cursive from the printed. In the first case, what entered into deriving spoken words from the written text seems to have been a kind of concealed process; in the second, deriving was more on the surface in that use of the two tables was part of the overt actions of the activity.

But suppose that in the second language-game the person uses the table in an unexpected way, although in a way that follows an understandable pattern – what we may take to be *his* understanding of the rule. Suppose, for example, he writes the cursive 'b' for the printed 'A,' the cursive 'c' for the printed 'B' and so on. Then again, suppose he uses a far more irregular rule – a rule that is very difficult for us to understand or that we cannot understand at all. Wittgenstein asks, 'Where is the dividing line between this procedure and a random one? But does this mean that the word "to derive" really has no meaning, since the meaning seems to disintegrate when we follow it up?' (PI §163). Not at all. The problem is that the rule has not been specified clearly. If it had been, competence in deriving would have been more evident. At least *part* of what makes an action 'deriving' is that it is done correctly, according to specified rules.

Wittgenstein has presented us with examples of ways in which 'deriving' might be applied to some cases of reading according to rules and where rules are not clearly specified. In the simplest case (the example of deriving pronunciation of words from the Cyrillic), deriving had 'a quite special garb, which had to be stripped from it if we wanted to see the essence of deriving. So we stripped those particular coverings off; but then deriving itself disappeared. – In order to find the real artichoke, we divested it of its leaves' (PI §164). So what remains? We were left not only with a concept that has no single essence, but which has been shown to be applicable to a 'family of cases' of deriving. Moreover, in the same way we also use the word 'to read' for a family of cases. 'And in different circumstances we apply different criteria for a person's reading' (PI §164). Deriving, like reading, is a family resemblance concept.

Is there some other intermediary between the written and the spoken?

It is obvious that Wittgenstein's rejection of deriving as an intermediating process does not rule out other mentalist strategies aimed at discovering the essence of reading. It might be insisted, for example, that reading aloud consists in seeing words and saying them aloud; that reading involves particular processes or consists in particular experiences related to seeing and saying either aloud or inwardly. But as we saw in the language-game where a pupil is taught to utter the sounds of a Cyrillic text (PI §159), words from the printed page need not be understood in order for them to be said aloud. More importantly, if reading is a particular experience, then the rule or rules employed to read drop out of the picture of what is needed to identify a certain activity as reading. With these considerations in mind, Wittgenstein acknowledges the mentalist might counter that a characteristic of reading is that words "'*come* in a special way." That is, they do not come as they would if I were for example making them up. – They come of themselves' (PI §165).

There are many ways we might describe this feeling that words come in a special way. One strategy quickly dispensed with is that printed words 'remind' a reader of their sounds:

> I should for example not wish to say: the printed word 'nothing' reminds me of the sound 'nothing' – but the spoken words as it were slip in as one reads. And if I so much as look at a German printed word, there occurs a peculiar process, that of hearing the sound inwardly.
>
> (PI §165)

Another language-game is introduced to explore the idea that, during the activity of reading, words come in a special way. Wittgenstein asks us to read the letter 'A' and then write the Roman 'a' (PI §166). Now we are asked: How did the sound of 'A' come to us when we read it and how did the movement of our hand come as we wrote the Roman 'a'? Of course, we are at a loss to answer these questions. Even if we look at a printed marking *unlike any marking we have seen before* and invent a sound that corresponds to it (e.g. the sound we make when saying 'U'), we cannot identify the way the sound came to us any better than we could in reading or writing a familiar letter. But is there not an essential difference to what lay behind the sounds that came to us in these cases? Well, yes. With regard to comparing the sounds we may speak when writing 'A,' 'a,' and the novel marking that produces the 'U' sound, Wittgenstein says:

> The difference lay in the difference of situation. I had told myself beforehand that I was to let a sound occur to me; there was a certain tension present before the sound came. And I did not say 'U' automatically as I do when I look at the letter U. Further, that mark was not *familiar* to me in the way the letters of the alphabet are.
>
> (PI §166)

To backtrack a bit, in PI §161 Wittgenstein asks us to say the numbers 1 to 12 and then to read those numbers off from our watch. Here he suggests that what made reading them off our watch an instance of reading was the fact that we were doing something different from counting 1 to 12 – that is the difference was a difference in situation, regardless of what subjective differences there were. We now have confirmation that this is indeed the point Wittgenstein is driving at in §166. The sounds of novel markings do not come in a special way due to their inherent qualities. Their coming to us is *connected* with the situation in which they are used. We may begin using a novel marking, say, as a shorthand character while taking lecture notes. With continued use we may suppose the 'tension' to which Wittgenstein refers will be reduced, if not disappear altogether. But this disappearance in tension cannot be attributed to a change in the marking itself. The tension will disappear, in part, because we become accustomed to the situations in which we use the mark. We have acquired a habit.

Let us put our finger on an error in thinking about reading that Wittgenstein is trying to expose. It does not just boil down to thinking that reading consists in neurophysiological processes, noticeable mental events and specific feelings. Rather, it has to do with the inference that because we can identify distinctive experiences associated with arbitrary marks, misspellings, unfamiliar words and so on, we assumed 'that ordinary reading is accompanied by normal familiar and uniform experiences which serve as criteria for reading' (Baker and Hacker, 1980, p. 646). We are thus tempted to turn our attention to those normal, familiar and uniform experiences in an attempt to identify the essence of reading. We may look to the 'extremely characteristic' look of the printed line and the 'enormously familiar' appearance of the words we read (PI §167). We may compare the way our eyes pass over printed lines with the way they pass over 'arbitrary pothooks and flourishes ... But what in all this is essential to reading as such? Not any one feature that occurs in all cases of reading' (PI §168). Without doubt, reading is marked, in part, by familiar experiences. Philosophical and psychological investigations into reading *seem* facilitated by comparing what is familiar and uniform in the practice with 'difficult cases.' However, such comparisons will not reveal what reading consists in or what, in all cases of reading, *must* obtain neurophysiologically, mentally, or in accompanying personal experiences of sensation.

Causes, reasons, influences and phenomenological differences

Previously we mentioned that when reading, a person may become aware of the sounds of words they are reading. These sounds seem to come from within, more or less involuntarily. Anyone skilled at reading has experienced this. Perhaps the printed words *cause* this inward hearing of word-sounds – this *feeling* that words come to us involuntarily when reading. Alternatively, perhaps this feeling might be better described as giving us *reasons* to make the sounds of words, or that letters exert a kind of *influence* on us. Wittgenstein (PI §169) dispenses with each of these attempts to identify a link between written words and utterances in reading.

In the first case, an unobservable feeling of causation would have to be interposed between the observable events of seeing words and saying them aloud. We would thus be led to seek out the experience of causation interposed between the words we see and our utterances. But it is difficult to tell how such feeling of causation could be experienced.

In the second case, giving reasons for reading is something that is said or thought, not felt. This is an observation about the grammar of giving reasons versus the grammar of talking about bodily feelings. It is difficult to tell how any reason for reading could be felt. Under pressure, we might say we can feel a kind of influence from printed letters – an influence not felt from a series of arbitrary flourishes or even somewhat familiar signs such as '§.' Again, when we look at a particular letter we are likely to hear immediately its sound from within. We will pronounce it more effort-lessly than '§' and, of course, far more effortlessly than an arbitrary flourish. With the aid of such thought-experiments, we can identify a *phenomenological or experiential difference* between saying a letter inwardly, saying it aloud and saying the sound of a sign such as '§' (PI §169). Ordinarily we will take these phenomenological differ-ences to hold the key to the door that conceals the essence of reading. By now it should be obvious that Wittgenstein maintains it is not in these phenomenological differences that we will discover the essence of reading.

Experiences of reading and the context of investigation: application of the example

Wittgenstein now offers a summation that reveals a most important angle to his investigation on reading that promises to be applicable to psychological investiga-tions into other cognitive performances. Comparisons between the reading of familiar letters, somewhat familiar signs and arbitrary doodles has led to the supposition that we feel a kind of influence from familiar letters that we do not feel from looking at somewhat familiar signs or doodles. We may have counted this feeling of influence as *the* defining feature of reading – an appealing conclusion, given what seems to occur in us when we read slowly, where we let ourselves be *guided*, so to speak, by letters. 'But this "letting myself be guided" in turn only consists in my looking carefully at the letters – and perhaps excluding certain other thoughts' (PI §170). What Wittgenstein means here is that in the context of thinking about the possibility of letters guiding us, we read slowly in order to isolate that experience, perhaps to the exclusion of others. Our endeavor to uncover the essence of reading has led us to focus our attention on phenomenological differences between reading familiar letters and other kinds of markings. In so doing, we have mistakenly identified a particular experiential difference with the difference between being influenced by letters and not being influenced by doodles. But this experiential difference (and perhaps others) has only been linked up with reading by a kind of examination that *presupposes* there must be an essence to reading and, in turn, requires that a certain kind of attention be paid to the act of reading *during reading* or *after reading*. Wittgenstein extends this point to what was at work in his earlier remarks having to do with mechanistic and mentalistic accounts of reading:

> We imagine that a feeling enables us to perceive as it were a connecting mechanism between the look of the word and the sound that we utter. For when I speak of the experiences of being influenced, of causal connexion, of being guided, that is really meant to imply that I as it were feel the movement of the lever which connects seeing the letters with speaking.
>
> (PI §170)

It is only within the context of investigating supposed connecting links between the written word and its utterance that one or more forms of connecting mechanisms, processes, or experiences become viable candidates for explaining what is essential to reading. It is our *form of investigation* that leads us down the road to the hypostatization of intermediaries between the written word and its spoken counterpart. Psychologists and research methods students might recognize this point as having some connection to response set as an extraneous variable in psychological experiments.

The point that our form of investigation influences what we pick out as relevant phenomena is applicable to all the forms of explanation for reading addressed by Wittgenstein thus far. But that is not all. There is also the temptation to connect the phenomena with something hidden. As Baker and Hacker (1980) put it: 'The hankering for a connection, material and causal, or spiritual and ephemeral, between letter and sound, rule of a series and the numeral written, meaning and application, understanding and use, is almost irresistible' (p. 648). The 'connection' referred to here is presupposed and unjustified. But it follows naturally from a particular kind of investigation informed by what McGinn (1997) labels the 'theoretical attitude.' It is this very attitude to which Wittgenstein (PI §90) refers, in his remarks on philosophical method (to be addressed in Chapter 7), when he says, 'we feel as if we had to *penetrate* phenomena.'

We see the heuristic purposes of Wittgenstein's method at work when he now purposefully gives way to the temptation to think that the written word might be said to *intimate* its sound to the reader, or that letter and sound might be said to form a *unity* – much in the same way pictures of the faces of famous men and the sounds of their names form a unity (PI §171). However, as we saw in the case of being guided, it is only within the context of an examination of the experiential phenomena of reading that we are inclined to think words intimate their sounds to us and that letters and sounds form a unity. *We simply do not ordinarily have these experiences as we read.* In other words, 'reading with the intention of finding out what happens when we are reading is a special case of reading and as such different from ordinary reading' (Feyerabend, 1978, p. 222). This becomes abundantly clear when we read a few sentences while not thinking about the concept of reading. Do this, says Wittgenstein,

> and ask yourself whether you had such experiences of unity, of being influenced and the rest, as you read. – Don't say you had them unconsciously! Nor should we be misled by the picture which suggests that these phenomena came in sight 'on closer inspection'. If I am supposed to describe how an object looks from far off, I don't make the description more accurate by saying what can be noticed about the object on closer inspection.

> (PI §171)

By 'closer inspection,' Wittgenstein has in mind the lens of traditional philosophy. The point can easily be extended to psychology as modeled on the natural sciences. Both traditions take as their departure the hypostatization of neurophysiological mechanisms, mental processes, or phenomenological experiences isolated through introspection while reading and thinking about reading. By contrast to these forms of investigation, Wittgenstein opts for a wide-angle view – a surview – of the grammar of words that are or might be used to describe the activity of reading. His method takes as its departure the whole of our reading vocabulary and explores connections between that vocabulary and others similar in kind and still others seemingly unrelated, in part to show that no single word captures the essence of what 'goes into' reading. In this, one implication for psychology is quite clear: begin your investigations into reading and other cognitive skills with a conceptual investigation, then go forward with empirical research that treats the cognitive skill *as a whole*.

The wider phenomenon of 'being guided'

But suppose psychologists are not convinced by Wittgenstein's employment of family resemblance to concepts related to reading or, for that matter, to any number of other cognitive performances, such as calculating, inferring, deciding and so on. Suppose they think the meanings of a number of concepts referring to cognitive performances are quite clear in the sense that there is something common to all instances where they are applied to describe those performances. For example, 'inferring someone's attitude,' 'inferring a conclusion from premises' and so on might have no common essence. It may very well be that treatment of any concept as a family resemblance concept will be thought to be unsatisfactory by those imbued with the methodology of physics and chemistry in ruling out a single essence behind the family of phenomena to which it is applied.

But there is another dimension to the spirit of Wittgenstein's notion of family resemblance as applied to psychological concepts. Its serves to inoculate us against false analogies and simplistic summations of psychological phenomena that lead to faulty first steps in investigations of those phenomena. One faulty first step is to think that reading while thinking about reading is the same as reading while not thinking about reading – that experiences of reading both without and within the context of investigations into reading are the same. The latter form of reading, which allows us to isolate specific experiences of reading, leads to the hypostatization that one or more of those experiences is *essential* to reading as a particular kind of experience. But 'what happens *while* one reads, means, or remembers something is not what reading, meaning or remembering consist in' (Baker and Hacker, 1980, p. 339), in part because any number of things might and might not be experienced while reading. As we have already seen, if someone denies that certain experiences were felt during reading we would not deny they were reading.

Wittgenstein's method of analysis often includes exploring applications of a word in ways that are just slightly dissimilar to applications that catch our attention originally. In PI §172 he does this by considering five cases where the expression 'being guided' might be used to describe various experiences. Eyes bandaged, we might be guided across a playing field by someone who leads us by the hand, or we might be led by the hand while resisting going where being led. We might be led on to a dance floor by a partner, being as receptive as possible to our partner's moves, trying to anticipate intentions and availing ourselves of the slightest pressures. We might go for a walk with someone and, while having a conversation, simply go wherever he goes. Finally, we may follow the lanes on a field track without paying any attention to the topography. As with Wittgenstein's examination of deriving, we can see in these five cases a handful of similar situations. 'But,' he asks, 'what is common to all these experiences?' (PI §172).

The question may be put differently. In the context of attempting to uncover the essence of being guided by things other than printed words, is there something about being guided in the foregoing cases that can be linked up with being guided by printed words? Is there an essence to being guided in all cases where the expression might be applied – a common strand of guidedness? One might respond by saying that in all the preceding cases (in addition to the case of being guided by letters), people were involved, that bodily movements or thoughts were part of each activity, that they took place in social contexts, or that social rules were involved. But such a response will not distinguish being guided from any number of other expressions used to describe the activities of people in social contexts (e.g., 'following,' 'using,' 'imitating,' 'blaming'). So why narrow our focus to being guided?

What is the point of this examination of other cases where we might describe others or ourselves as being guided? Why has Wittgenstein drawn our attention to cases seemingly unrelated to reading, albeit cases where 'being guided' is applicable? We might suppose that it has to do with his persistent defense against the temptations of the Augustinian picture of language, which reappears in the idea that being guided refers to a particular intermediary process (analogous to a 'thing') between the written word and its utterance. While this is indeed the case, there is more. Wittgenstein's demonstration of being guided as a family resemblance concept is reflective of his attack on essentialism. Again, this is the view that there must be something common to all instances of a concept's application that explains why we apply that concept.

When is it that 'taking great care' is *the* criterion for copying letters from one alphabet to another? (Or, for that matter, when is it that some other feeling or action might become *the* criterion?) 'What is done carefully' cannot be a criterion for skilled action, since only if I already know that an action is skilled can I apply 'carefully' to it. It makes no sense to drop a tea-tray carefully (PI §173). What about 'vomiting carefully'? The temptation is to try to deal with the variety of these accompaniments by saying '"No, it isn't *that*; it is something more inward, more essential"' (PI §173). Why would I want to follow this line of thought? One might be concentrating on only one of various feelings that accompany skilled practices. Or it might be that while I am carrying on the activity 'I notice nothing *special*; but afterwards, when I ask myself what it was that happened, it seems to have been something indescribable' (PI §175).

The persistent attraction of the particular experience

The remainder of Wittgenstein's remarks on reading explore further the implications of thinking that a particular experience – namely being guided or influenced while copying or speaking – might be identified as essential to reading. This insistence on particular experiences of being guided is met with the reminder that in thinking of being guided while reading is a particular experience; 'you are now *thinking* of a particular experience of being guided' (PI §173). All right, then, maybe there is something even more essential behind the experiences of being guided, such as looking at letters, making faces while reading, writing letters with deliberation and so on (see PI §174). But to say we are writing letters 'with deliberation' is to make an adverbial qualification to our action, not to isolate a particular inner or outer experience as differentiating writing haphazardly from writing deliberately. To do so would be tantamount to positing the same experience accompanying any number of things we do deliberately and so necessitate differentiating what otherwise must lie behind these to make them different actions in the first place.

The effort to isolate experiences of a certain performance through careful study makes it seem as if we can uncover something essential to and characteristic of that performance. But further reflection calls this into question. In making an arbitrary doodle on a piece of paper and then copying it, we may be said to have been guided by the first doodle. Everything was quite simple when copying the doodle, but on looking back and asking ourselves what happened when making our copy, it seems as if no description of what happened will satisfy us in terms of determining just what being guided consists in. Only then, when looking back at what happened, 'does the idea of that ethereal, intangible influence arise' (PI §175). The ethereal, intangible influence might be dubbed the 'experience of being influenced' by the doodle we copy. As part of an investigation into the phenomena of copying, such an experience is likely to be thought of as

> a connexion – as opposed to any mere simultaneity of phenomena: but at the same time I should not be willing to call any experienced phenomenon the 'experience of being influenced' ... I should like to say that I had experienced the '*because*', and yet I do not want to call any phenomenon the 'experience of the because'.
>
> (PI §176)

It is not that, in looking back on copying a doodle, we may be inclined to say 'I experience the because' from any specific memory of what occurred during copying. Rather, the inclination arises from looking at the experience of copying 'through the medium of the concept "because" (or "influence" or "cause" or "connexion")' (PI §177). Even in pretending to guide another person's hand along to help them copy a doodle, we make the same movements as guiding. We are thus inclined to call such hand movements 'guiding' even though no one else's hand is there. In this case, the movements and feeling of our hand are those of guiding, but they 'did not contain the essence of guiding, but still this word forces itself upon you. It is just *a single form* of guiding which forces the expression on us' (PI §178).

The application of these insights to the study of other cognitive processes and performances is not difficult to see. Cognition is the manipulation of meanings according to rules, principles, customs, conventions and so on. In every case, the same questions and temptations emerge. What are the criteria by which we identify instances of the phenomenon? Are there mental accompaniments that tempt us to propose a mentalistic essence for the phenomenon? How are our experiences when performing cognitive tasks relevant to our understanding of these tasks? Since, in human cognition, rules are somehow involved as guides to best or adequate practice, how are we to understand guidance in each of the many cases and contexts in which cognitive processes occur?

The upshot of this surview of 'reading'

The vast conceptual terrain covered by Wittgenstein's remarks on reading is striking, if not dizzying. First there were the hypothetical language-games involving reading-machines. These showed that specific neurophysiological states and/or processes cannot be used as criteria for applying the word 'reading' to machines trained to behave as if they are reading, calling into question the idea that future neurophysiological discoveries will shed light on the *meaning* of 'reading' or any other cognitive phenomenon. Second, there were the language-games leveled at mentalist claims that consciousness of mental phenomena provides criteria for reading. These language-games – of A's sham reading to B – showed that experiences accompanying reading or pretend reading *cannot serve as necessary or sufficient criteria for reading*. The language-game of counting 1 to 12 and reading the same numbers off our watch suggested that the two practices *are different due to their having taken place under different circumstances*. Then Wittgenstein entertained the inevitable attempt to define reading as deriving sounds from signs, introducing two language-games (pronouncing Cyrillic letters and copying printed letters in the cursive according to rules). Similar cases would be deriving conclusions from premises or summations from columns of figures. These cases show that defining reading as 'deriving' *does not illuminate the ways in which rules enter into the activity of reading*.

In addition, these language-games show that although rule-following enters into carrying out an activity like reading, *rules alone do not make an activity an instance of reading*. The phenomenological experience of words 'coming in a special way' while reading was then explored through the language-games of copying upper-case letters into lower case and making the sound of an unfamiliar marking. In both instances it was shown that whatever 'comes to us' while being engaged in these activities is not due to any one qualitative feature of the markings or any one experience of the activity. Rather, what comes to us and the way it comes to us *is connected with the situation in which the activity takes place*. Possible links between reading and the uttering of words were then explored, such as the idea that words cause the feeling that they come to us involuntarily while reading or that printed words give us reasons to let out their sounds.

A connecting link between these language-games is the idea that the experience of words coming to us is disjoined from the experience of one or more causes, while at the same time reasons are disjoined from feelings. Wittgenstein then anticipates that the next explanatory move would be to say that words 'influence' us. However, this only led us to a seemingly infinite set of phenomenological experiences – seemingly infinite because of the manifold contexts in which reading might take place – that might be singled out as the essence of reading. Finally, there was the case of being guided – an expression that, Wittgenstein showed, applies to numerous activities seemingly unrelated to reading and is therefore not apt for singling out the essence of reading.

Word use pertaining to reading shows reading to be *an ability that is exercised in many contexts*. Many words can be used to express and describe the phenomenological experiences of reading and their uses vary in accordance with a variety of factors, not the least of which are the reader's attentiveness to those experiences and the surrounding circumstances of reading. But there can be no *definition* of reading based either on phenomenological experiences or surrounding circumstances. Nor are we justified in concocting definitions of reading based on neurophysiological processes or mental experiences. Whether someone is able to read or not can be determined only through reference to public criteria in the contexts where we (or they) are justified in applying expressions such as 'reading,' 'has read' and so on.

Thus we encounter a rule of thumb for Wittgenstein's form of analysis: there is a *connection* between correct use of psychological concepts and their criteria of application. Moreover, both the use of psychological concepts and criteria for their use are connected with the surroundings within which the behavior to which the concepts are applied is manifest. Our *psychological reality* having to do with reading (and many other skilled cognitive performances) is not rooted in neurophysiological states and processes.

The explanatory regress apropos of the skill of reading aloud from a text is homogeneous, ending in simple habits into which we have been trained. Nothing need be inserted between the sign and the vocalization in order for us to have a mastery of the concept of reading, nor between prices of items on the bill (the check) and the total we are required to pay. We can tell fluent readers from beginners, pretending from really reading, and so on, just as we can tell who can add up accounts and who cannot. We can explain the differences between various kinds of reading from texts by reference to the habits of speaking (and writing) into which we have been trained.

The threshold fallacy

We can draw together the themes of this chapter by seeing the argument in terms of one of Wittgenstein's most powerful critical/analytical moves. We are faced with a seemingly intractable problem, an unanswerable question. The problem exists, so Wittgenstein argues, only because we have taken for granted that the question is legitimate. We must retrace our steps to the threshold over which we entered the room, and query the unthinking acceptance of the intelligibility of the question we have found so hard to answer.

Let us return briefly to the idea that, when reading aloud, letters of words cause my vocalizations. We might say that we 'felt a causal connection' between the letters and my vocalizations. What would this feeling be? We might try an experiment to compare what I feel when reading an unfamiliar lexicography compared to a familiar one. One might say 'I justify my reading by the letters which are there. This justification, however, was something that I said, or thought: what does it mean to say that I *feel* it?' (PI §169). Wittgenstein remarks in PI §170 that 'it would never have occurred to us to think that we *felt the influence* of the letters on us when reading, if we had not compared the case of letters with that of arbitrary marks.'

Why is this? It seems to happen when I say such words as 'guidance' and 'influence' to myself (PI §175). Again, in PI §177 Wittgenstein points out that 'when I reflect on what I experience in such a case I look at it through the medium of the concept "because" (or "influence" or "cause" or "connexion").' We are very much inclined to try to base our accounts of the exercise of abilities on just a single form of, for example, 'guiding.' The point of this paragraph in §177 is to remind us that what we observe or pick out for emphasis is often – in the sciences as in everyday life – a matter of the concepts we already have at hand. If we use the sort of words listed above, the question 'What is the link between sign and vocable?' seems entirely innocent.

In pursuing the topic of 'reading' we have tried to answer the question 'What is the link between sign and vocable?' Taking this question seriously *presupposes* that there *is a link* and that there is only *one kind of link* between text and spoken words. In this case, the quest for the link leads us to try to find it among features of the practice of which a skilled reader is aware or can be brought to notice. But there are many different practices in the generic category of 'reading,' which turns out to be a field of family resemblances. There is a huge variety of correlative subjective phenomena that can accompany reading aloud. Sometimes there are no subjective accompaniments at all. So there is no systematic and universal type of private experience that accompanies successful exercise of the skill.

At this point in the analysis there are two mistakes we might be inclined to make:

(1)   We can insist that there *must* be a common link, but it will have to be one of which no reader is consciously aware.
(2)   We can require that it will be of the same sort as *one* of the cases we have studied. In other words, we are not content with a catalogue of family resem- blances among particular cases. We hanker after a single 'essence' that unites them all.

If to ascribe a skill to someone is not to say anything about his or her state of mind or brain organization, what is it? To ascribe a skill to someone is to make a kind of generalized prediction. When presented with a task (a suitable text to read aloud from or to copy), the person will perform the task more or less correctly, according to the local requirements of the task. *This is not to deny that unless there is an appropriate process in the brain of the reader he or she will be unable to have and display the skill.*

Now that we have found our way through all sorts of temptations to the idea that the basic phenomena of psychology are skilled performances in which we make use of abilities, we encounter the notion of 'correctness' and related concepts. How are we to bring them into our discussion? Wittgenstein, anticipating and influencing much recent discursive psychology, turns to the notion of 'rule-following' as a metaphor to illuminate how it is that our performances can be seen to meet – or fail to meet – the local standards for correct and proper performances.

Learning point: from sign to spoken word

1. *The assumption of 'links'*

   (a) Inquiry into how rules, conventions, habits and so on enter into the performance of reading begins by considering the possibility of links between the sign and the spoken word.

   (b) But this tempts us to define reading in such a way that one or more essences of it can be identified and then investigated.

   (c) For example, we might think that in all cases of reading there is a process of 'deriving' a reproduction from a text, a musical score and so on. There is the text and there are the utterances. We link the text and utterance with a process of deriving.

   (d) Language-games of transcription in the form of deriving show that investigations into deriving get us nowhere in terms of knowing what deriving consists in and how rules, standards of correctness and so on enter into reading.

   (e) Other intermediaries are considered. For example, the mentalist might propose that in reading 'words come in a special way' or that printed words 'remind' the reader of their sounds. Or perhaps printed words *cause* the inward hearing of word-sounds.

2. *The context of investigation*

   (a) Proposed intermediaries gain their special character due to the various *situations* in which reading occurs. More than anything else, distinctive experiences of reading are connected with situations.

   (b) But there are a variety of experiences that people have from time to time while reading. But none of these – including a feeling of deriving, if there could be such a feeling – are ubiquitous and could serve as the single essence around which we could construct a definition of reading.

   (c) We must be on guard against the influence of special situations of reading that suggest particular experiences, processes and so on are essential to reading in ordinary cases.

   (d) There is no *link*. There is only a bare correlation between sign and spoken word. That is all that there is the domain of psychology, as Wittgenstein understands it. No single link can be identified, in part because reading is a family resemblance concept.

   (e) Psychological concepts required for a homogeneous explanation regress are *training* and *habit*, not cause and effect, since for the latter we can always ask 'What is the link?'

3. *The threshold fallacy*

(a) A seemingly intractable problem exists only because we made a seemingly innocent assumption.

(b) We are prone to ask: 'What is the link between sign and vocable?' The question is meaningful only if it makes sense to suppose ...

    (i) that there *is* a link and ...

    (ii) that whatever it is, it is common to all cases.

    (iii) Examples show no unique link, but only a family of different cases.

(c) However, we tend to say that there *must be* a common but invisible link ...

    (i) of the same sort as one of the cases we have studied or ...

    (ii) of a different sort from any we have studied.

We are not content with a catalog of family resemblances among particular cases, but hanker after *just one*.

Further reading

Baker, G.P. and Hacker, P.M.S. (1985), *Wittgenstein: Rules, grammar and necessity. An analytical commentary on the* Philosophical Investigations (Vol. 2). Oxford: Blackwell. (Specifically pp. 83–85 of Chapter 4.)

Feyerabend, P. (1978), Wittgenstein's philosophical investigations. In K.T. Fann (ed.), *Ludwig Wittgenstein: The man and his philosophy* (pp. 214–50). Sussex: Harvester Press.

Just, M.A. and Carpenter, P.A. (1980). *The Psychology of Reading and Language Comprehension*. Boston: Allyn and Bacon.

6 Rules and rule-following

Philosophical Investigations §§138–242

The goal of theory in cognitive psychology is to establish a
unified account of the brain's information-processing mechanisms, which can eventually be reduced to neuronal mechanisms,
at least to a significant extent.

L.W. Barsalou (1995), p. 185

Cognitive theory holds that I store a rule. Rules are widely used as
mental surrogates of behavior, in part because they can be
memorized and hence 'processed,' but there is an important
difference between rules and the contingencies they describe.
Rules can be internalized in the sense that we can say them to
ourselves, but in doing so we do not internalize the contingencies.

B.F. Skinner (1986), p. 87

Grammar – the rules of concept-formation and conceptual
deployment – provides for us the (logical) possibilities of
phenomena, not the other way around.

Jeff Coulter (1997), p. 299

Topics introduced: reductive explanation; normative constraints; 'rule' as a metaphor; implicit norms and explicit rules; following a rule versus acting in accordance
with a rule; causes and contingencies in rule-following; the paradox of interpretation; dispositions; authority of rules and justification; agreement; 'grammar' and its
autonomy

In managing our everyday lives with others we routinely distinguish, in our actions
and words, between two general kinds of regularities. First, there are regularities of
working mechanisms, including chemical and biological mechanisms. These are
caused regularities, in the sense that, once a mechanism is put into action, it will
'run its course' – assuming there are no other mechanical interventions. An electric
clock will keep good time until it malfunctions, its batteries lose power, or until a
finger stops its minute hand. Ice will melt when salt is applied to it.

Then there are *social* regularities, exhibited in the actions of persons and animals. We distinguish between the social regularities of persons and animals partly
because the former may be exhibited in both actions *and* language use, the latter
being a form of action not available to animals. So in baseball the umpire signals
and announces: 'Strike three! You're out!' whereupon the disconsolate batter re-

turns to the dugout. Or, on a crowded subway train, a mother instructs her twelve-year-old: 'Give up your seat for that elderly man' and the boy obeys.

Empirical research in the social and behavioral sciences is based, in part, on the exploitation of social and sometimes mechanical regularities for the purposes of extracting universal principles, or 'laws,' by careful observation and measurement. But while there is no disputing that the 'hard' natural sciences (e.g. chemistry and physics) are concerned with mechanistic regularities only, psychologists continue to debate whether or not – or the extent to which – the phenomena of human social and cognitive regularities can (or should) be explained in terms of causal mechanisms. Certainly humans need a brain to be social, to add up restaurant checks, to translate Arabic poetry, and to solve problems and make inferences. And it is true that the brain may be looked upon as a 'causal mechanism' of sorts. Still, it would be a stretch to say that brains are social beings engaged in social interaction. *People* – not brains – are social and *people* solve problems.

The quotation from Barsalou at the beginning of this chapter, from a review of J.R. Anderson's (1993) book *Rules of the Mind*, expresses the sort of reductive and mechanistic mindset of cognitive science that needs to be questioned seriously by any student of psychology. Anderson, working in the field of artificial intelligence (AI), maintains that to a significant extent human cognition is due to the interaction of millions of rules in a kind of competition to be applied moment by moment. As an extension of his earlier and well-known efforts to theoretically and empirically substantiate the workings of an 'Adaptive Control of Thought' (or ACT) system as a basis for human cognition, Anderson's new and improved system (Anderson, 1993) adds a 'rational' component to the ACT system that streamlines rule-application and conserves cognitive resources. Hence the new 'ACT-R' system.

In significant respects Anderson's ACT-R system resembles those of other AI theorists and researchers working since the 1960s. In seeking to construct a mechanical mind of sorts, researchers in AI posit a host of interacting mechanisms and processes (e.g. memory repositories and control or performance processes) and codes or rule-systems governing the workings of the system as a whole. Such models may differ in the extent to which the mechanisms of memory, perception, learning and so on work differently or in similar fashion (see for example Gardner, 1985, pp. 131–3).

It is true that modeling of this sort has contributed and will contribute to technological advances in computing, the building of robots, 'smart systems,' and so on. But our enthusiasm with respect to such technological advances should be tempered when it comes to comparing the 'rules' by which computing machines carry out their work and the rules people follow in their day-to-day activities. Is the concept of 'rule,' freely used in both contexts, stretched across the distant regions of a field of family resemblances? What is striking about the AI paradigm is its assumption of causation by mechanism and its reductive treatment of rules as no more than descriptions of regular sequences in machine behavior. We can assume that most AI proponents agree that the phenomena of social and intellectual regularities involve 'information processing.' It is a short step to the startling claim that the rules determining the flow of information are reducible to 'neuronal mechanisms, at least to a significant extent,' as Barsalou (1995) puts it.

Reductive explanations of psychological phenomena can be found in the writings of philosophers hundreds of years before the birth of modern experimental psychology and they are at almost every turn in psychology even today. We note B.F. Skinner's reduction of the regularities (or 'rules') of social action to contingencies of reinforcement, as expressed in the second quotation at the head of this chapter. In our view, the critique of reductive explanation is one of Wittgenstein's greatest potential contributions to psychology. His remarks on rules and rule-following, written during the age of behaviorism and before the cognitive revolution in psychology, are applicable to both behaviorism and to the kind of cognitivism that one finds in some interpretations of the computational models offered up by AI theorists, not to mention contemporary cognitive neuroscience. By exploring the ways the concept of 'rule' is used in relation to human social regularities, Wittgenstein shows that reductions of such regularities to the output of causal mechanisms is misguided. His investigations show that rules are neither parts of cognitive mechanisms 'in the head,' so to speak, nor the causes of what people do. Rules, however we may conceive of them, do not lay down future actions. Among other things, rules make it possible to determine whether what someone says or does is correct, proper, decent, or the opposite.

Providing a context for Wittgenstein's inquiry

Central as it is to psychology, an account of rules and rule-following is tied closely to our analysis of the concepts of skills and abilities in Chapter 5. Rules are relevant for a psychology based on the concept of action as the exercise of skills. Skilled activities require attention to *standards of correctness*. In this sense the postal worker delivering mail, the athlete playing a game, and the psychologist undertaking research are all very similar. If they do not want to muddle through their activities they will, at the very least, try to follow local standards of correctness. Granted, in between muddling and doing well at any activity there are many intermediate shades of competence, and the terrain of possible standards is as broad as the number of possible activities. For example, Dreyfus and Dreyfus (1986) outline five levels of learning competence humans can achieve while acquiring countless skills.

When it comes to clarifying the way we use the concepts of rules and rule-following, Wittgenstein's aims are rather modest. He does not aim to 'reform' the language of rule-following or to refine or complete a system of social rules. Nor does he seek to establish any form of 'psychology of rule-following.' In keeping with his philosophical method, his aim is clarity; that clarity in light of which confusions of thought and language-use about rules and rule-following will be dispelled.

We already know that, in Wittgenstein's view, when a person uses a word correctly we say they understand the meaning of the word. When a person uses a word on numerous occasions and in various contexts, we might say they 'know the rule for the use of the word,' although it would be unusual to use this specific expression. As we have indicated, the same framework of concepts is applicable to the problem of how we know *how* to perform a skilled task. We know how to perform the task because we know the rule(s) for performing the task correctly and, in so doing, 'carry out' the rule(s). Another way to say this is that using a word correctly or performing a task correctly can be thought of as following the rule relevant to using the word or performing the task. Also – and this is important – the cognitive phenomenon of 'understanding' is transformed into phenomena related to 'following the relevant rule.' Finally, there must be *sanctioning* within to one's local culture for using a word and performing a task in ways that members of the local culture count as 'correct.' This sanctioning makes possible *justification* for following the rule. So we have moved from rule-following, to skills and abilities, to understanding, to norms. We caution that this framework of topics associated with rule-following is not exhaustive.

Obviously a thorough account of rules and rule-following requires inquiry into other, related topics. And this is what Wittgenstein does. Grammar necessitates this topical movement. Furthermore, this movement should remind us of the important notion of family resemblance, introduced in Chapter 4. Following written instructions is a kind of rule-following. It is also possible to characterize a person who acts in a customary way as 'following a rule.' Rules to guide actions 'for the time being' can be formulated in no time. But can we work out a rock-solid definition of what it is to follow a rule that establishes the necessary and sufficient conditions for applying the concept of 'following a rule' to all rule-guided actions? Wittgenstein thinks not. 'Rules' and 'rule-following' are family resemblance concepts.

Another way to look at what we have sketched out thus far is to see it as the presentation of a simplified pattern of *normative constraints* on what someone does. For the purpose of summarizing this basic insight we can fill the 'space' of Wittgenstein's inquiry thus:

- 'what I *can* do' (ability)
- 'what I *may* do' (having the right/sanctioning by the local culture and justification)
- 'what I *do*' (exercising the ability rightfully)

By introducing the notion of normative constraints we are pointing out their logical connection with standards of correctness. Generally the alternative, cognitivist approach is to establish an empirical connection between the regular concomitant events of a sequence by projecting rule-following from such contexts as following written instructions or orders into the realm of hidden mechanisms referred to in explaining rule-following. As we have suggested, when pressed on the status of these hypothetical rules and mysterious processes of rule-following, cognitive psychologists tend to identify rule-following with neural activities. To make this step, however, presupposes a propositional model for rule-following, as if the paradigm case were to be the following of explicit instructions or obeying the orders of legitimate authorities.

One of Wittgenstein's main concerns in his extended discussion of rule-following is to show that explanations of customary, orderly, normatively assessable actions in terms of propositions – or formula-like, reductive representations of norms which guide (or 'cause') actions – are inadequate. His aim is to establish that for the vast majority of cases, 'knowing a rule' is not a matter of entertaining a proposition, but of having mastered a technique. In short, *rules are more often expressed in practices than in verbal or written instructions*. And certainly they are not expressed in material brain states or processes!

Rules as a metaphor for conventions, customs and practices

We all take for granted the conventions of correctness and incorrectness implied in what we say and do. Rarely are these conventions specified as explicit rules until we start to look at them as ways of describing what our socio-cultural situation requires us to say and do; for example, when someone breaks a rule. This is one reason why Wittgenstein is interested in the 'frameworks' we all take for granted. Part of the job of the psychologist, according to this point of view, is to express taken-for-granted frameworks as systems of rules. As we will see in this chapter, the explanation of psychological phenomena in terms of rules must be the principal explanatory paradigm in many fields where currently the concept of 'cause' is used routinely. The almost ubiquitous use of causal language in reporting the results of psychological research may be no more than a way of describing a correlation between antecedent conditions and subsequent behavior. It seems as if the use of this causal language implies that we also have unearthed the *agency* that brings about the behavior. But we have done no such thing. Persons are the sources of activity in human life. Using the word 'cause' or something equivalent to describe the conditions for a psychological phenomenon to occur tends to make us think we have explained the phenomenon. But in neglecting the role of the human actor we have only given the appearance of a psychological explanation.

How do we reveal the normative framework of some human practice? When someone does something different from what people expect there is usually some sort of reaction. People may, for the first time in their lives, feel obliged to formulate a rule justifying or vilifying the unexpected action. Here we have a situation in which an aspect of the normative framework begins to appear. In social psychology, Harold Garfinkel pioneered the technique of deliberately breaking common conventions to elicit the reactions of people who ordinarily took those conventions for granted. For example, Garfinkel (1967) instructed his students to treat the customers in a supermarket as if they (the customers) were staff; for example by insisting that customers should point out where to find things in the store. The reactions of the customers revealed the taken-for-granted conventions in accordance with which they carried out the routine task of shopping.

When we are trying to study the psychology of human beings scientifically, if we attend to the ways human beings explain their emotions, make decisions and so on, we see that in a great many cases these explanations have to do with fulfilling intentions in accordance with the local norms and cultural conventions. Thus, to a significant extent the project for a scientifically-minded psychologist is to bring out the relevant norms and to study how they are applied. For example, what are the norms for accepting someone's claim to have remembered something? For the most part, there are no 'memory traces' ready at hand to check the verisimilitude of an alleged recollection. This issue – which is grammatical in nature – has come to the fore in the phenomenon called 'false memory syndrome.'

Different cultures, different rules

Group A has some odd rules of behavior and strange ways of thinking, but they have been together a long time and they are settled into their ways. Many ways of acting other than their own they regard as 'criminal.' Along comes a person from Group B, who has lived with a very different set of rules. How does Group A regard the person from Group B? What do members of the former group do with respect to the member of the latter group?

In this example we are describing a situation familiar to members of many dominant cultures, where a person from an unfamiliar social group or class 'encounters' an immigrant, or person from a different social class. It is hoped that, rather than attacking the stranger, the locals probably will attempt to influence the newcomer to act in accordance with their own ways of living. Members of the dominant group 'correct' the stranger in various different ways. The two groups might be incompatible, but by and large the home-base group – if there are only a small number of immigrants – informally trains the newcomers in all sorts of subtle ways to behave properly. Perhaps an Austrian farm boy picks up so much of the local conventions for proper behavior that he can be elected as the governor of a populous state in the USA. One gets accustomed to the local ideas of social propriety. Sometimes the new person changes the society they encounter. The locals adopt the outlander's rules. There is no guaranteed way in which this is going to happen, but the study of how immigrants fit into the *psychology* of a new society reveals the overwhelming importance of rules and conventions.

Conforming to standards of correctness and occasionally exploiting them by breaking with those standards evidently are aspects of prime importance in human life. If a good deal of scientific psychology is to be transposed from the causes key to the rules key, a thorough understanding of rules and rule-following is necessary.

Implicit norms and explicit rules

Imagine a professional athlete, say, a football player in the USA. Obviously, he has played football for many years in order to achieve a level of expertise that has earned him a highly paid position in the National Football League. He is especially familiar with the countless 'ins and outs' of his position. He 'knows' his position to the point where there is little or no need for deliberative thought while he plays the game. Indeed, he has seen and experienced the negative impact of deliberative thought during football. The football player who 'thinks too much' is slow to respond, hesitant, unsure, and lacks the requisite aggression to play the game well. While the ball is in play, our football player simply reacts to contingencies, automatically recognizes what he needs to do, and goes about doing it. Significantly, consistent failure to do his job well results not in his coaches asking him to think more carefully about what he is doing, but to point out his mistakes and to train him to do otherwise without thinking deliberatively.

Our football player knows the rules of his game, but not necessarily all of the rules. Perhaps it has been years since he has read the rule book. But to be sure, over years he has learned the game and there have been points where he was made aware of a certain rule that he, one of his teammates, or a player on an opposing team has violated. So, for example, in order to prevent neck injuries, the rules of American football explicitly state that players will not take hold of an opponent's protective facemask. To avoid violating this rule, players are taught from an early age not to grab their opponents' facemasks while blocking or tackling. Thus, training in the proper ways to block and tackle includes attention to keeping one's hands away from the facemask until not doing so is second nature.

In contrast to our football player, the referees who preside over his games are very familiar with the many details of the game's rule book. More often than not, they are able to make calls more or less automatically, in the sense that they do not have to deliberate over what they have seen in order to blow their whistles when a rule has been violated. But as any fan of American football knows, on certain occasions it is unclear to the referees just what call or calls should be made during a game. So at times they confer on the field to deliberate. It is simply accepted that there are limitations even to *their* knowledge of the rules because sometimes events occur on the field that are unexpected or unusual.

We can think of it this way: the rule book of American football 'is at work behind the scenes,' so to speak, during the playing and refereeing of the game. But in what sense do these written rules work behind the scenes? How should we conceptualize this state of affairs? Generally speaking, cognitive science looks upon these rules as actually operating inside the heads of competitors and referees. (And why not the fans as well?) Or we might say that the rules *cause* the behavior of players and referees. Suddenly the notion of following the rules of football becomes a rather sticky business. For if the rules are inside the heads of players and if they *cause* the behaviors of players, why would any competent player break a rule? And does this perspective not rule out the possibility that a player might follow a certain rule without knowing it is in the rule book?

Shaping actions

Our actions are shaped by all sorts of influences. Wittgenstein begins to explore the problem of how we should express the psychologically central phenomena of actions being brought about by a person, but shaped by an external influence, by undertaking a surview of the uses of the phrase 'being guided by … '.

In the previous chapter, when we discussed Wittgenstein's remarks on reading, we saw that at PI §172 he gives some examples of the variety of ways someone can be guided by an external influence. These range from being tugged unwillingly around, through actively following a dancing partner, to unconsciously following a track on a country walk. He asks: 'All these situations are similar to one another; but what is common to all the experiences?' The answer that emerges in subsequent remarks is that there is only the obvious surface feature of these and other situations of being influenced by something external. There is no common *subjective* experience of being guided to be found in every case.

Where do we get the idea that there is a single common experience of this sort? In PI §173 Wittgenstein's interlocutor protests: 'But being guided is surely a particular experience!' to which Wittgenstein replies: 'you are now *thinking* of a particular experience of being guided.' So long as we are engaged in the guided activity, such as drawing a line parallel to another line 'with deliberation' (PI §174), we notice nothing special. The same observation applies to being guided by the shape of an arbitrary doodle in order to copy the doodle. But looking back on these processes of copying,

> when I ask myself what it was that happened, it seems to have been something indescribable. *Afterwards* no description satisfies me. It's as if I couldn't believe that I merely looked, made such-and-such a face, and drew a line ... and yet I feel as if there must have been something else; in particular when I say 'guidance', 'influence', and other such words to myself ... Only then does the idea of that ethereal, intangible influence arise.
>
> (PI §175)

Summing up the discussion in PI §177, Wittgenstein remarks that the use of causal talk in connection with being guided in this or that way amounts to acknowledging that what one did was influenced by an exemplar, rule, model, dancing partner, or some other external influence. Yet on close examination we see that there were a myriad ways in which one's actions are and can be shaped by such influences.

We turn now to a close study of the nature and role of rules in the management of human living. Our method, following Wittgenstein's advice, will be to conduct an overview of the uses of words relevant to rules and rule-following. In so doing, we will gain a gradual 'pre-empirical' understanding of the varieties of rules and rule-following, along with the varieties of socio-psychological phenomena related to 'rule-following.' Our discussion of Wittgenstein's remarks on rules and rule-following is highly selective. The topic has been quite controversial among Wittgenstein scholars. As is the case throughout this book, suggestions for further reading on the subject are provided at the end of the chapter.

The role of rules: metaphorical and literal

Wittgenstein's conception of human life and how the psychology of human action should be studied is built on our relations to rules and how we understand them. For most of our lives we are not so much passively subject to causes as we are guided by rules, conventions and customs, knowingly or otherwise. As we saw in the case of the football player, there is a difference between following a rule and *acting in accordance* with a rule. Sometimes we treat a rule as an instruction or an order: 'Do this!' Formal ceremonies are managed in this way. Graduation ceremonies at Oxford are still conducted in Latin. A newly appointed Dean of Degrees has been known to conceal a copy of the written list of rules in his or her academic hat as a guide to making the correct moves in the ceremony. But most of the time people are just doing things correctly without recourse to *explicit* instructions or commands. So, with little or no deliberative thought, we drive on the right-hand side of the road in France and the USA, pull up at traffic lights when they have turned red, speak the mother tongue fluently and correctly, and so on. In these less formal cases, if we happen to refer to rules we speak about them in more or less non-explicit ways. Contrast this with a social psychologist, who notes a set of rules that seem to be operative for a certain social group in a given context, for instance, in the case of people from one culture greeting people from another culture. What is the status of the social psychologist's notes? Are the notes a description of some unconscious mental process? Or are they metaphoric for habits and customs?

Our discussion of Wittgenstein's remarks on the cognitive skill of reading in the previous chapter revealed the fundamental insight that there is no particular mental state corresponding to and grounding a claim like 'Now I know how to follow the rules of reading.' Just before his remarks on reading, at PI §151, Wittgenstein asks us to imagine a situation where 'A writes [a] series of numbers down; B watches him and tries to find a law for the sequence of numbers.' The numbers in question are 1, 5, 11, 19 and 29. If B can continue the series, what did he learn? Did he specifically work out the formula $a_n = n^2 + n - 1$? Or did B just feel 'a certain feeling of tension, and all sorts of vague thoughts' until finally working out the series? Perhaps B only felt 'what may be called the sensation "that's easy"' and just continued the series. Clearly, there is a variety of possible admixtures of thoughts and sensations that B might experience while trying to learn the rule 'hidden' in the series written by A. These might include doubts, levels of confidence and embarrassment, perplexity, and even possibly an effortless and immediate realization that 'Now I can go on.'

Wittgenstein refers back to this example immediately after his remarks on reading, at PI §179:

> It is clear that we should not say B had the right to say the words 'Now I know how to go on', just because he thought of the formula – unless experience shewed that there was a connexion between thinking of the formula – saying it, writing it down – and actually continuing the series ... We can also imagine the case where nothing at all occurred in B's mind except that he suddenly said 'Now I know how to go on' – perhaps with a feeling of relief; and that he did in fact go on working out the series without using the formula. And in this case too we should say – in certain circumstances – that he did know how to go on.

In the next remark (PI §180), Wittgenstein points out that in the case just described it would be 'quite misleading' to call the words 'Now I know how to go on' a 'description of a mental state.' The grammar of expressions like 'to be able' and 'to understand' is much more complex than it might appear. They form fields of family resemblances, and *psychologists make general hypotheses about this sort of conformative conduct at their peril*. One advantage of grammatical analysis – which ought to be conducted before and alongside empirical research in psychology – is its potential to reveal the *complexities of phenomena* psychologists seek to investigate and explain. Also, on many occasions grammatical analysis has the potential to mitigate psychologists' need to formulate simplistic generalizations of their findings in the name of science.

Teaching: getting someone to follow a rule

Wittgenstein's remarks on cognitive skills and abilities, including reading, overlap with his remarks specifically on rules and rule-following. Our point of departure is PI §143, where Wittgenstein surveys all sorts of ways a person can get another person to follow a rule. He examines a language-game where A (whom we will call 'the teacher') gives an order to B ('the student') to write down a series of signs according to a formation rule specified by the teacher. The student is supposed to write down the natural numbers, 1, 2, 3, 4 and so on. The difference here is that instead of asking how the student can learn the rule, Wittgenstein wants to look at how the teacher can *get* the student to learn the rule. There are all kinds of ways the teacher can do this.

Wittgenstein says that first of all, the student might copy the numbers from those the teacher has written out. Or the teacher could guide the student's hand, perhaps saying: 'Look, you do it this way.' In the first case, suppose sometimes the student copies the numbers well enough, but writes them in the wrong order. The teacher might think the student has some sort of disorder, but after a while no such suspicions are warranted because the student can write the numbers properly and otherwise behaves normally. Gradually, the student gets the idea, writing 1, 2, 3, 4 and so on. Still, the student occasionally makes mistakes. These might be systematic (for example, the student might skip every fifth number after the number 10), or mistakes may occur due to the student's lack of concentration. But with effort mistakes are overcome until the teacher is satisfied that the student has learned the rules governing writing the natural numbers in order.

Now, to go beyond Wittgenstein's examples, imagine other ways the teacher might have taught the student. Here are just a few. After teaching the student to associate number-words ('one,' 'two,' 'three,' and so on) with their written signs, the teacher might have spoken the words in proper order over and over again until the rule for their sequence was learned. Or perhaps the teacher had the student write one number per page in a notebook, correcting each mistake until the notebook was complete. Then, the student could write out the sequence while referring to the notebook until the rule was mastered. Or the teacher could have used a slide projector to show the numbers, one at a time in proper order, while the student copied them. This process could have been repeated until there was a satisfactory result. There are many possibilities. The point is that teaching a student how to master a rule *of any kind* can be accomplished in many ways.

But what is the teacher of rules doing when they teach in one way or other? Well, the answer is that the teacher is training someone. But because there are so many possibilities in teaching even a single rule and because we can expect slight variations even in one approach to teaching a rule, there can be no one particular mental state that constitutes the teaching, much less one mental state that constitutes the learning. By teaching a rule we are not inducing a mental state common to all those who have learned the skill employed in skillfully exhibiting knowledge of the rule. As a further point in recognizing the complexities here, think of the differences in appearance and personality exhibited by teachers and learners in the instructional context!

Another avenue to consider here is the possibility that rules are coercive. Suppose you have added a devastating back-hand passing shot to your tennis game. You are playing with your employer, who is a vain but deeply flawed tennis player. Early in the match your passing shots are cracking down the line past her, and it is already clear that she has no chance of winning even one game. So what do you do? With the opportunity for advancement in your company hanging in the balance, you deliberately begin to give your boss a chance at winning. You perform your back-hand passing shots incorrectly. Because these shots are skilled behaviors that conform to a norm of correctness, rather than the result of the running of a causal mechanism, you can perform them incorrectly. If you were caused to 'emit optimal back-hand passing shot behavior' every time the ball came back from your boss's feeble return shot, then she would stand no chance of winning. You would have to continue to game, set, match, and pink slip with ease. But because tennis shots conform or fail to conform to norms of correctness and do not just happen mechanically, if you are with people with whom it would be impolite to win, you can let them win by purposefully playing badly. Note that this account is not inconsistent with the assertion by highly regarded athletes that they practice their skills over and over so that they (the skills) become 'automatic.' We note also that losing the match by playing badly purposively may be seen is acting in accordance with another rule, roughly: 'flatter the boss to keep your job and maybe even gain advancement.' In the human scene we can never escape the domain of rules, even if we are locked up for flagrantly breaking them.

Learning point: basics on rules and rule-following

Our problem is to set up a system of concepts for understanding orderly human practices that involve standards of correctness. Causal language eliminates the human actor as the agent who produces appropriate behavior.

1. *Understanding a practice is knowing a rule.* However, what is it 'to know a rule'?

2. *Rules in Wittgenstein's sense (I)*

   (a) 'Following a rule': This is acting on an explicit instruction (e.g. 'Do this if you want that'). This involves 'rule-expression' in the form of a proposition or statement (often in the imperative, verbal or written).
   (b) 'Acting in accordance with a rule': This amounts to behaving in an orderly way while carrying on some practice, or 'rule-expression exhibited in practice.'
   (c) Why is it that 'following a rule' and 'acting in accordance with a rule' are both normative? We apply standards of correctness of both kinds of practices.

3. *Explanatory format* (Note: We have introduced this terminology for convenience)

    (a) We are tempted to generalize the format of 'following a rule' to the case of 'acting in accordance with a rule' by introducing hypothetical rules 'in the mind.' Wittgenstein holds it is a major mistake to use 'following a rule' as a model for understanding the phenomena of 'acting in accordance with a rule.'
    (b) For 'rule-following' we have a heterogeneous regress. To terminate the regress, we shift from a hierarchy of rules (propositions) to a trained habit. Behaviorists omitted the regress. For 'acting in accordance' we do not have a regress, as rule-following terminates immediately in habit or trained performance.

4. *Teaching someone to follow a rule*

    (a) PI §143: A teacher instructs (trains) a student to write down the series of natural numbers. This can be accomplished in many ways.
    (b) Since there are so many ways such instruction can be carried out, it is unlikely that the teacher will be engaged in passing on a particular mental state to the student.
    (c) Whatever may be the state of mind of a learner, applying a rule correctly is the criterion of mastery.
    (d) The employee–employer tennis match language-game shows that rules cannot be coercive. Rule-following (and breaking rules) involves agency, choice.

Knowing a rule

Can we tell from what someone does whether he or she is following a certain rule, a rule which in some sense that person 'knows'? Can we know, *from their actions alone*, which rule they are following? Wittgenstein begins an extended discussion of this important question in PI §145.

Suppose that, as a teacher, you asked a pupil to write the series of integers from 0 to 9 to your satisfaction. When would you say the pupil 'knew the rule' for writing this series? Only when the pupil is nearly always successful. Certainly you would not give the student a pass mark if s/he writes the series correctly once in a hundred attempts. Now you want to teach the pupil to go further, into the teens, twenties, thirties and on to 100. You continue the series and draw the pupil's attention to the recurrence of the first series of units. Eventually the pupil writes 0–9, 10–19, 20–29 and so on. How do you know the pupil has understood the principle of constructing numerals to the base 10 – that the pupil *knows* this rule? There are at least two criteria: the pupil (1) goes on *independently* and (2) continues the series *correctly*. Correctness is not so much having the right thing in one's head as conforming to what the others are doing, however that conforming is achieved. It is no good thinking that because one is convinced that one is doing something correctly it is correct, particularly if *all* the others are saying that it is not correct.

The rule metaphor is intended *to cover everything that people do in a more or less orderly fashion* – including reasoning, remembering, acting in a mannerly way at table, dressing, driving and so on – *wherever the distinctions between doing something correctly and incorrectly, carefully and carelessly and so on can be applied*. (Recall Wittgenstein's remark about dropping the tea-tray carefully in PI §145.) In many cases rules are not taught formally. But they are learned nevertheless. In the educational movie *Acquiring the Human Language: Playing the Language Game*, Steven Pinker, a protégé of Noam Chomsky, insists that the rules of grammar are not taught to children learning how to use language. Like many who have accepted the reality of Chomsky's hypothetical mental machine, the 'language acquisition device,' Pinker speaks of teaching the rules of grammar as if teaching could only occur in formal settings.

This is an important problem for the psychology of learning. Sometimes a learner will just copy or 'imitate' what others do. (As any student of child development knows, this is an important point made by Albert Bandura.) Sometimes a teacher will guide the learner without formulating the rule explicitly. Sometimes an expert just corrects our systematic errors. The power of fashion is rather like that. In the USA, nobody said 'All men must have their hair short' during the 1990s. But suddenly a great many men in the USA began wearing short hair. Nobody announced in the mid-1960s that young men should wear their hair long.

Again, Wittgenstein wants to rid us of the temptation to think that explicit rule-following and acting conformatively consists in being in a certain mental state. This point becomes important in the basic research question as to how I know whether you are following a rule and, if so, which one. If I want to know whether you are following a rule I do not ask you to introspect and tell me what you are thinking or feeling. What do I do? Well, I see what you are doing and whether you do such things as correct yourself with the realization that a certain step you made did not conform to standards of correctness. I may try to find out how you came to be able to do it. There are other possibilities. Here is an example. College lecturers know that after about two or three meetings of a class, students tend to sit in the same places in the lecture hall. After a while the lecturer has a sense that he or she knows where each student is *supposed* to be. Nothing causes the audience to sit in these positions. If we are tempted to explain this phenomenon in terms of rules, we would not explain it in terms of the students following the lecturer's instructions. There is a practice, or a habit, or a custom to sit in the same place – or near the same place – in college lecture halls. Here we have a rule at work. So if I want to know if you are following a rule, *I see what you do*. I don't ask: 'Are we following rules?' On any given day, students might have all sorts of things in mind when entering the lecture hall, including 'Oh God, it's a lecture on Wittgenstein's psychology again!' Or, on any given day, one or more students might have nothing in particular on their mind at all when entering class. In so far as the behavior is normative, we will say that the students are following rules and conforming to customs. 'Knowing a rule' is a kind of cognitive metaphor for 'being able to do something correctly.'

This leads us to a topic of great importance for the methodology of psychology. How can we be sure that we have hit on *the* custom, norm, or rule, that is the key element in a research project?

The paradox of interpretation

Suppose you are in an examination room at a hospital for your yearly physical. Doctor Smith is explaining various aspects of your exam as she goes about her work. 'It's time for the old reflex examination,' she says. 'Cross your legs and relax them. I'll use this reflex hammer to tap the patellar tendon in your left knee. Then your body will follow the "patellar tendon reflex rule" and your leg from the knee down will extend.' After being given a clean bill of health, you reflect on Dr Smith's description of your reflex exam. Something strikes you as odd. '"Patellar tendon reflex rule"? My body followed a "reflex rule"? There are rules in the body? I thought *people* followed rules. How would my body know the meaning of a reflex rule?'

Our purpose in describing this language-game is to bring up some questions about rules and meaning. Ordinarily, we think of rules as meaningful because if a rule were not meaningful, it could not be followed. Also, it seems reasonable to suggest that in order to follow a rule in some normative practice, a person needs to know how to follow the rule case by case. But how does a rule 'get' its meaning? This question is relevant to psychology because we have seen that theorists in AI, psycholinguistics and other fields of inquiry propose that rules governing thought, language and so on actually reside in the brain. This is similar to Dr Smith's claim that a reflex rule resides in the body. But how could these bodily rules get their meaning? Does it make sense to propose that some rules are independent of meaning – that there are mechanical rules?

At the heart of these considerations is the notion of *interpretation*. To interpret is 'to explain to oneself the meaning of; elucidate,' or, 'to expound the significance of.' Must rules be interpreted in order to be followed? Or do rules 'speak for themselves'? We need a workable case to answer questions of this sort, and one case Wittgenstein explores is the 'sign-post.' In the following remark, a rule is compared with a sign-post and Wittgenstein hints at a possible grammatical connection between rule-following and interpretation:

> A rule stands there like a sign-post. – Does the sign-post leave no doubt about the way I have to go? ... But where is it said which way I am to follow it; whether in the direction of its finger or (e.g.) in the opposite one? – And if there were, not a single sign-post, but a chain of adjacent ones or of chalk marks on the ground – is there only *one* way of interpreting them?
>
> (PI §85)

To end this remark, Wittgenstein seems to leave open the question as to whether a sign-post will 'leave no room for doubt' or 'sometimes leaves room for doubt and sometimes not.' Because we can see whether a sign-post leaves room for doubt by observing people's behavior in relation to sign-posts, we are now in the realm of 'empirical' inquiry – not philosophical (or grammatical) inquiry. Still, it is possible that empirical inquiry cannot provide an answer to the question of whether rules need to be interpreted in order to be followed.

Wittgenstein has in mind only sign-posts that inform persons about which direction they need to travel in order to get to one or more places. And we should keep in mind that people encounter sign-posts while thinking of many different sorts of things, with various attitudes, and in various emotional states. But how do people learn to follow sign-posts in order to get to their destination?

At the very least we can assume that people are *trained* to react to sign-posts in certain ways. We might assume also that implicit in this training is learning to *interpret* the rule associated with sign-posts. But, as Wittgenstein has observed, 'is there only *one* way of interpreting them?'

Suppose a sign-post were constructed at Four Corners Monument – the only place in the USA where you can stand in four states at one time. The 'Four Corners Sign-post' has four signs pointing in the appropriate directions, inscribed with 'Utah,' 'Colorado,' 'New Mexico' and 'Arizona.' But there are other signs as well, including 'New York City – 2,254 miles,' 'Anchorage – 3,456 miles,' 'Los Angeles – 694 miles' and 'Caribou, Maine – 2,698 miles.'

Now suppose that Person A, who wants to go to Caribou, had to state clearly the rule that she follows for sign-posts. She might say something like: 'Go in the direction of the point of the sign inscribed by the name of your destination.' By her *interpretation* of the rule and given where she wants to go, this means she will go in the direction of the point of the sign inscribed with 'Caribou.' By so doing, her actions *accord with the rule*.

Now here is the problem. Wittgenstein (PI §85) questions whether there is only *one* way to interpret a rule. Couldn't *anything* be made to accord with a rule, just by adjusting one's interpretation of it? Along comes Person B. He also wants to go to Caribou. But his response to the 'sign-post rule' at Four Corners is rather different from that of Person A. Encountering the Four Corners sign-post, Person B travels in the *opposite* direction to the point of the sign-post inscribed with 'Caribou.' Then, after traveling 100 miles over one week away from and back to Four Corners, he checks to see if the Caribou sign is pointing in the same direction relative to the other signs. If it is still pointing in the same direction, he proceeds to Caribou. At a practical level, Person B's actions accord with Person A's interpretation of the sign-post rule because Person B ends up in Caribou. 'But why,' we may ask Person B, 'did you follow the sign to Caribou *that* way?' 'Because,' he replies, 'someone told me that on occasion, sign-posts can be incorrect. I wanted to take some time to check it.' Imagine the variations in action that can be seen ultimately to accord with the sign-post rule!

At PI §198 Wittgenstein's interlocutor asks: 'But how can a rule shew me what I have to do at *this* point? Whatever I do is, on some interpretation, in accord with the rule.' This is a statement of the 'paradox of interpretation.' People can be explicitly trained to follow rules and any rule can be interpreted in a variety of ways. But as we have described them, the vast majority of rules are learned without explicit training. Absurd as it seems, what Person B did can be looked upon as according with the sign-post rule 'on some interpretation.' Hence the paradox. How can a single rule be interpreted so variously and still be followed? How can a variety of actions accord with a single rule? This seems to run against the commonsense idea, suggested by Wittgenstein in PI §198, that the 'connexion' between one's actions and 'the expression of a rule – say a sign-post' is training. Training implies the instruction of *a particular way* of according with a rule. (Think of how firearms instructors train military recruits to disassemble and assemble their rifles.) But Wittgenstein's interlocutor questions the extent to which this observation really tells us what it means to follow a rule: 'But this is only to give a causal connexion; to tell how it has come about that we now go by the sign-post; not what this going-by-the-sign really consists in.' Wittgenstein responds: 'On the contrary; I have further indicated that a person goes by a sign-post only in so far as there exists a regular use of sign-posts, a custom' (PI §198).

What does 'going-by-the-sign' *really* consist in? Does it consist in something that *accompanies* the actions of going-by-the-sign, the actions themselves, or a combination of both? There are other possibilities. Wittgenstein's answer seems to be that a prerequisite for going-by-the-sign is a customary use of sign-posts. But to what extent can there be a 'customary' use when so many interpretations of the sign-post rule are possible? Furthermore, given the variety of possible interpretations of a rule, how can psychologists hope to construct a *scientific* use of the concept of rule-following toward establishing an understanding of human conformative conduct?

Here is Wittgenstein's reply to the possibility, expressed by his interoluctor, that one could never know what rule was being followed:

> This was our paradox: no course of action could be determined by a rule, because every course of action can be made out to accord with the rule. The answer was: if everything can be made out to accord with the rule, then it can also be made out to conflict with it. And there would be neither accord nor conflict here.
>
> (PI §201)

But, of course, we *do* make judgments as to whether actions accord with or conflict with rules. The argument of this paragraph is not an invitation to skepticism about rule-following explanations, but a disproof of the claim that there are unlimited ways of interpreting a rule. The very fact that umpires and referees successfully manage sporting games is enough to show that such judgments are not only possible, but routine! What follows? The premise that no course of action could be determined by a rule must be false, since it entails a false conclusion. (A *modus tollens* argument.) *The interpretative 'paradox' came from thinking that 'interpreting a rule' meant giving a unique description of the conditions for its application.* As Wittgenstein remarks, 'interpreting' mostly means substituting one expression of the rule for another, handier one.

If a rule is a proposition, be it in the form of an overt statement or in the form of tacit propositional knowledge, then an interpretation of it will always be required to apply it in any particular case. Most words that make up the expressed rule 'Black tie for formal college functions' need interpretation. What is meant by 'black tie' in this context? Is it different from 'black tie' in the rules for how to dress for a funeral? What exactly is to count as a 'formal college function'?

This can be expressed in yet another way. The idea that interpretations are always needed to mediate between a rule and an action in accordance with it is one particular case of the general principle that there must be a mediator between rules and actions in accordance with them. It seems to us quite clear that the heart of Wittgenstein's treatment of rules and rule-following is the wish to do away with this idea. If, on seeing someone doing something that seems to be embedded in a network of social practices – including assessing what has been done by standards of correctness and propriety – we want to know what rule that person is following, we must consult what the person is doing. *Rule-expression is in the practice itself. There is no gap between rule and action, since the action realizes the rule and rule is realized in the action.* It is easy to make a connection here with Wittgenstein's remarks on reading.

Dispositions and rules

It is with the relationship between dispositions and rules that we come very close to the heart of the matter with reductionist accounts of rules. Must we include states of the brain and nervous system in giving an account of human life in normative terms? Surely in acquiring a skill, say playing the clarinet, the brain and nervous system of the learner are changed and are maintained in a particular state. Wittgenstein remarks that 'the grammar of the word "knows" is evidently closely related to that of "can", "is able to"' (PI §150). Does the maintenance of an ability require a permanent state of the person who has it?

If one says that knowing the ABC is a state of mind, one is thinking of the state of a mental apparatus (perhaps the brain) by means of which we explain the *manifestations* of that knowledge. Such a state is called a disposition. But there are objections to speaking of a state of mind here, inasmuch as there ought to be two different criteria for such a state: a knowledge of the construction of the apparatus quite apart from what it does (PI §149).

Let us explain the concept of a disposition. Toward the beginning of Chapter 5 we distinguished between abilities and powers. The former pertain to people (or animals) and the latter pertain to things. Aspirin has a power to stop people feeling pain and to prevent blood clotting. It has this power because it has a certain chemical structure. It contains acetyl salicylic acid, originally extracted from the bark of willow trees. Useful though this schema is for the physical sciences, how does it work when applied to psychology? At the back of Wittgenstein's mind is something like the following. Someone recites the alphabet correctly. They display a certain skill. Is there anything here corresponding to the chemical composition of aspirin? We might ask for an account of the structure of the mechanism the person employs in reciting the alphabet. So we might think that between the time this person was unable to recite the alphabet and the point at which they could recite it, something *must* have happened to their brain.

Wittgenstein is hardly denying this obvious fact. Rather, he is pointing out something about word use. Whatever the mechanism is, it is irrelevant to our *assessment* of whether the learner has acquired the skill; that is, whether we should say 'Now he knows the alphabet!' Nor is there any particular mental state or process that must obtain if it is proper to say that someone can recite a poem. Likewise, nor is there any particular form of training in which a competent performer must have been engaged. It might very well be the case that various persons, performing the same skilled activity, are able to do so on the basis of different neuropsychological foundations upon which this ability depends. Whatever these states and processes may be, they can play no role in *establishing what it means* to say that someone is 'a skilled lacrosse player' or 'has an ear for music.' It does not matter what is going on in your brain *with respect to the conditions for the application of dispositional concepts* to a human actor, such as skills, capacities and ability to carry out the practices and customs of the culture.

Related to this point is a beautiful remark by the late John Gardner. In one of his books he says that clowns would be just as funny if they had nothing but sawdust in their heads. Don't you have to have *something* going on in your head? True enough. But the point has to do with the criteria for saying that someone is following a rule, or custom, or acting skillfully. We want to see whether you really know how to perform a back-hand pass. If playing tennis were like bringing out the analgesic efficacy of aspirin, I could find out if you can play tennis in two ways. I could say 'Here's the ball, show me a back-hand passing shot with lots of top spin!' Would it do equally well to put you through a PET scan to ascertain the state of your brain? Could I say 'Let's shave your head, put on these electrodes and then we will see if you can do a back-hand passing shot!' Why is this proposal ridiculous?

The thing that matters for the correct use of words in attributing to someone a disposition or skill is whether they can do what is required. Here is another example. It does not follow that because we all know how to use the word 'horse' that we must have the same brain structure sustaining our skill in using the word. Each of us will have some sustaining brain structure, but these may differ from person to person. What is more, there is strong empirical evidence in favor of the general principle that the same skills can be supported by different neural states and structures. The late Donald Broadbent studied the neurophysiological basis of the skill of reading. We can all read. But half of us, the females, make significant use of different parts of their brains from the other half, the males. To that extent there are different neurophysiological processes underlying the same skill. When reading, women generally use a broader area of the brain, less laterally distributed, than do men. But there are no discernible gender differences in adult reading capabilities.

Many things are going on when we play tennis. What accounts for our skill at the game is not something mental, either. What you are thinking when you are doing a back-hand passing shot has very little to do with your ability to do it. There are exceptions. If you have drawn John McEnroe in the local tennis club summer tournament, even though he has retired you are probably going to get so uptight thinking about his fame that your usual skills desert you.

This is not a kind of behaviorism. We must never lose the insight that the actions we are trying to understand are ultimately identified by *what they mean*, either to the actor or to the relevant local community. There is no unique, public, context-free description of what counts as a tennis shot, a memory, a solution to a problem, and so forth.

Do rules *cause* conforming behavior?

Figure 6.1 represents and summarizes what we have learned thus far about the relationship between rules, learning rules, and actions in accordance (or not in accordance) with rules. It can be looked upon as two right-angled triangles, each sharing a vertical base defined as the relationship between natural regularities/ training (at the $90°$ angle for both triangles) and normative actions (at the $50°$ angle for both triangles). The directions of the arrows are significant, as are their solid or dashed lines. Solid lines represent *necessary* grammatical relationships, while dashed lines represent empirical relationships.

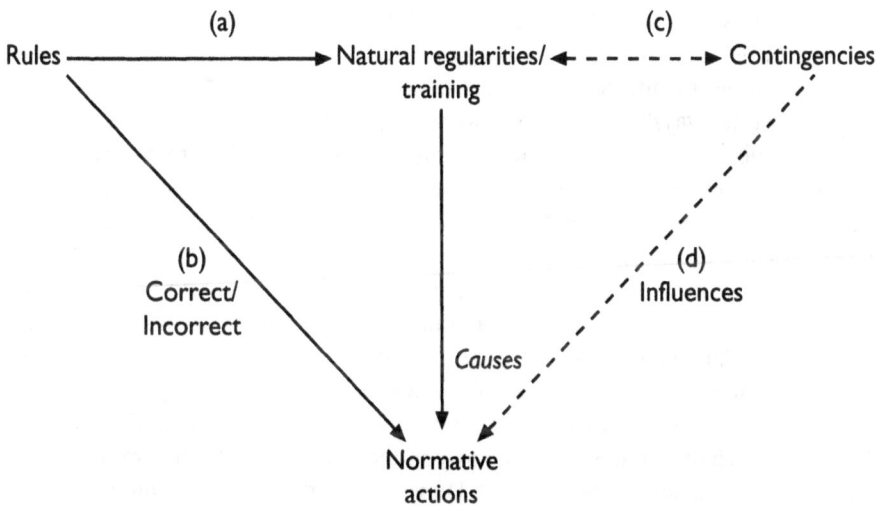

Figure 6.1

The following five paragraphs summarize Figure 6.1. It will be helpful to refer to each specific area of the figure while reading.

At (a) there is a necessary grammatical relationship between rules and natural regularities/training. As such, a necessary relationship between rules and normative actions is forged via natural regularities/training.

At (b) there is a necessary grammatical relationship between rules, standards of correctness and normative actions. All normative, rule-guided actions can be said to be carried out either correctly or incorrectly. There are varying degrees of correctness that can be tolerated.

At (c) there is an empirical interaction between natural regularities and training, on one hand, and contingencies on the other hand. Unexpected occurrences can always influence training. Also, there are contexts of training, including the expertise and personality of the trainer and/or learner.

At (d) the influence of contingencies on normative action also is not grammatical, but empirical. Contingencies may interrupt or break the bond between training and normative actions; for example, either preventing an action from being carried out or preventing it from being carried out in the way a person (or group) intends.

In italics, although *causes may* play a role in rule-following, grammar makes no provision for rules as causes of normative actions. Grammatically, the position of causes lies somewhere at the nexus of natural regularities/training, contingencies and the carrying out of normative actions. Grammatically, causes are to be subsumed under contingencies. For example, organic causes of memory loss (e.g. in Alzheimer's Disease) may prevent the unfortunate person from successfully carrying out a normative action. This would be a kind of causal contingency.

The foregoing can be summarized less formally. Keep in mind that when we refer to training, we are referring to both formal and informal training. Obviously training is an important and necessary component of rule-following and acting in accordance with rules. Culture consists of the beliefs, behavior patterns and products of groups of people that are passed from one generation to the next. This 'passing of the torch,' so to speak, largely rests on informal training. But whether we are speaking of informal or formal training, why do we train someone to do things in certain ways? Well, because we want them to be able to do these things.

It is sensible to train someone to do something correctly. (The really cruel thing would be to train someone to do things that are incorrect.) We can think of effective training as consisting partly in training someone to follow rules, which are set out either formally or informally, or with a mixture of formal and informal training. But in thinking of the subsequent behavior of the trainee, we would be mistaken to say that the rules 'cause' their behavior. Rather, the rules are the social or individual background which is drawn on in training. Once the training is complete the rules recede into the background, so to speak, as we account for why the person behaves as they do. At that point, other considerations move to the foreground. For example, the person's behavior might consist partly in the realization of a natural tendency, like being right-handed or left-handed. Do you eat with the fork in your right hand or your left? A natural tendency of this sort can be modified by culture, as anyone crossing the Atlantic can see readily.

What is the relationship between rules and actions? Rules inform us as to which actions are correct and which are incorrect. Could it be the case that a correct action did not accord with a rule? It could not; not because it would be difficult to do, but because the rule *determines* what the correct action is. Nothing could be incorrect and in accord with a rule, so the relationship between rules and actions is internal or conceptual. It is not necessary to do an experiment to discover this. Of course, we train people to follow the rules so they will do what is correct.

Unfortunately, everything is not lovely in the garden because there are contingencies. All sorts of things happen and all sorts of things go wrong in life. So contingencies can interfere with training and its results. The tennis player trained to make a great back-hand passing shot is victimized on match point by a bit of grit on the court, which makes her opponent's shot deviate slightly from its predicted path. Thus, what otherwise would have been a great return passing shot goes out of bounds. Our tennis player made all the correct moves, but the contingency of grit on the court resulted in her losing the match. This sort of thing happens all the time. New rules can be made in countless situations with little or no difficulty. (In more formal settings, we even have rules for changing rules.) If a person goes to the supermarket to buy one jar of Mexican salsa for $1.50, they might end up taking advantage of a sale in which two jars of salsa cost $2.50. In the broadened sense of 'rule' advocated by Wittgenstein, the manager of the supermarket has made up a new rule because the store is overstocked with salsa. This rule can work very well, so long as the store remains overstocked.

Insisting that rules are causes of behavior, someone might say that when I have learned to do something according to a rule, the steps in my behavior are in some sense already taken. This is perhaps a kind of fatalism. A certain merchant goes into the market in Bokhara to sell some carpets. As he walks into the market, across the crowd he sees the black-cowled skull-like figure of Death looking at him. So the merchant thinks he'd better get out of there fast. He leaves the market, packs up his carpets, and goes across the desert to Samara, the next market town. When he arrives he walks into the market and the first person he meets is Death. The merchant says: 'What are you doing here? I saw you in Bokhara!' 'Yes,' says Death, 'but I have an appointment with you in Samara.'

What is it that rules determine? It is, of course, the standards of correctness and propriety that will be applied by those who subscribe to the rule. What happens is subject to all kinds of contingencies, accidents and folly!

Where do rules get their authority?

At PI §187 the pupil claims to know what the teacher meant by 'add 2,' but the pupil does not act correctly after he has reached 1004. We dismiss his claim to know what the teacher intended and we try to remedy his failure. We do this by reference to the authority of the teacher as a representative of the local community, whose judgment 'counts.' But is this judgment merely an expression of personal conviction, and is that conviction all that supports a normative practice *qua* 'normative' practice? Wittgenstein hints at an answer to this question earlier in the *Investigations*, at §145: 'Now, however, let us suppose that after some efforts on the teacher's part he [the pupil] continues the series correctly, that is, as we do it. So now we can say he has mastered the system.' No; personal conviction is not enough to support a normative practice as such. There are standards to live by and rule-following is expressed in practices.

In §202 Wittgenstein emphasizes the above point by asserting that *thinking* one is obeying a rule does not amount to obeying a rule. Obeying a rule by thinking one is obeying a rule has no social support. In §206 he carries the thought further by comparing following a rule with obeying an order. We are trained to react to an order 'in a particular way.' But suppose some people react in one way and some in another, to both the order and the training? The one who reacts as we all do, that is, in conformity with the demands of society, is correct. 'The common behaviour of mankind' is the final arbiter (PI §206).

This 'common behaviour of mankind' as authority is ever present. In PI §§218–36 Wittgenstein comments on several ways one might symbolize the continuing authority of rules. To cite just a single example, one might think that rules are 'rails laid to infinity' (§218), such that the steps to take at the beginning of a normative task 'are already taken' (§219). *But this does not invite us to take rules as causes of regularities in conduct.* These symbolic images of rules given to us by Wittgenstein, like the 'rails' simile, are intended 'to bring into prominence a difference between being causally determined and being logically determined' (§220). Unlike a human authority, which might be capricious, a rule 'always tells us the same, and we do what it tells us' (§223). Does this mean we have no choice but to obey rules? Certainly not. But when I *do* obey a rule, 'I do not choose. I obey the rule *blindly*' (§219). Just think of the many rules people follow this way in the course of their daily lives, from wearing certain clothes to their bedding. Are we making 'choices' in the great majority of cases when we conform to local standards?

The key to understanding the orderliness of our lives lies in the realization that we are trained in certain procedures. One result of this training is habit. Nothing further needs to be offered by way of justification for what I do than that I have been so trained. The upshot is Wittgenstein's fundamental thesis that we commit ourselves to norms. Here again, the famous remark on obeying the rule '*blindly*' (in §219) is relevant. In the great majority of cases when we obey a rule we do not choose between one interpretation of the rule and another. What if we are asked *why* we do such-and-such? We may give reasons for doing so or we may say, 'I don't know.' But if we do cite reasons as justifications for what we do, we can only regress so far into them because 'my reasons will soon run out. And then I shall act, without reasons' (PI §211). In another well-known image Wittgenstein says: 'If I have exhausted the justifications I have reached bedrock, and my spade is turned. Then I am inclined to say "This is simply what I do"' (§217).

What does all this mean for the human sciences? Wittgenstein is intent on getting us to see that human life is grounded in commitments to certain customs and in the training people get in the skills and practices of everyday life. Why these customs and practices exist can be given only a historical explanation. They are constitutive of a 'form of life.' Obviously this is a perspective on rules that is very different from the 'rules-in-the-mind' perspective outlined at the beginning of this chapter.

Learning point: rules-in-practices

1. *Rules in Wittgenstein's sense (II)*

    (a)   The rule metaphor covers everything that people do in a more or less orderly fashion. This includes varieties of cognition. We must consider rules and rule-following whenever there are distinctions between doing things correctly or incorrectly, carefully and carelessly, and so on.
    (b)   There are implicit and explicit forms of training in rule-following (or mixtures).
    (c)   A major thrust of Wittgenstein's rule-following considerations is to rid us of the temptation to think that conforming to rules as standards of correctness is, in fact, to be in a certain mental state. Also, he shows us that rules are not causes of behavior.

2. *The paradox of interpretation*
    To show that rules and actions are internally related is to show that the model of rule-expression-as-proposition must not be generalized to cases in which the rule is expressed nowhere else but in the practice.

    (a) The sign-post example (PI §85) brings up the question of whether any action can accord with a rule. Is there only one way of interpreting a series of sign-posts?
    (b) PI §198: The interlocutor suggests that an interpretation – perhaps in the form of a proposition – be inserted between rule and action: Thus any action can be seen to accord with a rule.
    (c) PI §201: Statement and partial resolution of the paradox. Inserting an interpretation between a rule and actions in accordance with it makes us think that the interpretation gives us a unique description of the conditions under which the rule can be applied.
    (d) But since the insertion of an interpretation allows every course of action to be in accordance (or not in accordance) with the rule, the distinction between 'in accord with' and 'not in accord with' would have no application.
    (e) But 'in accord with' and 'not in accord with' are routinely applied. So an interpretation is not the basis upon which we act in accordance with a rule. There is no gap between rule and action into which an interpretation might be inserted because the action realizes the rule and the rule is realized in the action.

3. *Grammatical and empirical relationships*

    (a) The relationship between rules and natural regularities/training is grammatical, that is, 'internal' and necessary.
    (b) The same holds for the relationship between rules, standards of correctness and normative actions.
    (c) There is an empirical relationship between (i) natural regularities and training and (ii) contingencies. Contingencies also are empirically related to normative action.
    (d) Rules are not causes of normative actions. Causes are kinds of contingency. We might propose that training establishes a sign as a cause of behavior. But rules may be mandatory only as a custom in a social context.

4. *Authority of a rule*

    (a) PI §187: The authority of a teacher is representative of society (custom). Normative standards come 'from without.' Personal conviction (e.g. that one has mastered some system) is not enough (PI §145). Thinking that one is obeying a rule does not amount to obeying a rule (PI §202).

(b) PI §§148–52: Claims to mastery based on personal experiences are only accompaniments to understanding (mastery).

(c) Is the teacher, as a representative of society, the final arbiter of what is correct? Not really. Analogous to obeying an order, 'correctness' is assessed by reference to 'common behaviour of mankind' (PI §206).

(d) PI §§218–23; 238–9: Knowing a rule is not to have a representation of all future steps, but to be able to act correctly each time. The picture of rules as rails to infinity (PI §218), in which all the steps in following a rule are already taken, is intended to show the distinction between being causally determined and logically determined.

(e) What lies at the root of our justifications for doing what we do? This question opens up a regress of justification. My reasons for doing what I do 'will soon run out' and so, at some point, I must 'act without reasons' (PI §§211, 217).

(f) Thus we terminate justifications homogeneously, as a kind of habit. This is a point about the grammar of justifications for actions. It does not warrant the switch to a heterogeneous regress, or justifying actions in terms of material and efficient causes.

Agreement

Since rule-following in both its explicitly propositional form and as a custom or practice is so integral to our local social worlds, how does this come about? One powerful metaphor is that of 'agreement.' Wittgenstein uses this metaphor to warn us against making too rigid a distinction between agreement in language, customs, and so on on the one hand, and agreement as to what is true on the other. Of course, unless we had agreement in language – that is, how we use words relevant to our activities – we could not even begin to discuss whether or not some fact obtained. Unless we agree on what the words 'back line' mean we cannot discuss the question of whether the tennis shot is in or out. And, as Wittgenstein notes, people do not generally disagree about whether a rule has been followed or not. They sometimes do, of course. But agreement does not determine what is true or false. This bald distinction needs refining. In PI §242 Wittgenstein draws our attention to the *necessity* of some agreements as to matters of fact without which there would be no normative practices at all. Brenner (1999, p. 41) offers the example of the way colors cluster around red–orange and around blue–green as a kind of judgment which, without our agreement, there could be no refined grammar of color words.

Grammar, the 'autonomy of grammar,' and identifying a grammatical rule

We have referred already to 'grammar' on numerous occasions. Wittgenstein generalizes the concept of grammar to include all the rules, explicit or implicit, that are relevant to a practice. But although he is concerned primarily with the rules of language in the context of philosophical investigation, our concerns are broader. We have generalized it yet again to cover *sets of rules relevant to any normatively constrained practice*. We think that Wittgenstein would warrant our generalization.

It is important to emphasize that while persons may cite rules on occasion to decide whether something has been done or used correctly or incorrectly, the *quality* of the performance is not determined by the rule. A musician may play the notes as they are represented in the score, a kind of rule, but give an uninspired performance. Again, as Figure 6.1 on rules, training, contingencies and so on shows, a rule is inherent in a practice. As Glock (1996) puts it, a rule 'codifies existing practice, that is the prevailing practice' (p. 152). By writing down the music, Scott Joplin brought some jazz improvisations under a rule.

Here is an idea that we think psychologists of any kind should consider. In this and in previous chapters we have occasionally encountered the distinction between the grammatical and the empirical. Often, Wittgenstein appeals to the way things are in the world. But what is the relation between grammar and states of affairs in the world in Wittgenstein's later writings, particularly PI?

By 'grammar,' Wittgenstein is referring to all that is implicated in language-in-use. Grammar also refers to *possible* uses of words, so that a grammatical investigation will also explore possible and borderline/problematic uses of language. In the context of exploring grammar for the purposes of philosophical investigation (grammatical analysis) which, we have insisted, ought to be part of empirical research in psychology, Wittgenstein sees grammar as not wholly independent of the world in which it is used. Still, features of the world do not *determine* grammar. In this sense, grammar is 'autonomous.' But grammars make possible the identification of certain features of the world. For example, having learned the names of trees, by learning the rules for applying these names correctly, an undifferentiated forest springs to life as a complex pattern of different species. (See for example PI §§371 and 373.)

We put the main point of Wittgenstein's insistence on the autonomy of grammar thus: we do not – indeed cannot – justify a grammatical rule by pointing to a matter of fact, or state of affairs in the world. But here some caution is warranted. For we can justify a grammatical rule in so far as it reflects or is expressed in a community practice to which the rule-user belongs. For example, 'Red is a color' does not express some super-fact about a particular hue. 'Red is a color' expresses a *grammatical* rule, indicating the 'station in language' where the word 'red' is to go.

How many colors are there in the spectrum? We all agree that there are seven, represented in the acronym VIBGYOR. However, examining the spectrum cast by a prism and paying attention to the perceived difference between hues, we can easily see that there are six colors. Newton, as much an alchemist and magician as physicist, decided that the mystical number '7' better fitted such a God-given array as the colors. So he inserted 'indigo' between blue and violet. The grammar of color words is, to that extent, autonomous.

Rules and rule-following: the *Tractatus,* the *Investigations* and psychology

Grammatical rules express the standards of correctness for how we speak, write and think about things and events. In the *Tractatus* Wittgenstein set tautologies and self-contradictions as representing the boundaries of sense. The former were true in every situation and the latter in none, so neither were meaningful, according to the criteria of the picture theory. Tautologies could be thought of as expressing the rules of logic, the grammar of the perfect language.

In the *Investigations* this idea is refined and given a practical edge. Let us look at an example. Someone says 'Nothing can be red and green all over at once.' What sort of statement is that? Must I do a survey of colored objects to ascertain its truth? The test, implicit throughout the *Investigations,* is to consider the negation of the proposition. Can we find any situation in which the proposition 'Something (this) is red and green all over at once' can be used in a meaningful way? If we cannot imagine any situation in which these words would have a use, then the correlative affirmative statement is a grammatical rule, expressing some aspect of the way the words 'red' and 'green' are to be used. One can bring up examples that seem to run counter to this analysis. Isn't a piece of shot silk something that is red and green all over at once? This example serves to open out the field of family resemblances in the uses of color concepts. It shows that 'red' and 'green' are sometime used for hues (or colors as seen) and sometimes for color dispositions (or how something can be seen in the appropriate circumstances). Thurber writes (in *The Thirteen Clocks*): 'Something scuttled across the floor that would have been purple had there been any light to see it by.'

Let us now turn to a psychological example in which someone claims: 'Every action is intended.' Should I construct and administer a survey to ascertain whether indeed every action is accompanied by an intention? Surely not, since this is the expression of a rule that fixes the use of the words 'action' and 'intention.' As a qualification, we are thinking here of 'action' as it is used in more formal, philosophical circles. The form of words 'Some actions are not intended' has no application. If someone does something unintentionally *it does not count as an action.*

This has great importance for experimental psychology. Perhaps there are research programs into topics that are described by what amount to grammatical rules. The result of such research is pre-ordained and the money and effort committed to the programs might have been saved if a little more attention had been given to the language.

Another way of expressing this aspect of the role of grammar appears in PI §371 ('*Essence* is expressed by grammar') and §373 ('Grammar tells us what kind of object anything is'). The attributes of a horse could be divided into those which it has as a member of the species (equine quadruped) and those it has as an individual (e.g. 14 hands high and a palomino). The former are involved in the conditions for the correct use of the word 'horse' and would be cited in a formal rule-expression of the grammar of 'horse.'

Glock (1996, p. 154) has a nice example to illustrate how deep this principle goes. It may seem of no importance at all that 'The horse were in the field' is wrong, while 'The horse was in the field' is correct. In preferring 'God the Father, God the Son and God the Holy Ghost was on Mount Sinai' to the 'were' construction, we are taking sides in a deep theological issue – the meaning of the Holy Trinity. Since, in the vast majority of cases, propositional rule-expressions represent the prevailing standards of correctness of practices, as those change so will the status of the propositions that express them. This point is made clearly in several places in Wittgenstein's last book, *On Certainty*, published in 1972. For example, in that book Wittgenstein remarks rhetorically 'Is it that rule and empirical proposition merge into one another?' (Wittgenstein, 1972, §309). And in §321 of the same work he says: 'Any empirical proposition can be transformed into a postulate – and then becomes a norm of description.'

Conclusions: rules in psychology – 'psycho-logic' and computational models

The accent on rules as expressions of standards of correctness for customs and practices leads from causal-based psychologies to the discursive paradigm. Wittgenstein's influence has a positive side in qualified support of the methodology of 'psycho-logic' (Smedslund, 1988) and a negative side in the criticisms of computational models in cognitive psychology.

Despite its flaws, Jan Smedlund's (1988) program for the establishment of the conceptual relations immanent in the practices of a culture involves explicitly formulating such propositions as 'Every action is associated with an intention.' If this proposition expresses a grammatical rule, then the concepts of 'action' and 'intention' are internally related. This means that the concepts mutually determine meanings; that is, the uses of the words 'action' and 'intention' are necessarily connected. Consequently, there is no sense to be made of an empirical study of actions to see if they are accompanied by intentions. Something like the discipline of 'psycho-logic,' exploring conceptual relations among psychologically significant concepts, *must* be an essential component of all psychological research programs. For example, there are some necessary conceptual associations of the uses of the word 'embarrassment' that define the space in which empirical studies of this emotion should be set (Parrott and Harré, 1991). In the next chapter, in which we lay out the main features of Wittgenstein's 'method,' we will look more systematically at the role of linguistic analysis in the preparations for the empirical aspects of psychological research.

A few years ago there was great enthusiasm for the idea of computational models in psychology. The principle was simple: the rules of cognitive, social and other forms of orderly behavior are internalized as brain states. The source of this model of cognition was the running of programs on computers. Such programs consist of a set of rules of computation, each rule having a specific representation in the registers of the machine as a binary sequence. This was one aspect of the notorious conception of the mind as a loose cluster of representations. As Winograd and Flores (1986) have shown, the limits of this program soon became apparent.

Does this mean the end of the 'rule model' of cognition? Not at all. Wittgenstein is not arguing for the reality of a realm of hypothetical rules. On the contrary, the thrust of his argument is always towards the principle that, for the most part, the norms of a human practice are immanent in the practice itself. In so far as we make ourselves aware of the normative character of many of the performances in which we engage, we can express our intuitions in propositions. But this is secondary. The norms of most practices have their primary expression in the practice itself. This point has been made particularly clearly by the ethnomethodologists, led by Garfinkel (1967). Conformity to a norm is a matter of the shaping of action by the immediate context. Propositionally, expressed rules may have a role in giving justificatory accounts of what one has done. They rarely play a role in the genesis of the action. Even when one is following an explicitly formulated instruction there are innumerable contextual features that determine how the instruction is applied on this or that occasion.

Learning point: agreement and grammars

1. *Agreement*: Orderly life requires agreement. Agreement in what?

    (a) Agreement in rules or customs.
    (b) Only if we have that kind of agreement can we consider the truth or falsity of alleged matters of fact.
    (c) However, unless we agree on some very general matters of fact we could not have a system of customs or rules (e.g. the customs of the education system were once related to the empirical proposition 'education damages the health of women').

2. *Systems*

    (a) A relatively coherent system of rules is a *grammar*.
    (b) Wittgenstein includes all sorts of rules expressing all sorts of customs and so on in 'grammar.' For example, compare 'The horses was in the field' with 'God the Father, God the Son and God the Holy Ghost was on Mt Sinai.' (Theology of the Trinity.)

3. *Autonomy of grammar*

    (a) Rules are not descriptions of, or ultimately grounded in, empirical facts.
    (b) The status of a rule may change.

4. *Identifying a rule of grammar*

   (a) The negation has no application.
   (b) Testing with exceptions can lead to opening up of the field of family resemblances (e.g. colors as hues and as dispositions probes the status of 'nothing can be red and green all over at once').

5. *Grammar expresses essences.* Essence expresses what it is to count as an 'X.' Take for example 'horse.'

   (a) It is an 'equine quadruped' (specifies type).
   (b) It is a '14 hands high palomino' (describes a particular).

Further reading

Baker, G.P. and Hacker, P.M.S. (1984), *Scepticism, Rules, and Language.* Oxford: Blackwell.

Glock, H.-G. (1996), *A Wittgenstein Dictionary*. Oxford: Blackwell. (Specifically pp. 323–9.)

Schulte, J. (1993), *Experience and Expression*. Oxford: Clarendon Press. (Specifically pp. 115–19.)

7 Wittgenstein's method

Philosophical Investigations §§89-133

> We predicate of the thing what lies in the method of representing it. Impressed by the possibility of a comparison, we think we are perceiving a state of affairs of the highest generality.
>
> Wittgenstein, *Philosophical Investigations*, §104

> Wittgenstein distinguished sharply between conceptual, philosophical investigations and empirical, scientific ones. Conceptual investigation is logically prior to empirical theory building, and no factual discoveries as to what is signified by a given concept can have bearing on the philosophical clarification of that concept.
>
> Baker and Hacker (1982), p. 228

Topics introduced: conceptual (philosophical) versus empirical problems; the mind–body problem; conceptual confusion in psychology; regions of language; features of philosophical problems; philosophical therapy; faulty linguistic analogies; surface and depth grammar; memory 'stores'; reification; seeing conceptual connections; defining versus perspicuous representation

The present chapter is pivotal to our approach throughout the remainder of the book for two primary reasons, both of which have been hinted at in previous chapters. First, it provides a framework for psychologists to understand what Wittgenstein is aiming at in his investigations into the workings of psychological concepts. Second, it serves to inform psychologists how his method of conceptual investigation is relevant to empirical research and theorizing in psychology.

Our goals are to explore those aspects of Wittgenstein's method that are most relevant to empirical psychological investigations and the research programs of which they are a part. Others have made their own abstractions from Wittgenstein's writings, for example literary theorists (Perloff, 1996). We hope that the third part of the book, for which this chapter serves as a preliminary step, will provide what is needed for psychologists to recognize the import of Wittgenstein's form of investigation and its impetus.

Wittgenstein's later philosophical method – or cluster of methods – was developed in the interests of the resolution of *philosophical* problems. We must show how psychology, in its various attempts to attain the status of a science, has run into a wide variety of such problems which have, here and there, stood in the way of the development of a coherent scientific psychology. (This has been done before *many* times.) Before turning to the remarks in the *Investigations* that comprise Wittgenstein's mature explication of his method and its impetus, we need to provide some background to support this intuition.

The persistence of conceptual problems in scientific psychology

Let us start by looking at Wittgenstein's most famous remark on psychology that happens to be located on the last page of the *Investigations*, which we encountered previously at the top of Chapter 1. It begins: 'The confusion and barrenness of psychology is not to be explained by calling it a "young science"; its state is not comparable with that of physics, for instance, in its beginnings' (PI II, xiv, p. 232). Wittgenstein then compares psychology with 'certain branches of mathematics' – in particular set theory – and adds that while 'in psychology there are experimental methods and *conceptual confusion*,' branches of mathematics such as set theory are characterized by 'conceptual confusion and methods of proof.' Then he suggests that the experimental method in psychology cannot provide the means for psychologists to solve the fundamental problems of their discipline: 'The existence of the experimental method makes us think we have the means of solving the problems which trouble us; though problem and method pass one another by.' In the same way, using the techniques of mathematical proof cannot solve the fundamental problems of mathematics. In both cases, we must turn back to a deep and sustained examination of the conceptual basis of each discipline.

As with so many of Wittgenstein's remarks, there is more going on here than meets the eye. To begin with, we do not want to assume that Wittgenstein is expressing a general contempt for the idea of psychology as a science. Nor should we be misled into thinking his observations have become irrelevant with the onset of the cognitive revolution and advances in research methodologies, even though Wittgenstein's specific target is, by today's standards, antiquated.

Peter Hacker (1996) has traced the impetus for this remark to a chapter in Köhler's (1929/1947) *Gestalt Psychology*, entitled 'Psychology as a Young Science.' There Köhler compares the scientific psychology of his time with physics in its youth. He presumes that the parallel makes sense because the early physicists struggled to accomplish a transition from direct, qualitative measurement to more indirect, quantitative measurement of the phenomena of physics, the properties of material bodies. For example, while early physicists measured thermal properties of objects through direct, qualitative observation (e.g. simply feeling the object undergoing temperature change and reporting perceived changes in warmth or coldness), over centuries these rather unsophisticated methods were gradually replaced by increasingly sophisticated procedures involving the use of new devices to measure *quantitative* changes in temperature. Although these newer forms of measurement were comparatively indirect – employing instruments for measurement instead of the senses – they were more precise and served to expedite the establishment of functional laws (see Hacker, 1996, pp. 401–2).

At the same time the *concept* of 'temperature' underwent radical change within the discipline of physics. From meaning roughly how something felt temperature-wise, it was transformed into a name for one of the many forms that energy takes in the material world. Of course, with respect to the transition from qualitative to quantitative procedures and measurements, not all branches of the physical sciences proceeded at the same pace.

Köhler thought early psychologists, such as Fechner, had gone too far, too fast, with quantitative measurement. The experiments on sensation by Fechner and his followers did not involve qualitative descriptions of sensations. Experimental subjects were limited to what were thought to be unambiguous 'yes–no' type responses – for example, to judgments of weight increase – which were recorded and ultimately used to define a quantitative function linking the response series to the stimulus series (see Danziger, 1990, p. 138). Köhler thought this move to eliminate qualitative descriptions of sensations begged the question as to *what was being measured in the first place*. Fechner and his followers assumed the sensations they were measuring constituted 'psychological atoms or elements that could be incrementally added if they were of the same kind' (ibid.). Thus, 'thousands of quantitative psycho physical experiments were made almost in vain. No one knew precisely what he was measuring' (Köhler, 1929/1947, p. 44).

Köhler criticized the early behaviorists in much the same way. They had jumped the gun by devoting themselves to quantitative measurements of the organism's responses, leaving the project of making qualitative distinctions between *forms* of response up in the air. So Köhler held that psychology had yet to complete the fundamental work of direct, qualitative description of the very phenomena being studied. Psychologists had to admit the time was not right for their discipline to imitate the physical sciences in their mature form. Rather, psychology should try to emulate the physical sciences *in their immature form*. 'Otherwise we should behave like boys who try to copy the imposing manners of full-grown men without understanding their *raison d'être*, also without seeing that intermediate phases of development cannot be skipped' (Köhler, 1929/1947, p. 42). We hasten to emphasize that Köhler's caveat does not amount to his rejecting the idea that psychology might eventually achieve the status of the physical sciences in their maturity. He maintained that most psychological research *could be* indirect and quantitative – but only after psychology had amassed a wealth of direct and qualitative data.

Now it is to *this* idea that Wittgenstein objects in the final remark of the *Investigations*. Physicists have found their own way of identifying the phenomena that constitute the material world. These phenomena exist independently of human perceptual capacities, which have given way to the reactions of instruments and the properties of models, imagined mechanisms by which phenomena are brought into being and related to one another. The situation is rich in irony. Psychologists, purporting to have eliminated 'philosophy' from their discipline, have taken for granted a grossly distorted picture of the physical sciences, derived from the philosophical doctrines of positivism. In very brief form, we have set out a more realistic account to the methods of the physical sciences in Chapter 1. The realities of the methods of the physical sciences should be kept in mind as we assess the claims of past and present 'psychologies' to have successfully emulated them. The achievement of quantitative measures of properties of material systems is neither here nor there as a hallmark of the physical sciences.

At issue here is the idea that psychology will achieve a status on a par with the physical sciences only when solid correlations can be established between the qualitative observations emphasized by Köhler and the psychological events (or brain states and processes) that might be measured through indirect means (e.g. today's fMRI). Here is the problem. *We must use our ordinary psychological vocabulary to make qualitative observations.* 'All research participants reported feeling fearful immediately subsequent to perceiving the stimulus.' Now suppose stimuli that cause fear are studied qualitatively to the point where psychologists feel the need to embark on a research program to correlate the psychological phenomenon of fear with brain states and processes. What happens to our ordinary psychological vocabulary pertaining to fear when specific forms of brain activity are correlated with what has been observed qualitatively? Can it be dropped in favor of the neuropsychologist's vocabulary, which is used to describe the correlated brain activity? A situation of this kind poses no problem for a branch of physics like thermodynamics, since words such as 'hot' and 'cold' can be easily replaced with temperature concepts for the purposes of physics to which they bear only a historical relation. But to what extent can this be done with psychological concepts for the purposes of psychology?

We should not forget that humans do not just fear. They fear the bear that suddenly emerges from the forest. They fear losing their job. They fear that their son or daughter will be killed by a drunk driver. They fear that they will be lonely in their golden years, and so on. Adjacent to this cluster of concepts are many others, such as *Angst*, anxiety, dread, horror, terror and so on. Are we to assume neurophysiological correlates will be established for all these forms of fear and their degrees, in addition to all the other related psychological states, dispositions and what have you that our everyday psychological vocabulary expresses and describes so well? And from such a dizzying number of correlations, what sort of specialized vocabulary for the science of psychology might be constructed?

As we pointed out in the second part of Chapter 3, a vocabulary purporting to do this job has already been proposed in the guise of so-called 'eliminative materialism' (Churchland, 1981). It is so obviously a failure that it can serve as a warning to anyone who sets out down that road of converting our ordinary vocabulary to a vocabulary fitted for science. Considerable difficulties confront the very idea of constructing such a vocabulary, given the diversity and subtlety of the psychological phenomena that would need to be distinguished and unambiguously described. At the same time, there is the problem of how we could abandon our ordinary psychological vocabulary completely and still construct sentences describing the phenomena to be investigated and explained by indirect means. From where would we begin without our ordinary psychological vocabulary? Moreover, in order to identify the relevant neurophysiological states and processes from the myriad happenings in the human brain, we need to be able to identify the psychological phenomena independently.

The immediately foregoing is simply a requirement for proper scientific practice. Similarly, it is a mainstay of the scientific enterprise that our findings – in this case, correlations between qualitative observations and neurophysiological states and/or processes – are always provisional. But for reasons already given, the extent to which our findings in psychology are provisional is reflected by our psychological vocabulary! Remembering the discussion of skills in Chapter 5, where we considered Wittgenstein's remarks on reading in the *Investigations*, it is readily apparent that our psychological vocabulary pertaining to reading is extraordinarily rich and consists of a field of uses displaying various family resemblances. It is one thing to use fMRI to identify areas of the brain that 'light up' when a person is reading. It is quite another to identify which areas of the brain *always* light up when a person 'comprehends' what is read, is 'bored' by what they are reading, derives 'a spiritual experience' from a text, finds the text 'poorly written,' and so on. Even if we grant that, in principle, fMRI can correlate such experiences with specific brain states, it does not seem possible that a scientist will ever be able to look at an fMRI image and determine, for example, 'this person is reading, but they find what they are reading to be boring, poorly written and barely understandable' without having *independent* criteria for boredom, bad writing and understanding of a text. Let us reiterate that this is not a criticism of neuropsychology. It is a reminder of the linguistic conditions under which neuropsychology is possible.

To this point we have not addressed the final paragraph of Wittgenstein's remark at PI II, xiv, p. 232. There Wittgenstein says that while 'an investigation is possible in connexion with mathematics which is entirely analogous to our investigation of psychology,' such an investigation is not quite a mathematical nor a psychological investigation. (The investigation 'will *not* contain calculations,' for example.) He concludes by adding that the investigation 'might deserve the name of an investigation of the "foundations of mathematics".' What Wittgenstein seems to be saying here is that Köhler was wrong to blame the difficulties in psychology on its not having started at the same point as the physical sciences – with direct, qualitative descriptions. Psychology in its present state is better compared with investigations into the foundations of mathematics toward the latter part of the nineteenth and early twentieth centuries. What distinguishes investigations into the foundations of mathematics from early physics is that in the former case, the problems and issues were not framed in terms of adequate instruments and the concepts that would accompany new measuring techniques. Rather, the problems in psychology compare well with the problems that beset considerations of the foundations of mathematics in that they did and do stem from *conceptual confusion*. In order to address conceptual problems we do not need new instruments and new vocabularies. We need a way to identify the source of confusion and to relieve it. For example, the concept of 'intelligence,' as it appears in the testing of human abilities, is mistakenly treated as if it parallels a concept like 'valency' in chemistry, an unobservable property of the mind that explains the levels of problem-solving skill displayed by different people.

Besides our previous allusions to common misunderstandings of the line of argument of the passages in question (PI II, xiv, p. 232), we should add that Wittgenstein *never* denied that good work might be done correlating neurophysiological events with behavior and experience, or that what we now call neuroscience is somehow misguided or doomed to fail. As Hacker (1996, p. 404) puts it:

> On the contrary, it was at least an indirect part of [Wittgenstein's] aim to clear away the conceptual confusions that impede serious advances in these domains. For a

multitude of false pictures of the mental, misconceptions of the 'inner' and of its relations to the 'outer', misunderstandings of the very concepts that are being deployed in such investigations, is a primary cause of the poverty of empirical psychology. Clarification of the relevant psychological concepts is typically a prerequisite for posing fruitful questions amenable to experimental investigation.

If these 'false pictures' underlie so many of our problems in psychology and impede the discipline's progress, and if clarification of our psychological concepts promises to enable psychologists to pose the right questions to guide their research, questions must be raised as to how they might go about clarifying relevant concepts. We will explore Wittgenstein's own method of clarification, which we think is preeminently fit for the task. But first we need to address a more fundamental question. How can psychologists *learn to recognize* when they are under the spell of the false pictures, misconceptions and misunderstandings mentioned by Hacker above and how can they identify the *origins* of their conceptual problems so as to avoid them in the first place?

'Philosophical' problems

It is common knowledge that, as a prerequisite to recovering from their addiction, alcoholics must first acknowledge they have a problem with alcohol. Oftentimes the suggestion that there is a problem will be met with resistance. 'I am only a social drinker' or 'I can give up vodka martinis at breakfast anytime.' In some respects the analogy holds with psychologists who resist the suggestion that many problems in their research and theorizing are not empirical, but philosophical.

One reason for this is that the vast majority of psychologists do not understand the nature and origin of philosophical problems because they have not been trained to attend critically to the *concepts* with which they describe phenomena and formulate their problems. This is not to say that most psychologists are entirely ignorant of philosophy and are incapable of philosophical reasoning. So why the neglect?

One possibility is that psychologists hang on to certain aspects of the positivistic account of science when, unbeknownst to them, it has largely been abandoned by other scientific disciplines. In the *Tractatus* Wittgenstein offers a wholly positivistic account of meaning in which the meanings of words derive from the objects to which the words refer. Thanks to the insights of the later Wittgenstein and others, we now see this account as thoroughly misleading and inadequate. In order to be able to pick out the phenomena to which our vocabulary refers we must already have some idea as to what phenomena there are. Contrary to the strict empiricism of the positivistic point of view, we now see that although words do not create the world, what is available to us as phenomena is in part determined by the conceptual systems embedded in our language. Learning to see, feel, hear, touch and so on is all one with learning to talk, to manipulate and so on.

Physics never has been independent of philosophical – that is, conceptual – problems. For example, the distinction between average and instantaneous velocity, fundamental to the application of the calculus to kinematics, took two centuries to become well established and generally understood. 'Speed' is a very complex family of concepts, which must be disentangled and their interrelationships clarified. Similarly, the problem of teasing out 'energy' and 'momentum' as distinct physical properties from the generic concept of 'quantity of motion' occupied the subtlest scientific minds for two centuries. Furthermore, the era of philosophical work in physics is never over. For instance, the influence of the misleading picture of electrons as minute 'things' – that is, the influence of the analogy between the grammar of 'electron' and that of a typical thing-word, say 'bullet' – can be seen still to impede clear thinking in subatomic physics.

As a result of so much emphasis on a certain (distorted) picture of science during their training, psychologists often take it for granted that all or the great majority of problems encountered during the planning, carrying out and reporting of research can be solved through more research in the empiricist tradition. Meaning is presumed to have been taken care of by the positivistic principle of giving an 'operational definition.' This usually results in the selection of one use from a field of family resemblances, thus distorting the character of the phenomena under study. This leads to a neglect of the fundamental work of conceptual clarification, without which the empirical work can be rendered worthless. As we will see, even psychologists who appear to be quite philosophically inclined exhibit this mentality.

We do not deny that *certain kinds* of problems encountered during the course of empirical research can be solved through more research. For reasons already suggested, what we deny is that empirical research has any significant bearing on the elimination of false pictures, misconceptions and misunderstandings of psychological concepts that appear at every turn in psychology. It is therefore extremely important for psychologists to learn how to distinguish philosophical problems from empirical problems and to see that although these two kinds of problems *appear* similar, their origins (and significance) are quite different.

An illustration

We can illustrate the distinction between philosophical and empirical problems with a famous problem that is, to the embarrassment of psychology, still visible within the discipline: the problem of the interaction of mind and body. How can thinking of some action and deciding to carry it out bring about the processes in nerves and muscles that eventuate in a bodily movement? Any psychologist worthy of the label has heard of the 'mind–body problem.' It is a problem that has found no definitive solution over many centuries. It seems to arise anytime we ponder such questions as: 'When I decide to turn on a light, how can a mental process move my arm to reach for the light switch?' Questions of this sort imply a distinction between two realms. It appears there must be some unseen entity (the mind), states of which cause the material body to move purposefully. Instead of trying to develop an experimental program to deal with the array of similar problems in psychology, let us ask about the reference of words like 'belief,' 'intention' and so on. To what do they refer? Are their referents attributes of 'the mind'?

No one imagines that there is an experimental program explicitly aimed at solving the mind–body problem. But there are plenty of opinions out there, often masked as 'theories,' regarding its resolution. What we want to point out, however, are the mistakes in thinking that bring about the problem in the first place – not to mention its resolutions. Let us begin with the 'traditional' view, often put implicitly, that the mind is an immaterial substance and words like 'belief' refer to certain of its properties. This view distorts our understanding of the grammar of words like 'believe,' 'intend,' 'act,' 'try' and so on. We can escape from the thrall of the picture by a close examination of the actual uses of the key words in our list having to do with 'what the mind does.' It soon becomes clear that these words are not used to ascribe properties to an immaterial substance, but to ascribe to persons dispositions to act in certain ways. But here is a key point. *To treat these words as referring to brain states and processes is equally mistaken.* The word 'belief' is not a name for a state of any kind.

Instead of abandoning the distinction between mind and body, psychologists of various sorts and those outside of psychology, imagining themselves to be philosophers worthy of the task (e.g. Chomsky), have tried to make sense of this distinction in a variety of ways. As is well known, most American behaviorists (e.g. Watson) opted to reject the 'mind' component of the distinction altogether in favor of describing and predicting behavior only. For the most part, they abandoned (and at times ridiculed) the use of mental predicates in their descriptions of behavior, favoring the use of verbs pertaining to overt action. Yet the basis of the behaviorist point of view was that very distinction.

There were exceptions to the rejection of the 'mental' side from science. For instance, the behaviorist clinician Wolpe (1978) proposed that 'thought' obeys the same laws as those governing the mechanisms of motor action. While appearing to legitimize the use of certain mental predicates, this move was supposed to eliminate the need to locate thought in a realm independent of movement. On this view, we are mistaken to think that the mental predicates of our ordinary language, when used in concert with verbs of overt action, refer to anything other than the realm of the physical.

Wolpe's approach to the mind–body problem lends support to Rachlin's (1992, p. 1374) assertion that the behaviorists shared with today's cognitive scientists a deep concern with explaining the internal, efficient causes of behavior. The difference is that all cognitive scientists make free and easy use of mental predicates in their search for cognitive processes. But what specifically do the words that comprise our mental vocabulary (e.g. 'will,' 'intention,' 'thought') refer to and describe? There are numerous explanatory options. Maybe the words that comprise our ordinary mental vocabulary refer to nothing other than 'emergent properties' of active brain states.

We said it is important for psychologists not only to identify and acknowledge problems in their thinking, but to identify certain of those problems *as philosophical*, that is, *involving conceptual confusions* of various sorts. (To an extent, Wittgenstein never abandoned the idea of philosophy as 'critique of language.') Most philosophers and many psychologists now acknowledge that the mind–body problem is such a problem, in large part because there does not appear to be any way experimentation will clear it up (although empirical research is often cited to lend support to someone's advocacy of a 'solution' to the problem). So again, there are instances where psychologists have no trouble at all recognizing problems in their thinking as philosophical problems. But we would be mistaken to think that the process of identifying philosophical problems in psychology rests on the single criterion that experimentation cannot help us with them. Philosophical problems *are* conceptual problems. (We hope that so much will become evident below and in coming chapters.) How do we tackle these problems? Here is a sketch by Wittgenstein of what is involved.

> We feel as if we had to *penetrate* phenomena: our investigation, however, is directed not towards phenomena, but, as one might say, towards the *'possibilities'* of phenomena. We remind ourselves, that is to say, of the *kind of statement* that we make about phenomena ... Our investigation is therefore a grammatical one. Such an investigation sheds light on our problem by clearing misunderstandings away. Misunderstandings concerning the use of words, caused, among other things, by certain analogies between the forms of expression in different regions of language. – Some of them can be removed by substituting one form of expression for another; this may be called an 'analysis' of our forms of expression, for the process is sometimes like one of taking a thing apart.
>
> (PI, §90)

If Wittgenstein is correct, how do we know when the problem we face is 'conceptual'?

Four features of philosophical problems in psychology

Below we describe four characteristics of philosophical problems and their implications for psychology. They are 'intractability,' 'resistance,' 'faulty linguistic analogies' and 'connecting what should be disconnected' (or the converse, 'disconnecting what should be connected'). Our descriptions, aided by some insights from Wittgenstein, also serve to outline ways in which psychologists become captured in the web of a philosophical problem without knowing it.

Intractability

The mind–body problem and its various associated conundrums seem to be intractable. The best minds have failed to solve them. In a manuscript constructed by Wittgenstein in 1933 (known as the 'Big Typescript'), Wittgenstein set down a number of remarks on the nature of philosophical problems that would later make their way into the *Investigations*. These are to be found in a 'chapter' entitled 'Philosophie,' published in the book *Philosophical Occasions* (Wittgenstein, 1993). Among the remarks that did not make their way into the *Investigations* is one in which Wittgenstein (1993) says that the problems of philosophy, 'so tough and seemingly intractable,' are 'connected with the oldest habits, i.e., with the oldest images that are engraved into our language itself' (§90, pp. 183, 185). But despite their apparent intractability, theoretically inclined psychologists continue to believe such problems need to be solved in order for the business of psychology to proceed.

Alternatively, we may acknowledge the problem and do nothing about it, believing that when 'all the research is in' the problem will simply disappear. This seems to be Howard Gardner's (1985) view. He thinks cognitive science 'holds the key' to 'whether questions that intrigued our philosophical ancestors can be decisively answered, instructively reformulated, or permanently scuttled' (Gardner, 1985, p. 6). Moreover, since philosophy is 'external' to empirical psychology and since it is thought that certain philosophical questions will be answered by science, philosophers interested in cognitive science 'may ultimately recede from the scene' (ibid., p. 389).

Perhaps Gardner is right that cognitive science might enable us to reformulate age-old philosophical questions. But will cognitive science *answer* age-old philosophical questions – or even new philosophical questions? To think that science has this capability betrays a misunderstanding of the nature of philosophical questions. On Wittgenstein's view, the problems that result from taking philosophical questions as if they were like scientific questions arise from our uses of language, not lacunae in our knowledge of the world. The question 'How does a mental decision to shout act on the material lungs and vocal cords?' sounds like the scientific question 'How does an antigen act on a bacterium?' The damage has already been done when we frame the psychological question about decisions and actions in terms of the mind–body distinction.

Philosophical problems are not solvable because their status *qua* problems is owed to misunderstandings about *the ways we use our language*. Wittgenstein's method of philosophical analysis shows that these long-running conundrums are not 'problems' at all. The very idea of a 'problem' suggests that somewhere, if only we could find it, there is a 'solution.' Once we become clear on how our language works we can identify where we went wrong by following the false grammatical analogy that led to the illusion of a problem. In this way we can avoid the 'problem' altogether. Rather than a solution, we arrive at an *informed perspective* on how we tend to use language related to topics of interest within which there is no problem and therefore no place for attempts to find a solution. There is no 'solution' to the mind–body problem.

As we will see in more detail below and in subsequent chapters, Wittgenstein believes many of our philosophical problems originate in 'misleading analogies' in our uses of words. By uncovering these analogies we reveal how we conceived the problem in terms of the question of how two disparate 'substances' can interact. That is, we explore the grammar of words related to our problem by conducting a grammatical investigation. As we have seen, Wittgenstein's use of 'grammar' is rather broader than the customary use. It is important to reiterate that 'grammar' in Wittgenstein's writings refers not only to our actual uses of words, but also to *possible* uses of words as well. Needless to say, by analyzing our real and possible uses of words we will, at times, consider *impossible* uses. This is why Hilmy (1987, p. 129) says 'grammar, in that it is the ledger of our actual linguistic transactions, is, as it were, the ledger of the sorts of moves that are (can be) and are not (cannot be) made in a given "language game".' 'Grammar' refers not only to the *ledger of our linguistic practices* but also to the *ledger of meaningful actions of every kind* – facial expressions people make in various circumstances, modes of dress, ways of playing games, assembling furniture, worshipping God, gardening, preparing food and so on.

Since philosophical problems arise from misunderstanding of our uses of words and overlooking their possibilities of use, we go about solving a particular acknowledged problem by *identifying the grammatical analogy or analogies that led to our using words in the way that spawned the problem*. To return briefly to the 'problem' sketched above, we must examine the grammatical analogy that led to many generations of psychologists using the word 'mind' as if it referred to an immaterial substance. The origin of the illusion that there is a mind–body *problem* is rooted in a misleading analogy between our uses of the words 'mind' and 'body.' Clearly, our bodies are material. The problem arises in our (at least) implicit conception of the mind as an immaterial substance, the mental counterpart of the body as a material substance. So the mind–body problem manifests itself in our wondering how something immaterial can interact – indeed bring about – the movements of our material bodies. Neither attempts to reduce bodies to minds, as the idealists proposed, nor attempts to reduce the mind to the body as materialists have tried to do will work. Both projects presuppose the *meaningfulness* of the distinction.

Intractability is a sure sign that we have been going on using words in a certain taken-for-granted way and that this is what keeps the problem alive. Dissolving it consists in identifying the false grammatical analogies that have led to the uses that underlie the apparently intractable problem.

Resistance

According to Wittgenstein, a key feature of philosophical problems is that they take an emotional toll on us. Philosophical problems irritate us like a persistent itch or a personality conflict with a colleague. In the 1933 chapter 'Philosophie,' Wittgenstein (1993) compares his own philosophical efforts to the resolution of psychological problems through psychoanalysis. Although it is problematic to draw a line between intellectual and emotional problems in philosophy and psychoanalysis, Wittgenstein thought the difficulty in resolving philosophical and psychological problems was *primarily emotional* (Stern, 1995, p. 25). Also – and as mentioned previously – just as the clinician's efforts will be met by the patient's resistance, efforts to resolve philosophical problems will be met with resistance, much as alcoholics will resist acknowledging their drinking as a problem.

To this extent, Wittgenstein's is a method of *philosophical therapy*. For Wittgenstein, the goal of philosophical therapy is a kind of peace of mind. While most psychologists are not emotionally troubled by living with confusions of which they are hardly aware, the persistence of positivistic presuppositions in psychology, when every other science has all but abandoned them, might be seen as a form of resistance.

It is hard to get someone to adopt a wholly new way of looking at things. For example, it has been very difficult to get people to think of the mind as a process rather than as a substance. 'Thinking,' 'deciding,' 'classifying' sound well enough, but 'emoting' seems out of place as a word in this list. Part of the problem is that the grammar of 'mind' and what we might call the 'substance reading' of grammar pertaining to mind is tied in with a huge array of other concepts, beliefs and practices. For example, the Christian religion is deeply imbued with substance-like accounts of the soul. Soul and mind have always been related, but were welded into one by Descartes in the seventeenth century. This is a massive tradition to set aside, even for those who are now outside the religious community altogether.

Faulty linguistic analogies

We have already seen that some psychologists (e.g. Gardner, 1985) think it possible that philosophical questions on matters psychological can be answered through scientific investigation. We suggested that this view betrays a misunderstanding of the nature of conceptual (philosophical) questions. But it is also owing to our thinking that statements of such problems may look rather like statements of empirical or factual (scientific) problems, yet another misleading grammatical analogy. A question such as 'How is it possible to know what another person is thinking or feeling?' looks like 'How is it possible to know when a cake is baked?' (Here is an example of similarity in 'surface grammar,' a topic we will address below.) The differences between these sentences are prone to be obscured by assumed (but faulty) grammatical analogies between them. Because both questions are about possible knowledge, we might be led to believe that knowledge in both cases could be gained through hands-on investigation. We thus treat the grammars of these two questions as the same. But while we can be quite confident that empirical research will reveal criteria for establishing when a cake is baked (e.g. by investigating how well the ingredients have combined by seeing whether a skewer comes out clean), there are no empirical methods *to establish criteria* for knowing what another person is thinking or feeling. This does not mean that we do not frequently know what someone else is feeling, but there is no technique comparable to the use of the skewer.

Wittgenstein's way of identifying these faulty linguistic analogies is to explore the grammar of words involved in the analogies. We want to know why these two questions (and their answers) appear the same, yet are different. Why is one question philosophical while the other is not?

At this point we need to address Wittgenstein's (PI §664) distinction between a sentence's surface grammar and its depth grammar. This distinction, which refers to how sentences are constructed, is useful as a way of specifying one of the reasons why we tend not to recognize grammatical differences in linguistic expressions and are thus led to treat two very different kinds of questions (or statements) in the same way. One purpose of doing philosophy Wittgenstein's way is to explore the *philosophical implications* of a sentence's surface grammar which, although remaining the same, might depend on different depth grammars when it is applied in different contexts and for different purposes. For example, if we hear a piano being tuned while we are simultaneously in pain, we may say, 'It'll soon stop.' Obviously, what we mean by this expression depends on whether we are referring to our pain or to the piano. But, asks Wittgenstein (PI §666), 'what does this difference consist in?' Characteristically, he does not answer this question for us. He leaves it to us to find out these differences for ourselves.

For starters, we may compare the possibility of someone saying, 'Will you please stop tuning the piano?' with someone saying, 'Will you please stop being in pain?' Why would someone balk at saying the latter sentence? We can say, 'Oh come on! Quit crying!' But we hardly expect a person to stop their pain in response to such comments, which amount to our asking the person to tolerate or 'handle' their pain better. The pain-version of 'It'll soon stop' carries with it implications that are quite different from the piano-version. Clearly, we have come full circle, back to our previous example of knowing someone else's feelings versus when a cake is baked, except in that case we have two sentences with similar surface grammars that, lacking vigilance as to the workings of language, we may treat as having similar depth grammars. Psychologists consistently run into trouble when they fail to recognize the variety of possible depth grammars of a single expression or fail to recognize the different depth grammars of two or more sentences that have the same or similar surface grammars. There are two main ways that grammatical analogies can mislead us: suggesting connections where there are none and disconnecting concepts that should be connected.

Connecting what should be disconnected

There are plenty of grammatical analogies that criss-cross our language. Here is an example from contemporary work in the field of the psychology of memory. In presenting what we can remember to ourselves and others we tend to itemize recollections into 'memories.' To be able to present a recollection, it is presumed that there must a corresponding item in the mind, perhaps represented in some neural state at a certain location in the brain. Most of the time we are not remembering any particular item. 'Stores' are places where we keep things not in use at the moment. It seems natural to presume that there must be memory 'stores.' 'A memory' is a noun phrase, like 'an apple.' We may store the latter in the pantry. Surely we store the former in the pantry of the mind or brain? Theoretical work on neural nets and empirical work on the location of 'memories' discloses that, at best, the word 'store' is a *metaphor* that is exhausted in the apparently innocuous idea that somehow a person can, when called upon, picture or describe some past event, come up with a name, display competence in a mathematical procedure, and so on. In falling into the presumption that memories are entities we connect what should be disconnected. A grammatical analogy creeps in that must be resisted. Again, when it comes to memory, 'store' is simply a metaphor. We are tempted to think it is an actual *place* where memories reside! What justification do we have for giving in to this temptation? Well, of course, one justification is that damage to certain *areas* of the brain leads to memory loss or the inability to form new memories. But from this it does not follow that our brains have memory stores – in the sense of 'places.'

Here is another contemporary example. The use of new labels, which undoubtedly have correlates in our ordinary language and the vernacular of psychology, may display 'conceptual neglect,' 'conceptual limitation,' 'conceptual disconnection' and the like. For example, the mistake of reification in psychology may be regarded as a case where 'unwarranted connections' between concepts are made or assumed. We might think that 'anger,' 'grief,' 'anxiety' and so on are mental entities. This move privileges the noun form of this vocabulary while in fact there are only angry people, grieving families and anxious parents. The unwarranted connections here would be between the region or regions of language having to do with the grammar of entity-like beings, in contrast with the grammar of processes, such as 'being angry,' 'grieving' and 'being anxious.' Furthermore, the adverbial expressions refer to emotional experiences of people in specific circumstances. Without the person and his or her contexts of language use in the picture, it is impossible to grasp what is meant by this or that emotion expression.

Disconnecting what should be connected

In the context of analyzing the use of words referring to psychological phenomena, the notion of 'seeing connexions' (PI §122) reminds us that failing to notice connections between concepts referring to psychological phenomena leads to an incomplete picture of the *meanings* of those concepts, the contexts of their use, and the roles they play in the lives of humans (including psychologists). We will be reminded that a single concept does not stand alone, independent of other concepts, limited to just one use. (Note here the contrast with the *Tractatus*.) We can use the method of 'perspicuous representation' and attention to language-games to identify and label specific mistakes that place improper limitations on uses of psychological concepts.

Mistakes that come from not seeing connections may be identified as part of the overall ontology and metaphysics of mainstream experimental psychology, which presupposes that experimental control is essential to properly conducted experiments. We can see this in Schachter and Singer's (1962) famous experiment involving 'the creation of situations from which explanatory cognitions may be derived' (p. 382). Subjects injected with epinephrine and informed of its side-effects were considered to have an 'appropriate' explanation for their bodily state when they could offer 'an authoritative, unequivocal explanation' for that state, while those told they would have no side-effects from the injection were said to have 'no appropriate explanation' (Schachter and Singer, 1962, p. 383). But given their *prescription* of what counts as an appropriate explanation for a bodily state, it appears that these psychologists could not help but confirm the basic tenets of their cognition-arousal theory of emotion. Through something like conceptual limitation, emotion recognition is necessarily linked to recognition of a bodily state, while concepts used to express emotions – regardless of bodily states – are banished from the linguistic region of emotion concepts.

By this example we can also see that seeing connections is a *goal*. Establishing connections (or lack thereof) between concepts before undertaking empirical investigations into psychological phenomena helps psychologists avoid conceptual confusion in their planning of research and attempts to make sense of experimental results. Unwarranted analogies and metaphors used in the explanations of experimental results might also be brought into focus with an eye toward conceptual connectivity.

Relatedly, the polysemous meanings of words can be demonstrated through the use of intermediate cases in order to show that they are used by psychologists in convenient and restrictive ways. The tendency to 'legislate against' the uses of a word or words – exemplified in Schachter and Singer's (1962) experiment in addition to the popular survey studies in mainstream psychology – will be avoided.

Defining versus displaying concepts perspicuously

We might be tempted to believe that Wittgenstein's form of analysis will lead to 'a final analysis of our forms of language, and so a *single* completely resolved analysis of our forms of language' (PI §91). There is the danger of thinking that such an investigation, where 'we eliminate misunderstandings by making our expressions more exact,' will move us 'towards a particular state, a state of complete exactness; and as if this were the real goal of our investigation' (ibid.). This state is, of course, the kind of state Wittgenstein tried to achieve in the *Tractatus*. Also, it is reminiscent of the experimental psychologist's construction of operational definitions. Wittgenstein admits that the temptation to find a state of complete exactness

> finds expression in questions as to the *essence* of language, of propositions, of thought. – For if we too in these investigations are trying to understand the essence of language ... yet *this* is not what those questions have in view. For they see in the essence, not something that already lies open to view and that becomes surveyable by a rearrangement, but something that lies *beneath* the surface.
>
> (PI §92)

Fields of family resemblance can contract or expand as the cultural climate changes. For example, the once all-important concept of 'sin' has shrunk from its rich content to a mere synonym for bad behavior. (Who now can recite the lists of mortal and venial sins, or even knows the difference?) At the same time the semantic field of 'memory' and 'remembering' has expanded to include such refinements as 'implicit memory' and 'collective remembering.' We emphasize that Wittgenstein does not reject the latter form of expansion in principle. 'Such a reform for particular practical purposes, an improvement on our terminology designed to prevent misunderstandings in practice, is perfectly possible.' However, he qualifies this by adding: 'But these are not the cases we have to do with. The confusions which occupy us arise when language is like an engine idling, not when it is doing work' (PI §132).

Description of uses replaces abstraction of essences

Wittgenstein pursues the idea that the workings of ordinary language *can be described without theoretical preconceptions* – an idea that strongly implies he is promoting an impartial approach to the description of the 'rough ground' of language (PI §107). The *Tractatus* proceeded on the assumption that the smooth and ideal terrain of logic would reveal a formal unity of words such as 'sentence' and 'language.' The new descriptive method will show that these words (and others) do not have 'the formal unity that I had imagined' but are representative of a 'family of structures more or less related to one another' (PI §108). Wittgenstein's alternative to 'the *preconceived idea* of crystalline purity' of logical analysis is examination of the 'spatial and temporal phenomenon of language' rather than 'some non-spatial, non-temporal phantasm' (ibid.). Thus grammar is pitted against logic. In the following famous remark on his method, Wittgenstein makes it quite clear that his method of analysis is not aimed at discovering new truths and advancing theories. Rather, we may not advance any kind of theory [as an explanation of the actual uses of words]. There must not be anything hypothetical in our considerations. We must do away with all *explanation*, and description alone must take its place. And this description gets its light, that is to say its purpose, from the philosophical problems. These are, of course, not empirical problems; they are solved, rather, by looking into the workings of our language, and that in such a way as to make us recognize those workings: *in despite of* an urge to misunderstand them. The problems are solved, not by giving new information, but by arranging what we have always known ...

(PI §109)

What would such non-theorizing consist in? It would be an attempt to explain how words are used in terms of the hidden essences, the 'real meanings' that are presumed by those who try to establish unified and precise definitions. In Chapter 5 we saw the folly of this sort of premature attempt at precision in detail in the study of the skill of reading aloud from a text.

Description of the workings of language – or grammar, language-in-use – will assist philosophers and psychologists in overcoming certain habits of thought that militate against the development of sound scientific accounts of psychological phenomena. In preliminary conceptual investigations embarked upon to aid scientific research, nothing new is 'discovered' and so there is no need to advance theses or support hypotheses as in moving beyond scientific psychology to a study of the neurological tools with which we carry out our discursive activities. Everything we feel the need to know is open to view and the new method – a kind of arrangement – will remind us of what we already know and thus serve as a prophylaxis against conceptual confusion, wasted empirical endeavors, and faulty summaries of research results.

The method of perspicuous representation

The idea of a 'perspicuous representation' is crucial for understanding the characteristics and purposes of Wittgenstein's method and hints of a directive for psychologists as to how the method might be used in their research. Wittgenstein says:

a main source of our failure to understand is that we do not *command a clear view* of the use of our words. – Our grammar is lacking in this sort of perspicuity. A perspicuous representation produces just that understanding which consists in 'seeing connexions'. Hence the importance of finding and inventing *intermediate cases*.

(PI §122)

Then he adds: 'The concept of a perspicuous representation is of fundamental importance for us. It earmarks the form of account we give, the way we look at things' (ibid.). It seems that what Wittgenstein is getting at here is that in our efforts to represent the ways in which a particular concept is actually used – which may consist in showing examples of other words that occupy the region of language within which it works – it will sometimes be advantageous to compare its use with words of other regions of language. Indeed, it is difficult to imagine how a concept that is improperly used – as if it were used like words from another region of language – might be brought back to its proper 'place of use' without reference to at least two regions of language: one where the word 'belongs' and the one to which it has been improperly assigned. For example, psychologists have taken the word 'attitude' to refer to a persisting but hidden state of mind that causes a person to behave, talk and think in certain ways. It is still presumed by some psychologists that attitudes can be 'measured' by answers to questionnaires.

At this point we need to consider a problem, brought out for example by Lapierre's (1934) study of racial attitudes in the USA in the 1930s. Stumbling across the phenomenon by accident, he began a systematic study of how motel keepers treated Chinese couples, comparing what they did with what they said in answers to questionnaires as to their attitudes to accepting such couples in their hotels. There was no connection whatever between the answers to the questionnaires and the face-to-face behavior! The paradox is readily resolved by attention to 'grammar.' Attitudes are aspects of context-driven displays for a purpose at hand. We can display attitudes in what we say, in what we do and in many other ways. Traditional attitude studies made two conceptual errors. They failed to keep separate two domains of language: adjectives and nouns. The surface grammar of the word 'attitude' is noun-like, but when we come to describe its actual use it turns out to be adjectival, *qualifying what people do*. The second mistake was to assume that behind each of the many diverse uses of the word 'attitude' (and its synonyms) there must a common meaning, a linguistic essence. Putting these two mistakes together, we can slip into believing that there is a common cause, a hidden cognitive state, that causes our performances. No wonder Lapierre's study caused a stir!

As it stands, what we are proposing here is programmatic and the effectiveness of Wittgenstein's method as a form of analysis fundamental for the development of psychology as a genuine science has yet to be demonstrated. In addition, we have yet to answer questions such as how his form of analysis might dovetail with empirical psychology and how it differs from and might be preferred over other forms of conceptual analysis available to psychologists. But in closing the present chapter we want briefly to address the obvious question of whether the method might be too complex and unwieldy for the mainstream psychologist. Will mainstream psychologists be equipped with what it takes to perform such analyses – to trace connections and disconnections between regions of language in addition to seeing connections between concepts in the same regions of language? In another important remark for psychologists, Wittgenstein reminds us that his method only addresses that which is 'open to view' and as such, 'there is nothing to explain. For what is hidden is of no interest to us. One might also give the name "philosophy" to what is possible *before* all new discoveries and inventions' (PI §126).

Here we find a suggestion that there is a sense in which Wittgenstein's way of analyzing language might be easier to undertake than the day-to-day empirical activities of mainstream psychology. After all, what we need (concepts and their use) is right before us and anyone can describe the uses of words and the contexts in which they are used before undertaking empirical investigations. Such an 'undogmatic procedure' may or may not result in debates as to whether or not descriptions of concept use are accurate or even relevant. Of far greater importance are the realizations that we are, as psychologists, tempted to use concepts referring to psychological phenomena in certain ways and that we can shed light on other ways of using these concepts by setting up 'objects of comparison' that reveal not only similarities but dissimilarities in their use (PI §130). In setting up these objects of comparison we should 'constantly be giving prominence to distinctions which our ordinary forms of language easily make us overlook' (PI §132). The message is clear. There is no substitute for a thorough and comprehensive study of the conceptual systems that are in use in the language with which we conduct our lives. Köhler's (1929/1947) warning of the dangers of premature attempts to transform qualitative into quantitative concepts may be based on a misapprehension, but the spirit of caution is entirely worthy.

Not realizing that empirical research cannot answer conceptual questions, the psychologist will likely focus on how key terms embedded in such questions that serve as the impetus for research are defined and related. If a question like 'How is it possible to know what another person is thinking or feeling?' leads to designing a study or experiment to see what factors enable one person to know what others think, the psychologist will need to determine just what constitutes 'knowing' in such instances. Other words may be considered as well, and the meanings of still others (e.g. 'thinking') might be taken for granted. The effort to define concepts clearly is thought to reflect the rigors of a scientific psychology, so it is not surprising that some psychologists expend considerable effort defining concepts. But defining concepts is an extraordinarily tricky business. Whether formally worked out or implicit in the discourse or procedures of research, the definition of a term may make its way into the literature and soon it is used by just about everyone interested in the topic to which it applies. 'Theory of mind' is a good example in today's developmental literature. There is no guarantee that the phenomena that can then be picked out by those who understand the term have anything in common with the rich and diverse vocabulary which has been displaced. The advent of the term 'affect' is another case in point. There is no doubt that its widespread use distorts and impoverishes the psychology of the emotions, implying similarities where our attention should be on differences. The use of this word hints at the thesis that in all the diversity of emotions there must be a common essence.

In attempting to define concepts rigorously the psychologist can be misguided with respect to the workings of language. We will have occasion to address further Wittgenstein's position on defining specific psychological concepts in Part Three. For the time being, we will only note that it is not unusual for definitions of psychological concepts to be met with skepticism and for alternative definitions to be offered. This for the very reason that some psychologists tend to think that psychological concepts carry the same meaning in all the varieties of situations where they may be used, while others are intuitively aware of the variety of language-games into which a word like 'memory' can enter. Compare 'remembering a string of nonsense syllables,' 'remembering the picnic,' 'remembering where we were when Kennedy died,' 'remembering the Alamo,' and so on (Middleton and Edwards, 1990). The experimental context is only one kind of memorial situation.

Indeed, the rigorously established definitions in psychology can be seen as one kind of means by which psychologists seek to establish control in their studies and experiments. Thus the grammar of psychological concepts becomes restricted to those instances of their use in experimental studies by psychologists. As we pointed out in Chapter 3, experimental control then becomes a kind of conceptual control. The constrained experimental situation becomes the primary source of a word's meaning.

What needs to be done

Before conducting research, psychologists should explore the meanings of psychological concepts in a way that is entirely different from fixing meanings by definition and by reference to experimental procedures. They may take account of *numerous ways* the words in question are used, can be used and cannot be used. Again, Wittgenstein calls this kind of account a 'perspicuous representation' of our uses of words. What makes a remark or group of Wittgenstein's remarks a perspicuous representation is, as Baker (1991) puts it, their 'function in making "our grammar" perspicuous, by providing, for example, landmarks, patterns, analogies, or pictures, which enable us to find our way about in the motley of "our language"' (pp. 56–7). We can imagine, therefore, that a thorough attempt perspicuously to represent the use of a word or words might involve many examples of their use, but these examples will be assembled as *reminders* of ways in which the word or words are used. McGinn (1997, p. 14) summarizes a number of ways in which Wittgenstein assembles such reminders, including (1) imagining a variety of circumstances in which we would use a given concept or expression, (2) asking how we would teach it to a child, (3) asking how we would verify that it applies in a particular concrete case, (4) looking at the role of disagreement and the nature of the certainty that is possible in connection with it, (5) asking whether it would still be usable if certain facts of nature were different, (6) imagining what we would say in a variety of peculiar cases, and (7) comparing our use of an expression with an example provided by Wittgenstein.

These ways of assembling reminders can be extended with ease to the perspicuous representation of a word or words pertaining to psychological phenomena. As a positive effort toward clarifying such concepts, Wittgenstein's method may be used to describe (1) the use of mental expressions, (2) the circumstances of their employment, (3) the grammatical structures in which they are imbedded, (4) their 'behavior' in different circumstances that provide the grounds of their use (e.g. in teaching psychological concepts to children), and (5) the purposes behind the utterances in which they occur.

McGinn (1997, pp. 14–15) says the purpose of these and other techniques used by Wittgenstein is twofold. First, Wittgenstein wants to pit ideas of how a given concept is used (or 'works') – and these are invariably given at least implicitly in the various uses of psychological concepts in psychological theorizing and research – against the way(s) it *actually* functions. Second, he wants us to attend to the differences in the ways of using language that identify and characterize the different regions of our language. We have used the expression 'regions of language' at several points in this chapter. It is connected with Wittgenstein's metaphor of language as a city, which he describes early in the *Investigations*: 'Our language can be seen as an ancient city: a maze of little streets and squares, of old and new houses, and of houses with additions from various periods; and this surrounded by a multitude of new boroughs with straight regular streets and uniform houses' (PI §18).

In Wittgenstein's view psychologists are mistaken in thinking that empirical research can solve philosophical problems. That is one way philosophical problems are treated by psychologists – via blind allegiance to the methods of positivistic science. The other, owing in part to lack of training in rigorous philosophical thinking, is the inability to recognize certain problems as philosophical problems. In both instances, psychologists need to recognize that philosophical problems are identifiable by attending to their seeming intractability and, if the psychologist is so constituted, the emotional toll and resistance they will recognize in themselves. With recognition and acknowledgment, the origin of a philosophical problem can be revealed by looking for possible faulty linguistic analogies in the psychologist's uses of words. Rather than solving the problem, definitions of psychological concepts only set aside the problem for later, for someone else to tackle. The temptation to define in order to get clear on the 'real meaning' of a word is one sure sign that a philosophical problem has got hold of us. Instead of giving in to the temptation, we should first look to the many possible uses of words that are causing our problem. By so doing, we are likely to see where we have gone wrong in our thinking. The problem will simply cease to exist.

A qualification is in order. Are we saying that scientific research in psychology can go forward without definitions of key terms and even operational definitions? Not really. Above we acknowledged that psychologists have effectively expanded our memory vocabulary with such refinements as 'implicit memory.' Such terms are, of course, defined by psychologists. But they are defined for the practical purposes of theorizing and research *in psychology* and may conceal deep conceptual problems. Or perhaps, in some cases, they do not. Wittgenstein, we have seen, admits that for 'practical purposes' such 'reforms' are 'perfectly possible' (PI §132). He is saying they are possible in the sciences. But they are not the task of a Wittgenstein-informed analysis of language (see Baker and Hacker, 1980, p. 557). This seems to run counter to much of what we have said about the temptation to define, problems with operational definitions, essential meanings, family resemblance and so on. The conflict suggested here is rooted in our having forgotten about the 'directionality' of grammatical analysis and scientific research in psychology. Definitions of psychological concepts often conceal grammatical differences in their possible uses. Grammatical analysis – in part, the critical examination of linguistic analogies – reveals these differences. We have said repeatedly that such analysis should be prior to research. If definitions are needed for practical purposes, they will be informed by prior grammatical analysis. Among other things, the direction of analysis *before* research will result in more informed research programs, more thorough research and proper qualification of findings. Psychologists need to keep in mind that their definitions of psychological concepts will almost invariably lack the richness of use of those concepts in everyday life.

Learning point: philosophical problems in psychology

1. *Köhler's criticism of psychological concepts*

    (a) In physics, quantitative concepts have replaced qualitative concepts, with new devices and instruments.
    (b) In psychology such a replacement, if premature, eliminates the specificity of the phenomena.
    (c) Ironically, psychologists are captivated by a false picture of science: positivism. In this picture, phenomena determine the meanings of words. But words and discriminations of phenomena are learned together.
    (d) Wittgenstein argues that such a replacement is generally incoherent.
        (i)   Ordinary language specifies the phenomena in the first place.
        (ii) The concepts of the vernacular embrace complex fields of family resemblances with many dimensions of difference, e.g. 'fear.'

2. *Conceptual problems in psychology.* Psychologists need to learn how to distinguish conceptual problems that impede progress in psychology from empirical problems that require technical and experimental solutions.

    (a) Example: the mind–body problem arises because we mistake the grammar of the words 'mind' and 'body,' taking 'mind' to share a substance grammar with 'body.' This produces the intractable problem: 'How can mind and body interact?' The problem dissolves when we see that the concept of mind in the pair 'mind–body' is the result of a false grammatical analogy.
    (b) Features of conceptual problems:
        (i)   Intractability: here a grammatical investigation reveals the nature of the problem to be conceptual (i.e. philosophical).
        (ii) Resistance: persisting in positivistic presumptions in psychology may be a sign of resistance to radical revision of method that is required by Wittgenstein's insights.
    (c) Features of the dissolution of conceptual problems:
        (i)   Faulty linguistic analogies: realizing that similarity of surface grammar may conceal differences in depth grammar. Same or similar sentence forms may be used in different contexts in accord with different depth grammars. This shows up in a close study of uses.
        (ii) Attempting strict definitions instead of a perspicuous survey: for example, psychologists' definitions of 'memory' have excluded much of the range of the uses of the words 'memory'

and 'remember,' giving the illusion of thorough and successful research.

(iii)   A perspicuous representation assembles *reminders* of how
we actually use the key words and displays the differences
between *regions of our language.*

3.   *The method of perspicuous representation*

(a)   It addresses the *source* of our failure to understand the workings of
words. One major source is a limited view of the workings of
words.

(b)   It reminds us of what we already know: varieties of word-use. We
reveal similarities and dissimilarities in word-use by using objects
of comparison (language-games) that bring into prominence distinctions in use.

(c)   It is 'prior' to new discoveries, particularly in the social and
behavioral sciences.

Further reading

Baker, G.P. and Hacker, P.M.S. (1982). The grammar of psychology: Wittgenstein's
Bemerkungen Über die Philosophie der Psychologie. *Language & Communication*, **2**, 227–44.

Barnett, W.E. (1990). The rhetoric of grammar: Understanding Wittgenstein's method.
Metaphilosophy, **21**, 43–66.

McGinn, M. (1997). *Wittgenstein and the Philosophical Investigations*. London:
Routledge. (Specifically Chapter 1.)

SELF-TEST: PART TWO

- What assumptions constitute the Augustinian picture of language?
- How does 'stage-setting' differ from 'context'?
- What is the language-game of 'five red apples' meant to show?
- What is the block/slab game meant to show?
- Why does Wittgenstein liken language to a toolbox?
- Distinguish between form and function in language. Why is this distinction significant?
- Is language use always descriptive? Include the idea of 'performatives' in your answer.
- Why does Wittgenstein deny that there are linguistic essences?
- How does Wittgenstein show that meaning is not something mental?
- Discuss Bruner's 'request formats' as the development of a skilled linguistic practice.
- What are the components of an ability?
- What is mentalism? How could we show that the ability to read is not a mental state?
- Could a study of brain states tell us that someone is able to read?
- Compare homogeneous and heterogeneous explanation formats (or regresses).
- How are signs and spoken words related?
- What is the 'threshold fallacy'? Give an example.
- Give a description of the general account of rules to be found in AI.
- Discuss rules as a metaphor for conventions, customs and practices.
- Distinguish between following a rule and acting in accordance with a rule.
- Rules can be mastered in many ways. What are the implications of this?
- How do explanatory regresses of skilled normative activities terminate?
- What is the 'paradox of interpretation'? What does it show?
- Is knowing a rule to know all the steps in advance? Why or why not?
- What relationship holds between rules and actions?
- Where do rules and practices get their authority?
- What sort of agreements are needed for us to have a stable normative practice?
- What does Wittgenstein mean by a 'grammar' and the 'autonomy of grammar'?
- How do we know that a statement is serving as a rule of grammar?
- Why do we say the norms of a practice have their primary expression in the practice?
- How did Wittgenstein qualify Köhler's criticism of quantitative methods?
- Why is it important to distinguish between empirical and philosophical problems and how do we make the distinction?
- How can we dissolve the mind–body problem? What is the source of the problem?
- Discuss the main features of philosophical (conceptual) problems.
- Why do we not want to give in to the temptation to define psychological concepts?
- What are the main doctrines of Wittgenstein's method of perspicuous representation?

Part Three
APPLICATIONS

8 Cognition: thinking and understanding

> Most [cognitive] explanations treat behavior as the outcome of computation, and computation presupposes a medium in which to compute … [which has the characteristics of a language].
>
> *Fodor* (1975), p. 33

> What one wishes to say is: 'Every sign is capable of interpretation; but the *meaning* mustn't be capable of interpretation. It is the last interpretation.'
>
> Wittgenstein, *The Blue Book*, p. 34

> Speech with and without thought is to be compared with the playing of a piece of music with and without thought.
>
> Wittgenstein, *Philosophical Investigations*, §341

Topics introduced: cognitive psychology as the science of thought; language and thought; the fallacy of the mind behind the mind; the brain behind the mind; understanding

Psychology is presented to us as the science of thinking, feeling, acting and perceiving. These are among a certain group of characteristic activities that distinguish human beings from all other types of entities, inorganic or organic. Human beings are also the only beings that play football, compose, perform and listen to music, sacrifice members of their own species to placate imaginary beings, and form sexual relationships with members of their own gender. The Big Four above – thinking, feeling, acting and perceiving – have their special status because they are involved in all of the more specific activities characteristic of human beings.

The development of 'cognitive psychology' includes a revival of the notion that there are unobservable cognitive processes underlying cognitive activities, such as reasoning, calculating, remembering and the like. Psychologists are no longer content with a catalogue of correlations between stimuli and responses, even if they are cognitive stimuli and cognitive responses. They want to develop explanatory theories based on hypothetical mental processes, in much the same way that chemists develop explanatory theories based on hypotheses about the redistribution of atoms among the molecules involved in a chemical reaction. This is why we have included the quote from Fodor above from his famous book *The Language of Thought*. As is evident, Fodor (1975) juxtaposes two principles employed in explanations of behaviors that are the 'outcome' of cognition: 'computation' and 'a medium in which to compute' (p. 33). We hasten to add that the 'medium' to which Fodor refers *has the characteristics of language*. Hence the so-described 'language of thought.' Earlier, in the same book, he says that psychological explanations of the sort he aims to develop 'presuppose the availability, to the behaving organism, of some sort of representational system' (Fodor, 1975, p. 31). Note the admission that a representational system is *presupposed*. As a paradigm of explaining cognition, however, such presuppositions are precisely of the sort that Wittgenstein was most concerned to repudiate. In the twenty-first century it sounds blasphemous to suggest that there are no grounds for inserting a computational process and/or a language-like medium 'behind' the symbolic manipulations people actually carry out.

There is no getting round it. The 'take-off point,' so to say, for any conceptual contribution to scientific psychology – including Wittgenstein's – must be the way the vernacular concepts around 'thought' and 'thinking' *are actually used*. By attending to a preliminary study of the sort undertaken in this and following chapters, we can grasp both the scope of the field of relevant phenomena and free ourselves from certain illusions into which misunderstandings of the grammar of these concepts can lead us. One of these illusions is that there are hidden mental processes 'behind' the thinking we do in solving our everyday problems and getting on with our lives. In this chapter we will follow Wittgenstein as he unravels the complexities of the way the words 'thinking,' 'thought' and 'understanding' actually are used.

As we follow Wittgenstein we will find ourselves shedding prejudices and over-hasty generalizations of particular cases. As always with the method of surveyable representation, we will pay for the achievement of clarity with the need to acknowledge the complexity of a field of family resemblances between many subtly different ways that concepts are used. We will explore similarities and differences between thinking and other closely allied activities and we will explore the conceptual issues that emerge from reflecting on the evident – but poorly understood – ways that thought and language are involved with one another. The upshot will be a firmer grasp of a major conceptual field, one that plays a prominent role in the understanding of our own lives, and, in the setting of research projects, reveals their character more perspicuously.

We will begin by exploring two popular but mistaken presuppositions.

(1) Early exponents of cognitive psychology took for granted that speaking and acting are the public representation of a private domain of thought processes, in which cognitive activity *really* resides. Many cognitivists continue to think this way.

(2) Such private and sometimes hidden processes of thought were – and still are – assumed to accompany those actions we take to be 'rational.' The accompanying thought is what endows the processes with their rationality.

Our investigations will reveal that there are no good grounds for either of these presuppositions. Thinking is a task that people perform with all sorts of symbolic instruments, many of which are public and some of which are private. But there is no 'shadow world' of thought that consistently accompanies such performances and gives them their 'cognitive' character.

The place of thinking in human life

What distinguishes the meaningful use of language by a human being and the vocal utterances of a parrot? One obvious answer is that the 'thinking' behind human language use and the utterances of a parrot are different. Indeed, there is every reason to doubt that there is any thinking at all behind the utterances of a parrot; that is, unless one ascribes to the very simplistic view of thinking as information processing (e.g. Siegler, 1998). The information-processing perspective on thinking is overly broad and not supported by even the most rudimentary grammatical analysis.

One way of locating thought is to think of it as a process that accompanies the uses of language and gives expressions meaning. There must, according to this view, be two processes occurring when someone uses signs meaningfully: the production of the sequence of signs and the production of the sequence of thoughts that accompanies them.

Is this alleged relation necessary? Or is it contingent? If it is contingent and speech and thought are independent existents, then there could be speech without thought and thought without speech or some other deployment of signs.

What are the constituents of the flow of thought? They (the constituents) must be meaningful themselves. Here we get back to the notion of 'the language of thought.' But how do thoughts acquire meaning? We might think there must be another, shadowy companion behind the thought that gives meaning to the uses of symbols. But what gives this *companion* meaning? Another shadow domain that animates the shadow domain that animates our first-order acts of thinking? How many such domains must there be? It seems as if we have entered again into an endless regress. How can this regress be avoided and the meaningfulness of our private and public symbolic manipulations be preserved? Something is surely wrong in the way the problem has been posed in the first place. So we must address first the supposed relation between thought and language, that is, between thinking and speaking aloud to another or to oneself.

Are thought and language the 'same thing'?

A case might be made for distinguishing the thought and the linguistic act that expresses it. For example, Latin and German use different patterns of word order from English and French. Yet the thought expressed in a German, French and English translation of a Latin sentence is at least *meant* to be the same. Wittgenstein (PI §336) ridicules the French politician who claimed that French was unique in that the word order in French exactly matched the order of rational thought.

If thought and language are not the same thing, then perhaps thought is what *accompanies* sign uses of all kinds, including the uses of words. The discussion here would be conducted largely in terms of speech as the prime example of a sign system in action. It bears pointing out that the same arguments can readily be extended to cover the case of any form of sign use, be it gestures, flag waving, or deeply felt musical performances.

Wittgenstein presents us with two arguments that call for rejection of the idea that thought is a necessary but hidden accompaniment of meaningful speech. These arguments call into question proposals that thinking accompanies speech (or other forms of symbol use) or that thought is a material state of the brain.

The regress argument

We have encountered this argument in Chapter 5, where we discussed the foundations of having an ability. Now let us look more closely at what Wittgenstein has to say on the matter. We remind the reader that the psychology of musical performance is as much in need of this distinction as the psychology of speech, or for that matter with respect to any competent use of symbolic systems. There is a world of difference between an expressive and thoughtful performance of a concerto and a mere rattling through of the notes. People who played in the same chamber group in which Wittgenstein performed on his clarinet complained of his excessive devotion to playing every note exactly as written in the score.

One point we will be considering is whether thinking, as an accompaniment to the skillful use of symbols and signs, is necessary or sufficient for meaningful performance. If thinking is a process that necessarily accompanies meaningful activities (such as speaking), then we should be able to separate them and have the thinking without the speaking. A moment's reflection shows that the symbolic performance cannot be detached to leave the thinking as an independent process.

> While we sometimes call it 'thinking' to accompany a sentence by a mental process, that accompaniment is not what we mean by a 'thought'. – Say a sentence and think it; say it with understanding. – And now do not say it, and just do what you accompanied it with when you said it with understanding! – (Sing this tune with expression. And now don't sing it, but repeat its expression! – And here one actually might repeat something. For example, motions of the body, slower and faster breathing, and so on.)
>
> (PI §332)

Given the history of their science, many psychologists will scoff at the foregoing remark because it calls upon an 'outdated' form of investigation: introspection. But we should not be led to think that Wittgenstein ultimately wants to arrive at some kind of empirical result of his investigation. The remark serves to show, at least in preliminary fashion, that one can speak and act meaningfully without such speech and action being accompanied by anything. Inventing hidden cognitive processes and entities only adds to the confusion. In following up the remark, Wittgenstein examines the status of what an abstract noun suggests there might be when the vernacular expression is content with a verb. He suggests we look at the sentence: 'Only someone who is *convinced* can say that' (PI §333). Wittgenstein asks how adding 'conviction' as a mental state would help us to understand a sentence said with conviction. Where is the 'conviction'? He asks, 'Is it somewhere to hand by the side of the spoken expressions? (Or is it masked by it, as a soft sound by a loud one, so that it can, as it were, no longer be heard when one expresses it out loud?)' (PI §333). In a similar vein Wittgenstein examines the tempting but erroneous presupposition of a hidden mental entity in explaining the point of someone saying: 'So you really wanted to say … ' as if what the person '"meant"' was already *present somewhere* in his mind even before we gave it expression' (PI §334). There are all sorts of reasons why one might give up one form of expression for another. All that the original comment could do would be to offer an alternative version of what had been said.

We could call the mistake of projecting a half-hidden realm of thought behind the common uses of symbolic systems to perform cognitive tasks 'the fallacy of the mind behind the mind.'

Is thought a material state of the brain?

If thinking is the skillful use of symbols of many kinds to accomplish tasks and if there is no mind behind the mind, perhaps there is a brain behind the mind. Wittgenstein discusses this suggestion very briefly, but tellingly. What more would it add to our understanding of the rules of use and the meanings of words and other signs to insert a material background where the Cartesians and others had inserted a mental background? There is no need of a background at all. Thinking is there for all to see in its totality, as we follow the construction of discourse – verbal, pictorial, audible and so on.

Going further in the study of thought should not take us inside the human organism but out into the human environment.

> But didn't I already intend the whole construction of the sentence (for example) at its beginning? So surely it already existed in my mind before I said it out loud! ... An intention is embedded in its situation, in human customs and institutions. If the technique of the game of chess did not exist, I could not intend to play a game of chess. In so far as I do intend the construction of a sentence in advance, that is made possible by the fact that I can speak the language in question.
>
> (PI §337)

We must emphasize again that it would be a mistake to slip into thinking that Wittgenstein would have been hostile to neuroscience as a discipline. We can point out one reason for this by thinking over the above remark. A comparison is being made between intending to say a sentence and intending to play chess. Both activities involve following rules. Are the rules contained, as it were, in the intentions? Indeed, are the rules 'in' the mind of the speaker–player? The final sentence of the answer in §337 reveals the answer to be yes and no. It also brings into play the idea that intentions are embedded in their customary and institutional situations. As Hacker (1993b) says: 'They [the rules of chess] are present in the mind of the intending player only in the sense that he has mastered them and can say what they are' (pp. 179–80). So intentions are not independent of situations in which they are carried through. Nor are they entities of sorts, added on to speaking, playing chess, and any number of other activities.

Now why would this indicate that Wittgenstein would not be hostile to neuroscience? It is because the neuroscientist, being skilled at using language, must already be able to identify thinking and its varieties before she can embark on any study of the brain as the material instrument by the use of which a human being accomplishes cognitive tasks. What Wittgenstein *would* object to, of course, is the supposition that intentions can be identified as a set of neurophysiological correlates to accomplishing cognitive tasks. We should add the following empirical observation as well, which is similar to a point made in Chapter 5 when we discussed the cognitive skill of reading. Since 'an intention is embedded in its situation' and because there are so many situations in which one can intend, it seems implausible that neuroscience will arrive at an account of the neurophysiology of intention to fit the varieties of intending. Think of the great many situations in which one can 'intend' to read! One further point. *Rightly understood*, cognitive psychology is the study of the instrument by means of which people accomplish discursive acts. Neuroscience could never replace cognitive psychology because it *depends* on cognitive psychology.

Language as the prime vehicle for thinking

In the *Investigations* Wittgenstein presents us with many lines of argument that dispense with the idea that every cognitive performance must be accompanied by a hidden process which shadows it and gives it its unique character. We can only scratch the surface of the main thrust of his investigations on this topic here. At this point we return to the question of the relation between language and thought, specifically addressing the question of whether we might be bold enough to see them as one.

In many cases language and thought are in a sense identical, since we often use language as the means by which we think. As Wittgenstein puts it: 'When I think in language, there aren't "meanings" going through my mind in addition to the verbal expressions: the language is itself the vehicle of thought' (PI §329). In §317 Wittgenstein brings out a fundamental error of the kind he was so good at uncovering. Why would anyone come to think there was thought as well as the words (or other symbols) that are its vehicle? In the discussion of the expression of feelings in Chapter 9 we will show that there could not be a language in which meanings are fixed by private experiences. Of course, there are pains and expressions of pain. We learn the uses of words like 'pain' by substituting verbal expressions for natural expressions (see PI §244). In this way we can acquire a vocabulary for expressing some domain of experience without the need to learn the words by ostension or pointing to exemplars.

Might we not be attracted by a misleading parallel between propositions as expressing thoughts and cries as expressing pains? In the latter case there are pains as well as expressions of pain. In the former case there are not two things, the thought and its propositional expression. There is only one thing: the proposition. That is how the thought 'exists.' We should take note, then, that there is, at best, a family resemblance between the two uses of 'express.' There are expressions of feelings in gestures, grimaces and exclamations. Then there are expressions of thought in propositions. There are similarities and there are differences.

Following this further, we find ourselves with a profoundly important reversal to the simplistic view that places thought independent of and behind language. The point is nicely summarized by Glock (1996, p. 360): 'What we think is determined by what we would sincerely say and do, not by what images and words may flit across our minds.' If we consider what we might call 'lightning-like thoughts,' Wittgenstein remarks that 'I can see or understand a whole thought in a flash in exactly the sense in which I can make a note of it in a few words or a few pencilled dashes' (PI §319). That is, in the latter case we express the thought in a sketchy sort of manner.

A more profound and subtle connection between thought and the symbols which we use to express it emerges if we consider how thoughts are to be identified and individuated. The subtle point simply is that to say what one is thinking is to do the whole job. In PI §502 Wittgenstein offers a comparison:

> Asking what the sense is. Compare:
> 'This sentence makes sense.' – 'What sense?'
> 'This set of words is a sentence.' – 'What sentence?'

In the first case, would I repeat the same sentence to answer Wittgenstein's query 'What sense?' Of course not. That would accomplish nothing. Instead, I would likely offer some other sentence or set of sentences to make the sense of the sentence clear. I would not try to conjure up some mental picture or feeling or something like that (although I might draw a diagram and explain it, again, using other words). Having offered the sentence, that is all that can be required. In the second case I speak or write some words and say 'This is a sentence.' To Wittgenstein's query ('What sentence?') would I speak or write the same sentence? What else could I do?

The same point comes out in PI §503 thus: 'If I give anyone an order I feel it to be *quite enough* to give him signs. And I should never say: this is only words, and I have got to get behind the words.' Exactly the same point is at the center of J.L. Austin's (1975) famous account of performative utterances, which we discussed in Chapter 4. If I have said 'I promise ... ' there is no room for questions about the sincerity or otherwise of any alleged mental accompaniments. Having said the words I am thereby committed to the relevant performance. Applying this point to the understandings the speaker can have of his or her own words, Wittgenstein points out: 'But if you say: "How am I to know what he means, when I see nothing but the signs he gives?" then I say: "How is *he* to know what he means, when he has nothing but the signs either?"' (PI §504).

We seem compelled to drive a wedge between signs and their meanings, just as we seem compelled to propose that thought is a hidden accompaniment to speech. Amidst his remarks on method in the *Investigations*, Wittgenstein seems to ridicule the very idea that words and their meanings should be given separate (but related) status: 'Here the word, there the meaning. The money, and the cow you can buy with it. (But contrast: money, and its use.)' (PI §120). The key point is again very well expressed by Glock (1996). Summarizing Wittgenstein, he says the 'essential link between thought and language is that the capacity for having thoughts or beliefs ... requires the capacity to manipulate symbols, not because unexpressed thoughts must be in language, but because the expression of thoughts must be' (Glock, 1996, p. 361). And this includes even (and especially) the *expression* of thoughts to myself!

The connection to psychology

Can the empirical aspect of the study of cognitive psychology pass beyond the realm of signs and their skillful manipulation by competent people? Only in a very limited sense. Surely thus far we have every indication that hypotheses about the inner lives of people might not count as 'explanations' of what people do. In the same vein, explanations in the domain of psychology might do no more than suggest the projects in which people are engaged – publicly and privately. On the other hand, an important place is reserved for the study of the 'vehicles of thought' as such, and the means by which an active thinker manages them. There is the game of tennis as a socio-cultural phenomenon, with its rules by which the shots and the movements of the ball are given meaning. However, there is also the independent study of the physics of ballistic missiles and of elastic strings. These sciences are required in order to understand the vehicles by which the meaningful shots of tennis are performed by active agents engaged in a match. Neither Bjorn Borg nor John McEnroe thought like physicists. But they do have bodies and brains that make any of their activities possible.

To be more specific on what all of this has to do with psychology and cognitive psychology in particular, we hope it is evident that Wittgenstein's insights potentially are fundamental to bringing an adequate cognitive psychology to life.

> How does the philosophical problem about mental processes and states and about behaviorism arise? – The first step is the one that altogether escapes notice. We talk of processes and states and leave their nature undecided. Sometime perhaps we shall know more about them – we think. But that is just what commits us to a particular way of looking at the matter. For we have a definite concept of what it means to learn to know a process better. (The decisive movement in the conjuring trick has been made, and it was the very one we thought quite innocent.) – And now the analogy which was to make us understand our thoughts falls to pieces. So we have to deny the yet uncomprehended process in the yet unexplored medium. And now it looks as if we have denied mental processes. And naturally we don't want to deny them.
>
> (PI §308)

What, then, are we doing when we construct models of cognitive processes, for example by employing the analogy between cognition and computation, say, in a connectionist network? We are not offering a hypothesis about the nature of something that we may eventually come to observe. We should be clear that this kind of model-making is not parallel to the use of the ion model in chemistry. In the latter case we have some idea of the domain to explore to see whether there or are not ions, charged atomic particles, and how they behave. Nor is our computational model merely heuristic, a device for neatly summing up what we have observed, though it certainly has this role. It cannot be a picture of a *hidden* mental process. Taken within the framework of scientific realism, it must have an interpretation as a possible structure of a possible neural mechanism by which a person could perform the task which it has been used to model. Of course, there *are* mental processes. They are what we take note of when we pay attention to our thoughts and feelings. They are as much in need of modeling in some suitable medium as are the overt acts of speaking and other meaningful performances.

When we make models of cognitive processes – for example Baddeley's (1998) 'loops' in his model of certain kinds of remembering – *we are not representing hidden cognitive processes*, but the structure of actual symbol manipulation. Beyond that, such models could only be representations of brain processes. But these are nothing like a language.

The circumstances of understanding

In the gamut of concepts with which we describe our cognitive activities, 'understanding' plays an integral part. In the context in which Wittgenstein highlights the concept, in simplified form it is used to express a person's belief that a technique has been mastered. At the same time to say one understands some procedure expresses a certain confidence that one knows how to go on with a task in hand. In PI §§152–5 the context is roughly 'understanding what one is required to do.' The task at hand is arithmetical and elementary. The pupil is required to continue a series initiated by the teacher. In this situation to say 'Now I understand' is more or less to say 'Now I know how to go on.' (The case is similar to the case of teacher teaching the pupil to read in Chapter 5.)

What do declarations like 'Now I understand' amount to? Suppose the pupil supports the claim to understand by reciting what seems to be the relevant formula. Evidently, merely saying that the formula has occurred to me does not mean that I know how to go on. What would suffice? Is 'Now I understand' a description of a process occurring behind the saying over of the formula? We already know that Wittgenstein would deny this. 'If there has to be anything "behind the utterance of the formula" it is *particular circumstances*, which justify me in saying I can go on – when the formula occurs to me' (PI §154). We say we understand or otherwise in a wide variety of cases. If it were the particular circumstances of each situation that were constitutive of 'understanding,' then there would be no generic phenomenon of 'understanding.' In a case of family resemblance semantics there must be similarities *as well as differences* in use between the family members.

If the construal of understanding is not to be yet another example of the 'mind behind the mind' fallacy, then perhaps it is best construed as having 'a special experience,' as Wittgenstein suggests in PI §155. Suppose the person who understands how to go on examines their experiences. Suppose further they identify a particular experience connected with their being able to go on – to grasp the principle. Is that the end of the story? No. From our point of view, 'it is *the circumstances* under which he had such experience that justify him in saying in such a case that he understands, that he knows how to go on' (PI §155).

What does Wittgenstein mean by 'the circumstances'? Understanding and/or having understood is shown or displayed in what one does. Understanding is not simply conforming behavior. Yet conforming behavior is necessary to support a claim to have understood. Understanding is expressed in what one does. Just as in the case of thinking, which is expressed in words and does not exist apart from word use, so is understanding expressed in displays of mastery. One cannot then confess to not having understood, nor be convicted of not understanding, because to actually go on shows one is *able* to go on, and being able to go on just is the mastery that is shown in going on according to the rule – having 'grasped the principle,' as Wittgenstein puts it.

What is Wittgenstein's advice? 'Try not to think of understanding as a "mental process" at all' (PI §154). Whatever the degree of conviction I may have, to 'understand in a flash' is a kind of hypothesis about what I will be able to do. Understanding is not a mental process. Nor is it a feeling that comes to me when contemplating what I must do. Surface grammar leads us astray. 'Lend*ing*' is an activity. 'Understand*ing*' is not. I show that I have understood by acting in any one of a variety of relevant ways. To understand is to have acquired a certain skill or capacity.

Wittgenstein's treatment of cognitive psychology

Many cognitive practices are carried through by the public use of words and other symbols in social and material contexts. The very same cognitive tools can be used for private and personal acts of thinking. In light of these claims there are three deep questions to be answered. First, how are the meanings of such words and other ancillary vocabulary to be established for current use in performing cognitive tasks, remembering that public uses must be established prior to private uses? Second, how are these vocabularies actually used in *performing* the relevant cognitive tasks? And third, how are the vocabularies we use to *describe* cognitive tasks to be understood?

There is a pressing need for philosophical analysis and reflection apropos of these questions, since in some important cases there are 'false pictures' of these processes embedded in both professional and lay psychology. If the 'pictures' were taken seriously, the words we use routinely in everyday practices could not have the meanings that they seem to have. To remedy this situation the false pictures must be rejected. At the same time we need to understand how they came to seem natural and inevitable. Now we can see why the method of surveying the uses of the words in a certain vocabulary is a key procedure for setting psychology on the right track.

In the chapters to come we will study the following five main domains of psychology.

(1) Private and personal subjective experiences (such as feelings of pain and seeing of colors) of which each and only one person is conscious, yet about which public conversations can be carried on using a vocabulary everyone understands. The 'false picture' that inhibits understanding of these private experiences is that of meanings-as-objects-signified, a picture that makes the acquisition and use of a public vocabulary for private experiences impossible.

(2) Past and future events that are not available to anyone at the present moment. How can we talk about these events? What can such words as 'remember,' 'expect,' 'hope' and so on mean? The false picture that inhibits

our understanding of these events is that of cognitive processes as descriptions of current representations of the past and future. How could we ever know that any current thought or image was a representation of a past or a future event?

(3)   We talk about what we are going to do by using a vocabulary that includes such words as 'intend,' 'intention' and so on. How can such words serve in explanations of what someone does? How can we accommodate the fact that an intended action is defined in terms of the intention that was realized in doing it? The false picture that inhibits our understanding of the relation between intentions and future behavior is the explanation of action in *causal* terms. Is talk of 'the will' an appropriate vehicle for explaining actions causally? Is willing like trying?

(4)   In the psychology of the emotions the causal pattern of explanation surfaces again, for example, in a confusion between targets of emotion and causes of emotion. The role of bodily feelings evident in emotional experience, too, need careful analysis. Wittgenstein's analyses lend support to the current move to a cognitive account of emotions as social acts.

(5)   In the final chapter we discuss applications of Wittgenstein's insights and method to difficult problems encountered in understanding certain perceptual – predominantly visual – phenomena. Is the grammar of our color vocabulary independent of what we know about the physics and physiology of the causes of color experiences? In answering this question Wittgenstein leads us to such problematic questions as why there are no uses for the phrase 'transparent white,' again following out the consequences of certain grammatical analogies. The final topic will be the phenomenon of seeing aspects of ambiguous figures, the explanation for which must be sought in some other domain than that of retinal images. On this topic, Wittgenstein's writings tie in with the great twentieth-century debate between Gibson and Gregory on how these phenomena are to be accounted for.

In each case, by a surview of how the relevant words are actually used and by eschewing premature theorizing about them, we can escape from the spell of the inhibiting 'false' picture. (1) In the case of public discussion of private feelings, language is being used *expressively* rather than descriptively. (2) In the case of talking about the future, the words we use stand for *general prescriptions* rather than future particulars, while we regulate talk about the past by social *negotiations* and not by 'archeology.' (3) In the case of the expression of intentions, these statements are not descriptions of states of mind but are used to make *public commitments* to act in a certain way in the future. (4) In the case of emotions, our vocabulary is and must be established in public performances, as these are embedded in all sorts of social situations. Bodily feelings cannot be the source of the meanings of emotion words. (5) In the case of color words, our color vocabulary has meaning, so to speak, 'as a whole.' Its relative independence from physics and physiology is shown in the way certain features of how we talk about colors reflect linguistic conventions. The phenomenon of seeing aspects is neither physiological nor cognitive, but partakes of both explanatory frameworks.

In none of these cases is language used to describe hidden or theoretically motivated cognitive processes. It is that assumption that leads us astray and its cure is to use the results of our surviews to throw out the tempting but misleading pictures that have lain at the root of so much muddle and confusion, especially in academic psychology.

Learning point: thinking as the skillful use of symbols

1. *Wittgenstein's targets:* that there is an unobservable domain of thinking 'behind' symbolic manipulations. This domain confers rationality on overt cognitive processes, public and private.

2. *Thought and language.* Are there meanings behind meaningful uses of language? No, since this would entail a regress of meanings.
    Is thinking nothing but using language? Thinking cannot be detached from thoughtful activities.

    (a)   Reference to brain processes is redundant for identifying thinking. The rules of rational symbol use are socially based. In human life, language is the most important human tool for thinking. The parallel between a verbal expression of pain and verbal expression of thought is misleading.
    (b)   Thinking need not be verbal, but expression of thought must be symbolic and is usually verbal.

3. *Cognitive psychology*

    (a)   There is no need to hypothesize processes and states over and above the manipulation of symbols. There is no justification for supposing that such processes and states await discovery.
    (b)   'Understanding' is a family resemblance concept expressing beliefs as to one's competence in some cognitive task.

4. *Applications*

    (a)   To the problem of the sources of the meanings of words for private feelings and other subjective phenomena.
    (b)   To the problem of the meanings of the words we use for thinking about the future and the past, including 'hoping,' 'remembering.'
    (c)   To the problem of how the expression of intentions and acts of willing are related to what a person subsequently does. The argument is expressly contrary to the use of a causal paradigm for these phenomena.
    (d)   To the problem of the meanings of words for emotions and disposing of the myth that they get their meanings from bodily feelings.

(e)   To the problem of how color words get their meanings in public language games, and how we should understand the strange phenomenon of 'seeing aspects' of ambiguous figures.

These are not the only applications of the method of surveyable representation to topics that interest psychologists. The general thrust of these applications and the results of such overviews, however, can serve as guidelines to other applications.

Further reading

Baker, G.P. and Hacker, P.M.S. (1980). *Wittgenstein: Understanding and meaning. An analytical commentary on the* Philosophical Investigations (Vol. 1). Oxford: Blackwell. (Specifically Chapter 6.)
Vygotsky, L.S. (1962). *Thought and Language*. Cambridge, MA: MIT Press.

9 Subjectivity, expression, and the private-language argument
Philosophical Investigations §§243–315

> In fact, it is just this feature where we find, in what follows, the
> defining criterion of the Völker-psychological. A language
> cannot be brought into existence by an individual.
> > Wilhelm Wundt, from *Elements of the Völkerpsychologie*
> > (1912)

> 'I can only *believe* that someone else is in pain, but I *know* it if I
> am.' – Yes: one can make the decision to say 'I believe he is in
> pain'. But that is all. – What looks like an explanation here, or
> like a statement about a mental process, is in truth an exchange
> of one expression for another which, while we are doing
> philosophy, seems the more appropriate one. Just try – in a real
> case – to doubt someone else's fear or pain.
> > Wittgenstein, *Philosophical Investigations*, §303

Topics introduced: the private-language argument, private experience of bodily feeling; ethology and natural expressions; the substitution principle; primary and secondary language-games; physiognomic language-games; expressive (first-person) versus descriptive (third-person) language and the asymmetry principle; the beetle in the box simile; grammatical remark; numerical and qualitative identity; applications to color words and personal identity

The 'private-language argument' (hereafter 'PLA') employs a complex web of analyses and arguments sparked by the question of whether a single individual could create a language by associating words with his or her own personal and private experiences. Perhaps the point of such a language would be to reflect on one's own experiences for one's own purposes. Such a language would be unintelligible to others, and have no public use. But is such a 'language' possible?

In the course of demonstrating the impossibility of setting up a private language more or less so described, Wittgenstein examines the conditions under which our common vocabulary of feeling words is established. This discussion brings to the fore the important distinction between *expressive* uses of words and their *descriptive* use. He considers a number of examples to delimit the role of each speech form in psychologically relevant discourse. Another strand in the argument explores the seemingly obvious parallel between subjective states, such as pain, and things in the material world. Pains have locations and temporal boundaries, and so do things. Herein lies another temptation: to take the parallel further into presuming an entity-like mode of being for feelings. This is one of the misleading presuppositions that feeds into the fantasy of the private creation of a language for one's own feelings alone, as if the words of this language could be given meaning by being associated with entity-like feelings.

The quote by Wundt above, translated by our friend Dr Jim Lamiell of Georgetown University, serves to show that the idea of a private language is not a mere passing consideration for some psychologists. But why? In Wundt's (1912) case, the 'defining feature' of his 'Völkerpsychologie' lies in recognizing that the 'psychological findings that emerge from the collective nature of human life ... cannot be explained in terms of the characteristics of individual human consciousness because the latter requires the interaction of many such consciousnesses.' Since language use is dependent on the interaction of many consciousnesses, there can be no language 'brought into existence by an individual.'

But of what relevance to contemporary psychology are considerations of private language? Not only is the possibility of a private language 'tacitly presupposed' in the writings of many philosophers since Descartes, including those of classical British empiricists and Kantians; it is presupposed in 'contemporary cognitive representationalism' (Glock, 1996, p. 310). It is presupposed, for instance, in Fodor's (1975) 'language of thought' doctrine, which we mentioned in Chapter 3 and discussed further in Chapter 8. While Fodor would deny that the language of thought is private in the sense that it is not 'made up' by individuals – that it needs input from an environment of language-users – he cannot deny that such a 'language' is highly individualistic. It 'runs,' so to speak, in the heads of individuals. So too with Chomsky's 'language acquisition device' which, being programmed into the human brain, is responsible for spitting out grammatically well-formed sentences as children develop. (But again, this device is in need of input from the environment.) We want to suggest, therefore, that what Wittgenstein says in the PLA is, in principle, applicable to these contemporary views on thought and language.

Wittgenstein's considerations of the impossibility of a private language have more direct and profound consequences for how a coherent scientific psychology might be set up, particularly with respect to the range or domain of the phenomena that can be 'data' for such a science. We have mentioned before that the demise of classical behaviorism was more a matter of inanition and disenchantment with its effectiveness as a paradigm for a scientific psychology than the result of an in-principle demonstration of its deep logical flaws. The PLA disposes of the prohibition on including subjective states in the domain of the phenomena of psychology by demonstrating the grounds for the public intelligibility and reliability of what people say about their personal and private experience. At the same time this disposes of the philosophical grounds for the behaviorist restriction of the domain of psychological phenomena to that which can be publicly observed. This restriction had its ultimate source in the 'Problem of Other Minds,' that is, the seeming impossibility of obtaining any unmediated knowledge of the thoughts and feelings of another person.

Nothing could be more familiar to us than the displays of feeling of our fellow human beings and even our pets. Yet the feelings that are so displayed are *immediately present* only to the mind of the other being. I may 'know' how you are feeling from your behavior, but I do not have to take note of how I am behaving to know how I am feeling. This seeming truism raises the question of how public displays and private feelings are related in general.

Hacker (1993a) sets out three apparent features of the way we deal with the thoughts and feelings of others. Each of these features implies a duality between personal experience and public knowledge that has distorted our ways of thinking about the mind.

(1) We tend to think of 'the mental' as a world in significant ways different from the world of objects and events we inhabit. Nevertheless – and because we model the grammar of this mental world on the grammar of the physical world – 'we will be prone to populate [the mental world] with objects, states, events, and processes which we conceive to be, as it were, just like physical objects, states, events, and processes, only immaterial or etherial' (Hacker, 1993a, p. 17).

(2) The grammar of our linguistic expressions about the world includes notions of the independence of that world and its objects both from human beings and from our descriptions of them. Objects in the material world can be owned, shared and so on by human beings, but these relations are not inherent in the nature of the things themselves. I may, to some extent, associate my Maserati Bi-turbo Quattroporte with my sense of self. But this relation is quite contingent. It is possible to remain myself and to trade it in for a Mini Cooper. Contrast this with our relations to the states, events, and processes of the '"inner world" ... [which] are essentially owned' (Hacker, 1993a, p. 17). The stuff in my mind is *my* stuff. No one can experience this stuff like I can. It is mine in a specially intimate sense because in a way it is what I am.

(3) The owned inner contents of each individual's mind are associated with privileged access to those contents. Anyone and everyone has access to parts of the physical world, but only I can access the private contents of my mind by means of introspection. No one else can know what I am thinking and feeling as I can. Whereas I can be sure about these matters, other people can only conjecture from what they see and hear me do.

So here we have three related dualities laid down, it seems, in the very grammar of our ways of talking about personal experiences. There is the *inner–outer duality*, the *public–private duality*, and the *duality of privileged and unprivileged access*. These have all had a prominent place in the grammar of the discourses of mainstream psychology. Also, it will be abundantly clear that these dualities have a ring of the Augustinian picture of language (see Chapter 4). To say the least, any philosophical analysis that might show these dualities to be chimerical will have profound implications for the ways psychological phenomena are conceived, investigated and related.

The private language argument

One source of the idea that there is a private and personal mental realm, with states of mind experienced only by the person who 'has' them, is the evident privacy of bodily feelings, such as pains, aches, itches, tickles and so on. Yet we share a diverse and refined vocabulary to talk about how we feel and to understand how others feel. In other words, the three dualities outlined above are bridged routinely in everyday conversation. But this fact leaves us with a difficult problem if we continue to subscribe to the principle that the meaning of words is that to which they refer or what they denote. The word 'itch' seems to denote a private feeling. How does this word and all the other words we use for referring to our private experiences become established as part of a publicly usable vocabulary that every-one can understand? Is this an empirical question, a philosophical question, or a mixture of both?

It seems evident that no one can experience the bodily feelings of another person. The meanings of many words are acquired by a 'teacher' pointing to examples of what the words denote. But how can words for private mental 'somethings' ever be taught? There seem to be no public exemplars of private feelings. The teacher cannot point to the learner's feelings and the learner cannot experience the teacher's feelings. Even if the teacher were to induce a feeling in some well-established way, the question of the *nature* of the private experience would still be open. Suppose the teacher says to the learner: 'Now I'm going to give you a Chinese burn just above your left wrist by gripping that area of your arm with both of my hands and rending my hands in opposite directions until you feel the "burn."' Is it the case that the pupil feels the same 'pain' as that of the teacher when the teacher has experienced a Chinese burn? Only if we were assured of the answer to this question could we argue that the meaning of the word 'pain' in such a case could be established by attending to the experience it denotes.

The problem of meaning modulates into a corresponding question about knowl-edge. How do I 'know' that something I have said has amused my friend? Well, I have said something and my friend smiles and laughs. Surely this action of mine and my friend's response depend on a common feature of human life. When people are amused they have a natural tendency to smile and they might laugh. But suppose we go further and ask how it *felt* to be amused? How do we know that everyone feels much the same bodily feelings when they are amused? How could we make an interpersonal comparison? When my friend is amused she might feel as I feel when I have indigestion. Compare this with establishing which of two people is the taller. All we have to do there is stand them back to back and look.

Yet we *can* talk to one another about our feelings. For example, sometimes it is very important to inform a doctor about our pains as accurately as possible, quali-fying the mere declaration of being in pain with such epithets as 'throbbing,' 'sharp' and so on. If we were to try to hold on to the Augustinian account of meaning as the object signified by a word, it looks as if we could never learn a vocabulary for discussing our private feelings. Since we *do* have a mastery of such a vocabulary something must be wrong somewhere in the analysis we have just presented!

Here is a second puzzle. How could a person use a feeling word consistently if he or she had only their own private feelings to go on? Does a person have to attend to his or her public behavior to identify the feeling? Surely not.

Try remembering a painful or pleasurable bodily feeling. For the most part we remember the circumstances, but not the feeling itself. We cannot revive an actual feeling of pain. We remember that we were in pain, or we remember an occasion of pain, but not the pain itself. The same thing goes for other sensory modalities. Few people can remember the specifics of smells or tastes. Think about a favorite taste. Suppose it is 'the taste of Tin Roof Fudge Pie.' One can surely remember the occasion, but one cannot conjure up the very taste. (This, however, does not rule out being able to identify the taste of Tin Roof Fudge Pie in a blind tasting. But here we have a different use of the concept of 'remembering.') If we try to go by the phenomenology of qualitative experiences we are lost for words.

The private-language argument shows, among other things, that *the personal quality of experiences could not be the foundation for a language with which to discuss those experiences with other people.* As we have said, there are no public exemplars to serve as the referents for learning many words of one's mother tongue. This is particularly the case with bodily feelings of the kind we have already mentioned. Only *displays* of such feelings are public.

But what if someone argued that we can learn about what sort of feelings we experience by learning the *categories* of feeling from exemplars? For example, someone might learn the general category of pain by being shown pictures of people in pain, then by matching their expressions with those pictures when they are 'in pain.' This will not work either, since the feelings can be experienced only by the person whose feelings they are! There is no 'matching of experiences' in our example. Nor could there be. Wittgenstein (PI §263) points out that it would do no good to concentrate our attention on bodily feelings in order to make an ostensive definition of pain that could be used in future experiences of pain. 'Pain' was something felt yesterday. How does anyone know that the feeling they have today is the same feeling they felt yesterday?

To pose another question, might not the private-language-user have recourse to standards of correctness he or she conjures up in their imagination? This would amount to having an imaginary list of sensations consisting in the sensations themselves and their names, with which sensations could be compared at any time. We would have to imagine that the accuracy of the table has already been established by previous experience. Characteristically, Wittgenstein (PI §265) compares this strategy with a person checking to see if they have remembered the time of departure of their train by consulting an imaginary timetable. How does this person know that the imagined timetable is correct? He would have to emerge from his subjective domain and consult the 'real' timetable. The same would hold for an imaginary sensation list. Checking the accuracy of that list would put anyone in a rather strange situation: '(As if someone were to buy several copies of the morning paper to assure himself that what it said was true.)' (PI §265)

The clue to resolving these problems with the language of feelings and other private experiences lies in the fact that we remember the *circumstances* of an experience, though admittedly we cannot recall or relive the experience itself.

Taken at face value, the considerations so far advanced seem to lead to a paradox. On the one hand, there seems to be no procedure by means of which words as names for private feelings, thoughts and so on could be established. On the other hand, we use these words freely and for all kinds of practical talk, such as medical consultations, without running into the impasse of mutual incomprehension.

The troublesome presuppositions

In considering the communication and understanding of private experiences of bodily feeling, Wittgenstein reveals two common presuppositions, neither of which is defensible when brought to light. The first presupposition is that all words other than grammatical particles (like 'and' or 'is') are *names*. This proposition, or what amounts to the denotational theory of language mentioned in Chapter 4, has been the target of several lines of criticism from the very first paragraph of the *Investigations*. If this principle were true, feeling words like 'itch' would have to have the grammar of words for objects in the world. As we have seen, this presupposition runs counter to the conditions under which these words must be learned.

The second presupposition is that sensations – or what we will call 'bodily feelings' – are mental objects rather like physical objects, albeit immaterial. This presupposition is deeply entrenched in our ways of talking. It goes back to the psychology of ideas as mental atoms, developed in deliberate imitation of Newtonian physics in the seventeenth and eighteenth centuries.

From these two presuppositions it follows that there could be no possibility of interpersonal communication about certain kinds of feelings, because there could be no guarantee that two people meant the same experience by the feeling words they used. Furthermore, there would be no possibility of a person having a stable sense of what his or her own bodily feelings were from day to day. How could people be sure that they had remembered their past feelings correctly? But we *do* communicate about private feelings. You can tell me whether you were disappointed or overjoyed about your grade on your half-term paper and you can tell the doctor where it hurts. In turn, most of the time your teacher and your doctor understand you effortlessly. Furthermore, you have little difficulty in re-identifying a feeling as 'the same' feeling you had previously. This is illustrated by the fact that in certain cases you may want to repeat the experience over and over again, and in others to avoid it in future.

Ethology is a branch of biology that, among other things, deals with the expressions by which animals display their subjective states. Dogs growl and bare their teeth when angry, cats purr when contented. There is a human ethology too. People express pleasure, happiness and satisfaction by smiling, pain by crying and groaning, and so on. Wittgenstein suggests that language gets a footing in the subjective domain of individual experience by the substitution of verbal devices for the natural expressions with which we display 'how it is with us' in public. We will discuss a specific remark in the *Investigations* pertaining to this suggestion below. But, as is always the case with Wittgenstein, we will need to be on guard against our own supposition that the suggestion of replacing natural expressions with linguistic expressions amounts to an empirical claim. The suggestion itself is rooted in grammar.

There is an internal, grammatical relation between a public display and the private state it expresses. This means that the public display would not be a display of, say, pain unless the person or animal tended to display just 'this' reaction when in pain. If someone has a tendency to smile, they are not, *ceteris paribus*, in pain. Of course, there is the language-game of 'putting a brave face on it' and smiling when hurt. But this is a way of displaying courage and stoicism only if there is what has been described as a 'primary language-game' in which smiling and feelings of pleasure are internally related. We will use the expressions 'primary language-game' and 'secondary language-games' at various points in this and in remaining chapters. Put simply, a 'primary language-game' involves a sketch of what kind of training at least one participant needs in order to acquire a vocabulary and take part in more complex language-games. Certain vocabularies are acquired in primary language-games and, in the case of the vocabularies of bodily feeling, these games are based on natural expressions. By contrast, a 'secondary language-game' is never based on a natural expression. It is based on a primary language-game. A person could not 'put a brave face' on their pain without already having mastered the primary language-games that involved their learning to use the word 'pain' (or related words) when they are in pain. Below we mention that 'insincerity' is an example of a secondary language-game.

To continue, in PI §289 Wittgenstein remarks that to use a word without a justification, that is without empirical evidence for applying it, does not mean that we cannot use it without a right. When I use the word 'jolly' to express how I feel on some sunny morning, I am not able to justify it in the sense that I cannot point separately to the joyful feeling and then wonder whether I have found the right word. Feeling joyful and being ready to express this by saying 'I feel jolly this morning!' are part of the same complex state.

Descriptions, on the other hand, are verbal devices which are, in a certain sense, independent of that which they describe. A description can be incorrect. The grammar of descriptions involves not only truth and falsity, but also such associated concepts such as 'certainty,' 'knowledge' and 'evidence.' However, the private feeling displayed in an expressive act *is not evidence for the truth of the expression*. My pains are not evidence for my avowing that I am in pain. This is why Wittgenstein makes the following observation which, without qualifications of the sort we have provided, sounds remarkable: 'It can't be said of me at all (except perhaps as a joke) that I *know* I am in pain. What is it supposed to mean – except perhaps that I *am* in pain?' (PI §246).

The irrelevance of the subjective relation between word and bodily feeling for understanding how the words of a vocabulary get their meanings can be brought out in another way (PI §271). Let us suppose that a person cannot remember the connection once established between the word and the bodily feeling, but yet uses the word as everyone uses it in the proper public circumstances. The supposition that they have forgotten the connection between word and feeling surely is empty, like a wheel that turns without being connected to machinery. We turn now to present these important arguments in more detail, beginning with Wittgenstein's famous suggestion that natural expressions of pain are replaced by more refined, linguistic expressions.

Learning words for feelings and other 'private' mental phenomena

The substitution principle

How is the feeling vocabulary established?

> How do words *refer* to sensations? – There doesn't seem to be any problem here; don't we talk about sensations every day, and give them names? But how is the connexion between the name and the thing named set up? This question is the same as: how does a human being learn the meaning of the names of sensations? – of the word 'pain' for example. Here is one possibility: words are connected with the primitive, the natural, expressions of the sensation and used in their place. A child has hurt himself and he cries; and then the adults talk to him and teach him exclamations and, later, sentences. They teach the child new pain-behaviour.
>
> 'So you are saying that the word "pain" really means crying?' – On the contrary: the verbal expression of pain replaces crying and does not describe it.
>
> (PI §244)

The economy with which this passage presents us with powerful new psychological ideas is astounding. Here are the three main points:

(1)   Human beings are born with a repertoire of natural expressions of feeling that are readily understood by other people. One can tell the difference between a cheerful infant and a miserable one.

(2)   How do we get a vocabulary of bodily feeling started? Where do the words come in? We *substitute* verbal, linguistic expressions for the natural expressions (the 'substitution principle'). The ability to substitute linguistic expressions for natural expressions involves training. (Another way to put this is to say that the link between a linguistic expression and a natural expression of bodily feeling is learned.)

(3)   What are the functions of the verbal substitutes? At first they must be more or less the same as the natural expressions (e.g. crying) the substitutes replace. The original behavior is *expressive,* not descriptive. The verbal substitutes are, therefore, primarily expressive too.

Physiognomic language-games

We did not learn to talk about 'being in pain' or 'being hungry' by learning to describe something presented to each one of us. What we did was learn to substitute 'My knee hurts' for crying. We must bear in mind the difference between the conditions under which the uses of words are established – primary language-games and all the other secondary language-games that become available to people once the primary uses are established. We like the term 'physiognomic language-games' (from Hintikka and Hintikka, 1986) as a convenient label for the situations and contexts in which the 'feeling vocabulary' is established for public use.

From the point of view of psychology, the force of the PLA is strongly non-behaviorist, since verbal expressions replace natural expressions of feeling. *But neither form of expression describes the feeling.* The point of the substitution principle is to highlight the commonality in grammar between a verbal expression and a natural expression. Thus the interlocutor's suggestion, in PI §307, that Wittgenstein is 'really a behaviourist in disguise' who claims 'at bottom ... that everything except human behaviour is a fiction' is met with the retort: 'If I do speak of a fiction, then it is of a *grammatical* fiction.' The fiction so identified through analysis of grammar is the idea that something lurks behind expressions of bodily sensation (see Hacker, 1993b, p. 133).

The asymmetry principle: the grammar of first-person *expressive* talk and third-person *descriptive* talk

There is another grammatical distinction implicit in the PLA of very great importance for psychology and other of the behavioral and social sciences. Disciplines such as psychology cannot be based upon a theory of meaning in which meanings are established by attaching names to mental entities. So when someone talks about his or her own disappointments, feelings of being in love, stomach aches and so on – including such cognitive matters as 'feelings of conviction' – what sort of statements are these? Are they descriptions of our feelings and subjective states of mind? If they are, then the words we use and the feelings we have are independent of one another. This means that questions of truth and falsity come in, for the words may not match the feelings.

Wittgenstein points out that this interpretation of talk about our subjective and private experiences must be mistaken. We have already seen that if I know the meaning of the word 'pain,' I cannot be incorrect about whether I am experiencing a pain. It is not like being incorrect about an item of clothing: 'That's not a scarf. It's a cravat!' It makes no sense to correct myself by admitting that it wasn't pain I felt after all, but that it was amusement. Talking about how I feel is not a description of my state of mind but an avowal of how I feel. Avowals can be sincere or insincere, but they cannot be true or false. This distinction will become more clear as we follow the argument in more detail.

The distinction we are after is reflected in the difference between the grammar of first-person speech and third-person speech. In the first-person I say 'I'm very disappointed that I did not get the Nobel Prize' or 'Since the car crash I have had a terrible pain in my back.' With this kind of talk, according to Wittgenstein, I am expressing how I feel. This is because the tendency to use these words is *part of what it is* to be disappointed or to be in pain. Should I have no tendency to use these words I am not disappointed nor am I in pain. I cannot use them incorrectly on this or that occasion, but I can use them insincerely. 'Insincerity' is a secondary language-game, since using words like 'disappointed,' 'overjoyed,' 'pain' and so on deceptively depends on the existence of the primary language-games in which this vocabulary is established.

If, however, we are talking in the third-person and say 'She is disappointed because she lost the match' or 'He has a pain in his foot since he did so much digging,' then we are reporting something, describing what we think somebody is feeling. In this sense, our tendency to use these words is independent of whether the person so described is disappointed or in pain. It follows that we could be wrong about how it is with them. Such a third-person statement might be true or false. It is based on whatever evidence we can gather, such as her bursting into tears or his rubbing his foot vigorously and grimacing. What is more, descriptions attract the concepts of doubt and certainty. I tell you that I've seen the first cardinal of the season today. You might have your doubts and say 'Are you sure? It's rather early in the year for cardinals.' I reply that I glimpsed a flash of red in the woods. But still you might judge my claim to be false. Perhaps it was not a cardinal but someone in a red plaid jacket. Now suppose I say that I am in terrible pain. What if you say 'Are you sure? It was only a mosquito bite.' All I can possibly say is that I am telling you this because of the acute pain I am feeling. There is no gap to be filled between the evidence for what I am experiencing and my avowal. The tendency to utter these words is part of the way one *displays* one's feelings or one's state of mind. I can be wrong about the bird being a cardinal, but I cannot be wrong about the feeling being an intense pain, if I know how to use the word.

Again, in making a first-person statement about my feelings I am making an avowal. I am expressing how it is with me, sincerely or insincerely. In making a third-person statement about somebody else's feelings I am describing that person's feelings correctly or incorrectly. In the first case I need no evidence. In the second I must go on the signs I see or hear. These distinctions between the grammar of first-person expressive talk and third-person descriptive talk can be categorized as the asymmetry principle.

Resolution and diagnosis of the paradox: the beetle in the box simile

The final thrust in this part of the argument comes in two famous passages (PI §§293, 304) concerning the status of feelings in relation to our public expressive vocabulary. In these and surrounding remarks Wittgenstein argues that the bodily feelings as the topics of subjectively oriented discourse can play no role in the language-games by which the meanings of the vocabulary for this type of discourse are established. There is no guarantee whatever that the private feelings of all those people who display similar expressive performances are alike in relevant ways, or even that they are actually experiencing anything at all in some cases.

If I say that it is only from my own case that I know what the word 'pain' means, can I not say the same of other people too? Asks Wittgenstein, 'How can I generalize the *one* case so irresponsibly?' (PI §293). Someone tells me that he knows what pain is, speaking from his own case only. How could that be? Now Wittgenstein sketches out the famous 'beetle in the box' simile:

Suppose everyone had a box with something in it: we will call it a 'beetle'. No one can look into anyone else's box, and everyone says that he knows what a beetle is only by looking at *his* beetle. – Here it would be quite possible for everyone to have something different in his box. One may even imagine such a thing constantly changing. – But suppose the word 'beetle' had a use in these people's language? – If so it would not be used as the name of a thing. The thing in the box has no place in the language-game at all; not even as a *something*: for the box might even be empty …

(PI §293)

Think of a bodily feeling as a beetle and think of the box as your mind. Now think of the bodily feeling, like the beetle, as 'an it,' an entity, in your body. Finally, think of other people as having entities of this sort in their bodies and suppose you can talk with them sensibly and with ease about these entities. Why would these entities have 'no place' in our conversations pertaining to them?

To understand the full thrust of this simile it will be useful to consider how you could grasp the meaning of the word 'beetle' in public talk. You could not grasp this meaning by reference to whatever is in another person's box because they might have quite different things in their boxes. Suggesting that our private experiences are like taking a look at the beetle in our box highlights the tendency we have to think that feelings in our bodies are thing-like, as beetles are things. That is to say that, if the grammar of the language of bodily feelings is based on the model of object and designation, the object drops out of consideration as irrelevant. We must be able to learn how to use the word without being able to compare objects. We can learn words for bodily feelings without comparing bodily feelings. To an extent, this also supports the idea that first-person language pertaining to bodily feelings is expressive.

Wittgenstein sums up these considerations in §304. The interlocutor accuses him of declaring that the feeling of pain is 'a nothing,' since it plays no direct role in fixing the meaning of a pain-word. To this Wittgenstein replies:

Not at all. It [the feeling of pain] is not a *something*, but it is not a *nothing* either! The conclusion was only that a nothing would serve just as well as a something about which nothing could be said. We have only rejected the grammar which tries to force itself upon us here.

We should take the words 'some*thing*' and 'no*thing*' quite literally as the proposal that 'things' play no role in the meaning of 'pain.' In other words, pains and other bodily feelings are not mental entities, or thing-like beings known only to he or she who has them. Also, what greater difference could there be between a case in which someone puts on an act of being in pain when feeling nothing and when that act is expressive of the discomfort he or she feels 'as pain'? The point of the argument is to make clear the nature of the primary language-games in which one acquires the relevant vocabulary, which do not require teaching by pointing to a common refer-ent. Once the vocabulary is acquired, it can be used to refer to a private feeling because having the feeling and having the tendency to a certain expression are internally related, being part of the same psychological complex. But in both the case of *learning* words and the case of *using* words once learned, the relation of words to experience is expressive and not descriptive. Again, the statements in which the words appear are avowals, not assertions.

Breaking the analogy between material things and mental entities

Another lesson to be drawn from the PLA is that the mentalistic states of affairs, which we are expressing, are not mental objects – if our paradigm case of an object is an ordinary material thing. The uses of words to express bodily feelings and the like do not follow the same grammar as the words for material things (§§253, 254). We need to look more closely at the background of the 'beetle in the box' simile to get clear about what sort of 'existence' private feelings actually have.

In the seventeenth and eighteenth centuries philosopher–psychologists tended to think of the contents of the mind as 'ideas,' or mental entities that are in many respects like material things. Indeed, the concept of a mental 'content' was consciously modeled on the physicist's concept of a material atom or 'corpuscle.' According to this principle, words for mental entities obey the same grammar as words for material entities. In particular, there seemed to be no deep problem about determining whether the idea of the pain of being stung today was the same as the idea of the pain of being stung yesterday. Frequent reference was made to ideas as color sensations, without any doubts being raised about their criteria of identity. For example, Locke (1690/1972) offers a comprehensive theory of 'ideas,' including 'ideas of sensation,' without being troubled by any identity questions.

But in order to talk about something as an object we need to satisfy two main conditions. These 'identity criteria' for objects have to do with how to apply the concept of 'sameness.'

At this point we need to introduce the notion of a 'grammatical remark.' We encounter a number of these in Wittgenstein's later writings. Grammatical remarks having to do with psychological concepts are, in part, identifiable on the basis of their showing logical connections between words and the psychological phenomena to which they refer or which they express. Malcolm (1995) has explained it thus: 'a true grammatical remark is a "truism" since it merely spells out some feature of our familiar use of an expression' (p. 85). For example, the statement 'There is no bluish yellow' is a statement about a particular facet of our color vocabulary. Thus grammatical remarks are rather different from empirical generalizations. As part of a grammatical analysis, the truisms revealed through describing the uses of words represent the possibilities and limitations of words as they are used to express and refer to psychological phenomena. That is, part of the function of a grammatical remark is to point out rules of use.

Now, if it is a grammatical remark that another person cannot have my pains, what does this imply about the uses of the word 'same'? Wittgenstein asks:

> What counts as a criterion of identity here? Consider what makes it possible in the case of physical objects to speak of 'two exactly the same', for example, to say 'This chair is not the one you saw here yesterday, but it is exactly the same as it'. In so far as it makes *sense* to say that my pain is the same as his, it is also possible for us both to have the same pain.
>
> (PI §253).

If a being is to be treated as one of a kind of thing, one has to be able to say whether it is the same thing as was encountered before. Philosophers call this 'numerical identity.' Jill is sitting in numerically the same chair as she sat in last week. It has a recognizable pattern of scratches and a barcode label on the back with the same pattern. Using another sense of 'same,' Anthea and Jill are sitting in chairs that are the same, since both chairs are standard-issue lecture-room chairs. The chairs are the same in the sense of having very similar attributes. But they are *numerically* distinct. Philosophers call this 'qualitative identity.'

There are well-established criteria by means of which we settle questions about both the numerical and qualitative identity of material things. PI §§258, 261, 265 and 270–72 cover the case of seemingly immaterial objects. One thrust of these remarks is the question: What is the basis of judgments of sameness and difference of my own bodily feelings?

Imagine pricking yourself with a pin and then doing it again and asking yourself about the qualitative and numerical identity of the two pains. What would be the criteria for settling whether there had been one or two pinprick pains, and, if two, whether they were qualitatively identical? Does the expression 'same pain' follow the same rules of use as the expression 'same cup'?

Let us now look at Wittgenstein's way of resolving this question, starting with PI §258. We are to imagine someone trying to keep a record of a recurrent sensation (or what we will call a 'bodily feeling'). The first thing to do is to try to give meaning to the sign 'S' (for sensation) that is to be used to record the occasions when the person has the experience. Suppose we try to give 'S' meaning by concentrating on the feeling, by trying to do subjectively what one would do to establish a meaning of a word for a material thing (for example, by pointing to an exemplary instance). To this end we associate the sensation with the sign 'S' and write the sign on the calendar for every day we experience the sensation. Wittgenstein observes first that 'a definition of the sign cannot be formulated.' Why not? One reason is that we cannot provide an ostensive definition of the sign 'S' because, as Wittgenstein suggests, we cannot point to the sensation 'in the ordinary sense' even if we concentrate our attention on the sensation and 'point to it inwardly.' This 'ceremony,' as Wittgenstein calls it, would not achieve the goal of impressing upon us the connection between 'S' and the sensation itself. Nor would it enable us to remember correctly the connection between 'S' and the sensation in the future because 'in the present case [we] have no criterion of correctness. One would like to say: whatever is going to seem right to me is right. And that only means that here we can't talk about "right"' (PI §258).

This latter point means that since I have no way of telling whether I am using 'S' for the same experience, I cannot even have the idea of incorrect or correct use of 'S.' So I cannot make use of the idea of 'being right' here – or of 'being wrong' for that matter.

But if I cannot make use of 'S,' how can I suppose that the sign has a definite meaning? It might mean anything. When talking about sensations it is difficult to put ourselves in the position where we have, as yet, no mastery of sensation words. It is difficult to see what it would take to achieve that mastery. Even if I ask you to prick yourself with a pin and call that 'S' and then do it again and call it 'S' again, all this is happening in a framework of concepts and practices that are already established.

We could try to recover the 'original position' by thinking about an entirely novel bodily feeling. But then, how would you know that you are having another identical experience of that novel feeling? You say that you remember how it felt on the previous occasion. But this remembering must be supported by evidence. Compare the case in which you say that you remember the unique type of cake you had at my place last time. I am serving it again. Doubts can be settled by a glance at the recipe book. How do I know that I remembered the novel bodily feeling correctly a second time if the only way I can decide whether I have done so is by remembering it?

We are now familiar with the differences between two kinds of identity, between numerical and qualitative identity – the two senses of 'same.' Numerical identity concerns the persistence in being of the very same object and qualitative identity refers to two things with the same or similar properties. These are among the 'grammatical' rules for talking about things. The grammar that links pain to a person means that this sense of 'same' – as in 'having the same pain' – can only be qualitative. Even in the case of Siamese twins, about whom we might say that they 'both feel a pain in the same place,' their pains are only qualitatively identical (see PI §253).

'The proposition "Sensations are private" is comparable to: "One plays patience by oneself"' (PI §248). This is a grammatical remark. We can identify it as such since we cannot imagine the state of affairs that would be described by its opposite. In PI §251 Wittgenstein asks what it means to say that one 'can't imagine the opposite of this ... ' In many cases, being unable to imagine the opposite is not a failure of our imaginative powers, as if the task were too difficult. Why is it so difficult to imagine the opposite of 'Sensations are private'? The reason is that, in this case, there is nothing to imagine! Forming its 'opposite' – 'Sensations are public' – looks like a proposition alright. But it says nothing at all because *it makes no sense!* In other words, to be 'this pain' it must be 'this person's pain,' experienced by this person alone. We need to be careful here, however, because from this it does not follow that other persons cannot 'understand' this person's pain.

In the course of the argument outlined thus far the following insights have been developed:

(1) The Augustinian conception of language is shown to fail in yet another context, since words for bodily feelings are learned in language-games that do not involve pointing to an exemplary feeling.
(2) First- and third-person uses of psychological words obey radically different grammars; the first-person is expressive and the third person is descriptive. (This is the asymmetry principle.)
(3) Bodily feelings (and other private mental 'entities') are not mental 'things.'

To what sort of beings can we ascribe feelings?

Is the fact that words for bodily feelings can only be applied to people and beings like people simply a consequence of the way that feeling-words must be learned?

Wittgenstein, always getting away from the naïve idea that our problems with knowledge of other minds are to be put down to some matter of fact, sets about arguing that the tie between persons and feelings is also grammatical. In PI §281, Wittgenstein's interlocutor protests: 'But doesn't what you say come to this: that there is no pain, for example without *pain-behaviour*?' To which Wittgenstein responds: ' – It comes to this: only of a living human being and what resembles (behaves like) a living human being can one say: it has sensations; it sees; is blind; hears; is deaf; is conscious or unconscious.'

What about the fact that we ascribe feelings to inanimate things, such as a pot in a fairy tale and dolls in ordinary life? Wittgenstein admits that 'we do indeed say of an inanimate thing that it is in pain: when playing with dolls for example. But this use of the concept of pain is a secondary one' (PI §282). In other words, attributing pain to a doll is not a language-game in which we establish our customary usage of 'pain' and related concepts. A child can say her doll is 'in pain' only if she is already accustomed to using the concept. There is no justification for ruling out fantastic uses of sensation concepts, so long as we have already mastered their use in ordinary circumstances. It is important to add that this mastery does not emerge from private experiences. This is why Wittgenstein asks whether having got the idea of pains from my own experience I can transfer it to objects outside myself – to a stone, for example.

> Look at a stone and imagine it having sensations ... And now look at a wriggling fly and at once these difficulties vanish and pain seems able to get a foothold here, where before everything was, so to speak, too smooth for it.
> And so, too, a corpse seems to us quite inaccessible to pain. – Our attitude to what is alive and to what is dead, is not the same. All our reactions are different.
>
> (PI §284)

Again, the point is grammatical. In using words as we do, it is not that we are summing up a number of discoveries about the inner states – or lack of them – of stones and corpses. If there is no place for expression in the things in question, then there is surely no place for what usually is expressed in any form of life.

The same analysis applies to the question of why we always ascribe pains and other sensations to people and not to their bodies or parts of their bodies. It is not the rapidly beating heart that is excited, nor the broken foot that is in pain. There is a comprehensive language-game around persons, including such matters as which person is to be comforted and so on. One does not comfort a foot. As Wittgenstein says much later in the *Investigations*: 'A smiling mouth *smiles* only in a human face' (§583).

It might be beneficial to bring up another point here. Some readers will have noted that a number of the foregoing points are applicable to debates over the humane treatment of animals. Even a cursory application of Wittgenstein's views to such debates would take us beyond the purposes of this text. However, the remark we have quoted above where Wittgenstein compares our reactions to a stone and a wriggling fly (PI §284) gives some indication as to why members of some cultures have debates about the humane treatment of animals and 'animal rights' in the first place. There are very good reasons to regard the notion of 'animal rights' as dubious. But there is no doubting that such ideas emerge in significant respects from our ordinary uses of concepts pertaining to bodily feelings – to the cases in which we are inclined to ascribe pains to non-human, animate beings. So much is obvious. What we are suggesting is that, in significant respects, the notions of 'humane treatment of animals' and 'animal rights' emerge from the contexts in which 'pain seems able to get a foothold.' Beyond that, things get very complicated as the language-games of 'rights and duties,' 'what it is to be human' and so on must be considered.

To end this chapter we will turn to some applications and examples of topics in psychology to which the lessons we have learned from Wittgenstein's PLA can be applied. These will serve not only to reinforce some of the lessons, but to provide impetus for applying general ideas of the PLA to other topics. We will address only two topics: sensations of color and personal identity. The former, along with a more in-depth presentation of Wittgenstein's treatment of color concepts in Chapter 13, carries implications for the psychology of perception. The latter (personal identity) carries implications for the wider psychology of personality and perhaps more focused research on identity formation.

Learning point: the private-language argument

1. *Context of the argument.* The PLA consists of a web of analyses directed against the claim that a single person could create their own language by associating words with his or her own private experiences. The conclusions of these analyses ramify to several issues in psychology.

   (a) It is yet another strike against the denotational theory of meaning.
   (b) It effects a dissolution of the problem of subjectivity: its purpose is to show how public knowledge of private mental phenomena is possible.
   (c) It exposes three bogus dualities:
      (i)   The 'inner–outer' metaphor for the mind–body distinction.
      (ii) The 'subjective–objective' duality for types of experience a person has of mental–material domains.
      (iii) 'Privileged–non-privileged access' for the relation of the person to mental–physical experience.

2. *Force of the argument.*

   (a) To answer the following questions:
      (i)   Could there be a language, the words of which are given meaning by denotation of one person's mental phenomena and usable only by that person?
      (ii) How is a public language for reporting private experience established and what is its grammar?
   (b) The problem of how words for bodily feelings can have public meanings emerges only if one assumes that 'pain' and similar words

are *names* for mental entities, with a grammar similar to words used for material entities. It is a mistake to treat 'I have a pain' on the model of 'I have a red shirt.'

(c)   The descriptive–expressive distinction:

    (i)   A description, P, of X must be independent of X because P could be wrong.

    (ii)   A tendency to express one's private condition in a certain way *is part of what it is to be in that condition.*

3.   *How a subjective 'bodily feeling' vocabulary is learned*: By substituting a verbal expression for natural expressions, so that the words inherit the grammar of expression.

(a)   An expression and what it expresses are internally related, in that that expressed phenomenon would not be that phenomenon unless there was a tendency to express it in a certain way. For example, unless one had a tendency to smile and so on, one's state would not be 'happiness.'

(b)   'I'm in pain' inherits the expression-grammar from natural expressions of pain, and so *is not a description* of one's state, but is internally related to it.

(c)   In consequence, the use of such words as 'know,' 'certain' and so on, in the context of expressive uses of language, is seriously misleading.

4.   *The problem of correctness*

(a)   PI §258 illustrates the intractability of the problem of correctness in the circumstances in which the PLA paradox arises. (This is the diary and 'S' example.)

(b)   Undertaking to use a word in a certain way does not help to bridge the gap between uses of the word at different times, or recognizing the feeling as the same as before.

(c)   In PI §265 the analogy of using an imagined timetable to check an imagined departure shows the emptiness of subjective criteria of correctness. (This is the train departure example.)

(d)   In PI §271 the example of trying to imagine that someone has forgotten what feeling the word 'pain' refers to is incoherent – even if that someone uses 'pain' correctly.

5.   *Private experiences are not mental entities.* To bring out the difference between material things, such as a bottle of wine, and the objects of private mental experiences, such as feeling a pain:

(a)   We distinguish between numerical (same thing again) and qualitative identity (one the same as another, that is, having properties in common). Language-games featuring material things include both senses of 'same,' while language-games featuring private experiences can make use only of qualitative identity.

(b) PI §271: we observe that everyone may be experiencing something different when each uses a certain word, say 'beetle.' This shows that the object–designation picture of meaning for the subjective realm is mistaken.

6. *Implications for participating in the human form of life*

(a) Only of beings that do behave in distinctive ways expressive of their subjective states can we say that they are 'in pain,' 'amused' and so on. Some hint of 'humanness' is necessary.

(b) This does not rule out ascribing feelings to dolls in fantasy. But there can be no language-games ascribing feelings to stones.

Applications and examples

Sensations of color

The target of Wittgenstein's discussion of color words is a feature of Russell's (1918) proposal for a perfect language based on words for elementary sensations or 'sense data.' The words of such a language should take their meanings from private sensations, so that the relation between words and that to which they refer would be incorrigible. Russell believed that one could not be wrong about the private, sensory experience one was having then and there, and made much of visual sensations (colored patches in the visual field for example) as the basis for a language which would be immune from any kind of error, factual and philosophical. Again, psychologists have much to learn about perception from Wittgenstein's discussion of the general issue of how our color vocabulary is established and used. We remind readers again that in Chapter 13 we explore a wider range of questions concerning color words than the simple cases discussed at this point.

Phenomenologists assume that it is possible to 'bracket' the thing-like aspects of a red apple and attend only to the red hue, the color. But can I not use 'red' both for the barn in Northern New York of which I speak and for the patch in my visual field that corresponds to the color on my palette from which I will choose to paint a picture of the barn? Or do the two uses of 'red' here do duty specifically for two distinctive tasks – speaking about the barn and seeing a color patch in my personal field of vision? One would be for describing things we can all see. Another would be for describing something known only to the speaker, a patch in the visual field.

What am I to say about the word 'red'? – that it means something 'confronting us all' and that everyone should really have another word, besides this one, to mean his *own* sensation of red? Or is it like this: the word 'red' means something known to everyone; and in addition, for each person, it means something known only to him? (Or perhaps rather: it *refers* to something known only to him.)

(PI §273)

In the next paragraph Wittgenstein points out that saying 'red' *refers* to something private, rather than *means* something private, does not help us to grasp its function. Worse, it suggests that the red patch in the visual field is a kind of thing. We have already seen the difficulties that arise when we slip into treating bodily feelings as if they were thing-like.

Where does the temptation to fall into this piece of nonsense come from? A person does not have the feeling of pointing into him- or herself when they reflect on the color of the sky. But maybe a person has that feeling when they perceive the sky. The diagnosis of what has gone wrong is revealed by a parallel case.

> Someone paints a picture in order to shew how he imagines a theatre scene. And now I say: 'This picture has a double function: it informs others, as pictures and words inform – but for the one who gives the information it is a representation of another kind: for him it is the picture of his image, as it can't be for anyone else … And what right have I to speak in this second case of a representation or piece of information – if these words were rightly used in the *first* case?
>
> (PI §280)

Of course, I have no right. The picture has already informed others of what the theater designer thinks. There is no second stage at all. All he could do to show others what he had imagined would be to paint another picture. All anyone could ever do would be to compare two such pictures. Here again we have a situation closely paralleling that for bodily feelings. Picturing an image is rather like expressing what one senses, rather than describing it. If there is no independent access to what is pictured, then the 'truthfulness' of the picture has no place in the discussion.

The language-games in which people with normal vision come to learn color words must be based on public exemplars, perceivable by anyone. These are the primary color language-games. Only in secondary language-games can one talk about one's perceptions of color. Once established, one can use these words to talk about private experiences – how it looks to me – as well as to describe public objects. We might imagine Monet explaining to a friend why he chose a particular shade of green, one that was related to the private experience of color he experienced when looking at the lily pond. Or in the case of auditory perceptions we might imagine Mozart reflecting on how to achieve 'the tone color' he needs to express Don Giovanni's shock as the statue marches into the dining room.

When basing the possibility of language-use on words learned by pointing to exemplars, the word 'red' can get its meaning only derivatively from the public use of the word to describe public objects. This again is a kind of parallel to the case of feelings. Only if there is a way of establishing meaning in some language-game or public procedure could there come to be a use of a word for referring to private feelings.

Personal identity

This analysis also applies to another case of great importance in psychology, the sense of personal singularity. Just as saying 'I'm happy' expresses my emotion or mood, so using the first-person expresses my sense of self. It is not that 'I' refers to an inner being, the one who perceives. For that 'I' is none other than the person. 'I' *expresses* the point of view from which the world is perceived, including that part of the world that is the perceiver's own body.

What is it to be just *this* unique human being? How is individuality experienced? Do all cultures experience individuality of the human person in similar ways? These are some of the deep philosophical questions at the heart of the human sciences. We often use the word 'identity' to discuss these matters.

The two main senses of personal 'identity'

There are two senses of 'identity' in English-speaking cultures. Each answers a different level of question about the individuality of a human being. In contemporary English we have a relatively new use for the word 'identity.' Now it is often used to mean not 'which person this is' but '*what sort* of person this is.' This meaning of 'identity' appears in concepts such as 'ethnic identity' and derivatively in expressions such as 'identity politics.' This refers to basing one's political allegiance on such matters as cultural or racial origins, rather than on an 'objective' appraisal of policies. What we might label the 'traditional' meaning of identity survives in questions like 'Which particular person is this?' 'Identity' in this sense appears in concepts such as an 'identity parade.' The police use this procedure to pick out a particular person, not a person of a certain type. The phenomenon of 'identity theft' involves simulating the singularity and identity of someone else's personhood.

When we look more closely at this second main pattern of use we find that there are two aspects of personhood that are important. The first is the 'fact of identity,' or the idea that a person is the 'same person' at different times and in different places. Such a being can be picked out from others, perceived by other people as the one they had previously encountered. Dogs, of course, are adept at making such identifications. This presupposes that a person lives along a continuous path in space and time. In turn, it presupposes that the person is embodied in the same material thing throughout life and wherever that person may roam. There are criteria, including empirical tests (such as DNA identification), that succeed or fail to identify the person involved. Generally speaking these are invoked only in hard cases, such as occasionally arise in law. Dogs, of course, use different criteria of personal identity from those used by people to tell whether someone is already known to them. But dogs are remarkably effective at picking out their masters from others.

The second aspect of personhood related to identity as a particular person is 'the sense of identity.' This is simply a person's continuous sense of being just 'this person,' or 'me.' This is closely tied up with the point of view from which one perceives the objects of the world outside the envelope of one's body, as well as the parts and dispositions of limbs and so on of one's own body. Ordinarily, no tests are required for a person to check whether he or she is the same person as yesterday. There is no place for getting it incorrect. The idea that one could say 'Perhaps, after all, I'm really you!' is nonsense. Thus – and following the same line of thought as Wittgenstein at points in the PLA – I cannot really be said to *know* that I am the same person who fell asleep in the same bed. I can question whether it is the same bed, but what sense could we make of my questioning myself as to whether I am the same person? To use such expressions opens the way for other related concepts, such as 'doubt' and 'certainty.' I may surely doubt that my beliefs about myself are accurate or correct. However, that presupposes that I have no doubt about who I am – in the sense of which person, namely me. So the point here is very similar to Wittgenstein's claim that it makes no sense to 'know I am in pain' (PI §246).

How can these 'identities' be studied?

Issues around the fact of identity – that a person is the same person at different times and in different locations – are evident in all sorts of social and legal practices. There are ways of using physical characteristics of people to decide questions of identity. Most cases can be settled by similarity of physical appearance, as in police identity parades. Some cases need more sophisticated criteria based on the uniqueness of fingerprints and of each person's genetic code. In hard cases, the law courts make use of more psychologically oriented tests. For example, in cases of inheritance of a fortune, someone's claim to be the long-lost heir may be suspect. In cases like this the claimant may have to satisfy the court that he or she genuinely remembers events that could have been known only to a real descendant.

The sense of identity is subjective. It is my sense of my own continuous being as just the person I am. In normal life, no one uses criteria to decide whether they are the same person as they were yesterday. It would make no sense to discover that I was actually someone else. The strange cases of amnesia, of people becoming convinced that they have a previous existence (perhaps as an ancient Egyptian), and so on, only throw the normal case into sharper light. To remember that *one* was once the Pharaoh Akhenaton presupposes a robust sense of personal identity in the present.

How can such a subjective and private matter be studied in a way that would qualify as a genuine contribution to psychology? We can make use of the psychological phenomenon of the discursive expression of subjective states, just as we did in the case of private feelings. Just as in that case, we must give an account of the primary language-games in which the language of personal identity is established for public use.

The principle with which we are now familiar could be put something like this: *Words to be used for expressing features of subjectivity cannot be learned by procedures in which the word is to be learned by being associated denotatively with the feature in question.* In the case of the expression of the structure of my conscious experience we must look to the public language-games in which the relevant expressions are mastered. What are they?

Only English and the Germanic languages have a word that does duty for the various concepts that are related to the individuality and identity of persons. Here is a catalogue of the uses of the word 'self' that will help us keep track of the various aspects in which persons can be individuals.

(1) Sometimes 'oneself' simply means 'this person – the one talking.' 'I did it myself' means that the speaker was the only person engaged in the activity.

(2) Sometimes 'self' is used to refer to personal identity in the sense of the continuous and unique trajectory that a human being lives through in space and time. At each moment, a person has a unique point of view from which to see the world and from which that person acts upon the world. This depends on the public fact of embodiment. Consciousness is structured from within a perspective centered 'in the body', so to speak.

(3) Sometimes 'the self' or 'self concept' refers to the ever-changing totality of beliefs a person has about his or her powers and capacities, knowledge and so on. Of course, each human being has a variety of life stories, modulated to fit this or that audience and situation.

(4) Sometimes 'self' means the impression of the nature and character of the person that is created in other people by what that person does to present or display personal characteristics in public.

Each of these forms of language-game is rooted in common, public ways in which the individuality of a human being is manifested. However, John Locke (1690/1972, Book II, Chapter XXVII, §15) offered a fable about people who exchange selves, the exchange depending on the private sense of identity a person has and which would be expressed, for example, by the use of the pronoun 'I.' He imagines the following situation. A poor cobbler and a prince fall asleep in their respective beds. On waking, he who remembered going to sleep as a prince wakes in the bed and body of the cobbler. The complementary experience befalls the cobbler. One remembers his past as a cobbler, and the other remembers his past as a prince. Thus 'personal identity' for each of the victims of this event is *continuity of consciousness*. 'I am the prince!' is not a description of the poor fellow's status. It is an expression of who he is.

The expression of a sense of personal identity

We have followed Wittgenstein's important distinction between describing a personal, subjective state to someone else, with all the possibilities of misunderstanding, and an expression of a personal subjective state, using one of the natural means of expression we inherit with the rest of our bodily equipment. We learn various linguistic devices that are substitutes for natural expressions. To apply this insight to the sense of self we notice that the personal pronouns form a system with which personal identity is expressed. Our working hypothesis will be that 'I' does not refer to my individuality. It *expresses* it. To be able to use 'I' is part of what it is to have a sense of personal identity.

There is an important distinction between anaphoric pronouns (third-person) and indexical pronouns (first-person and second-person).

Anaphoric: the reference of the pronoun is fixed by a name or some other definite referring expression elsewhere in the same discourse. 'Patricia joined George on the platform and she expressed her sorrow for the victims.' The referent 'she' is fixed by the referential force of 'Patricia.'

Indexical: reference is fixed by knowing who the speaker is. Someone says: 'I am deeply concerned about the fate of the hostages.' Who is deeply concerned? The speaker, and we only know who that is by being present at the moment of utterance, or by a report from someone who was there. The same sentence, used elsewhere, indexes someone else as deeply concerned.

There are many indexical devices in English and other languages, including 'here' and 'now.' Each is used to index the content of a statement with the current location of the speaker ('here' means 'near the one who is speaking') or the time of the utterance ('now' means 'at the same time as this utterance'). Wittgenstein sketches this conception of the first-person in PI §410:

> 'I' is not the name of a person, nor 'here' of a place, and 'this' is not a name. But they are connected with names. Names are explained by means of them. It is also true that it is characteristic of physics not to use these words.

The last sentence no doubt refers to the principle that the laws of physics are or purport to be true everywhere and at all times. Their content is not to be indexed with particular places, nor moments.

There are four possible indexical features expressed in the use of the first-person in some language systems or other. Particular grammars may or may not represent all of these features:

(a)   location of speaker in space
(b)   location of the speech-act in time
(c)   moral standing of the speaker
(d)   social standing of the speaker.

Indo-European languages express only (a) and (c) in the first-person. But in all languages except English, the second-person singular pronoun takes two forms, 'tu' and 'vous' in French, for example. One has to attend to one's relative social standing to the person addressed in choosing whether to use the 'T' or the 'V' form (Brown and Gillman, 1960, Chapter 1). Many Oriental languages express (a), (c) and (d) in the first-person singular. For example, in Japanese, 'watakushi' expresses a higher social status for the speaker than does 'watashi.' Some South East Asian languages express (b) as well. In Kawi, the classical language of Indonesia, first-person pronouns are inflected for tense and location. 'I/here/now' is lexically distinguished from 'I/there/then,' and so on (Mühlhäusler and Harré, 1990, pp. 108–10).

   In PI §411 Wittgenstein links the use of pronouns to express one's sense of self with the expressive character of feelings-talk by contrasting the different uses of 'this' and 'these' to the relation between person and 'entity,' expressed by the use of the pronoun 'my.' Compare 'Are these *my* books?' with 'Is this sensation *my* sensation?' Any suggestion of a parallel between these examples is soon dispelled when we realize that the relation between me and my books is contingent, and the question is open to Yes or No answers. However, the relation between me and my sensations is *grammatical*. The question 'Is this sensation *my* sensation?' makes no sense, since if the sensation is a sensation at all it *is mine*. Confusion arises, says Wittgenstein, 'because one imagines that by directing one's attention to a sensation one is pointing to it' (PI §411). Only in the material domain can a person point to something. (From this it does not follow that Wittgenstein brooks an 'immaterial domain'!) The use of 'I' can be acquired only in the public domain in which it is an indexical, qualifying what is said by the relevant characteristics of the person doing the speaking. Exploiting the fact of personal identity allows anyone to know who committed him or herself to the content of a speech-act. This is the primary language-game in which mastery of the first-person pronoun is achieved. Once mastered, the secondary language-games of the expression of the sense of personal identity become possible.

There is, as yet, no substantial body of research on the acquisition of the means of indexical self-expression. One major study that throws light on the process is the famous study, by Bruner and Sherwood (1976), on the peek-a-boo game. This game can be observed in a great many cultures, some of which ultimately end up with rather different identity concepts than those with which we are familiar in our post-Christian world.

The game involves a familiar care-giver hiding behind something like a towel, at which point the infant becomes alarmed and even distressed. The care-giver takes away the towel and the infant displays considerable relief, even joy. Bruner and Sherwood (1976) see this phase as the infant being exposed to the problematic continuity in existence of the hidden care-giver. The game is played for months, during which the infant's anxiety disappears and playful enjoyment becomes the dominant tone. The focus shifts from the infant's growing sense of the care-giver's continuing identity to a growing sense of its own identity. The child knows that it does not cease to exist even though it cannot be seen by the mother. Here begins the establishment of a robust sense of personal identity. The accompanying vocalizations herald the development of a mastery of indexicals, ultimately the most potent of all, the pronoun 'I.'

The lessons of this chapter

We can include bodily feelings and other private experiences among the data of a scientific psychology because there are public expressions of feelings, public expressions of images seen and so on. Our ordinary vocabulary is adequate, since it was not learned by attending to personal and private exemplars. There is no need for a 'private language' to be able to discuss private experiences. Nor is one possible. But here is an important qualification: the fact that we could not have a private language does not mean that 'private experience' cannot be part of the domain of a scientific psychology.

Persons, not their bodies or parts of their bodies, have sensations. Persons feel things occurring with their bodies. So the person concept cannot be dropped in favor of body concepts, or concepts for parts of bodies, such as brains.

Identity criteria for mental states of all kinds must include bodily displays. Persons, the bearers of psychological attributes, must be embodied.

The sense of self is researchable for the same reason as private experience can be part of the field of study in scientific psychology. There are ways in which one's sense of one's own personal being is routinely expressed. Among the most enlightening of these means are the personal pronouns. The primary language-games in which their use is acquired exploit the fact of personal identity, the unique personal embodiment of each person in the material/social world. Then it becomes possible to express one's sense of one's own identity as a unique consciousness.

Learning point: extensions of the application of the expression principle

Reminder: Words for subjective (private and personal) states of mind must be learned in language-games based on the public – not the private – use of these words.

1. *The case of color words*

    (a) Color words are sometimes used to refer to private perceptions of color, private auditory sensations and so on, by artists, for example.
    (b) 'Red' must be learned by reference to public exemplars, as part of a system of color contrasts. In normal cases, it makes no sense to ask whether our perceptions of color are the same or different. We can think of the expressive use of 'red' as meaning that I am having the color *sensation* that you would have if you were looking at the same public object.
    (c) The same applies to other sensations such as taste, sound and so on.

2. *The case of personal identity*

    (a) 'Fact of identity' means the numerical identity of persons. 'Sense of identity' is uniqueness of personal point of view (center of consciousness).
    (b) 'Self' has two main uses: this person, and this subjective point of view.
    (c) Personal identity is expressed by the personal pronoun 'I.' First-person uses qualify the content of the utterance with the point of view of the speaker in space and time, and with commitment (personal responsibility).
    (d) 'I' must be learned in the context of language-games, which depend on the 'fact of identity', that is, the means by which others know where the speaker is and what sort of moral character he or she has.

Further reading

Brenner, W.H. (1999). *Wittgenstein's* Philosophical Investigations. Albany: SUNY Press. (Specifically Chapter 3.)

Hacker, P.M.S. (1993a). *Wittgenstein: Meaning and mind. An analytical commentary on the* Philosophical Investigations (Vol. 3, Part I, Essays). Oxford: Blackwell. (Specifically Chapters 1 through 3.)

Werhane, P.H. (1992). *Skepticism, rules and private languages.* New Jersey and London: Humanities Press. (Chapters 1 and 7.)

10 Thinking about the future and past in the present
Philosophical Investigations §§437–45 and 572–86

[A person] has ... anticipations of the future, and these of two sorts. The common name for both sorts is expectation, the special name for anticipation of pain being fear, and for anticipation of its opposite, confidence. And on the top of all, there is judgment, to discern which of these states is better or worse ...

Plato, *Laws*, I.644c

Now hope that is seen is not hope. For who hopes for what is seen? But if we hope for what we do not see, we wait for it with patience.

St Paul, *Epistle to the Romans*, 8.25

It is in what is said that an expectation and its fulfillment make contact.

Wittgenstein, *Philosophical Investigations*, §445

Topics introduced: meaning and future/past reference; expecting, hoping and wishing; criteria for expecting and hoping; the meaningfulness of unrealistic wishes; implicit prescriptions of type versus particular fulfillment; memory research in the tradition of Ebbinghaus; recollection versus recognition; caused remembering; the concepts of remembering and forgetting; remembering dreams; primary language-games of remembering

We like to think that human lives unfold as developments of a known and recoverable past into an anticipated future. But in fact often our recollections, both individual and collective, are inaccurate and our anticipations of the future ill judged. Nevertheless, thinking in the present about the past and the future are of enormous importance to humans. How much time we spend reminiscing and planning! These activities presuppose abilities to manage past- and future-directed thoughts and actions. Wittgenstein has much to offer the conception and design of psychological research programs into these important skills from his observations of the grammars of key terms we use to express ourselves, apropos of past and future.

This chapter is divided into two parts. In the first we examine Wittgenstein's remarks on future-directed language and thought, focusing on expecting and hoping. In the second part we look at thinking and talking about the past – what psychologists usually refer to as memory. In both parts we encounter familiar themes, such as the possible roles of inner (or mental) states and processes, the temptation to mark a clear distinction between the inner and outer, primary versus secondary language-games, and often unnoticed details of the grammar of psychological concepts related to memory and future-directed thought.

I Thinking about the future: expecting, hoping and wishing

We begin at PI §437, where Wittgenstein thrusts us into a philosophical quandary. Wishes, hopes and expectations all seem to be forms of thought, but they seem to be forms of thought with a special character. When I express an expectation, for example, I seem to know in advance what will satisfy the expectation. But of course my expectation of something does not 'contain,' as it were, what I expect. More or less the same goes for wishes. When my wish is met by, say, a phone call from my friend, I know *that event* is the satisfaction of my wish. Just look at the reaction of an adolescent who wishes his new 'girlfriend' will call. Look at the excitement on his face and in his actions when the phone rings and her name and number appears on Caller ID. His wish for her call is satisfied. But how does this happen? How does an event satisfy a wish, an expectation, a hope? What is the link between the boy's wish-thought and the girl's phone call? Does his wish-thought determine what will satisfy it, even though the girl has yet to call? Does the fact that his wish is satisfied make his wish-thought a 'true' thought? What kind of thought is it anyway?

Questions of this sort also apply to planning, intending, requesting and so on. Even the seemingly unproblematic arrival of the dish I ordered some minutes before raises deep questions. What is the relation between my saying 'I'll have some of your Tin Roof Fudge Pie' and a slice of it arriving at my table? Actually there are two questions here. First, how does the requesting bring about the hoped-for thing or event? And second, how can my request be 'meaningful' if the thing or event to which it seems to refer does not now exist? One clue is that expressions seeming to refer to currently non-existent events must be meaningful if we are to realize that our wishes are *not* fulfilled.

At the end of PI §437 Wittgenstein seems to be warning us against the temptation to think there is a necessary relationship between a wish and that which satisfies it, whereby a wish must be satisfied by a *particular* something. But this seems to run against the grain of our ordinary way of thinking about a wish and its satisfaction. Only a phone call from my friend will satisfy my wish that she will call. So what can be the meaning of Wittgenstein's admonition: 'Whence this *determining* of what is not yet there? This despotic command?' (PI §437)? The answer, to be elaborated in this chapter, runs as follows: I cannot wish for a *particular* event or thing, since it may never occur or come to pass. However, I can wish for a *type* of event or thing. In so doing I may envisage or describe a concrete event or thing in detail. I wish or hope for the thing I want. Must whatever comes to pass be *exactly* like what I wished for in order for it to count as the satisfaction of my wish? The same applies to expectations. My friend calls alright, but instead of praising me – which is part of what I expected – she berates me for something I did the day before. I expected *a* phone call and that is what I got. But in a sense, I did not expect *this* phone call.

To explore the question of the kind of connection that will obtain between a thought expressed as a wish or expectation and a future state, in six remarks (PI §§439–44) Wittgenstein discusses two models of how wishes and expectations might be fulfilled. The discussion of these models throws light on the problem of the meaningfulness of thoughts about the future.

Expectations and their fulfillment: models of the fulfillment relation

Here is Wittgenstein's general suggestion. The expression of an expectation and its fulfillment are related in the same sort of way as something that had been unsatisfied is related to that which satisfies it. 'What is our prototype of non-satisfaction?' asks Wittgenstein in §439. He offers two illustrations. For the first, he uses a metaphor derived from his engineering background. An unsatisfied wish might be thought of as being like a hollow cylinder and a satisfied wish as that cylinder now fitted with something like a piston (§439). In the second illustration he asks us to compare an unsatisfied wish with a feeling, like hunger (§440). Having an apple might bring to an end one's hunger. Is that which annuls a wish, an expectation, want, and so on, properly said to be that which 'satisfies' it? Let us examine these models of fulfillment built on concrete instances of the application of the concept pair 'unsatisfied/satisfied.'

Model 1: satisfaction is the achievement of a perfect physical match

In this case, the piston fits the cylinder. This neatness of fit seems unrealistic. Metaphorically, a hollow cylinder is an 'unsatisfied' cylinder and the well-fitting piston is that which satisfies it. But how well does this work as a metaphor for satisfied and unsatisfied wishes and expectations? Must the satisfying event or thing be an *exact* fit to the unsatisfied state of the person wanting, wishing for, or expecting something? Here is a different example. Restaurants often display pictures of the dishes they serve. When ordering dinner in such a place I do not get – nor do I expect to get – an *exact* replica of the dish displayed on the photo-menu. Yet the dish I receive may well satisfy my expectation as expressed in my order. I expected a double cheeseburger and I got one. A perfect fit is not required.

Another weakness of this model is that the cylinder and piston are *logically independent*. There might have been cylinders in a machine that never required pistons. By contrast, a wish and what fulfills it are not logically independent. To be *that* wish is to wish for *that sort of fulfillment*.

Model 2: a want is satisfied if I get something that causes me to stop wanting, hoping and so on for whatever I hankered after

That which stops me wanting something need not have been what was originally wanted. Just because a bowl of cheese and broccoli soup brings to an end my wishing for clam chowder, it does not follow that I *really* wanted, hoped, or wished for cheese and broccoli soup. Wittgenstein remarks: 'Saying "I should like an apple" does not mean: I believe an apple will quell my feeling of nonsatisfaction.

This proposition is not an expression of a wish but of nonsatisfaction' (PI §440). So the fulfillment of a wish is not like simply having that which brings about an end to one's hankering for something.

A resolution

The puzzles inherent in these models are resolved if we realize that when I express an expectation, wish, hope and so on, I am implicitly *prescribing the type* of 'thing' I want. I may use a particular something in thinking about my wants, but I am using that particular as an exemplar, to stand for a kind of thing or event. I am not describing the actual thing that, in the future, will satisfy my want. Now we can understand what Wittgenstein means in the third epigraph leading the present chapter: 'It is in what is said that an expectation and its fulfillment make contact' (PI §445). (We have made corrections in the original translation of this remark.) Typically, types are expressed through words. It is with words – but not only with words – that we can express something general. The colloquial 'I'll try some of your Tin Roof Fudge Pie' clearly is a request for something of a certain *sort*.

This insight bears directly on the question of meanings. How do expectations get their meaning *as expectations* if the objects and events which give them meaning only occur after the time at which the person expressed an expectation of this or that event? Expecting seems to be a case of thinking about something that does not now exist. Clearly there is still room for the misleading influence of Augustinian assumptions; that is, *in order for a word or phrase to have a meaning there must be a corresponding object or entity that gives it a meaning*. But in the case of thoughts about the future – and, as it will turn out, the past – there are, when we have such thoughts, no such particular entities.

Remembering more or less correctly is thinking about the past, about something that did exist but no longer does so. Expecting, hoping and so on are thinking about the future – about something that does not now exist but might exist. Again, how can expressions in use at this moment, which seem to refer to currently non-existent events, have meaning? In the case of thinking about the future, the event to which we seem to refer may never happen. Yet we can think about it. In the case of the past, the event that seems to have been referred to never can be recovered. Yet we can think about it.

Wittgenstein's general solution to the meaning problem is already implicit in his analysis of the grammar of concepts like wishing and wanting. I cannot use a particular event to establish meanings, since it may never exist. However, I can use a *type* of event in establishing meanings without presupposing the existence of any actual event. I can think about the type with a verbal specification or with an exemplar.

What if one's wish or hope or expectation is focused on something logically impossible, something that could not exist? We have phrases to express the folly of this kind of hankering (for example, 'wishful thinking'). Moreover, expecting something that could not exist is not only silly but seems to violate the grammar of the concept of 'expectation' itself. It would be a stretch indeed for someone to expect something that they knew could not happen.

Are expectations, hopes and wishes 'mental states'?

Having established that the content of a future-directed thought is general at the type level and does not refer to a particular event or thing, we can now look more closely into the psychological aspects of these cognitive performances. When someone says she is expecting someone to arrive, it is tempting to assume they are describing a certain state of mind that will be displayed in various preparatory activities. Compare this mentalism with the proposal that, for example, expecting clear skies might be displayed entirely in *what someone does*. I see my friend Tom preparing his fishing gear and I say, appropriately, 'I see you're expecting good weather for fishing.' What are the criteria for my coming to know that Tom is expecting good weather for fishing? Questions of this sort are the pressing questions to be answered before we can even imagine what a research program into any future-directed form of thinking might look like.

'Misleading parallel: psychology treats of processes in the psychical sphere, as does physics in the physical' (PI §571). For a time in the history of Wittgenstein scholarship a topic of much debate was the charge that he was a behaviorist 'in disguise.' But one could hardly find a stronger and more concise departure from behaviorism than this remark! What do we make of this 'misleading parallel'? Hacker (1996, pp. 405–9; 446–9) provides a noteworthy account of the entirety of PI §571 (and surrounding remarks) that, in some respects, exposes for psychologists the wide-ranging implications of Wittgenstein's remarks on psychological concepts. However, our purposes for citing §571 are more narrow. We want to ask: what are the phenomena that should be studied, however indirectly, when the topic is 'thinking about the future and the past'?

I am expecting someone. Or I am hoping or wishing for something. From the perspective of another person, my ways of expressing expectation, a hope, or a wish seem to amount to my being in a certain state of mind. According to this suggestion the state of mind will be displayed in things I do. It is at this point that we meet up with the 'misleading parallel' referred to in PI §571. For as much as psychologists only can observe what people do, they *presuppose* something behind that 'doing' which occurs in the 'psychical sphere' – a state of mind and/or mental process for example. The parallel, of course, is that physicists do much the same sort of thing when they observe the movements of bodies or the phenomena of electricity, report their observations and construct explanatory theories. But while the physicist is justified in supposing that unobservable forces and so on are behind the movements of bodies, psychologists are mistaken in supposing that unobservable mental states and processes are behind expecting, hoping and wishing – not to mention seeing, hearing, feeling and willing (Hacker, 1996, p. 406).

Well, must there not be something behind the overtly displayed evidence of expecting, hoping and wishing? Expecting someone or hoping for something is like knowing something. This knowledge can be displayed in giving a correct answer to a question. Being able to do something is displayed in an adequate performance. So hoping for something might be displayed in my looking out the window and keeping an eye out for the person delivering the mail. But what are the *criteria* for our coming to know that someone is in such a state as expecting, hoping, or wishing – before the expected, hoped-for, or wished-for event comes to pass? Do these criteria involve examining the expecting person's state of mind or corresponding physiological processes? Let us look closely at two cases.

'Expecting'

'Expectation is, grammatically, a state; like: being of an opinion, hoping for something, knowing something, being able to do something' (PI §572). But in what sense is expectation *grammatically* a state? Hacker (1996) suggests that in this remark, Wittgenstein is hinting at a distinction between surface and depth grammar. The surface grammar of expecting, being of an opinion and so on *makes it look* as if these concepts refer to states of a person. 'Knowing that the battle of Hastings was fought in 1066 is surely not a persistent state in which a person finds himself' (Hacker, 1996, p. 450). So Wittgenstein's comparison between expectation and what it is 'like' (e.g. knowing something) needs to be treated with caution. We need to examine carefully the depth grammar of expectation versus having an opinion or knowing something. Like ourselves, Hacker (1996) regards examination of *criteria* for expecting (versus, say, having an opinion) as the key in getting clear on how the surface grammar leads us astray.

When someone says 'I'm expecting him to come' or '"I hope he'll come" – is this a *report* about his state of mind, or a *manifestation* of his hope?' (PI §585). Is this state of expecting a continuous conscious awareness of something? (Compare this with the proposal that knowing when the battle of Hastings was fought.) Or does it mean that the person in question is *disposed to do certain things*, from a range of activities verbal and otherwise, typical of someone who is expecting something (PI §583)?

If someone were to say 'I keep on thinking of his arrival,' then that would be a report of a current state of awareness, and, in that sense, it would be a report of a state of mind, perhaps continuously observable by the speaker. But how do we distinguish between a reading of a statement as a *report* and a reading of it as an *expression of what I am disposed to do*? Is it because I am in a different state of mind in the one case that is different from the other? There might be no such difference, or indeed, no such states of mind in either particular case. To make the distinction between a report and an expressed manifestation (e.g. of expecting) one must take account of *what led up to the utterance*, rather than accounting for anything in the current situation (PI §586).

'Expecting' is a family resemblance concept, par excellence. Sometimes its use indicates a persisting state of mind, sometimes a disposition that can be manifested in indefinitely many ways, with no continuous conscious accompaniment. When our use of 'expecting' is dispositional, there need be no explicit thought in the mind of the host of his friend's imminent arrival. Sometimes occurrent manifestations of a disposition will be displayed, such as setting out the tea cups. But on other occasions we would be justified in saying that someone is expecting someone even though the expecting person has prepared nothing in advance. Because of these diverse possibilities, we can see that 'expecting' is not a mental process, like thinking. Nevertheless, thoughts can express expectations.

The general question is posed in PI §§574–7. Is expecting a species of thinking? Or is it rather a species of action or behavior – something someone expresses in what he or she does? Clearly, thinking something in particular never is necessary for someone to be properly said to be expecting something. But still there must be some manifestation of 'expecting' as a disposition. In §576 Wittgenstein gives the example of someone excitedly watching a fuse burn down toward an explosive. Although this person does not say anything so explicit as 'I am expecting an explosion,' we would certainly be inclined to say that he or she is expecting it.

Laying out the implicit scheme for these concepts, we get something like the arrangement shown in Figure 10.1:

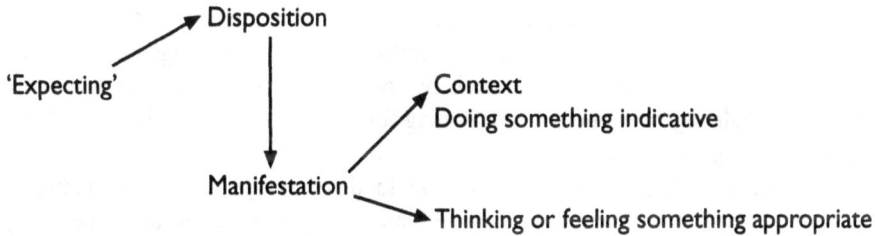

Figure 10.1 Scheme for concepts

It is important to emphasize that any of these 'doings' and 'thinkings' could be used for something other than expressing an expectation. I can go down and check my mailbox for all sorts of reasons. We need to take the context into account. Depending on the antecedents and surroundings of the expression of expecting, either an action or a gesture could be sufficient to justify an onlooker saying that someone is expecting something. In this context, the action or gesture is expressive of what I am generally disposed to do (PI §§583, 584, 587).

If, on seeing someone point a gun, someone says 'I expect a report' and the shot is fired, do we compare 'an expected shot' with the shot that actually occurs in order to find out if there is a match (PI §442)? No. There is no *particular* imagined shot present that we might compare with the real shot. The word 'shot,' used to express the expectation, does not refer to a specific future shot. 'Shot' merely exemplifies the kind of sound that will fulfill the expectation. Questions of fulfillment are settled by whether the particular event that occurs is *of the same type* as the one imagined. The relation between an expectation and what occurs is not an individual-to-individual relationship. It is a type-to-instance relationship. There may be differences between the instances of the type in question. Sometimes they matter and are enough to upset the event as a fulfillment of the expectation. Sometimes they do not.

'Hoping'

We need to take similar steps to locate the grammar (and psychology) of 'hoping.' In every case when someone could correctly be said to be 'hoping,' is that person in a certain mental state; for instance, 'imagining some desirable future event and longing for it'? Is 'dreading' what we say of someone who is imagining some undesirable future event and fearing its occurrence? Having a certain image in mind is indeed to be in a certain mental state. But is there some *image* typical of someone who hopes for something? If this were the correct way of representing the character of what these words are used for, 'hoping' and 'dreading' would be mental states. Are there any alternatives?

Is it the case that to be hoping for something is to be disposed to carry on some definite style of behavior, relevant to that for which one hopes? Is my dreading the arrival of the police nothing but a tendency to look for a safe back exit, to destroy incriminating papers and so on? Clearly, if I leave a stack of seditious literature on the table I can hardly be said to be dreading the arrival of the KGB!

Perhaps the comparison with expressive actions will be illuminating. Is a display of the characteristic marks of hoping expressive of a mental state, like groaning is expressive of being in pain? Is there a specific physiognomic language-game for hoping – something we could research by using video recordings of situations where we would say that a person was hoping for something? Here we seem to have a way of linking mental states with behavioral displays.

Wittgenstein takes considerable trouble to develop the distinction between being in a certain occurrent state of mind and being disposed to do some thing from a limited repertoire of things. For example, in PI §577 he points out that if I give an account of 'I am expecting him' as 'I should be surprised if he didn't come,' I am expressing what I am generally disposed to do in a certain (but non-necessary) way. I could have used some other phrase or a display of some other sort to express my expectation. This contrasts with the case in which I gloss my 'expecting' declaration as 'I am eagerly awaiting him,' which suggests that thoughts of his imminent arrival occupy my mind. This is a kind of thinking. Maybe this case is different enough from 'his coming does not occupy my thoughts' to warrant a different verb.

Neither the hypothesis of a definite mental state nor of a specific form of behavior will do. Having a certain image in mind is not a necessary feature of hoping. There is nothing whose display is definitive of what it is to hope. There does not seem to be a distinctive and unique inner connection between the character of displays or declarations of hoping and what is hoped for. One could not infer what someone hopes for from how that person is displaying a hope. I keep glancing out of the window whether I am hoping that Federal Express will bring me a copy of a new book I have ordered or whether I am hoping that Domino's Pizza will find my apartment. Though I must be disposed to think or do something germane to the realization of my hope, there is no tight inner connection between how one expresses a hope and what it is to be hoping. It is not like the tight inner connection between groaning and being in pain.

Perhaps, on closer examination, we will see that there must be an 'outer connection.' This raises the question of the meanings of words that purport to be descriptive of that for which I hope. What is the status of the direct object of 'hoped for ... '? Is it the future event itself that gives meaning to the image or the words, or the display that anticipates it? But that event does not now exist, so how could the event give meaning to the items in question that carry the content of my present hope? Is it the future event as an accompaniment of what fulfills the hope (or expectation)? No. The future event is the fulfillment *in so far as it is of the appropriate kind*. The psychology of 'wishing for something' can be analyzed along similar lines.

An exemplary tale: 'The Monkey's Paw'

The key point that specific thoughts and actions concerning the future can only be exemplars of types of possible events is brought out very well in a story familiar to Wittgenstein, that of 'The Monkey's Paw.'

A father and son are playing chess while the mother looks on. Later in the evening there is a knock on the door and a family friend, a sergeant who was once in the Indian Army, calls in. He is full of traveler's tales. This night he shows the family a monkey's paw that has the power to fulfill three wishes for the person who holds it. The sergeant expresses reticence about what had happened to the first person who made use of the power, except to say that his last wish had been for death. The sergeant himself already made his three wishes. These had proved disastrous. As a result, the sergeant throws the paw in the fire of the family's home. But the father pulls it out straight away. Eventually, the sergeant agrees to give him the paw. That night, holding the paw in his hand, the father wishes for £200. But nothing happens then and there. Next day, a man arrives at the house with news that the son had been killed in an accident in the factory where he worked. The firm had agreed to compensation. How much? – £200! Grief stricken, the father and mother settle into a dull routine of mourning, until one night the mother realizes that two more wishes remain. So she takes the paw in her hand and wishes for her son to be alive again. Nothing happens immediately. But after a few minutes, just long enough to walk from the cemetery, there is a loud knocking on the door and the mother rushes to open it. Her husband, realizing that she would open it to an animated but rotting corpse, picks up the paw and wished the son back in his grave again before the door can be opened (Jacobs, 1902).

Two difficulties with Wittgenstein's solution

Wishing for the moon

We use phrases such as 'wishing for the moon' to criticize unrealistic wants and wishes. The moon, though a real thing, cannot be possessed. What of wishes for impossible things? Surely these performances are meaningful, since only if someone understands the expression of the wish can it be criticized. We might think that the resolution of the problem of the meaning of descriptions of a future that does not yet exist fails for the case of a future which *could not* exist, since there is no viable general concept of which the fulfillment would be an instance. We think that Wittgenstein's response would simply be to emphasize that the expressions of such wishes are idle, not connecting with anything else in our form of life. Such talk has only the appearance of a language-game. That is to say, wishing for the moon is nonsense.

Stealing to order

People do, from time to time, hanker to have a famous work of art in their own personal collection – not necessarily to display, but to gloat over. Sometimes this desire may become so obsessive that a person with the necessary resources hires a gang of villains to steal the work. Here we seem to have a case of hankering for a unique particular. The person who hankered after Munch's *The Scream* wanted *that* painting, not a painting *like that*. When the collector received the canvas it did indeed fulfill his expectation. This example does not seem to present a problem for Wittgenstein's solution to the meaning question, since the work of art to which the expression 'Munch's *The Scream*' refers does currently exist. What is general is the 'moment of possession,' which may be realized in all sorts of ways.

Summary

Is there a definite answer to the question 'What is the present state of someone thinking about the future?'? What we have just brought to light shows that:

(1)   No necessary or particular mental state is required.
(2)   No necessary or particular bodily state or movement must be displayed.
(3)   There are generic dispositions to think/do a variety of things, which *only in a certain context* express hopes, wishes, wants, expectations and so on.
(4)   Fulfillment consists in the event hoped for or object desired exemplifying the same *type* as the expectation invoked.

Learning point: thinking about the future

How can a proposition expressing a thought about the future have meaning if the object of that thought does not yet exist, or may never exist?

1.   *Problems that an adequate account must solve*

(a)   How do I know that this event fulfills my hopes and so on?
(b)   What is the link between my present wish and its fulfillment?
(c)   Does the wish-thought determine what satisfies it?
(d)   Does the fulfillment make the proposition expressing my thought true?

2.   *Models of wish fulfillment*

(a)   PI §439: A cylinder determines what will fit it (a piston of a certain size). Must there be a perfect fit? This serves as a weak model, since cylinder and piston are *logically independent*. (There can be cylinders with no pistons.)
(b)   PI §440: A want (wish) is fulfilled by whatever stops a person wanting or wishing for something. I stop wanting clam chowder

when I have had some cheese and broccoli soup. But this does not show that I did not really want clam chowder.

3.   *Wittgenstein's implicit solution*

   (a)   In thinking and speaking about the future I am prescribing the *type* of thing I want, wish for and so on, but not the particular thing. For example, giving an order from a photo-menu, the particular photograph represents the type of dish.
   (b)   The remarks comprising PI §§437–44 warn against thinking that a fulfillment must be given by an anticipated particular.
   (c)   PI §445 says that an expectation and its fulfillment 'meet in language.' That is, the language-game of talking about the future invokes only general concepts, not particulars, which serve only as exemplars.
   (d)   'The Monkey's Paw' illustrates the 'general prescription/particular fulfillment' distinction.

4.   *Are these cognitive phenomena really mental states?*

   (a)   Feelings and thoughts of many kinds can go with any one of these modes of thinking, such as wishing, wanting, expecting, hoping and so on.
   (b)   No continuous pattern of conscious thought is required for an ascription of a continuous expecting or hoping to be proper.

5.   *Other questions*

   (a)   Can I wish for what could not exist? I can only *seem* to do so by playing an 'empty' language-game.
   (b)   Can I wish to own an *objet d'art* that is unique? There is no problem of meaning here since that object exists now. The puzzle is about what might exist but does not exist now.

II   Thinking and talking about the past

In some respects, much of the experimental research devoted to the psychology of remembering has been conducted within a framework of concepts and techniques pioneered by Ebbinghaus (1885). To discover the laws of recollection, he devised material to be remembered that was shorn of all meanings and thus all associations. He tested his own memorial capacities to recall items from his experimental material in different circumstances and at different times. That is to say, his was a case of '$n = 1$' research that included context and time as independent variables.

Whatever the merit of Ebbinghaus's work, it suffers from two serious drawbacks as an implicit model of what people do when they remember and think about the past. We do not have in mind the usual criticisms of his work: that he relied on introspection and that his research suffered from multiple-treatment interference. Rather, the first problem is that in *real life*, the cognitive states that express remembered items and the cues to recover them never are entirely shorn of meaning. Consequently, they are never wholly free of contextual and other associations with other items. The second problem is related to the $n = 1$ status of Ebbinghaus's research. The era of studies on statistical populations did not remove the fact that each individual did his or her memorial task(s) alone.

Many more recent studies on memory employ the kinds of material used by Ebbinghaus, to be remembered by individual participants that are part of a sample. So we are not holding up Ebbinghaus as a straw man. Furthermore, his imitators carried on one further unsatisfactory aspect of his work. For the most part, they studied 'recollection' rather than the more common phenomenon of 'recognition.' How many musical tunes can you recall when given their title? Now compare this with how many tunes you can recognize when presented with them. Similarly, few can recall the details of a journey that they traverse with ease every day, recognizing each twist and turn and junction as they come to it. This neglect is all the more startling in that the type of psychologist who continues in the Ebbinghaus tradition is prone to test the students under their care by requiring them to select the correct answer from a set of alternatives – the multiple choice test. This depends not so much on recollection as it does on recognition.

We do not want to suggest, of course, that the tradition of Ebbinghaus still dominates psychological research on memory. Rather, we only want to suggest that remembering is an enormously complex cognitive skill, the details of which have and continue to pose problems for empirical researchers and theoreticians of memory. Perhaps by familiarizing ourselves with its complex conceptual terrain, the grammar of remembering and related concepts can be opened up to enrich ongoing and future research.

Below we discuss a modest selection of Wittgenstein's remarks related to remembering, beginning with some remarks found in *Zettel* (Wittgenstein, 1967) that clear the way for addressing the mistaken assumption that there is some kind of inner process of remembering. Then we relate Wittgenstein's views on the grammar of remembering to the notion of 'collective remembering' before making a very brief suggestion about future research on the 'primary language-games' of remembering.

How is the past mediated to the present?

What sort of relation links some past event to my present recollection or recognition of it as something I once encountered? Wittgenstein wants to contrast the irrelevance of any causal link in understanding the language-games of remembering with the importance of links between the *concepts* of 'past,' 'present,' 'remember,' 'forget' and so on. In *Zettel* we find the following remark:

I saw this man years ago: now I have seen him again, I recognize him, I remember his name. And why does there have to be a cause of this remembering in my nervous system? Why must something or other, whatever it may be, be stored up there *in any form*? Why *must* a trace have been left behind? Why should there not be a psychological regularity to which *no* physiological regularity corresponds? If this upsets our concept of causality then it is high time it was upset.

(Wittgenstein, 1967, §610)

At first reading this seems to be a very odd assertion. How could a present recognition be a kind of remembering unless it was related in some way to what now exists, in the nervous system or somewhere else? The suggestion is simply that *the meanings* of the concepts of 'remembering,' 'recognizing' and 'forgetting' cannot depend on knowledge of states and processes in the nervous system.

The immediately foregoing sentence is very important and should be read carefully. We are discussing the *meanings* of concepts like 'remembering' and 'forgetting.' Wittgenstein is not asserting that remembering and forgetting have nothing to do with physiology – any more than he asserts that running up the stairs has nothing to do with physiology. 'Remember,' 'forget,' 'recognize' and other words having to do with the cognitive skill of remembering were in use long before there was any significant understanding of neuropsychology. Such words are used successfully by people who, in our times, have little or no knowledge of how their brains work. Wittgenstein's point in the above remark is that whether some activity or display of remembering *is remembering* cannot rest upon the character or even the existence of physical traces in the brain. Also, he is suggesting, characteristically, that insisting there *must be* memory traces held in the brain is evidence of a certain sort of temptation – even perhaps amounting to a dogmatic insistence.

There are two reasons why the meaning of remembering cannot depend on neurophysiological processes, storage areas in the brain and so on. The first is implicit in the above quotation. We make judgments about the verisimilitude of acts of remembering without having any knowledge whatever of the state of the brain of the person who has offered a recollection of some past event, or who has claimed to recognize something that he or she had encountered before. To that extent a grammatical relation is forged between remembering and skills and abilities, discussed in Chapter 5.

The second reason goes much deeper. How can one tell that an image of some event – or a statement describing some happening in which one believes one took part – is an act of remembering unless one can recognize the event portrayed or described *as past*? But one only comes to have a sense of the past when one has mastered the practice of remembering. Grammatically speaking, 'past' and 'remember' are internally related. The criteria for correct application of each of these terms are not independent of one another. Toward the end of the *Investigations*, Wittgenstein (PI II, xiii, p. 231) comments: 'And how does he know what the past is? Man learns the concept of the past by remembering.' There is no ancillary neurological criterion to hand.

At another point in *Zettel* we find the following: 'But if memory shews us the past, how does it shew us that it is the past? It does *not* shew us the past. Any more than our senses show us the present' (Wittgenstein, 1967, §663). There is no 'mark' that identifies what one is currently experiencing as 'the present' either.

> Nor can it [memory] be said to communicate the past to us. For even supposing that memory were an audible voice that spoke to us – how could we understand it? If it tells us e.g. 'Yesterday the weather was fine', how can I learn what 'yesterday' means?
>
> (Wittgenstein, 1967, §664)

There is a common element in these seemingly paradoxical questions about the past. It is what we might take, at first blush, to be the innocuous idea that the past we talk about *must be represented in the present*. But now we are not talking about the past event, but about its present recollection. We are no further forward with this picture of what remembering is, since we have no way by which we could judge whether the recollection we are using to access the past is accurate, or is a recollection at all.

These apparent problems simply vanish if we give up the false picture we are inclined to use. It is the picture that led us into trouble. False pictures about the workings of psychological concepts are often related to the technologies of the day. With respect to memory, the family album of holiday snapshots might be the culprit for people in the photographic age. Perhaps our problems have come from thinking of visual images of past events as if they were like photographs. We have good reason to think that photographs have a measure of verisimilitude stronger than mental images, however forceful the feelings we have of the 'pastness' and the truth of our images. The family photograph album does indeed contain records of the past. The camera may lie, but never wholly. The image in the family album was caused by a past event. Yet the album is a material thing having a public existence.

When someone reports a past event with the claim that he or she remembers it, what is the report about? Since the past happening does not now exist, we are inclined to say that the report must describe something that does now exist, such as a 'memory item' in the mind/brain. It is as if the person offering the recollection attends to a trace or a private image of what once happened, as if everyone had his or her private photograph album or video tape in their heads.

Can this mentalism account for the way we accept some memory claims and reject others? It cannot, simply because the same problem arises with the image as it did with the report. How does anyone know that his or her image is authentic? While we stay within the individual mind and the private video show or photograph album, there are only other reports and other images with which to compare it.

The moral to be drawn from this and similar cases is that *we should look for something public to authenticate putative memories*, be they expressed as images, as propositions, or in any other form. Often we rely on other people's recollections to check against our own. We would then use a coherence criterion to judge the verisimilitude of our own memory convictions. Alternatively, we could check material traces, in material forms that one presumes are known to be fairly resistant to corrosion and decay. There might be old letters, concert programs, an attic full of discarded furniture, a gravestone of a much loved pet and so on.

A memory report is about the past event, not about any present image or trace of it. This can be compared with the case of pain. An expression of pain is learned in a public language-game, a behavioral context, but it refers to or is about a private experience. Though we know if someone is in pain from their expressions, say crying, the word 'pain' does not describe the crying. In like manner, remembering the past is learned in a present language-game, but it refers to or is about a past experience. In each case we have an inaccessible referent at the heart of a common-place cognitive activity with which everyone is familiar and performs with confidence. We must now feel our way further into the language-games of remembering.

An inner process?

The first illusion to get out of the way is the familiar 'inner process.' Is remembering a public activity or is it really an inner process of which such public activities as telling someone what happened or making a drawing of a memorable event are the (inessential) outcome? In line with many of his psychological studies, Wittgenstein wants to shift away from this sort of account. At PI §305 his interlocutor asks: 'But surely you cannot deny that, for example, in remembering, an inner process takes place.' To which Wittgenstein responds:

> What gives the impression that we want to deny anything? When one says 'Still, an inner process does take place here' – one wants to go on: 'After all, you *see* it.' And it is this inner process that one means by the word 'remembering'. – The impression that we wanted to deny something arises from our setting our faces against the picture of the 'inner process'. What we deny is that the picture of the inner process gives us the correct idea of the use of the word 'to remember'. We say that this picture with its ramifications stands in the way of our seeing the use of the word as it is.
>
> (PI §305)

In the next remark, PI §306, Wittgenstein points out that when someone says that there has just taken place in them an inner process of remembering, it is to say no more than that he or she has just remembered something.

At this point we need to return to the remark, cited previously, that occurs toward the end of the *Investigations* (PI II xiii, p. 231). There Wittgenstein asks us to imagine a person who remembers for the first time in their life and says: 'Yes, now I know what "remembering" is, what it *feels like* to remember.' Then Wittgenstein asks: 'How does he know that this feeling is 'remembering'? ... – Does he know that it is memory because it is caused by something past?' Now we have run full circle, back to the internal relationship between the words 'past' and 'remember.' Except at this point we can link the observation of the relationship with PLA (Chapter 9). Suppose we ask: how could a person know in the future what remembering felt like unless he could remember what remembering felt like? Putting the question this way makes it seem as if a certain 'feeling of remembering' could serve as a criterion for knowing that one is remembering. But of course how remembering feels cannot be a criterion for an experience to be one of remembering.

A more direct link with the PLA pertains to memories as private images. Since the past happening does not now exist, we are inclined to say that the report must describe something that does now exist, as if the person offering the recollection attends to a trace or a *private image* of what once happened. But for something to be a recollection we must know that what it represents happened in the past. However, our only access to that event, for the most part, is via recollections. We seem to be running in circles. One way out is to examine the criteria – if there are any – of how we can *know* we have remembered something correctly. The issue of criteria in remembering correctly comes out in the following extended remark, which speaks to the temptation to think that what *corresponds* to words, such as color words, must exist 'somewhere' in order for such words to have meaning. That 'somewhere,' of course, will be 'inner,' as a memory. It can be laid down in a set of cellular assemblies, for instance, that are activated by the environment in an event in one's life after the event that is remembered. So, for example, we can think of a real sample of color, laid out on a table before us. It is the *only sample* of *that* color in the world. Also, we have a word for that particular color. Then we can think of a corresponding sample of that color in memory, laid in a set of cellular assemblies. When the cellular assemblies are activated, say by someone uttering the color-word, a mental image of the color pops up in our mind's eye. Suppose now that we destroy the 'real' color sample. What remains? Our memory of it. *That* color sample is not destructible like the real color sample.

> But what if no such sample is part of the language, and we *bear in mind* the colour (for instance) that a word stands for? – 'And if we bear it in mind then it comes before our mind's eye when we utter the word. So, if it is always supposed to be possible for us to remember it, it must be in itself indestructible.' – But what do we regard as the criterion for remembering it right? – When we work with a sample instead of our memory there are circumstances in which we say that the sample has changed colour and we judge of this by memory. But can we not sometimes speak of a darkening (for example) of our memory-image? Aren't we as much at the mercy of memory as of a sample? … – Or perhaps of some chemical reaction. Imagine that you were supposed to paint a particular color 'C', which was the colour that appeared when the chemical substances X and Y combined. – Suppose that the colour struck you as brighter on one day than another; would you not sometimes say: 'I must be wrong, the color is certainly the same as yesterday'? This shews that we do not always resort to what memory tells us as the verdict of the highest court of appeal.
>
> (PI §56)

To shed a bit of light on this remark we only need to think about how memories are 'negotiated' in courts of law. Are the memories of witnesses treated as being always veridical? It is hoped not. Memories are 'colored' by all sorts of influences. The comparison of memory images to corresponding samples in the real world is highly instructive when we question 'where memories reside.'

Then there is the case of reporting dreams. We seem willing to treat the telling of a dream as a recollection of something that happened when one was asleep and which one has remembered. But there is no possible use for a criterion of correctness in this case! The issue will strike us as important or empty depending on the interest of the question we might ask about the verisimilitude of the report. Obviously, if someone took the Freudian account of the role of dreaming seriously, the accuracy of the report would indeed matter.

Whether we remember something rightly is not always determined by how the memory seems to be. It is often a matter of public and material matters that we use to distinguish genuine memories from fantasies. Remembering must be established as a human practice in a language-game (or games) that more than one person can play. The upshot of Wittgenstein's relatively few remarks on remembering is in keeping with much of his commentary on psychological matters: the concept of remembering cannot be established by reference to a private inner process. There could be nothing intrinsic to that process that would mark it off as what remembering 'really is.'

Collective remembering

More recent developments in the psychology of remembering can be used to illustrate that Wittgenstein's plea to undertake a surview of relevant concepts can influence a branch of psychological investigation. Family resemblances in the ways the word 'remember' and related expressions are used open up in at least one new field of research, *collective remembering* (Middleton and Edwards, 1990).

One of the varieties of collective remembering is marked by such conversation openers as 'Do you remember ... ?' These expressions initiate discussions of some long-past event in the history of a family, a group of army veterans, a school reunion, a Thanksgiving dinner party and so on. Each individual engaged in the conversation contributes more or less significantly to the gradual development of a common version of some shared occasion. Research into such memorial conversations has shown the importance of the role of one or more members of the group as censors of individual contributions. Someone has or takes on 'memorial power,' accepting or rejecting suggestions to be incorporated in the common story (Middleton and Edwards, 1990).

Another study illustrating the importance of attending to the grammar of 're-membering' has been Dixon's work on collective remembering among older people (e.g. Dixon and Bäckman, 1995). Set a memory task, say to recall incidents in a video, if tested individually, younger people do better than their elders. However, when the remembering task is performed collectively, there is little difference between the level of performance between groups of younger and older people.

A third example begins from such commonplace expressions as 'Remembrance Day,' 'Remember the Alamo!' and so on. Such phrases are used for public and social memorial performances. Every society not only ceremonially marks important occasions, such as anniversaries of the '9/11' attack on New York and Washington, but also constructs public monuments as mnemonics, reminders of the lives of important people and great events. Washington DC is rich in such memorials. Abraham Lincoln gazes out over the Mall, while the soldiers depicted in the Iwo Jima Memorial draw the eye on Route 50 while one drives into Rosslyn, Virginia, just across the Potomac River from Washington.

Collective forgetting occurs as well. Those who would expunge memories of a painful past destroy the monuments meant to recall it. One of the most powerful images of the fall of Sadam Hussein was the dragging down of a huge statue of the dictator from its plinth. There is much yet to be discovered in the ways collective remembering and forgetting are 'done' (Middleton and Edwards, 1990).

So far as we know, none of the collective remembering studies was inspired directly by Wittgenstein's overview of remembering and related concepts. Nevertheless, they highlight the contrast between the narrowness of Ebbinghaus's studies and the breadth and realism of the work only hinted at here.

What are the primary language-games of remembering and recognizing?

Wittgenstein's grammatical investigations suggest that little children *must learn* the difference between remembering, imagining and dreaming, and that to a significant extent this learning process occurs in the setting of primary language-games. But why is there a glaring lack of research on these important, socially embedded processes of intellectual development? Is it because the laboratory is an inappropriate setting for such investigations? Perhaps so. But that is not all. Clara and William Stern, in their 1909 monograph *Recollection, Testimony, and Lying in Early Childhood*, suggest that even when developmental investigations are embedded in the ordinary contexts of young children's lives, certain aspects of what might be termed the 'negatives' of development (such as 'lying') often are overlooked. But what about the positives, such as 'recall'? It is not that these are overlooked, of course. It is that, amidst the all of this recall, there are 'false yes's and no's [that] hardly stand out as something unusual' (Stern and Stern, 1909/1999, p. 28). Furthermore, the Sterns observe that very young children are rarely questioned by their care-givers, and, when they are so questioned, responses are more susceptible to errors than 'spontaneous testimony.'

One aspect of the Sterns' work that is significant for present purposes is their accounts of the social contexts of remembering and clear indications that care-givers are intimately involved in helping their children to distinguish between, say, correct and mistaken recollections. We offer a single example from accounts of their first daughter, Hilde. The Sterns say that Hilde's first 'freely occurring' correct recollection occurred at 19 months, when Hilde wondered aloud where an adult guest of the family (Anna) had gone after a five-day stay at their home. On each morning during Anna's stay, Hilde conversed with Anna while each was still lying in their respective beds. (Anna occupied a room next to Hilde's and the two conversed through the door that joined the rooms.) Two days after Anna had departed, Hilde 'called out from her bed early in the morning "*Anna!*" and asked her mother: "*Where is Anna?*" With that she glanced at the door of the room where Anna had been staying' (Stern and Stern, 1909/1999, p. 11).

One problem with the Sterns' method of recording their observations is that often they do not include the care-giver's response to recollections of the sort described above. But we may assume that an explanation followed. For example, we might expect the care-giver to have said something like: 'Well, Hilde, Anna left a couple of days ago. She was only here for five days. You liked Anna, didn't you?'

In our view, a language-game of this sort is absolutely essential to the young child's learning the skill of correct recollection. Already we can make three important observations about these language-games. First, implicit in this 'teaching of memory' is a distinction between correct recollection and fantasy. Children often are fearful of ghosts that inhabit their rooms of a given night. What is the character of the language-games that ensue when the care-giver rushes into the screaming child's room? How do these primary language-games differ from those that support correct recollection? Second, in connection with these questions there is an implicit position taken with respect to *knowledge* of events that are remembered correctly and *expectations* regarding the details of recollection. In the great majority of cases, care-givers do not query their children with respect to the precise details of what is recalled. Thus, implicit standards of what is to count as a 'correct' memory are set up, and these standards in no way reflect the sort of detail required by witnesses in courts of law. *That* Anna stayed with the Sterns is never in question! Not that putative memories are never questioned. So much is clear in the Sterns' account of mistaken recollections. At this point we need to remind ourselves of Wittgenstein's view on the matter. When the correctness of a memory is in question, its authentication does not come from something 'inner.' As we have said before, authentication occurs in the public domain. Our third and final observation returns us to the inherent connection between 'remembering' and the concept of 'the past.' Clearly, Hilde's recollection of Anna could not have occurred without Anna having stayed with the Sterns – in the past.

Mainstream developmental psychologists of memory might object that an analysis of the sort we have undertaken above, which includes empirical observations of an individual child, are not generalizable and therefore lack scientific status. Indeed, toward the beginning of their monograph the Sterns (1909/1999, p. 3) defend their method of 'psychography' – or 'the psychological studies of individual children over time' – against this very criticism. What we wish to point out is that grammatical analysis, in a manner of speaking, 'shows the way' to generalizability. This is to say that the grammar of the primary language-games of remembering, for instance, shows the workings of our concepts *as they are used*, how they *could be used*, how they *cannot be used*, and so on.

Furthermore, the method of grammatical analysis, when combined with empirical observations, has the potential to set in motion the questioning of unwarranted assumptions about psychological development. Is the notion of 'cognitive constraints' a mere assumption? We think not. The Sterns' record of the development of their daughter Hilde reveals numerous observations that anticipate Jean Piaget's well-known thesis of developmental cognitive constraints that bear on any attempt to account for the primary language-games of remembering and other skills. Nor does grammatical analysis necessarily deflate certain assumptions made by proponents of the information-processing approach to development. The fact that adults make adjustments in accordance with implicit knowledge of children's memory skills is shown in the many contexts of adult–child language-games. But it is important to realize that children are surrounded by innumerable conversations having to do with remembering, and there is every reason to suggest that children can 'play the game' before they are *fully capable* of playing the game.

What assumptions lack warrant? With Wittgenstein's help, we have shown that the assumption of an inner process of remembering is conceptually vacuous and that a memory is not deemed correct by a process of comparing the memory – say, as a 'mental image' – to a past event. Again, to say that an inner process *must have occurred* while I remembered something is simply to say that I remembered something. We do not check the veracity of my memory by looking at the inner process. Nor does the inner process inform correct use of 'remember.' But from this it does not follow that, for instance, brain-imaging studies can tell us nothing about the 'mechanics of memory.' Learning about these mechanics is very important as further progress is made to help persons with disease processes and brain injury affecting memory.

But the mechanics, as we come to know them, will tell us nothing about what it *means* to remember. The language-games of remembering are, contrary to a scientistic attitude on ordinary people's knowledge, very well in order.

In summary, without empirical evidence to the contrary there is no reason to deny that, if the thrust of Wittgenstein's writings on remembering and many other psychological concepts is correct, there *must be* a pattern of primary language-games in which the remembering skill is established. Parallel to these, there must be others in which lying is distinguished from legitimate flights of fancy. (In our view, the Sterns' (1909/1999) research shows this to be the case.) So to this extent at least, a rich field of research awaits the Wittgenstein-inspired developmental psychologist.

Learning point: thinking about the past (remembering and forgetting)

1. *Remembering and recognizing*

   (a) The word 'remember' is not used for the routine exercise of recollective skills. (Psychologists' new expression is 'implicit memory.')
   (b) 'Recognize' is not used for familiarity, but in special cases like surprise (PI §§601–3).

2. *Possible account*

   (a) 'Remembering is describing a present representation of a past event.'
        (i)   Problem 1: How do I know present image and so on is of a *past* event?
        (ii) Problem 2: How do I know that the image is *correct*?
        (See PI II, xiii, p. 231: Remembering is not a *description* of a present experience but of a past event.)
   (b) The photo album example. PI §§604–5: 'representation' is the misleading picture.
   (c) Wittgenstein is not denying an inner process, only a misleading picture of an inner process (PI §305). However (PI §306), 'inner process' talk is redundant, since genuine and spurious cases of remembering are not distinguished by reference to inner processes.
   (d) PI p. 231, xiii: There are no characteristic 'remembering experiences.'
   (e) All of these problems melt away if the metaphor ('picture') of 'describing a representation of the past' is abandoned. This leaves us with a research project.

3. *Opening up the field of research*

   (a) What are the remembering language-games, correcting, authenticating and so on, for example 'collective remembering' and 'memorial power'?

(b)   What are the primary language-games in which we acquire the uses of 'remember,' 'recognize,' 'forget' and so on?

Further reading

Glock, H.-G. (1996). *A Wittgenstein Dictionary*. Oxford: Blackwell. (Specifically pp. 184–9 and 241–3.)

Stern, D.G. (1991). Models of memory: Wittgenstein and cognitive science. *Philosophical Psychology*, **4**, 203–18.

Intending, willing and acting
Philosophical Investigations §§611–31 and 635–82

Movement is the natural immediate effect of feeling, irrespective
of what the quality of the feeling may be. It is so in reflex action,
it is so in emotional expression, it is so in the voluntary life.
   William James, *The Principles of Psychology*, 1890, p. 1135

When I raise my arm I do not usually *try* to raise it.
   Wittgenstein, *Philosophical Investigations*, §622

Human will is the ability to act for reasons.
   Anthony Kenny (1963), Preface

Topics introduced: responses and actions; intention and future-directed thought; causal explanations of action; the grammar of intention; commitment; willing versus trying; persons as sources of active human conduct; contexts of action

The quote from William James (1890) above appears to blur the distinction between personal activities (or movements) that result from things that happen to us and our *intended* activities. In Chapter 6, where we discussed the 'paradox' of interpreting a rule, we considered how odd it would be to think of our response to a patellar tendon reflex test as a form of rule-following. There is no 'patellar tendon reflex rule.' When we respond to the patellar tendon reflex test, we respond to something that happens to us. Now contrast this with signing up for a language course at the local community college. While there are many things going on in my life at the time, I do not think of my signing up for a course as the direct result of antecedent events that have happened to me. I would like to improve my German and I intend to take a course in order to do so.

   It is striking that James's (1890) view, which we have simplified a great deal, is by no means antiquated in contemporary psychology. Even today many psychologists think of an intention to do something simply as one link in a causal chain. Implicit in this view is the idea that intention is a kind of chimera. By contrast, the great majority of philosophers today distinguish between mere bodily movements or responses and *actions*, the latter being linked with intentions. So from their perspective, the response to a reflex test is not an action. Things become more complicated when we consider whether running away from a charging bear constitutes an action. In a sense, we 'intend' to get away from the bear, save ourselves from harm, and so forth. But in doing so we are not using deliberative thought.

Visitors to Banff, Canada, are well advised to learn what to do if they encounter a grizzly bear when setting out on a hike in the Canadian Rockies. They might deliberate on an imaginary encounter. But they do not 'plan' to get away from a grizzly bear in the way that they plan their trip to Banff.

'Response,' 'action,' 'intention' and similar concepts have complex meanings and are related in complex ways. We admit to having generalized and glossed over many difficulties thus far. But it seems natural to think of intentions as future-directed thoughts. Thus, perhaps any psychology of deliberate action must involve the psychology of future-directed thoughts. The apparently obvious question for psychologists to try to answer is this: 'How is a present intention related to the action that would fulfill or realize that intention in the future?' Such a question appears similar to questions posed in the first part of the previous chapter. But there are differences.

The foundation of a good deal of recent and contemporary work in the field of intentional action is set by the following question: What is the best way of account-ing for actions – by treating them as events that happen and finding their 'causes' or by treating them as meaningful actions and giving reasons for them? This is the traditional dichotomy argued over for millennia, and questions surrounding the dichotomy are not just a matter of practical advantages and disadvantages of an explanatory strategy. It involves the concept of the 'person.' The 'causal account' deprives people of agency, of control over their actions, while the 'reasons account' at least restores the human person as a being capable of rational choice. We believe Wittgenstein's ultimate aim was to restore the agency of persons in the face of the causal account (though he does not declare this overtly). Let us begin by contrast-ing the two ways that we can think of how the future is brought about. This necessitates the important distinction between (1) an event or happening described in terms of movements of the body and (2) actions or bodily movements interpreted within some framework of meanings. We will try to maintain this distinction throughout the discussion to follow.

The traditional causal account

There is a causal version of both mentalism and behaviorism. According to the former, meaningful actions are the result of the operation of mental causes. Accord-ing to the latter, bodily behaviors are the result of environmental causes. In neither version is the human being actively engaged in producing the meaningful action or the behavioral event. Intended personal powers are not admitted as the ultimate source from which actions or bodily events flow. The person is a passive responder.

Turning to the mentalistic version of the causal theory, we must surely ask: what could these mental causes possibly be? One promising candidate is intentions. This seems to be the force of such a colloquial conversation as 'Why did you go down town this morning?' to which someone might reply 'Because I intended to do some shopping.'

This pattern of explanation, which seems straightforward, is highly problematic. The use of the word 'because' seems to suggest that the cited intention purports to be the cause or part of the cause of the behavior in question. However, there is a rather simple reason why this way of interpreting the conversation will not do. Causal explanations are based on the principle that the cause and the effect are logically independent. According to Hume (1739/1978), it is not a contradiction to conjoin an assertion that an event of the type of the cause existed, but an event of the type of the effect did not. 'She took the aspirin but her headache still was just as painful' is not a logical contradiction. 'He used only black paint but the chair was a brilliant white' is. A cause could occur without the usual effect occurring, and the effect could have been brought about by some other cause than usual. We have to *discover* what brings about a certain event. We cannot deduce it from a description of the alleged effect.

If we look more closely at how we recognize what people do, it is clear that an *intention is not independent of the event it is supposed to cause*. To interpret a certain event as a particular intended action one needs to know what the actor's intentions were. Did he raise his finger at the auction to make a bid, or did he do it to brush away a fly? Similarly, we often only know what someone's intention was when we have seen what they eventually did. Hesitating before the dessert trolley, my friend finally chooses the Tin Roof Fudge Pie. One may even have this experience oneself, realizing only after the event what one really intended to do. Generally, an intention is identified as just this intention by reference to the action antecedent to it. And an action is identified as just this action by reference to the intention supposedly precedent to it.

As Anscombe (1957) points out in a very Wittgensteinian spirit, what we identify as the intention behind an action depends on the context. Someone pumping water in a courtyard may be intending to fill the tank and intending to poison the inhabitants at the same moment – and by performing the same action. How could both be the cause of the pumping of water? Interpreting actions as causes does not seem plausible.

A second promising candidate for the mentalistic causes of action is an act of willing, a volition, a thesis examined by Anthony Kenny (1963). The idea that volitions precede and cause actions is very old indeed. Perhaps the idea comes from the effort that we sometimes need to make to get something done. 'I had to force myself out of bed this cold morning.' We then slip into the hypothesis that there are invisible acts of willing, volitions, at the root of every action. There are all sorts of problems with this proposal. Here is a very simple one. If I have to force myself to get up, the forcing or willing is itself an act. Must I not have willed it too? It seems that for every act of willing there must an another act, the willing to will it. And so an abyss of willings would open up in front of anyone trying to give a comprehensive psychological account of what someone did. So explaining actions by citing volitions, acts of will, does not seem plausible either.

Our age-old philosophical habits have left us with a set of problems that seem at once interconnected and intractable. What if we consider the possibility that the seeming intractability is the result of serious misunderstanding of the grammar of words having to do with intentions and with the efforts needed to bring about what one intends?

Wittgenstein's project

Wittgenstein's examination of the polysemous meaning of concepts having to do with the explanation of action leads to a blunt rejection of the causal account. The traditional analysis, he sets out to show, is the result of serious mistakes in our grasp of the grammar of words like 'intend,' 'will' and so on. These mistakes come about because we have assimilated their grammar to that of words for mental states or processes. The project will be to free ourselves from the spell of these grammatical models. Let us now turn to a close study of a group of words intimately involved in the explanation of action.

A grammatical investigation is an investigation of our linguistic practices. In this case we are concerned with practices related to future-directed thought and action. So we are not really investigating the thoughtful antecedents of action. Rather, we are trying to gain an overview of a complex of practices that include thinking, saying and doing, in one integrated package. And herein lies the danger: we may think that our language, which we use to express future-directed thought, is agentive (expressing our intentions) while unknowingly slipping into the stance that leads to a causal account directing our attention to what precedes an action. We come easily to think that something stands between our future-directed and agentive language and the events in reality that can be interpreted as realizing our intentions. We can resist this tendency only by a careful and comprehensive review of the grammars of the relevant expressions with which our accounts of what we do and plan to do are offered. We will see that there are no detachable antecedents to what we do that could stand alone as causes.

The grammar of 'intend,' 'intention' and so on

There is no doubt that intentions play an important role in the explanation of actions. If someone does something unintentionally we think very differently of the person and the action from cases in which the very same action is done intentionally. Knocking someone over unintentionally in a crowded subway is quite different from knocking someone over intentionally or deliberately. What is it that is absent in the first kind of case and present in the second? We are tempted to think that an intention to do something functions rather like a cause, bringing it about that the relevant action occurs, in a way somewhat like the way a material cause brings about a physical effect. Yet at the same time, we are ready to say that some person brought about the event in realizing or fulfilling an intention. Now the intention does not look like a cause at all.

In PI §§588–92 and at points thereafter Wittgenstein explores the claim that an intention is a certain state of mind, or rather that to be intending to do something is to be in a certain state of mind.

> 'I am revolving the decision to go away to-morrow.' (This may be called a description of a state of mind.) – 'Your arguments don't convince me; now as before it is my intention to go away tomorrow.' Here one is tempted to call the intention a feeling. The feeling is one of a certain rigidity; of unalterable determination. (But there are

many different characteristic feelings and attitudes here.) ... I say at the end of a quarrel 'All right! Then I leave to-morrow!'; I make a decision.

(PI §588)

There are all sorts of possibilities here. It is clear also that the very same feelings may accompany cognitive phenomena other than intending. In PI §592 Wittgenstein dismisses the suggestion of an accompanying 'mental undertone' as what it is to intend something by declaring an intention, for example, to go away.

What, then, is 'an intention'? What is displayed in the declaration of an intention? The solution is not hard to find. *Declarations of intention are acts of commitment.* That is, there is an internal relationship between intention and the language-games of making public commitments in which I display what I mean to do. Such language-games therefore are primary. But they are not predictions, so assessments of them in terms of 'probability' are not appropriate. We can, however, assess them in terms of their sincerity. Once the primary language-game of committing oneself to a future course of action is in place, we can derive secondary language-games such as making private commitments, concealing our intentions and so on. Though an act of commitment to perform a certain course of action, like the cause of an effect, must precede the fulfilling of it, we must resist the temptation to go any further with this grammatical analogy. The phrase 'an intention' must be used warily, since nouns suggest entities, and, in this case, there are no such entities. Finally, we should bear in mind that as in other cases of thinking about the future, the grammatical role of a description of what I intend to do is to stand for a general prescription (a type) of the kind of action I propose to perform. Here we have a connection with the grammar of thinking about the future, discussed in the previous chapter.

In PI §659 Wittgenstein asks what the telling of an intention adds to a report of what I do. It tells someone something about *myself,* not something that was going on at the same time. But what does the telling of my intention do? It does the work of *committing myself* to fulfilling the intention purposefully.

In line with the parallel that seems to exist between displaying an intention and expressing a feeling, PI §647 reminds us that it is perfectly natural to see the expression of an intention in the behavior of animals. But this does not amount to 'getting into the head' of, say, a cat stalking a bird. Perhaps a human verbal performance of an act of commitment has its roots in a primary language-game of the natural expression of intention. Again a research question emerges for developmental psychology. Is there a process of verbal substitution for natural expression in this case, as there was with the establishment of a vocabulary for the public expression of feelings?

In short, the grammar of 'intend,' 'intention' and so on *is more like the grammar of 'promise' than it is like the grammar of 'cause.'* It also has some resemblance to the grammar of 'pain' in that its role is expressive, though not of a subjective experience.

The grammar of 'willing,' 'trying' and related concepts

Imagine waking one autumn morning, surprised at how cold your bedroom has become overnight. You hesitate getting out of bed to ponder your impending discomfort, perhaps thinking: 'It's cold in here! I knew a cold front was coming in overnight! Why didn't I turn on the heat?' To get out of bed you will need to put thoughts of this sort aside – at least enough to exercise your will by throwing down the covers and putting your feet to the cold floor.

Now consider a slightly different case. You go to bed hopeful about a job interview the next morning. When your alarm sounds, you just spring out of bed with hardly a thought. When putting your feet to the cold floor you realize that you forgot to turn on the heat because a cold front was imminent.

Thinking they 'contain in miniature form the data for an entire psychology of volition,' James (1890/1983, p. 1133) describes similar examples in his chapter entitled 'Will' in *The Principles of Psychology*. So long as an 'antagonistic representation' (thoughts of your bedroom's coldness) is not on your mind, the representation of movements related to getting out of bed will awaken movements that are the representation's object (getting out of bed). In other words, without the inhibiting or 'blocking' effect of the antagonistic representation of coldness, there will be no thoughts to inhibit the well-established and habitual motor discharges required for getting out of bed each morning. So in the first example above, the blocking effect that stands in the way of exercising your will and putting these habitual motor discharges to work has to be overcome before you get out of bed. In the second example, the motor discharges of getting out of bed are not inhibited at all. Precisely at this point in the *Principles* we find the familiar quote from James that leads this chapter. Again, 'Movement is the natural immediate effect of feeling, irrespective of what the quality of the feeling may be. It is so in reflex action, it is so in emotional expression, it is so in the voluntary life' (James, 1890/1983, p. 1135).

Here we have the bare essentials of James's 'ideo-motor theory of voluntary movement' which, in part, proposes to explain willful movements in terms of anticipations of feelings that bring about movement. In cases where there are no blocking representations, willing just happens immediately. In this sense and without a blocking representation, willing is similar to the passive experience of, say, a reflexive movement. However, willful voluntary acts are higher-level acts that order and regulate established movements, without which we would be unable to anticipate the consequences of those movements (see Wild, 1969, p. 249).

By contrast, we can think of willing not as an experience, but as an action. Willing is something we do and entails *trying* to get out of bed, despite the cold. It is not that there is no trying with James's ideo-motor theory. It is just that the trying is preceded by an experience of willing that seems to happen of its own accord. The alternative to James's theory holds that willing does not just happen. It is, rather, a kind of voluntary bringing-about.

James's ideo-motor theory is not specified as one of Wittgenstein's targets in the remarks now under consideration. But manuscript evidence shows that Wittgenstein had James's views on voluntary action very much in mind while laying out his preliminary remarks on willing and voluntary action. James is referred to explicitly in PI §610, for example. Also, one can hear the echoes of Schopenhauer in the parenthetical 'the "will" too only "idea"' in §611. According to Schopenhauer (1818/1995, p. 67), 'every movement, although always a manifestation of will, must, nevertheless, have a cause from which it is to be explained in relation to a particular time and place' (see also Hacker, 1996, pp. 587–8).

Wittgenstein's considerations on willing at PI §§611–28 take the shape of a dialectic between these two views on the will, the first (James's) being a typical empiricist perspective and the second being anti-empiricist (Hacker, 1996, p. 535). So Wittgenstein's interlocutor begins with the claim that 'willing too is merely an experience' (PI §611), leading Wittgenstein to suggest immediately that raising his arm is not simply something that happens, like the reducing of one's heart rate, say, after being startled. Willing is something we do (PI §612). It is true that, to a large extent, experiencing the subsiding of one's heart rate is not like the Jamesian experience of willing. But minus the Jamesian blocking representations, willing just occurs, like a decrease in one's heart rate after being startled. So to this point it appears that Wittgenstein sides with the anti-empiricist perspective on willing – that it is something one does.

But if willing is not just something that happens to me, how do I *do* willing? When I raise my arm, am I engaging in a willful act of *bringing about* the raising of my arm? Initially, it appears that grammar allows for my bringing about willing. Just as I might bring about a stomach ache through over-eating, I can bring about my will to swim by jumping into the water (PI §613)! But now it seems I am engaged in willing willing. The regress points to a grammatical feature of willing:

> I can't will willing; that is, it makes no sense to speak of willing willing. 'Willing' is not the name of an action; and so not the name of any voluntary action either. And my use of a wrong expression *came from our wanting to think of willing as an immediate non-causal bringing-about* [emphasis added].
>
> (PI §613)

Just to be clear, Wittgenstein's 'wrong expression' relates to his tentatively entertaining the notion of 'bringing about' willing, which leads him to entertain the notion of willing willing.

As a psychologist, I can perform an experiment on the relation between stomach aches and food consumption by having research participants ingest large amounts of certain foods. So long as they consume these foods voluntarily and in sufficient amounts, I can think of some participants as bringing about their own stomach aches. That is, participants asked to continue eating even after they are full might be thought of as bringing about their stomach aches by continuing to eat voluntarily. So long as they are eating voluntarily, I can (to some extent) avoid getting caught in a causal nexus in explaining their *behavior*, although of course I have the option to revert to a causal (physiological) explanation when it comes to explaining their *stomach aches*. In the former case, there is no problem in thinking that these research participants are bringing about a stomach ache, and doing so willfully.

We have italicized a phrase in PI §613 (above) to emphasize that what drove Wittgenstein to entertain the idea of willing is not merely the proposal that willing is part of a causal nexus. Rather, he indicates quite clearly that there is something else that lies at the root of thinking of willing as 'an immediate non-causal bringing about.' We hasten to add that when Wittgenstein identifies the 'misleading analogy that lies at the root of this idea' as the establishment of 'a mechanism connecting two parts of a machine' (PI §613), he is not just finding fault with the Jamesian account of willing in favor of the anti-empiricist account. For even if we think of willing as an action, the grammar of willing does not support the proposal that willing is a form of 'doing something' either. The basic idea is that in constructing a psychology of willing-as-action we will probably be prone to identify a psychological *instrument* with which action is brought about.

If we think of willing as an action that involves a special instrument to get something done, we may regard the instrument as (1) being employed as part of a process that just happens to persons or (2) being actively engaged by persons. PI §613 is a point where these two explanatory roads diverge, each consisting in three remarks. The first (PI §§614–16) investigates the idea that we bring about voluntary movement by doing something psychological – say, by wishing – which then causes movement. The second (PI §§617–19) explores the idea that there is a physiological causal chain of movement that the will, as a psychic instrument, may directly instigate or interfere with (see Hacker, 1996, pp. 535–7). While the latter considerations appear Jamesian, it is not until PI §§624–6 that a perspective more clearly like James's comes into focus. The three groups of remarks identified immediately above will be our focus, although we will consider a few additional remarks as needed.

Psychologically bringing about and causing bodily movement

At first, Wittgenstein dogmatically denies that raising his arm involves using an instrument to bring about the movement of his arm, or that a wish is instrumental (PI §614). In response, his interlocutor suggests that if willing 'is not to be a sort of wishing, [it] must be the action itself. It cannot be allowed to stop anywhere short of the action' (PI §615). Note here the implication that James's blocking representations can play no part in blocking actions that result from willing. But why the contrast with wishing? The answer is simple: if I will to do something but fail to do it, I would only have wished to do it. Thus we are faced with the possibility that willing and wishing are related to *trying*. I will to do something, try to do it, but fail. Wittgenstein (PI §615) thus offers a number of examples of possible willful acts, one of which subtracts the 'ordinary sense' of action from willing (e.g. 'imagining something,' like someone's face from long ago). Finally, he observes that overt actions are not all that we will. It seems that along with willing to speak, to write, or to lift something, I can will to try, to attempt and to make an effort. *So willing is not a concept exclusively used in connection with overt actions.*

We can conclude one thing about voluntary action and its relation to *wishing*. The first two sentences of PI §616 constitute a grammatical remark, in that the grammar of voluntary action excludes the possibility that such action results from wishing. The idea that when I raise my arm I do not wish it to go up can be contrasted, for example, with wishing it will be sunny. But while the grammar of voluntary bodily action must be distinguished from the grammar of wishing in this way, the *character* of our voluntary action may be related to wishing or hoping. When I express my hope or wish to draw a circle faultlessly, I am using a grammar related to *how well* I draw a circle. But the voluntary action of putting my hand into motion, to put pen to paper, and to draw a circle, is not the result of my wishing or hoping to draw a circle. In this case, wishing or hoping is related to the nearly impossible task of drawing a circle by hand faultlessly. But does this mean that wishing and hoping are special psychological things we do in order to draw a perfect circle?

The will as a psychic instrument in a causal and physiological chain

The will as 'cause of action' theory (or 'dual-aspect theory') has been presented in great detail by O'Shaughnessy (1980). He expresses the theory in two new psychological laws. There is a psychological law linking intending with trying or striving, and there is a second law linking striving with acting. Willing is a kind of striving. It is just this conception that Wittgenstein seeks to undermine.

Wittgenstein was well aware of the stubborn insistence that the will is some kind of ghostly hand at the helm of human voluntary action. Sections PI §§617–19 explore the idea that there is a physiological causal chain of movement that the will, as a psychic instrument, may directly put into motion or interfere with. Note that a distinction of this sort – between the will as an instrument and a causal mechanism – implies that the will must be, in some sense and to some degree, 'informed' of how the causal instrument works. Now Wittgenstein employs an experiment of sorts to dispel this illusion. In crossing your middle finger over your index finger, you may find it difficult to move your index finger in a particular way if a friend points to it and says, 'Now move this finger downward and upward.' But you may find it easier to move your index finger as instructed if your friend touches it at the distal joint. What has happened here? Is it that the touching of your index finger gave information that can be used by your will to move your finger as instructed? If so, we would be obliged to consider the possibility that the will needs such information to execute a voluntary movement.

What is the active source of human conduct?

The discussion in PI §§618–28 is a close examination of various ways that some antecedent event or state might be proposed as a cause or activating condition of what someone does. None of the proposals survives critical analysis. We are left with the *person* as that which brings about a voluntary action. Wittgenstein does not expressly draw this conclusion. But it is not hard to see that this is one major thrust of these remarks.

Wittgenstein's account of willing and of voluntary and intended actions is generally directed against the temptation to assume that these words refer to separable antecedents to an action. This temptation comes, in part, from assuming that explanations of human action must follow a cause–effect pattern. More subtly, it comes from a familiar error: treating the grammar of verbs like 'to will' and 'to intend' as if they referred to distinct and separable steps in a sequence of events that culminated in an action, say raising one's arm intentionally. The error in question is treating these verbs as if they were grammatically similar to the verbs we studied previously in this chapter, namely, 'to wish,' 'to want,' or 'to hope,' which are used to refer to antecedents, though not *causal* antecedents of some event. Says Wittgenstein: 'When I raise my arm I have *not* wished it might go up. The voluntary action excludes this wish' (PI §616). The wish is not part of the action. Is willing it? There are cases where 'hope,' 'wish' and so on are relevant to how an action turns out. However, their relevance is to *how* an action is performed, not *that* it is performed.

We have seen that in PI §613 Wittgenstein remarks that 'willing' is not the name of an action, and so not the name of a voluntary action. There is a standing temptation to follow certain superficial grammatical similarities between 'willing to do something' and 'trying to do something.' They do have something in common. The effort we 'feel,' which is a feature of both willing and trying, can lead us astray. Clearly, 'trying to do X' and 'doing X' are both actions that a person can perform. If willing is a necessary antecedent for every action, then one must will to try to do X. This shows that the grammar of 'trying' cannot serve as a model for understanding 'willing.' To put it simply, *'willing' is not a species of 'trying.'*

In PI §§627 and 628 Wittgenstein makes it clear that a voluntary movement should not be thought of as an empirical consequence of a volition. The picture 'volition plus action' is a misleading version of the generally misplaced cause–effect pattern. In PI §620 Wittgenstein asks to what 'I do … ' refers. It refers to nothing that could be experienced. We should add that like many first-person phrases, 'I do … ' is a way for a person to take responsibility for an action. There is no 'doing' separable from what is done. In like manner, a decision is not a separable antecedent of the statement of an intention. It is what is expressed in that statement (PI §631).

Though one can predict what someone will do from that person having declared a firm intention to do it, this is nothing like predicting that someone will be sick after having taken an emetic! Suppose I say: 'I am going to take two powders now and in half an hour I shall be sick.' Here there are two predictions: one as to what I shall do and the other as to what will happen. The declaration was not made on the basis of an observation of behavior. It was an act of commitment. The prediction as to what will happen is based on empirical evidence of the effect these powders have on someone who ingests them.

> I do not want to say that the case of the expression of intention 'I am going to take two powders' the prediction was a cause – and its fulfillment the effect. (Perhaps a physiological investigation could determine this.) So much, however, is true: we can often predict a man's actions from his expression of a decision. An important language-game.
>
> (PI §632)

Occasionally, presidential elections are won or lost on firmness of conviction as expressed by the political combatants. An important language-game indeed! But more to the point, the common feature of each occasion allowing one to make a prediction does not mean that both should be assimilated to the cause–effect pattern. The performance that follows a declaration is not caused by that declaration, nor by anything separable from the action itself. The performance is what *fulfills* the declaration or commitment.

The upshot of all this is already made clear in PI §618. The source of an action is not any prior mental or material state or event. It is the person-as-agent. We have the result of a grammatical investigation that not only bolsters humanistic perspectives of human psychology and action, but flies in the face of reductions of action to material and efficient causes at work in the nervous system, perhaps brought about by prior conditioning or what have you.

We can add further dimensions to Wittgenstein's surview of the uses of the 'will' vocabulary. For example, we call someone 'willful' if they persistently refuse to take any notice of what other people have to say, perhaps even acting contrary to advice. (College instructors are familiar with the 'willful' student.) The point of this attribution is to emphasize the person as active agent, confirming the general line we have been extracting from Wittgenstein's remarks in this section. Again, the phrase 'a willing helper' can be used to praise someone who does not need to be told or cajoled into giving a hand, one who acts on his or her own accord. In both examples the point is the same: persons are the ultimate sources of activity in the human world. They are the unmoved movers.

The message for psychologists

How do some established psychological explanatory formats fare with respect to Wittgenstein's insights?

Psychologists have long used the concept of 'attitude' as an enduring mental state that is causally implicated in the genesis of actions. Philosophers, with an interest in psychology, have offered the belief–desire pair as the basic format for the explanation of what people do. This leads to the idea of a mental mechanism that is activated in appropriate circumstances.

It should be clear by now that it is a mistake to use a cause–effect schema for studying the relation between expressed intentions and people's intended actions. Rather, we should study the context – particularly the discursive context – in which such actions are performed. Do not say 'in which such actions occur'! If we must identify a cause or source of activity it must be the whole person. A similar privileging of the person as the ultimate source of action is to be found in the recently recovered 'personalism' of William Stern (1939). Though Stern's psychology was developed nearly half a century before Wittgenstein's later philosophy, there is a remarkable affinity between them.

The explanation of what people do must surely be one of the prime targets for psychological science. Yet the voluminous literature on the subject is rife with unexamined presuppositions and conceptual confusions, some of which Wittgenstein's overview of the relevant language-games has brought to light. Most publications in this domain, from philosophers like Davidson (2001) to psychologists like Ajzen (1991), are almost too painful to read. Antiquated notions of causality jostle with radical misunderstandings of the use of intention talk. An article by Werner Greve (2001) goes a certain way towards putting things right. At the end of an admirable critical summary of the psychological literature of the last thirty years, Greve remarks, rightly, that 'human actions are more than mere behavior ... Intentions, expectations and evaluations, as a point of principle, cannot be causes of behavior. Rather, they are central constitutive conditions of action ... ' (Greve, 2001, p. 447). Correlations between these constitutive items and actions do not show that they are their causes. However, Greve has not fully shed the old metaphysics, since he remarks that 'a prediction of an action by referring to an earlier assessed (asked) intention does not prove that the intention has caused the action but this intention has remained stable and dominant' (ibid.). Here we see signs of the old intention-as-mental-entity. Significantly, Greve sums up his analysis by remarking that we lack a psychological theory of intentional action.

Although admirable, Greve's (2001) diagnosis falls short in two important respects, remediable by attention to Wittgenstein's insights on this matter. First, in Greve's analysis the role of active agents is not fully realized. So people as authors of their own actions are not fully in focus. The second shortfall concerns the role of declarations of intentions that are neither (1) logically related to the type of action contemplated (whether described in public or private) or (2) overt or covert states of mind. To declare an intention is a kind of promise, an act of commitment. The promise to oneself and others remains in force. That is why actions can be predicted from declarations of intention. Once we have fully grasped the nature of declarations of intention, disabusing ourselves of the idea that they are descriptions of some state of mind, we have our missing psychological theory of intentional action.

This would be a quite different kind of research program from that of neuroscience, in which the efficient causal antecedents of bodily movements take center stage. In the context of neuroscience, a person's movements are stripped of personal and social meaning, since the scientific project is to look for events in the brain that precede bodily movements. In the context of psychology proper we must look for the plans, aims, projects and intentions to the achievement and fulfilling of which personal effort is directed. Just as in the case of remembering, criteria are to be found in the public arena.

The developmental dimension

Once again Wittgenstein's analysis leads us to questions for the developmental psychologist. What are the public language-games in which the expression of intentions becomes established as a discursive practice, something done with words? Is there a moment in the life of a young child acquiring the skill of expressing intentions that is comparable to the learning of practices of expressing feelings verbally? Remember that to express an intention is not only to indicate the type of event one intends to bring about, but to *commit* oneself to whatever is necessary to bring it about.

The ability to express what one wants to have is at least a necessary condition for acquiring the skill of expressing what one means to do. Jerome Bruner's work on 'request formats,' discussed in Chapter 4, has made some empirical inroads in this regard. Again, he shows that one component of the skill of expressing intentions may well arise as a public (request-format) language-game. Not far distant from this language-game must lie the games in which the practice of *commitment* to perform something becomes established. No doubt many established lines of research have the potential to at least inform the unfolding of commitment practices. But so far as we know, the step from requesting something to committing oneself to doing something or to obtaining something has not yet attracted the attention of development psychologists. Here too language-games will be the core of the process by which these discursive skills are established. But our guess is that they begin to be played more in the playground than in the nursery.

We now move forward to another topic, the complications of which are well known to psychologists and historians of psychology: the emotions.

Learning point: intending and willing – the psychology action

1. *The 'picture' that animates many traditional studies of action is cause–effect*

   (a) Behaviorism proposed direct and indirect environmental causes.
   (b) Mentalism proposes mental causes. (Freudian psychodynamics is another example.)

2. *Intending*

   (a) Comparing unintentional with intentional action tempts one to propose 'an intention' as the cause of the latter type of action.
   (b) Are intentions to act mental states? In PI §588 Wittgenstein examines a variety of mental states, none specific to intending.
   (c) In PI §590 it is suggested that saying what one intends to do is to make a public commitment to a course of action.
   (d) In PI §647 this discussion is linked to the PLA, since there are natural expressions of intending.

3. *Willing*

   (a) Is there always a volition between planning an action and acting? In PI §613 Wittgenstein argues that if willing were a mental act I would have to bring it about (will to will).
   (b) But the will is not an instrument for getting things done (PI §614).
   (c) Willing is not a species of trying, but this apparent parallel tempts us to insert a prior act (PI §§618, 619, 622, 623).
   (d) What are some other language games of 'willing'?
      (i) 'Willful' is not taking any notice of others.
      (ii) 'Being a willing helper' is acting as an independent person.

4. *The primary language-games of expressing intentions*

   (a) Effortful stretching by an infant towards a desired object is accompanied by sounds 'of effort.' (Request formats.)

   (b) The vocalizations become detached from the reaching, and serve to accomplish acquisition of objects in its stead.

   (c) Care-givers elaborate these vocalizations into requests.

Further reading

Greve, W. (2001). Traps and gaps in the psychological explanation of action. *Psychological Review*, **108**, 435–51.

Hacker, P.M.S. (1996). *Wittgenstein: Mind and will. An analytical commentary on the* Philosophical Investigations (Vol. 4). Oxford: Blackwell. (Specifically Chapter 5.)

Peters, R.S. (1969). *The Concept of Motivation.* London: Routledge and Kegan Paul.

12 The emotions

Selections from *Remarks on the Foundations of Psychology; Philosophical Investigations*, Part II, ix, pp. 187–9

> 'I must tell you – I'm frightened.' 'I must tell you – it makes me shiver.' And one can say this in a *smiling* tone of voice too. And do you mean to tell me he doesn't feel it? How else does he *know* it? – But even if it is a piece of information, he doesn't read this off from within.
>
> For he couldn't cite his *sensations* as proof of his statement. *They* don't teach him this.
>
> Wittgenstein, *Last Writings on the Philosophy of Psychology*, §39

Topics introduced: causes of emotions; James's hypothesis; cognitive theories; plan for the treatment of psychological concepts; sensations and emotions; genuine duration, synchronization, degrees, qualitative mixtures and characteristic course; directed and undirected emotions; objects of emotion as targets; natural expressions and primary language-games of emotion; the role of context; intentionality of emotions; transitive and intransitive emotion verbs; immediate experience; emotion knowledge; facial feedback hypothesis

Although Wittgenstein's many remarks on and related to the emotions have attracted considerable attention from philosophers, his impact on psychological research on the emotions has been limited primarily to his conception of family resemblance (e.g. Fehr and Russell, 1984; Parrott and Harré, 1991, 1996). One major contribution to this relative lack of interest on the part of psychologists is that the literature on Wittgenstein and the emotions is marked by contrasts between his views and psychological theories that are antiquated by today's standards. For example, Budd (1989) and Arregui (1996) focus on the perspectives of James (1890/1983) and Descartes (1649/1958) respectively. Furthermore, any psychologist looking into what Wittgenstein has to say about the emotions will find James's theory in focus. Does this warrant the assumption that Wittgenstein's writings on the emotions also are antiquated – that they have little bearing on persistent theoretical and methodological problems in the psychology of emotions? Absolutely not. This is why a presentation of his relevant remarks in light of his philosophical method, juxtaposed with more recent perspectives on the emotions found in contemporary psychology, is long overdue.

Our purpose here is to fill this conspicuous gap in the literature not only on Wittgenstein and the emotions, but also on the general psychological literature on the emotions. For this and the final chapter we will draw upon remarks from Wittgenstein's writings other than the *Investigations*, in particular Volumes 1 and 2 of *Remarks on the Philosophy of Psychology* (Wittgenstein, 1980a, 1980b).

As we have said, the present chapter goes beyond previous works on Wittgenstein and the emotions by contrasting his remarks on the subject with those of contemporary psychological theories of emotion instead of the principal target of Wittgenstein's remarks – James's famous theory. But rather than leaving James entirely out of the picture, our strategy is to indicate the extent to which two of his principal theses – that emotions are caused and that sensations must play a role in emotional experience – are still widely held and are at the center of ongoing debates in contemporary psychology.

Causation and emotion displays

It is not unusual for psychologists to anticipate and defend themselves against the charge that theirs represents a 'causal' theory of emotions, while at the same time failing to address what does and does not constitute a cause in the first place. This lack of specificity often leads to a strange admixture of causal and non-causal rhetoric. For example, Frijda (1988) argues that his 'laws of emotion,' which are 'assumed to rest on underlying causal mechanisms that generate them' (p. 349), are in some ways subject to reason and voluntary capacities. Besides the question of whether his so-called laws are, in fact, non-empirical and even tautological, there is the question of just how a law, understood as describing the workings of causal mechanisms, can include as part of its articulation presumably non-causal and intentional capacities. Frijda (1988) emphasizes that by 'law' he means 'primarily empirical regularities.' But how can his laws of emotion account for surprising or unexpected emotional responses to certain events, or the fact that people sometimes show no emotion in situations where we would expect strong emotional responses? Do such responses (or lack thereof) not count as 'lawful' empirical regularities as well? Questions of this sort may explain why some psychologists of the emotions resist the idea that logical analysis can be fruitful for establishing the relations between the bodily expression of an emotion and emotion concepts (e.g. Frijda, 1992; Laird and Bresler, 1992).

As already suggested, part of the problem is that psychological accounts of the emotions aimed at explaining how bodily responses to events and so-called 'objects of emotion' are attended to, evaluated and identified as 'emotional,' consistently fail to specify their philosophical mode of explanation. That is to say, the psychological literature on the emotions is consistently devoid of the terms that make up the standard fare of philosophical accounts of the phenomena discussed in psychology. Granted, Wittgenstein's is not what we might regard as standard-fare philosophizing either. But he is quite clear (and painstakingly thorough) on his philosophical *modus operandi* and his views on causes as they related to social norms. As we saw in Chapter 9, Wittgenstein holds that the foundation for certain forms of refined, normative sensation and emotion expressions are instinctive, natural expressions. His remarks on rule-following (PI, §§185–242) illuminate how his particular notion of causality might be applied to emotional experience, expression and description. As we saw in Chapter 6, he distinguishes *between following a rule* (that is, obeying an explicit instruction) and what we have called *acting in accordance with* (or acting in an orderly way, the norm in play in such a case being expressible as a rule).

We must resist the temptation to invent a repertoire of hidden instructions to account for the orderliness and conformity we can see. People are trained in these ways and act out of habit. Wittgenstein argues that *rules do not cause future behavior*. Thus, what we might call 'normative causes' (or rules) are not the causes of human action in Hume's (1739/1978) sense of cause as that which is regularly correlated with some type of event. Note the similarity between Hume's cause-as-regularity and Frijda's (1988) notion of laws as resting on empirical regularities. Along with a mechanistic model of human cognition, the Humean concept of causality is the keystone of explanation in traditional patterns of psychological research. Nor should Wittgenstein's sense of normative causes be equated with Aristotle's notion of 'final cause' or the 'wherefore,' the 'good,' or 'the "end" of any generation or change' (Aristotle, trans., 1960, p. 9), although we will see later that Wittgenstein does regard emotion expression and description as intentional. Rather, on Wittgenstein's view, normative principles *establish* social norms or what is to *count* as an action of a certain kind, such as responding to an event angrily, lovingly, anxiously, calmly and so on. In turning to perspectives on the emotions from James onward, when referring to causal accounts of the emotions other than Wittgenstein's we will assume with some confidence that they are, at the very least and with exceptions noted, Humean in spirit.

Jamesian and neo-Jamesian perspectives

By all accounts James (1890/1983) presents a Humean causal theory of emotions. But as is well known, the novelty of his theory is that two main aspects of the traditionally suggested sequential ordering of object of emotion, 'mental affection' and bodily expression of emotion, are reversed. This innovation is based on the grounds that if the traditional ordering were true we would feel no impulse to run from danger if we did not feel the bodily manifestation of fear first (James, 1890/ 1983, pp. 1065–6). Thus, when I see a bear (object of emotion) there is a bodily manifestation of fear and then the 'mental affection.'

With the exception of Dewey (1894/1971), who held that relevant value judgments should be put on an equal footing with the object of emotion and bodily perturbations in accounts of emotional experience, those who investigated the emotions immediately subsequent to James focused on the causal mechanisms of bodily feelings (e.g. Watson, 1919). Over a half century later, Tomkins (1982) proposed that affect is the primary innate biological motivating mechanism and as such, should replace drives as the primary human motive. But by positing an intervening motivating *mechanism* he only reinforces the Jamesian thesis that emotions are caused. His view poses no challenge to the supposed link between sensations and emotional experience. In response to claims by self-perception theorists (e.g. Laird and Bresler, 1992) that facial expressions inform people about their attitudes, experimental manipulations were introduced by neo-Jamesians to show that there is an interaction between an emotional stimulus and an innate motor response (such as the smile) as the determinant of emotional experience. Reference to an innate response involving facial muscles may be taken to at least imply a causal account of emotions and supports James's claim that sensations are necessary for emotional experience. With respect to James's assertion that emotions are caused and sensations are necessary for emotional experience, then, little has changed with the arrival of the so-called 'facial feedback hypothesis.' We will have more to say about facial feedback below.

Cognitive approaches to the emotions

Like neo-Jamesians, psychologists who came to view emotions as having a cognitive component have not, on the whole, seriously challenged the fundamental Jamesian thesis that sensations are essential to emotional experience. For example, Schachter and Singer (1962) famously proposed that 'a general pattern of sympathetic excitation is characteristic of emotional states' (p. 380). To cite a more recent example, Lazarus (1984) says 'an emotion is not definable by behavior, subjective reports, *or* physiological changes: its definition requires all three components' (p. 125). Also, Laird and Bresler (1992) propose that 'facial expressions, and other expressive actions, arousal, action, and contextual information all contribute to the experience of emotion' (p. 224) and regard their version of self-perception theory to be 'constitutive' rather than causal. By constitutive, they mean that lower-order elements of emotional expression – such as scowls and tremblings – 'are constituents of a high-order whole. The relationship between smiling and happiness is not logical, it is a part–whole relation' (ibid., p. 227). The entire emotional sequence, they say, begins with appraisal of the object of emotion, 'followed by behavior and recognition of the norms of behavior in relation to the object,' then a feeling that integrates 'the behavioral and situational information' and then use of the information for guiding further behavior (ibid., p. 229). One problem with this approach is that it does not account for what subjects regard as emotional feelings but which are not easily associated with a particular object of emotion. People can feel anxious without *knowing* why they are anxious. By de-emphasizing the role bodily sensations play in emotional experience, these researchers must resort to emphasis on evaluation of the object of emotion.

Similarly, some cognitive theories that explore processes of evaluation of bodily sensations and the object of emotion regard bodily sensations as primitive responses, while cognitive evaluation is taken to be the result of some kind of higher-order function. We do not want to go so far as to claim that most cognitivists believe emotions are caused. Rather, we believe that to this point cognitivists simply have failed to offer a satisfactory account of how the cognitive component of emotional experience is *not* caused. It is in this sense that, with regard to causes, neo-Jamesians and cognitivists are more or less on the same footing. The cognitivist challenge lies in articulating how cognition relates to emotional experience without ultimately reverting to the use of causal language (as does Frijda) or, as in the case of Laird and Bresler (1992), articulating how emotional feelings can be experienced and expressed without reference to an identifiable object of emotion.

Averill (1974, p. 179) holds that problems with articulating a cognitive account of emotional experience are related to the ambiguous nature of the word 'cognition,' which often is used to refer to rational and deliberative activity, even though deliberate and rational thought is only one aspect of cognition. It is on the basis of this observation that he appeals to two logical connections between statements about emotion and emotion phenomena. The first is from Kenny (1963), who observes that the very use of emotion concepts implies objects as their target. The second is from Peters (1962), who says that the distinction between recognizable emotional states implies cognitive appraisal and that cognitive appraisal is integral to what we mean by 'emotion.' These positions – especially Kenny's – are Wittgensteinian in spirit, though we will see that the extent to which emotional states can be distinguished (and therefore imply cognitive appraisal) depends on whether we are talking about first-person present-tense *expressions* of emotion or third-person *descriptions* of our own or another person's emotions. We will see also that Wittgenstein's conclusions on these and other matters run contrary to the neo-Jamesian spin on self-perception theory, which claims that 'we know about ourselves in the same way that we might know about others' (Laird and Bresler, 1992, p. 223).

To summarize, we regard neo-Jamesians and cognitivists as more or less on the same footing when it comes to their positions on the role sensations and causes play in the explanation of emotional experience. While cognitivists may protest that their approach leaves open the possibility that emotions are not caused, our position is that despite efforts by social constructionists to present alternative, non-reductionistic and non-causal accounts of the emotions (e.g. Parrott and Harré, 1991), psychology awaits a convincing argument showing that cognition is not causally linked to emotional experience – roughly in the Humean spirit of causation. The many experiments on cognition inspired by Schachter and Singer (1962) show that, at the very least, the issue of the necessity of citing causes as they relate to emotional experience is underemphasized. Thus we have little other recourse than to conclude that three primary problems in modern psychological theories of emotion, attributable to the fallout of James's (1890/1983) theory, are the problems of how sensations, causes and cognition are *conceptualized* by psychologists.

Toward a complete description of emotional behavior

To provide a framework for addressing Wittgenstein's remarks on the emotions we will begin with an account of his 'plan for the treatment of psychological concepts,' which comprises two remarks (Wittgenstein, 1980b, §63, §148), the first of which we will refer to as the 'initial plan' and the second its 'continuation.' Wittgenstein did not consider all the statements in the plan as definitive, but rather as useful for bringing to mind questions and possible answers about the criteria needed for including any number of psychological phenomena under a particular psychological category and for indicating possible relations of concepts within and between categories. Although Wittgenstein's organization of psychological concepts includes sensations, images and emotions, we will be concerned with the categories of sensations and emotions only.

Before proceeding we need to emphasize that the idea of 'sensation' in the philosophical literature is rather different from its definition in psychology. In psychology, 'sensation' is reserved to describe the results of activity in sensory receptors. 'Perception,' on the other hand, involves a psychological interpretation of what is sensed. In philosophy, 'sensation' is used in such a way that in many cases makes implicit reference to sensation *and* perception (in the psychological sense). In Chapter 5, particularly where we discussed the cognitive skill of reading, we avoided this ambiguity by using the expression 'bodily feeling.' Below we will not do so, in part because Wittgenstein often uses 'sensation' in his remarks on the emotions.

Sensations and emotions: some similarities and differences

In the initial plan, the 'inner connexions and analogies' of sensations are characterized through reference to '*genuine duration*' (Wittgenstein, 1980b, §63), meaning that a person can say when a sensation begins and ends. In addition, it is possible to experience two sensations simultaneously (synchronization) and to speak of sensations as having 'degrees and qualitative mixtures.' For example, I can say my toothache is getting worse (degrees) and perhaps feel a coldness that accompanies pain when I draw in air across a carious tooth (qualitative mixtures). Finally, sensations have a 'place of feeling in the body' and inform us about the external world (Wittgenstein, 1980b, §63).

Like our statements about sensations, our statements about emotions might express the experience of genuine duration. That is, it makes sense to say that an emotion begins and ends. And like experiences of sensations, emotional experiences are expressed in characteristic ways. Wittgenstein admits that this *implies* specific emotions might result from specific sensations. 'Thus sorrow often goes with weeping, and characteristic sensations with the latter. (The voice heavy with tears.) But the sensations are not the emotions. (In the sense that the numeral 2 is not the number 2.)' (Wittgenstein, 1980b, §148). Now this remark calls for some elaboration. Arregui (1996) suggests the parenthetical sentence that ends the remark is intended to introduce a logical distinction between matter and form. Described materially, '2' represents a numeral, while described formally it is a number. But the number 2 is not an entity added to the numeral 2. Rather, the number 2 is the numeral's definition. Similarly, the relationship between sensations and emotions is one of *matter and form*. 'Mental experiences or organic modifications make up only the matter of emotion' and so 'sensations or organic modifications and emotions are not two different realities but two different descriptions of the same reality' (Arregui, 1996, p. 329). We should emphasize that this interpretation should not be taken to mean Wittgenstein holds that sensations are necessary for emotional experience.

Another way sensations differ from emotions is that the latter have a 'characteristic *course*' and 'do not give us any information about the external world. (A grammatical remark.)' (Wittgenstein, 1980b, §148). Like Ryle (1949), Wittgenstein distinguishes between emotional dispositions, directed emotions and undirected emotions. In the initial version of the plan, the distinction between dispositions and directed and undirected emotions is followed by the claim 'that the emotions can colour thoughts' (Wittgenstein, 1980a, §836). The grammar of directed emotions is shown through reference to an object of emotion, whereas the grammar of undirected emotions makes no reference to such objects. I fear *something*, whereas in certain situations I may experience anxiety without being able to specify why I am anxious. Take my anxiety before participation in a sporting event. I may not be able to specify whether I am anxious about the possibility of losing, being embarrassed in front of a large crowd, or the pressures of winning the game. In the case of directed emotions Wittgenstein makes it clear that the *object of emotion is not the cause of emotion*. When using words to express an emotion my expression refers to the object of emotion. 'The language-game "I am afraid" already contains the object' (Wittgenstein, 1980b, §148). So, like Averill (1974) and Kenny (1963), Wittgenstein regards the object of emotion as the emotion's *target*, not its cause. 'Thus a face which inspires fear or delight (the object of fear or delight), is not on that account its cause, but – one might say – its target' (PI §476).

Is this a mere preference on the part of Wittgenstein to treat objects of emotion as targets of emotion, as opposed to James (1890/1983), who regards objects of emotion as causes of emotion? No. Mere preference is ruled out by grammar, or the ledger of our linguistic practices. For the *possibilities* of our linguistic practices rule out the notion that objects of emotion cause emotional experiences. Take the previous example of anxiety before a sporting event and Wittgenstein's suggestion that emotions color thoughts. While I may not be able to identify the exact reason for my anxiety before participating in a sporting event, I probably associate it with the event in which I am about to participate. But the event itself does not *cause* my anxiety. By saying emotions color thoughts, Wittgenstein is suggesting that emotions are subject to reason (and are therefore not caused). By reasoning that a sporting event is of little importance when compared, say, to the outbreak of war, I may reduce my anxiety. Sensations, on the other hand, do not color thoughts. That is, sensations feel the way they do regardless of how I may think about them, although it is possible that I may direct my attention from them in order to get on with the business at hand.

The penultimate statement of the plan's continuation is somewhat ambiguous and appears to contradict what we have said thus far about objects of emotion not being causes of emotion: 'Typical causes of pain on the one hand, and of depression, sorrow, joy on the other. Cause of these also their object' (Wittgenstein, 1980b, §148). Is Wittgenstein saying that typical emotions are caused, or that the typical causes of pain are to be distinguished from the objects of emotions because emotions are not caused? The case of the object of emotion as a special kind of cause will be considered in more detail below when we elaborate further on Wittgenstein's rejection of causal accounts of emotional experience.

Context, ethological foundations and the crossroads of socialization

Now we turn to a remark that concludes the second half of Wittgenstein's 'plan for the treatment of psychological concepts,' which likens the description of sensation behavior to the description of emotion behavior. Expressions of sensation and emotion, says Wittgenstein, can only be *fully* described 'along with their external occasions. (If a child's mother leaves it alone it may cry because it is sad; if it falls down, from pain.) Behaviour and kind of occasion belong together' (Wittgenstein, 1980b, §148). Surrounding circumstances play an essential part in the complete description of pain or emotion behavior and context *may include* the perceived role of the object of emotion.

We will return to what Wittgenstein has to say about the role context plays in the expression and description of emotion. For the moment our focus is on his assertion that a complete account of emotion behavior and of the behavior associated with sensations must also address the question of how sensation words are learned and the contexts in which they are learned. Again, as discussed in Chapter 9, at PI §244 Wittgenstein suggests that through training, certain forms of natural pain expression are replaced by more refined linguistic expressions. So the expression of painful sensations through, for example, crying, is replaced by verbal expressions such as 'That hurts!' We do not think Wittgenstein would frown upon our substituting the word 'fear' for 'pain' and 'emotions' for 'sensations' in order to illustrate how context plays an essential role in the learning and socialization of emotion behavior. Like pain behavior, certain more refined emotion behaviors (including the use of emotion words to express emotions) are based on primitive, natural expressions. The child in Wittgenstein's example at §244 might just was well be afraid as in pain. Perhaps he is both afraid *and* in pain. This is what Anthony Kenny has in mind when he says:

> A child runs to his mother, and she says 'Don't be frightened' or he trembles and she asks 'What are you afraid of?' Emotion-words are not taught simply as a replacement of emotional behaviour; for what behaviour is characteristic of a particular emotion depends not only on the nature of the emotion in question but also on the object of the emotion.
>
> (Kenny, 1989, p. 60)

A complete description of the child's behavior as 'emotional' or 'resulting from pain' depends on our knowing what the object of emotion is and/or the event (object) that causes pain. This may be what Wittgenstein (1980b, §148) is getting at when he likens the causes of pain and emotion through reference to their object. Still, Wittgenstein's interchangeable uses of 'cause' and 'object' to compare emotional and sensational experiences is unfortunate and may lead us to believe that he warrants causal accounts of emotional experience and expression.

What Wittgenstein calls 'the primitive form of the language-game' is based on instinctive reactions to objects and events: 'Language – I want to say – is a refinement, "in the beginning was the deed"' (Wittgenstein, 1980, p. 31). 'Our *acting* lies at the bottom of language-games' (Wittgenstein, 1972, §204). Clearly there is a connection here with what we have described as 'primary language-games.' As with learning more refined pain behavior, the learning of more refined emotion behavior cannot occur without its 'primitive form,' or natural expressions of emotion. From this we can gather that physiognomic language-games and the primary language-games of emotion expression are very much alike. Furthermore, they are not based on the young child's capacity to think. Indeed, Wittgenstein even goes so far as to say that language itself 'did not emerge from some kind of ratiocination' (Wittgenstein, 1972, §475).

Wittgenstein's position that a child picks up relevant words and sentences that are added to its repertoire of emotional expressions amounts to a view of emotional development that is not only ethological, but anti-rationalistic. His analysis of grammar shows that natural expressions of emotion behavior (which are not learned, but expressed instinctively) are the foundation upon which more refined forms of expression are learned. But there is one further dimension to all of this. Applying a remark from his book entitled *On Certainty*, it seems clear that more refined (linguistic) expressions are learned also on the basis of trust and not subject to doubt. 'The child learns by believing the adult. Doubt comes after belief' (Wittgenstein, 1972, §160). Here we have a connection with Anthony Holiday's (1988) argument that a language-using society preserves the norm of truthfulness by sustaining sincerity and trust. Thus, in learning language, children naturally gain fundamental 'moral powers.'

The *initial learning* of more refined forms of expression does not depend on the child thinking through the meaning, proper application, consequences and possible contexts of the use of words taught as replacements for gestures, facial expressions, cries and so on. These factors come into play later, when an increasing number of natural expressions are replaced by more refined linguistic expressions. The concept of 'fear' or 'pain' is learned when language is learned (PI §384) and the analysis of the use of such concepts branches out to other concepts that are learned along with more refined expressions.

Meaning, understanding and intentionality: some ramifications for studies on early emotional development

At this point we turn to discuss ramifications of the foregoing for studies of early emotional development before discussing intentionality in early emotional expression. The vast literature on early emotional development strongly suggests that researchers have been primarily interested in more refined (linguistic) forms of emotion expression. Quite often the emotional lives of children are studied at a point when they are linguistically competent enough for the first transitions from natural emotion expression to more refined forms of expression to be, so to speak and in terms of early development, ancient history. We do not mean to say that the crossroads between natural expressions and more refined forms of expression have not been of interest to some researchers. Rather, we want to suggest that *in terms of conceptualizing emotion behavior*, the focus of emotion development research seems to be on emotion recognition and understanding as opposed to very early *expression*.

One ramification of the emphasis on more refined forms of emotional expression in early development is that questions regarding motivation, intention, meaning and understanding are conflated with questions regarding later forms of emotional expression and description. But we add that researchers tend to conflate the idea that early emotional expressions (natural expressions) are intentional, that is 'about or because of something' with the quite different idea of 'intentional' – in the sense of 'directed to some end or goal.' For example, consider the question that begins Harris's (1989) otherwise excellent book on emotional development. He asks, 'How does the child come to understand that another person is feeling happy or sad, angry or afraid?' (Harris, 1989, p. 5). Reviewing the transition from Darwin's (1872) claim that infants instinctively know the meaning of facial expressions to research on universal cross-cultural facial expressions and studies on infant facial expressions associated with the introduction of various independent variables, Harris (1989) concludes 'there can be little doubt that expressions of happiness, anger and distress are systematically produced' (p. 13). At the very least, the notion of 'systematic production' implies intention in the second sense (that is, directed toward some goal). But what kind of intention is involved in the very early production of emotional expressions and how does this relate to understanding the emotions of others? This is to ask: *Are emotional expressions produced in order to convey meaning, and, if so, does the child know the meaning conveyed?* As natural and responsive expressions, they do not necessarily communicate *intended* meaning. Adults, who can also naturally express emotions (learning language does not eliminate the ability to express emotions naturally), have the linguistic competence that enables them retrospectively to supply meaning (explain, provide criteria) for their emotional reactions. But because the child's training in the use of more refined emotion expressions is based on natural expressions, the meaning of which can only be inferred and responded to (at times instinctively) by care-givers, the meaning of those natural expressions is established not by the child, but by the child's care-givers.

By this way of thinking, a natural expression of distress is not tantamount to an implicit use of the concept of distress by the child. But it is not necessary to posit a cognitive capacity of 'self-recognition' to fill in the epistemological gaps in our understanding of children's experiences of emotion. Young children's natural expressions of emotion are, in many cases, immediately responded to by care-givers without deliberative thought, and, as Wittgenstein would have it, at some point supplied with meaning by care-givers. By the same token, early responses to facial expressions are natural responses not produced through an understanding of the *explicit meaning* of facial expressions.

External occasions and the intentionality of emotional expression

The idea that more refined forms of emotional expression replace natural expressions of emotion indicates that any effort to present a complete description of emotional behavior must take into consideration the social framework within which the behavior takes place. Because natural expressions are not necessarily purposeful, we must establish the conditions that allow for more refined, purposeful expressions intended to bring about responses from others. We have suggested that in order for another person to understand fully what I am communicating through an emotional expression, s/he must be aware of that to which my emotion is directed. So what about undirected emotions? Is it possible for another person to understand my expression of an undirected emotion? In the initial plan and its continuation, Wittgenstein has little to say about what is necessary for a complete description of behavior expressed during the experience of undirected emotions. But in the *Blue Book* (Wittgenstein, 1958), after exploring the grammar of such words as 'expecting,' 'wishing' and 'longing,' he introduces a grammatical distinction between cases where we know what we fear and cases where we experience fear of nothing in particular. The grammatical distinction consists in our recognizing that verbs such as 'fearing' are intransitive, while expressions like 'I feel fear' are transitive.

> 'I fear' will be analogous to 'I cry'. We may cry about something, but what we cry about is not a constituent of the process of crying; that is to say, we could describe all that happens when we cry without mentioning what we are crying about. Suppose now that I suggested we should use the expression 'I feel fear', and similar ones, in a transitive way. Whenever before we said 'I have a sensation of fear' (intransitively) we will now say 'I am afraid of something, but I don't know of what.'
>
> (Wittgenstein, 1958, p. 22)

The grammatical distinction between transitive and intransitive uses of verbs referring to emotional experiences is not intended to show that one or other kind of expression is necessarily associated with a known object. But recall that Wittgenstein (1980b, §148) says 'the language-game "I am afraid" already contains the object.' So does the statement 'I am afraid of something, but I don't know of what' already contain its object? Wittgenstein's answer is that in such cases '"Anxiety" is what undirected fear *might* be called, in so far as its manifestations are related to those of fear' (Wittgenstein, 1980b, §148).

What use, then, is the distinction between transitive and intransitive verbs referring to emotional experience? For Wittgenstein, the distinction is useful in pointing out the 'queer' use of the expression 'to know' in the expression 'I am afraid of something, but I don't know what.' If, after using an intransitive verb to express an undirected experience of fear, I come to know what it was that actually made me fearful, 'is it correct to describe my first feeling by an intransitive verb, or should I say that my fear had an object although I did not know it had one?' (Wittgenstein, 1958, p. 22). To answer this question, Wittgenstein turns again to the relationship between the grammar of sensations and emotions by introducing the analogy of 'unconscious toothache.' Like the claim that we may be experiencing an unconscious toothache, using an intransitive verb to express an objectless emotion requires a different kind of use of the expression 'to know' and so our investigation of the grammar in such cases shifts from the grammar of emotions to the grammar of 'to know,' 'knowing,' 'knowledge' and so on (ibid., p. 29). The upshot is that when finally learning of what we are afraid, we are 'getting to know better' our emotional behavior.

This is another example of how emotions can color thoughts. It is a theme to which Wittgenstein often returns throughout his later writings: emotion language (like other forms of expression) does not occur within a vacuum, but spreads out into other suburbs in the city of language. The idea that the use of words for describing and expressing emotional or other psychological experiences is based on our 'pattern of life' introduces a certain amount of indefiniteness for their meaning in various contexts. 'The pattern of life, after all, is not one of exact regularity' (Wittgenstein, 1982, §211). This position calls into question the restrictive contexts of experimental studies on emotional behavior and claims to the effect that a 'basic stock of human concepts' found in any language can be established and explained (Wierzbicka, 1999).

That there is an intentional component to emotion behavior is strongly implied in the two ideas that (1) emotions color thoughts and (2) it is necessary to discuss external occasions to achieve a complete description of emotion. The intentionality of emotional behavior is elaborated further by Wittgenstein in a number of remarks that follow the continuation of the plan. But first, he offers 'pain' as a comparison. How can the concept of pain be characterized by referring to the occasions on which it occurs? 'Pain, after all, is what it is, whatever causes it! – But ask: How does one identify pain? The occasion determines the usefulness of the signs of pain' (Wittgenstein, 1980b, §149). The *usefulness* of a sign of pain shows that pain behavior is intentional and Wittgenstein elaborates on the concept of pain as being 'imbedded' in our life and having 'very definite connections' with other techniques of expression (ibid., §150). But while an expression of pain must be 'surrounded by certain normal manifestations of life,' the expression of sorrow or affection is 'surrounded by even more far-reaching particular manifestations of life' (ibid., §151). For example, 'emotional attitudes (e.g. love) can be put to the test, but not emotions' (ibid., §152). It makes no sense to say there is a sensation attitude or that sensations can be put to the test. Here is another reason why Wittgenstein is inclined to say that 'emotions can *colour* thoughts; bodily pain cannot. Therefore let us speak of sad thoughts, but not, analogously, of toothachy thoughts' (ibid., §153). One way to sum this up is to say that *the intentionality of emotional experience is more far-reaching than the intentionality of sensation experience.* Besides the fact that pain, for example, 'has the characteristics of sensation and fear does not,' it is not possible for pain to consist only of thoughts (such as misgivings) like fear and hope (ibid., §153).

That Wittgenstein connects hope with an emotion like fear is significant, as it expands upon his view that the expression of emotions is surrounded by more far-reaching manifestations of life than the expression of pain or other sensations. 'Hope can be called an emotion' because like fear, anger and joy, 'it is related to belief, which is not an emotion. There is no bodily expression typical of belief' (ibid., §154). Furthermore, 'belief is not any kind of occupation with the object of belief. Fear, however, longing, and hope, occupy themselves with their objects' (ibid., §155).

There is one final aspect of Wittgenstein's characterization of the intentionality of emotion concepts that fully expands their connection with external occasions. The examples of fear, longing and hope may give us the impression that he wants to assimilate emotion words to the same kind as dispositional words. However, this would be an incomplete account of their explanatory function. To explain why I am fearful or sad I implicitly set the action to be explained not only in the context of my own behavior, but in the wider social context. In addition, explanation of my emotion may include giving a reason and/or justification for my actions that are connected with my emotion. Thus, as Bedford (1986) puts it, 'emotion concepts ... are not purely psychological: they presuppose concepts of social relationships and institutions, and concepts belonging to systems of judgment, moral, aesthetic and legal' (p. 30).

A snapshot of Wittgenstein's comparative aspects

As a reminder, Wittgenstein did not consider the statements that comprise his 'plan for the treatment of psychological concepts' as definitive. There are several open ends to his comparison of criteria for statements about sensations and emotions. The following organization of his remarks is intended, in part, to illustrate these open ends, which are labeled with parenthetical question marks. This 'snapshot,' as we call it, facilitates a comparison between the grammar of sensation and emotion concepts respectively. It points out clear similarities and differences in the two grammars. Clear similarities in the two grammars are marked with an asterisk under the heading of sensations.

As indicated, the comparative aspects of Wittgenstein's plan that are open-ended have to do with the synchronization, degrees and qualitative mixtures and course of emotions, and questions of whether we may regard sensations as directed, their causes always identifiable and as sometimes intentional. Wittgenstein does not rule out that emotions may be synchronized. His point that the intentionality of emotions is manifest in the many connections a verbal expression of emotion has with other emotions and emotional dispositions seems to indicate that they can be synchronized. I may express both apprehension and fearfulness at the same time, but of course it does not follow that all emotions can be synchronized. In a passage where he questions James's (1890/1983) claim that it is impossible to imagine an emotion without corresponding bodily sensations, Wittgenstein says: 'If the death of a friend and the recovery of a friend equally caused us to rejoice or – judging by our behaviour – both caused us sorrow, then these forms of behaviour would not be what we call the expressions of joy or sorrow' (Wittgenstein, 1980b, §321). It appears, then, that sensations and emotions are similar in that some may be synchronized while others may not.

Do emotions have degrees? Wittgenstein does not address this question in the plan, presumably because its answer is so obvious: a person may express increased

SENSATIONS	EMOTIONS
*Genuine duration	Genuine duration
May be synchronized	Sometimes synchronized (?)
Degrees	Degrees (?)
Qualitative mixtures	Qualitative mixtures (?)
Place of feeling in the body (localized)	No place of feeling in the body
*Characteristic expression behavior	Characteristic expression behavior
No characteristic course	Characteristic course (?)
Give information about external world	Give no information about external world
Never dispositional	Sometimes dispositional
Directed (?)	Not always directed
Caused	Not caused (object not the cause)
Cause not always identifiable (?)	Object not always identifiable
*External occasions for complete description	External occasions for complete description
Do not color thoughts	Color thoughts
Expression sometimes intentional (?)	Intentional far beyond sensations
*Language-games replace natural expressions	Language-games replace natural expressions

or reduced sadness over time. The question of qualitative mixtures is more difficult, as consideration of this possibility puts us in the position of wondering whether we are actually referring to the synchronization of emotions. That emotions can be synchronized and have degrees seems to indicate that a person can experience qualitative mixtures of emotions. As for the question of characteristic courses of emotion, we do, on occasion, express expectations regarding how long emotions will last, how sad, for example, someone will be and so on.

As for the open-ended sensations, we may view sensations as directed. That is, referring to the cause of a sensation is a kind of directedness, even though my expression of sensation experience may be considered responsive. The question of whether the cause of a sensation is always identifiable is also not addressed by Wittgenstein in the plan, perhaps because it is obvious that we are unable to identify many sensations we experience throughout our lives. Wittgenstein says sensations may be intentional since the expression of pain can be useful to us. But the expression of pain or other sensations may, at times, only be reactive and so it seems that in those instances they are not intentional in the sense of our achieving goals, meeting desires and so on.

Differences in expressions and descriptions: the asymmetry principle revisited

Now we return to the topic of emotion knowledge. At the beginning of the initial plan Wittgenstein characterizes psychological verbs in general 'by the fact that the third person of the present is to be identified by observation, the first person not' (Wittgenstein, 1980b, §63). Elsewhere, he asks whether the field of the psychological should be called 'experience' and whether psychological verbs should be called 'concepts of experience': 'Their characteristic is this, that their third person but not their first person is based on grounds of observation. That observation is observation of behaviour' (Wittgenstein, 1980a, §836). When a person says she 'feels conviction,' she does not infer the feeling of conviction from her words, tone of voice, 'nor yet the actions arising from the conviction' (ibid., §710). On the other hand, when I observe conviction in another person's face I do so through observation of behavior characteristic of conviction. 'One speaks of a tone of conviction because there is a *tone* of conviction. For the characteristic mark of all "feelings" is that there is an expression of them, i.e. facial expression, gestures, of feeling' (Wittgenstein, 1980b, §320).

Here again we have a statement of the asymmetry principle, which we encountered in Chapter 9. Wittgenstein drives a grammatical wedge between first- and third-person references to or expressions of psychological experiences. He points out that first-person verbal expressions of thought, perception or emotion are not made on the basis of anything. Another person's understanding of what I am thinking, perceiving or emotionally responding to will be made on the basis of behavioral observation (Budd, 1989, pp. 11–12). But we should not be led to believe that from another person's point of view my inner life is hidden, whereas from my own point of view it is not. Properly understood, the asymmetry principle states that my inner life is *expressed* and therefore *not hidden* from myself or others.

The predictable response to the immediately foregoing is that at times I may choose not to reveal my inner states, thoughts and what have you. But we must remember that Wittgenstein is referring to first-person present-tense *expressions* of emotion here and how they are involved in establishing the meaning of an emotion vocabulary in primary language-games. Emotional expression does not involve a process of inner observation because first-person experience of emotion is *immediate*. We can attribute the fictive impression that emotional and other kinds of expression are based on inward observation of bodily occurrences to a misunderstanding of the grammar of first-person expressions. However, it would be a 'mistake to deny that such inner states exist, for this concedes that the notion of an inner state is perfectly in order and anger, for example, just doesn't happen to be such an inner state' (Fogelin, 1987, p. 190). But we caution that denying that the meaning of first-person expressions of psychological verbs – associated with sensations, emotions, dispositions and so on – are linked to some kind of inward reflection is altogether different, despite that fact that the notion of an inner state and the process of inward reflection are both conceptually problematic.

How, then, are we to articulate the kind of knowing involved in, say, determining whether or not I am fearful or just nervous? Arregui (1996, p. 326) suggests knowledge of this kind as falling under the class of what Anscombe (1957) calls 'the class of things known without observation' (p. 14). An example of knowledge without observation is our ability to know the position of our limbs, say, while lying in bed under the covers. It is not as if concentrating on the feel of my mattress or sheets will tell me the position of my left leg. Nevertheless, a healthy person can *say* what position their leg is in and this would be an expression of awareness and *knowledge* about the position of their leg. Emotion knowledge is similar in the sense that a person cannot marshal evidence to show they are correct in labeling their emotion.

> There is point in speaking of knowledge only where a contrast exists between 'he *knows*' and 'he (merely) *thinks* he knows.' Thus, although there is a similarity between giving the position of one's limbs and giving the place of one's pain ... one ordinarily *knows* the position of one's limbs, without observation, but not that being able to say where one feels pain is a case of something known.
>
> (Anscombe, 1957, p. 14)

Likewise for Wittgenstein (1980b, §63): 'One knows the position of one's limbs and their movements. One can give them if asked, for example. Just as one knows the place of a sensation (pain) in the body.'

To follow another example of Anscombe's (1957), to say the least it would be difficult for someone to understand what I meant if I complained of a very sore foot while nursing my hand. Taken together, my verbal and bodily expressions would be recognized as incongruous and understanding what I meant would require some sort of inquiry on the part of an observer. However, I would simply be incorrect if I said my leg was straight while it was, in fact, bent. Wittgenstein extends this distinction to the emotions in the following very important remark, which is quoted at the beginning of this chapter:

> 'I must tell you – I'm frightened.' 'I must tell you – it makes me shiver.' And one can say this in a *smiling* tone of voice too. And do you mean to tell me he doesn't feel it? How else does he *know* it? – But even if it is a piece of information, he doesn't read this off from within. For he couldn't cite his *sensations* as proof of his statement. *They* don't teach him this.
>
> (Wittgenstein, 1982, §39)

This remark supports Wittgenstein's arguments denying that sensations are emotions and elaborates on the role context plays in first-person present-tense verbal expressions of emotion. But his ultimate point is that while verbal expressions of emotion are taught as replacements of natural and instinctive reactions, the teaching itself *does not amount to a lesson on how particular sensations must be associated with either verbal or natural expressions*. We are simply never taught which sensations ordinarily are associated with particular emotions. We *are* taught which *objects* go with various emotions.

Wittgenstein on facial feedback

To conclude this chapter we want to address a collection of remarks by Wittgenstein on an area of research in psychology whose theoretical difficulties he anticipated –

the so-called 'facial feedback hypothesis.' Wittgenstein's remarks on facial feed-back and related topics tie together several theoretical topics that have plagued the psychology of emotions. His discussion is aimed, in part, at showing (1) that specific bodily feelings are not identifiable as components of emotional experience and (2) that first-person present-tense *expressions* of emotion *are not necessarily based on cognitive evaluation of bodily feelings*. Wittgenstein is therefore at odds with one of the definitive statements of self-perception theory, which emphasizes the role sensations play in emotional experience and asserts that 'the experience of emotion is a cognition' (Laird and Bresler, 1992, p. 228). More importantly, Wittgenstein is also at odds with neo-Jamesians working in the area of facial feedback research (for example, McIntosh, 1996), who hold that *induced facial expressions initiate corresponding emotional experiences* and that *feedback from facial expressions inform people about their emotions*. With regard to the assess-ment of both self-perception theory and facial feedback research, the facial stimulation studies that Laird and Bresler (1992) cite as research on facial feedback to support their theory were inspired by the theory of self-perception. On the whole, the difference between neo-Jamesians and cognitivists on the issue of facial feedback appears to hinge on the extent to which the feedback is connected with some kind of cognitive process or innately put to use without cognitive input.

Wittgenstein readily concedes that imitating certain facial expressions might induce physiological manifestations of emotion or that play-acting might produce an emotion (see for example Wittgenstein, 1982, §§414–15). But while a facial expression might bring about an emotion, it does not follow that the emotion is composed of bodily sensations (Budd, 1989, p. 160). Suppose we grant that the muscular feeling of a smile is part of feeling glad. We may just as well ask where the other components of gladness reside in the body. But Wittgenstein asks, 'do you really feel them, or do you merely conclude that they *must* be there? ... Why are you supposed to mean *them*, when you say you feel happy?' (Wittgenstein, 1980a, §456). Do we say, for example, '"Now I feel much better: the feeling in my facial muscles ... is good"? And why does that sound laughable, except, say, when one had felt pain in these parts before?' (ibid., §454). It would also be laughable to say that 'gladness is a feeling, and sadness consists in not being glad. – Is the absence of a feeling of a feeling?' (Wittgenstein, 1967, §512). What exactly is it about fear that is so frightful? 'The trembling, the quick breathing, the feeling in the facial muscles? – When you say: "This fear, this uncertainty, is frightful!" – might you go on "If only I didn't have this feeling in my stomach!"?' (Wittgenstein, 1980a, §727).

Although Wittgenstein denies that bodily feelings can be specified as compo-nents of specific emotions, he does not deny that we may be aware of bodily feelings when we experience an emotion. When I am anxious and my anxiety is frightful, I may be conscious of my breathing and the tightness of muscles around my mouth. But 'does that mean I find these feelings frightful? Might they not even signify an alleviation?' (Wittgenstein, 1980a, §730). Joy, for example, 'is mani-fested in facial expression, in behaviour. (But we do not say that we are joyful in our faces.)' (Wittgenstein, 1967, §486). Just because joy is *manifested* in behavior it does not follow that joy *is* a certain feeling around the mouth and eyes or an inner feeling. '"But 'joy' surely designates an inward thing." No. "Joy" designates nothing at all. Neither an inward nor any outward thing' (ibid., §487). 'I should almost like to say: One no more feels sorrow in one's body than one feels seeing in one's eyes' (ibid., §495). The feelings that accompany emotions do not constitute the emotional experience and are insufficient for first-person present-tense identification of emotion.

First-person *past-tense* identification of emotion may be partially – but not wholly – based on recognition of bodily feelings. As for present-tense experiences, Wittgenstein appears to say that rational, deliberate, or even unconscious identification of emotions has more to do with external occasions (context) than cognitive evaluation of changes in one's bodily states. So is Wittgenstein's ultimately a cognitive perspective on emotion?

Whether or not there is a cognitive component to emotion recognition depends on whether we are referring to first-person present-tense *expression* of emotion, present-tense *observations* of emotion by others, or descriptions of emotion after the fact by ourselves or others. To be sure, *there is no occasion upon which a first-person present-tense expression of an emotion is a description, because emotional experience is immediate*. If expressed at all, first-person present-tense experience of emotion is expressive only. It is not descriptive, and therefore not cognitive – if by 'cognitive' we mean the upshot of a process of ratiocination, the consulting and evaluating of evidence, and so on. Suppose a person cries out 'Help!' Does this person 'want to describe how he is feeling? Nothing is further from his intentions than describing something' (Wittgenstein, 1982, §48). The trouble with thinking that immediate, first-person experience of emotion is cognitive is illustrated in the following remark:

> How can you *look* at your grief? By being grief-stricken? By not letting anything distract you from your grief? So you are observing the feeling by *having* it? And if you are holding every distraction at a distance, does that mean you are observing *this* condition? or the other one, in which you were *before* the observation? So do you observe your own observing?
>
> (Wittgenstein, 1980a, §446)

Like first-person experience of emotion, in many circumstances a person's understanding and description of another person's emotion is immediate. Yet it is unclear whether immediate descriptions are purely natural, instinctive reactions.

> 'We *see* emotion.' – As opposed to what? – We do not see facial contortions and *make the inference* that he is feeling joy, grief, boredom. We describe the face immediately as sad, radiant, bored, even when we are unable to give any other description of the features. – Grief, one would like to say, is personified in the face. This is essential to what we call 'emotion'.
>
> (Wittgenstein, 1980b, §570)

Wittgenstein's denial that we make inferences in order to understand which emotion another person is experiencing when they are expressing an emotion seems to rule out a cognitive component to understanding the emotions of others. But this only applies to present-tense observations. With description, we are no longer referring to immediate experience, but events of the past. Therefore, *context* comes into play with regard to understanding our own and others' emotions. Determining whether or not the words 'I am afraid' are a description of a state of mind 'depends on the game they are in' (Wittgenstein, 1982, §412).

> The phrase 'description of a state of mind' characterizes a certain *game*. And if I just hear the words 'I am afraid' I might be able to *guess* which game is being played here (say on the basis of the tone), but I won't really know it until I am aware of the context.
>
> (Ibid., §50)

There is a cognitive component to another person's past-tense description of my emotion. Still, we are left with the question of how people are able to understand the emotions of others. In the *Investigations* Wittgenstein asks:

> What is fear? What does 'being afraid' mean? If I wanted to define it at a *single* shewing – I should *play-act* fear. Could I also represent hope in this way? Hardly. And what about belief? Describing my state of mind (of fear, say) is something I do in a particular context. (Just as it takes a particular context to make a certain action into an experiment.) Is it, then, so surprising that I use the same expression in different games? And sometimes as it were between the games?
>
> (PI II, ix, pp. 187–8)

In his interpretation of this remark, Schulte (1993) says 'it is the nuances, the shades and colourings of my expressions which make it possible for others to tell what I feel' (p. 133). In cases of natural expression of emotion our reaction to another person's emotion *may be* instinctive. But in the case of more refined forms of emotional expression, our reaction (understanding) depends on our having been similarly taught those more refined forms of expression.

Learning point: emotion, sensation and judgment

1. *Explanations of emotions*

    (a) Problems with a causal account about the incorporation of meanings.
    (b) Problems with a rule-following account over the role of implicit rules.
    (c) Problems with a cognitive account over the incorporation of feelings.

2. *The Jamesian perspective*

    (a) Caused bodily reactions precede cognitive interpretations.
    (b) Sensations, which are caused, are necessary to emotion experience.

3. *Cognitive approaches*

    (a) Emotions as 'fusions' of bodily reactions with cognitive appraisals.
    (b) Emotion concepts imply targets. Thus, there is intentionality.
    (c) A distinction is made between emotions based on primary cognitive appraisals from those based on primary bodily reactions.

4. *Emotion and sensation*

    (a) Similarities in temporal perspectives.
    (b) Dissimilarities:
         (i)   The 'object of emotion' is not the cause of the emotion.
         (ii) Undirected emotions color thoughts (moods).

5. *Learning emotion words*

    (a) It is like learning sensation words, by verbal substitution for expressive displays in primary language-games.
    (b) Expressive displays are not based on thoughts.
    (c) Refined expressions replace natural expressions.

6. *'Knowing' in relation to emotion*: is there a parallel with knowing sensations?

7. *Emotion expressions* are surrounded by 'manifestations of life' as, for example, 'hope' is related to 'fear.' These presuppose beliefs.

Further reading

Parrott, W.J. and Harré, R. (1996). *The Emotions*. Thousand Oaks, CA: SAGE.
Schulte, J. (1993). *Experience and Expression: Wittgenstein's philosophy of psychology*. Oxford: Clarendon Press. (Specifically Chapter 8.)
Wierzbicka, A. (1999). *Emotions Across Languages and Cultures: Diversity and universals*. Cambridge: Cambridge University Press.

13 The grammar of some perception concepts

Philosophical Investigations §§398– 401 and Part II, xi; selections from *Remarks on Colour*

> We do not want to establish a theory of colour (neither a physiological one nor a psychological one), but rather the logic of colour concepts. And this accomplishes what people have often unjustly expected of a theory.
>
> Wittgenstein, *Remarks on Colour I*, §22

> Think of a picture of a landscape, an imaginary landscape with a house in it. – Someone asks 'Whose house is that?' – The answer, by the way, might be 'It belongs to the farmer who is sitting on the bench in front of it'. But then he cannot for example enter his house.
>
> Wittgenstein, *Philosophical Investigations*, §398

> Hence the flashing of an aspect on us seems half visual experience, half thought.
>
> Wittgenstein, *Philosophical Investigations*, II, xi, p. 197

Topics introduced: domains of conscious awareness; perspectives on visual perception; framework statements; logical analysis versus analysis by physics; color exclusion; transparency; color-blindness and the human form of life; 'dawning' and 'continuous seeing' of an aspect; the 'visual room' and private ownership; interpretation; duck–rabbit and other visual illusions; the grammars of 'to see' and 'to see as'

The psychology of perception is concerned with what people see, hear, touch, taste and smell, and the means by which these are accomplished. Since the seventeenth century the phrase 'conscious of' has become more widely used to refer to the relation between a human being and of what he or she is aware. People are conscious ... of what? It has long been realized that there are ways in which the presence and properties of various features of the environment, including the human body itself, seem to be sensed by people without them becoming consciously aware of them. Wittgenstein's interest was exclusively concerned with the concepts we use to record, discuss and manage that which we experience consciously.

There seem to be three domains of objects and events of which people are consciously aware. First, there is the material world of shaped and colored things, arranged in space, and the events we are aware of as these things change in all sorts of ways. Second, there is the ever-changing domain of bodily sensations. Finally, there are the thoughts and the images that chase each other through our minds. Note that there seems to be a clear distinction in these domains between the 'inner' (private) and 'outer' (public) domains. Human begins are conscious of objects and events around them (the first domain, the outer). Then there is consciousness of bodily sensations, thoughts and images of 'the mind's eye' (the second domain, the inner). One might prefer to split this second domain into second and third domains, thinking that the mind/brain is different from the rest of the body.

Each domain has its characteristic vocabularies with which we express our experiences to ourselves and to others. In Chapter 9 we studied the conditions for the meaningfulness of the vocabulary of bodily feelings. In Chapters 10, 11 and 12 we have done the same for various forms of thought. In this chapter we turn to a study of the meaning conditions for the *vocabularies* with which we describe some of the visual characteristics of things and events in the world.

The history of philosophy reveals a morass of muddles and mistakes in the grammar of perception concepts as grievous and egregious as those we have already diagnosed in the domains of bodily feelings and thoughts. Our focus will be on the vocabulary that has developed to express our experiences of color, and on the problem of what sort of descriptions we should give of the subtle visual phenomena of the experience of shape and spatial organization of what we see, that seem to be neither purely visual nor purely interpretative. These experiences include seeing likenesses between faces, becoming aware of the multiple aspects of such puzzling things as the picture that can be seen as two faces or as a flower vase. Visual illusions served Wittgenstein as a platform for reflecting on the language of vision. These investigations will enable us to begin to get a just appreciation of the verbs 'to see' and 'to see as.'

Psychologies of visual perception

Attempts to understand how people perceive the world around them, and the states and configurations of their own bodies, go back to antiquity. In the seventeenth century, the philosopher–psychologists of the era, such as Thomas Hobbes and John Locke, took for granted that sensations were mental entities impressed on the mind by the effect of emanations from material things reaching the sense organs and eventually the brain. How brain states give rise to perceptual experiences was then – and remains to this day – a mystery. Whether the air of mystery is a product of conceptual confusion is ultimately the question that a Wittgensteinian approach to this branch of psychology should attempt to answer. From the discussion in Chapter 9, we can be sure at least of this: the seventeenth-century conception of sensations as mental entities is a massive error. The analogy between the grammar for describing material things and for reporting sensations led to such theories as the primary and secondary quality doctrine. One group of sensations was primary, such as sensations of shape, and resembled the 'real' qualities of material things, while another group of qualities, such as taste and color, was secondary and did not resemble the states of material things that caused a person to experience them.

In the eighteenth century George Berkeley not only dismissed Locke's analysis of visual experience, but made the first systematic attempts to use the geometrical configuration of the movements of the eyes to analyze the source of our ability to see objects as three-dimensional things. These pioneering studies secured the dominance of the sense of sight in the research programs of philosophers and psychologists, to the neglect of touch, hearing, taste, smell and the sense of the movement and positions of parts of the human body.

The great German psychophysicists of the nineteenth century, Gustav Fechner, Johannes Müller and Hermann von Helmholtz, had unraveled some of the correlations between physical stimuli and the sensations of which a person is consciously aware. However, we do not perceive just sensations. We are aware of colored patches, no doubt, but we see a three-dimensional world of things. We are aware of sounds but we hear articulate speech, rhythms and melodies. We are aware of pressures on the skin, but we feel shapes and textures. What is the relation between bodily sensations and perceptions? The brain and the neural components of the perceptual systems must play a crucial part in integrating the one into the other, so it would seem. What processes were these organs performing?

In the twentieth century two major general explanations of the cognitive processes that are the basis of our powers of perception were on offer. J.J. Gibson (1965) built up a comprehensive account that was based on a rejection of the traditional principle – of Locke and others – that perceptual experiences are compounded out of simple sensations. According to Gibson, the perceptual systems of vision, audition and so on are mechanisms that automatically extract higher-order invariants from sensory stimuli. These invariants are the things we see, hear and touch. For example, the visual perceptual system actively explores the retinal patterns produced by the electromagnetic flux in which people are embedded. The activities of the brain-as-analyzer are supplemented by deliberate activity by the person or animal exploring its environment. By contrast, Richard Gregory's (1970, 1998) equally comprehensive theory was based on the principle that perception is cognitive – a kind of reasoning. According to him, perceptions literally are pictorially presented hypotheses as to the existence and nature of things and events in the material environment affecting the various sensory organs. When a person perceives something, a kind of implicit reasoning is employed. Gregory's studies focused almost exclusively on vision, and his overall approach owes a great deal to interpretations of such phenomena as ambiguous figures and illusions.

The approaches to perception by Gibson and Gregory follow a divergence in principle as to how perceptual systems work and how they should be studied. On one hand, we have the psychology of perception as a kind of mathematical analysis concerned with the causal processes of perception, identifiable in the brain and nervous system (Gibson). On the other hand, the psychology of perception is a study of the construction of meanings and the uses of rules. Which approach is best? Could both be correct? Wittgenstein's grammatical investigations into the concepts we use to express our visual experiences seem to offer a point of view that partakes of both Gibson's and Gregory's emphases.

Framework statements

Wittgenstein wrote on color concepts on and off during the final eighteen months of his life. His literary executors organized these remarks into a three-part book entitled *Remarks on Colour* (Wittgenstein, 1977), which we will refer to hereafter as ROC. Let us begin with five remarks in which Wittgenstein says explores the concept of 'seeing' in this book.

> Could a 'Psychology' contain the sentence: 'There are human beings who see'? Well, would that be false? – But to whom would this communicate anything? (And I don't just mean: what is being communicated is a long familiar fact.)
>
> (ROC, III, §328)

> Is it a familiar fact to me that I see?
>
> (Ibid., §329).

> We might want to say: If there were no such humans, then we wouldn't have the concept of *seeing*. – But couldn't Martians say something like this? Somehow, by chance, the first humans they met were all blind.
>
> (Ibid., §330)

> And how can it be meaningless to say, 'there are humans who see,' if it is not meaningless to say there are humans who are blind? But the meaning of the sentence 'there are humans who see', i.e. its possible use at any rate, is not immediately clear.
>
> (Ibid., §331).

> 'You see the tree, the blind do not see it'. This is what I would have to say to a sighted person. And so do I have to say to the blind: 'You do not see the tree, we see it'? What would it be like for the blind man to believe that he saw, or for me to believe I couldn't see?
>
> (Ibid., §321)

What is Wittgenstein getting at in these striking statements? He is offering an outline of the conceptual framework for the concept of 'seeing' (and, hence, seeing something *as a certain color*). The possible use of the sentence 'There are humans who see' is 'not immediately clear' because we live in a world of the sighted and our words for seeing and our color vocabularies are geared, so to speak, toward the sighted. Consider these questions: 'Do the blind believe sometimes they can see?' 'Do the sighted believe sometimes they cannot see?' It seems absurd that we would say to someone: 'You see the tree, the blind do not see it.' Why?

> There seem to be propositions that have the character of experiential propositions, but whose truth is for me unassailable. That is to say, if I assume that they are false, I must mistrust all my judgments.
>
> (Ibid., §348)

We must be careful to not mistake propositions that express the *framework* of our ways of thinking, and so are not subject to doubt, for those that are experiential (empirical) and are subject to doubt. 'Human beings can see' is just such a proposition. To put this another way: what it is to be a human being is to possess the sense of sight. Of course, this is not to say that non-sighted persons are not human beings! It only serves to point out the *grounding of our color concepts* in the notion of 'what it is to be a human being.'

Color concepts

In Chapter 3 we mentioned that color concepts played an important role in Wittgenstein's transition from his Tractarian to his 'later' philosophy. In the *Tractatus* he held that, like other concepts, there is a *necessary or a priori logic* to color concepts. So first, 'white is lighter than black' states a logical relation between 'white' and 'black' that cannot fail to hold between these concepts (Wittgenstein, 1921/1961, 4.123). Second, being colored is a 'form of objects'; that is, objects must have some color – and so therefore being colored is one of the essential attributes of objects (§§2.0131, 2.0251). One can render a transparent flask in a painting, but in so doing the flask will not be colorless. If it were colorless, no one could see it! Certain cunningly curved windows are 'invisible' in this sense.

For several reasons the internal relations among perceptual concepts mentioned above cannot fail to obtain. They are given with or partly constitutive of the color terms we use. The color of a certain object often is essential to what it is – how it is described and as what it is identified. For example, the sky at night is said to be 'black' and a baseball is said to be 'white,' not because these are matters of fact that might have been otherwise. A red ball about the size of a baseball is a cricket ball. Allied to such statements are others drawn from empirical research on the physics of light. The sky is black because no incident solar radiation is refracted by the sky at night, and a baseball is white because the pigment of the cover reflects light of all wavelengths. Thus we have a kind of split between considering the logical analysis of color words in the first group of examples, and the study of color phenomena in physics in the second group. The same sentence can be used to express a conceptual relation in one context and a matter of physics in another. In these cases, the words 'white' and 'black' are embedded in different patterns of connections with other words.

What about the logic of 'color exclusion,' such as when we express our grasp of the color spectrum in a statement such as: '"A is red" necessarily excludes "A is green"'? The notion of color exclusion means that simultaneous ascriptions of different colors to a point in the visual field are *logically inconsistent*. This seems to run counter to the Tractarian view that all meaningful words are independent terms in the sense that they point to particular things or states of affairs and their meanings are acquired in this way. The statement '"A is red" necessarily excludes "A is green"' seems to depend on the notion that red and green are related – that color concepts *form a system*. In his post-*Tractatus* philosophy, Wittgenstein thought the uses of color terms might form a 'propositional system,' whereby propositions about color are compared with reality not individually, but all at once. Written out fully, such a propositional system would express relations such as 'A is red, and not green, and not yellow, and not blue ... ' and so on. The upshot is that if color words form a system, *color language does not consist of a vocabulary of elementary names.* (See Chapter 3.) Besides, who can locate the elementary object 'red'? In expressing the structure of this system, we may identify statements such as 'Nothing would count as red and green all over' as *grammatical propositions* (or grammatical remarks) that *express a rule* about our use of the words 'red' and 'green.' Still, there is the question of the source of these rules. It seems odd to say that these rules are just conventions.

The irrelevance of theories of color to Wittgenstein's grammatical inquiry

In ROC, Wittgenstein shows that as a study of grammar, the analysis of the uses of color words cannot be *based* on the physics of color, in which hues are distinguished by the wavelength of the electromagnetic radiation which cause us to perceive color. Nor would such an analysis count as a *phenomenology* of color, or the relations between colors as we experience them. It is neither a commentary on Newton's physics of color and its successors, nor on Goethe's phenomenology of color experiences, although these and other accounts of color are addressed in Wittgenstein's analysis. So we are not working toward a *theory* of color, but a *description* of the possible and impossible uses of color concepts in various circumstances. Our project is to explore the grammar of our color vocabulary. Wittgenstein makes this clear early in ROC:

> We do not want to establish a theory of colour (neither a physiological one nor a psychological one), but rather the logic of colour concepts. And this accomplishes what people have often unjustly expected of a theory.
>
> (ROC, I, §22)

What is it that we expect a theory of color to accomplish? A theory will represent an explanation of color that gives us the satisfaction of 'knowing' scientifically the nature of color, how we perceive color, perhaps by what neural mechanisms, and so on. But why does Wittgenstein resist the notion that we can 'know' about color concepts by constructing physical or phenomenological/psychological theories? Consider the following observations about transparency:

> Why is it that something can be transparent green but not transparent white? Transparency and reflections exist only in the dimension of depth of a visual image. The impression that the transparent medium makes is that something lies *behind* the medium. If the visual image is thoroughly monochromatic it cannot be transparent.
>
> (Ibid., §19)

> Opaqueness is not a *property* of the white colour. Any more than transparency is a property of the green.
>
> (Ibid., §45)

> And it does not suffice to say, the word 'white' is used only for the appearance of surfaces. It could be that we had two words for 'green': one for green surfaces, the other for green transparent objects. The question would remain why there existed no colour word corresponding to the word 'white' for something transparent.
>
> (Ibid., §46)

> When we're asked 'What do the words "red", "blue", "black", "white" mean?' we can, of course, immediately point to things which have these colours, – but our ability to explain the meanings of these words goes no further! ...
>
> (Ibid., §68)

Why is it that something can be transparent green but not transparent white? This question and others like it cannot be answered by theories of the physical properties of green and white materials and the electromagnetic radiation they transmit or reflect. Nor can they be answered strictly in terms of personal color 'experiences' or 'physiological reactions' that occur inside us. Rather than having to do with empirical evidence, such questions have to do with the grammars of words such as 'green' and 'white' in contexts where we see transparency or opacity. This is why Wittgenstein says our explanation of the meanings of certain color words 'goes no further.' In explaining the meanings of these words, we have 'reached bedrock.' Our justifications for calling a ripe tomato 'red' can go no further. That 'our spade is turned' is shown in the way a ripe tomato might play a central role in one of the primary language-games in which someone masters the use of the word 'red.'

The connection between the grammar of color concepts and teaching practices

The consequence of the immediately foregoing discussion is to say that the *grammar* of, for example, 'white glass,' is different from the grammar of our means of description of glass of other colors. Our grammar of color concepts does not include the possibility of white transparent glass. Is this because white reflects most incident light (the physical properties of white), while colored glass does not? Yet red glass transmits light, so why do we not call clear glass 'transparent white,' since it transmits all wavelengths? A certain kind of answer leads us to a Tractarian position. Does our color language mirror reality? Is our color language necessarily rooted in the properties of things? Is there a one-to-one correspondence between a color word and a color? Are color words only ostensively defined? The answer to all these questions is no, although ostensive definition plays a crucial role in our explanations, justifications and evaluations of our uses of color words. (To the question, 'What is red?' we might point to a sample of red.) Running the risk of sounding behavioristic, it is the grammar of words for describing white and other colors that *shapes* our thinking about the possibility of transparent white. But neither the grammar nor the physical properties of white *determine* our thinking about whatever we see to be white.

> 'White water is inconceivable, etc.' That means we cannot describe (e.g., paint), how something white and clear would look, and that means: we don't know what description, portrayal, these words demand of us.
>
> (ROC, I, §23)

> When dealing with logic, 'One cannot imagine that' means: one doesn't know what one should imagine here.
>
> (Ibid., §27)

> From the rule for the appearance of transparent coloured things that you have extracted from transparent green, red, etc., ascertain the appearance of transparent white! Why doesn't this work?
>
> (Ibid., §29)

> *Why* can't we imagine transparent-white glass, – even if there isn't any in actuality? Where does the analogy with transparent coloured glass go wrong?
>
> (Ibid., §31)

It is not immediately clear what transparent glass we should say has the *same colour* as an opaque colour sample [e.g., white]. If I say, 'I am looking for glass of *this* colour' (pointing to a piece of coloured paper), that would mean roughly that something white seen through the glass should look like my sample. If the sample is pink, sky-blue or lilac, we will imagine the glass cloudy, but perhaps too as clear and only slightly reddish, bluish or violet.

(Ibid., §24)

The remark immediately above reveals the grammar that shows the impossibility of the notion of 'white water' (in §23), an expression used by 'white-water rafters.' Is it that the grammar of our color language *determines* our thinking about white, so that we cannot 'ascertain the appearance of transparent white' (§29) or be able to 'imagine transparent-white glass' (§31)? How do we *learn* the possibilities and impossibilities of our uses of color words?

What is there in favor of saying that green is a primary colour, not a blend of blue and yellow? Would it be right to say: 'You can only know it directly by looking at the colours'? But how do I know that I mean the same by the words 'primary colours' as some other person who is inclined to call green a primary colour? No, – here language-games decide.

(Ibid., §6)

Imagine a *tribe* of colour-blind people, and there could easily be one. They would not have the same colour concepts as we do. For even assuming they speak, e.g. English, and thus have all the English colour words, they would still use them differently than we do and would *learn* their use differently ...

(Ibid., §13)

The answer to our question (how do we *learn* the possibilities and impossibilities of our uses of color words?) is *teaching practices* (including personal trial and error) – the language-games of learning the uses of color words in varieties of context. A person may believe green is a primary color. But that belief would be based on their not having seen or experienced for themselves what happens when blue and yellow are mixed. It is through activities like mixing and use of colors that we learn that our color concepts form a system, the relations of colors within that system, and that our color vocabulary is *driven by practices* (e.g. mixing colors, drawing in a coloring book, painting, and appreciating works of art and colored icons). Others can have different color vocabularies and color systems (e.g. a color-blind tribe).

Color vocabularies are not acquired as substitutes for public expressions of sensations of hue

In Chapter 9 we saw that at PI §244 Wittgenstein suggests that the learning of certain sensation words (e.g. 'pain') is based, in part, on the replacement of natural expressions by those words. In learning certain sensation words we are learning new, more refined, pain behavior. In ROC, I, §57 Wittgenstein says:

['I feel X'
'I observe X'
X does not stand for the same concept in the first and the second sentences, even if it may stand for the same verbal expression, e.g. for 'a pain'. For if we ask 'what kind of pain?' in the first case I could answer 'This kind' and, for example, stick the

questioner with a needle. In the second case I must answer the same question differently; e.g. 'the pain in my foot'. In the second sentence X could also stand for 'my pain', but not in the first.]

Note that the remark is bracketed. This means Wittgenstein may have been dissatisfied with it. Nevertheless, it says something about the relationship between our uses of sensation and color words if we extend the case of 'I observe X' to the observation of something (which is, of course, colored). As Wittgenstein points out, in the statements 'I feel pain' and 'I observe pain' the word 'pain' is a different concept. I can say 'I observe my pain' but I cannot – so Wittgenstein claims – say, 'I feel my pain.' Why not? It is because 'I feel my pain' would simply be put as 'I feel pain.' In the former case, it is as if we would undertake an investigation as to whose pain I am feeling. This would be a first-person present-tense expression of pain. Could I 'observe' my pain if I were asked by a doctor to be more precise in my response to his questions? There is a sense in which such an example is *like* a third-person description of pain.

In ROC, III, §61 Wittgenstein asks, 'How do people learn the meaning of colour names?' Well, we do not replace natural color expressions with more refined verbal expressions of color. It appears that color words are not expressive, although we can use them to express (e.g. 'That sunset is incredibly orange!'). We are inclined to say: *color words seem to be 'located' in the descriptive suburb of the city of language.*

If we adopt the apparently obvious alternative, that color words are learned by pointing to color samples, this suggests that we could learn the words one by one in public language-games, just as we learned the words for bodily feelings one by one. We might even extend the notion of 'expression' to color, thinking of someone choosing a color from a palette as expressing the hue of an imagined element in a scene to be rendered in paint. But this suggestion runs into difficulties with the necessity to make a place for the logical relations between colors, in that if someone says something is blue, I can deduce that it is not yellow, green, red and so on. Hues are determinates under the determinable 'color.' It seems that color words are *learned as a system*. This was our conclusion from the above discussion of the role of practices in acquiring the color words of our tribe.

What are these practices? What purposes are served by this color system? For the most part, the color system is one among various schemes by which we make discriminations significant for our way of life. As motorists we must be ready to discriminate red, amber and green. As art critics we must be ready to discriminate many more shades, with a richer system of color concepts. Vocabularies of color words are not made meaningful by reference to a set of distinctive items given by nature, whether these be visual sensations or public samples.

Color-blindness and the human form of life

Our color vocabulary is limited by grammar (the logic of color concepts) *and* the human form of life. Part of the latter (and, more obliquely, the former) is the possibility of color-blindness. We have already encountered the comparison between those who are and are not color-blind. Now we will explore this comparison further for another purpose. People who are color-blind do not 'have' the color concepts of normally sighted people. So much is obvious. But how do we know this?

> Do the normally sighted and the colour-blind have the same concept of colour-blindness? The colour-blind not merely cannot learn to use our colour words, they can't learn to use the word 'colour-blind' as a normal person does. They cannot, for example, establish colour-blindness in the same way as the normal do.
>
> (ROC, I, §77)

> ... I can observe what colour judgments a colour-blind person – or a normally sighted person, too – makes *under certain circumstances*.
>
> (Ibid., §82)

> People sometimes say (though mistakenly), 'Only I can know what I see'. But not: 'Only I can know whether I am colour-blind'. (Nor again: 'Only I can know whether I see or am blind.')
>
> (Ibid., §83)

Under certain circumstances, color-blind people make different judgments about the matching of things of similar and different colors from those with normal sight. For example, when presented with a heap of strands of wool of many colors, they do not sort them into piles as most people do. They might put all the red and the green strands in the same heap, insisting that they are 'more or less the same color.' We establish color-blindness by observing these judgments (ROC, I, §82). They (the color-blind) seem to be playing a different language-game, or cannot participate fully in our language-games.

But the basis upon which color-blind people do not 'have' the same color concepts as normally sighted persons is *not* that color-blind people lack a certain kind of private experience (ROC, I, §83). Our review of the private-language argument in Chapter 9 should have inoculated us against the idea that each person may mean something different by 'blue' when they say, for example, 'The colors of the Estonian flag are blue, black and white.' The grammar of color words is fixed by their use in public practices, such as matching objects of the same colors and differentiating those of different colors. The sensory experience of hue plays no role.

The basis upon which the color-blind do not 'have' our color concepts is that they *lack the perceptual abilities* to participate fully in our language-games having to do with color (e.g. 'I love that purple stitching in your dress!' 'Did you see that incredible red in the sky this morning?'). Color-blindness plays a role in the human form of life in that we can imagine people of various cultures coming to some understanding that members of their tribes are color-blind, in that certain of their public practices are different from those of the majority. Nothing is added to the conceptual distinction between the normally sighted and the color-blind by coming to understand that the basis for color-blindness is physiological and to know, in detail, the details of their physiology. We can imagine tribes where it is believed color-blindness is indicative of magical powers, or the result of the 'evil eye.'

What would happen if a psychologist in the country of the color-blind were to discover that a few people made a distinction between some of the strands of wool in a certain heap undifferentiated by the majority of the locals, insisting that they were distinguishing them by color? The fact that some people see a reddish tinge at the very end of the violet part of the color spectrum suggests that there is a place for the concept of 'greater discrimination.' Would the psychologist in our example conclude that 'there must be another color'?

If so, a place would have to be found for it in the existing system of color words – just as we can add 'infra*red*' and 'ultra*violet*' to ours, though very few of us can see them.

Learning point: the grammar of color concepts

1. *Vision*: 'Human beings can see' is not a statement of fact, but a specification of a conceptual framework. The concept 'color-blind' finds a place only in our conceptual system. It would have no place in the framework of a color-blind tribe.

2. *The learning of color words*: Generally, Wittgenstein is against the idea that color words are learned by paying attention to sensations of color or isolated color samples.

    (a) Color words are learned *as a system*. They are learned, in part, in the process of making certain kinds of distinction between groups of things.
    (b) Words for hues are organized as determinates under a determinable, and hence stand in logical exclusion relations to one another. In learning 'red' one is learning 'not green,' 'not orange' and so on.
    (c) Color vocabularies cannot be explained by:
         (i)   'Newtonian' physics. (Our color vocabularies do not match precisely the color spectrum, nor do they identify color density.)
         (ii) Nor are meanings fixed by reference to something like Goethe's phenomenology of color hues. (There is no possibility of comparing subjective color experiences.)
    (d) Cultural history: Why not 'transparent white' for 'clear'? This is not one of our language-games.
    (e) Painters' talk of shades of color is a secondary language-game.

3. *Color-blindness* is disclosed by a matching task, a public language-game. A color-blind person could not know he or she was abnormal from private experiences, but only from differences in the performance of certain color-relevant public tasks.

4. The *grammar of color words* is fixed by participating in public language-games, not by the physics of light nor by private sensory experiences.

Seeing shapes and spatial relations

The look of things – interior and exterior

Another major aspect of the world-as-visually-perceived is something we might call the 'spatial organization' of things in the world, including the relations of components of individual things. In Part II of the *Investigations* Wittgenstein discusses various visual phenomena of this sort, beginning with a contrast between such expressions as 'I see the tree' and 'I see a likeness between the father and son in the family portraits.' Consider the latter case. I show a friend a picture of my father and myself, pointing out our likeness. Pressed by my friend to specify the likeness between my father and myself, I might say, pointing: 'Don't you see it? Look here. Look at my brow, nose and chin. Now look at his.' Suppose my friend is unconvinced. What do I do now? In desperation I might opt to reproduce the pictures, say by drawing my face and my father's face in such a way that the likeness is more apparent. But will this exercise amount to reproducing the *likeness*? Would it be odd to say that a painter, reproducing a picture of twins, is reproducing their likeness? One might say so. But really, reproducing the likeness between myself and my father amounts to nothing more than reproducing parts of the picture of me and my father. (The same would hold for a case in which I simply make a photocopy of the father–son picture.) One implication of this is that although I or another person can see the father–son likeness in my drawing, I cannot really 'portray' the likeness. I am unable to do this, as it were, in the physical world. Now we will be tempted to think the likeness is an inner mental phenomenon. If the likeness cannot be realized outside, it *must be* realized inside.

Suppose that, with some effort, my friend finally notices a certain likeness between me and my father in the picture. 'Oh, now I see it!' he says. Wittgenstein suggests that we call my friend's experience the 'dawning' of an aspect of something seen. In this case, it dawns on my friend that there is a likeness between myself and my father in the picture. But upon first viewing the picture my friend was aware that it is a picture of me and my father. Using Wittgenstein's (PI II, xi, p. 194) terminology, this would amount to a 'continuous seeing' of an aspect. Wittgenstein offers several illustrations intended to bring about the former (dawning) experience as what we might call 'workable cases' in the conceptual investigation of seeing shapes and spatial relations. The most famous of these is Jastrow's 'duck–rabbit,' which is shown on the page in the *Investigations* cited above.

To continue with our example, we might ask: what happens when the likeness between me and my father in the picture dawns on my friend? As we have already said, one temptation is to construe this dawning as a personal or private experience. After all, my friend might say: 'Yes, *I* see a likeness.' Is my friend seeing this likeness in his personal, private, 'mind's eye?' Marie McGinn (1997) suggests that, in considering Wittgenstein's remarks on seeing aspects, we consult a few of his remarks prior to Part II of the *Investigations* on the so-called 'visual room,' primarily PI §398. Here Wittgenstein's interlocutor proposes that when imaging or seeing something, 'I have *got* something which my neighbour has not.' This means that a visual experience or imagined visual image is 'owned,' so to speak, by the person having the experience or imagining the image. It is important to point out, as does McGinn (1997), that Wittgenstein acknowledges the validity of the interlocutor's temptation. 'I understand you', says Wittgenstein. It just seems reasonable that, like a dream that seems to occur in one's own head, an imagined visual image is 'one's own.' '*I* had a dream last night.' 'I had the *same* dream that you had!' Preposterous! *My* dream is *my dream*, just as my imagined visual image is *my* visual image. However – and this is very important – when we examine the *purpose or purposes* of such expressions, we see that the notion of ownership here is quite odd. It is on this basis that Wittgenstein responds by declaring the words 'I have got something which my neighbour has not' really 'serve no purpose.' Why? Because in order for these words to make sense the interlocutor would need to be able to talk about 'having the private experience.' And this would, in turn, require that the alleged mental something was a kind of entity, something which could belong to me and, as such, would be something other than myself – that is, something that I could 'have.' Here I am. Here is my possession.

We are not just talking about 'figures of speech' here. We are talking about grammar. Take the case of the visual room. I cannot do anything with this room. For example, I cannot do anything *in* it. The temptation to say that I could do something in the visual room is rooted in my wanting to use the same form of expression about the visual room as the material room in which I sit. This is the point of our quoting the remark about the farmer and his house at the beginning of this chapter. It is easy to shift from talk about objects that represent to 'representations.' But then, with this shift, the grammar shifts as well. Perhaps this shift should form the basis of an approach to the psychology of perception that is free from the illusory model of perceiving-as-internal-imaging. We must beware, above all, of trying to invent such a relation on the model of the relation between a person and the objects that anyone can see.

Obviously Wittgenstein is taking the notion of 'ownership' here quite literally. It is easy just to assume that the same word – or related words – is applicable to 'inner contexts' of privacy and ownership. A *real* farmer sitting outside his *real* house can *really* go inside the house. An imagined farmer sitting outside an imagined house is in an entirely different situation. But actually, he is in no *real* 'situation' at all! Again, we are not just talking about figures of speech.

'Seeing aspects'

We now can proceed to Wittgenstein's investigations on seeing aspects. The investigation begins with some global reflections on the suggestion that the phenomena involved in 'seeing X as Y' are to be explained as differing *interpretations* of what is seen. Already Wittgenstein has hit upon a particular view on perception that relates to a controversy in scientific practice central to his day: to what extent does *interpretation* play a role in scientific practice? Or, as Gillies (1993) puts it, is observation 'theory-laden'? Contributions to answering this question on the part of empirical psychology, addressed by Gillies in chapter 7 of his excellent book, show conclusively that research by psychologists on the perception of ambiguous figures like the duck–rabbit and Necker cube suggest that observation *is* theory-laden, or involves interpretation based on prior experience with objects and their relations in the world. Indeed, as Gillies (1993) points out, such figures played a central role in Richard Gregory's (1970) cognitive/interpretative theory of perception mentioned toward the beginning of this chapter. Again, we can contrast this view with perspectives on perception, more in the Gibsonian vein, that propose that the relation between perceived things and perception is more direct and comprehensive than Locke thought. (Locke, you will remember, proposed that perceptual experiences are compounded out of simple sensations.) So really, in addressing the interpretative side of visual experience, Wittgenstein has something to say about the fundamental assumptions behind the perspectives of Locke, Gibson and Gregory. To simplify, we can say that he is exploring the validity of (1) visual perception as colored patterns and structure, or sensing, in which patterns and structure, 'cause' our visual experience, or (2) visual perception as sensations plus thoughts, whereby we interpret what we see 'as something.' A general outline of these perspectives is taken up by Wittgenstein on pp. 193–4 in Part II of the *Investigations*.

I see the picture of the duck. Then, with some coaching, I see it also as a rabbit. Is interpretation an add-on to this dawning of an aspect? If so, I might be able to answer the question 'An interpretation of what?' by making reference to a common something that is interpreted in two or more ways. Another famous picture, the black Maltese Cross on a white ground that alternates with a white cross on a black ground, can be seen as one or the other, but never as some third something in need of interpretation. (The Maltese Cross is shown at PI II, xi, p. 207.) The locution 'seeing as … ' has its home ground, so to say, when there are alternative 'seeings.' This is the upshot of those aforementioned 'workable cases.'

The change from a picture-duck to a picture-rabbit can be described as a perception. But, strangely, if I draw what I see in each case, the drawings are the same! This suggests a tempting step: perhaps the duck and the rabbit I see become 'inner pictures,' images in the mind, and that is why I cannot draw them separately – now as a duck and now as a rabbit. But the inner picture is modeled on the 'outer picture.' Would not the same common pattern of lines be reproduced inwardly, imagined as a duck and then as a rabbit? Making the duck–rabbit an inner picture to explain how we experience a change from one to the other moves us no further in explaining this experiential phenomenon. However, it does put us in the position to take the interpretative stand, *à la* Gregory. The picture does not change, but our *interpretation* of it does change. Further support for this comes from the fact that a person looking at the duck–rabbit may say they 'suppose' it is both a duck and a rabbit or it 'looks like a rabbit now,' and their verbal expressions may take the form of conjectures. These forms of expression imply cognition, interpreting.

On the other hand, Wittgenstein indicates that expressions pertaining to perceived changes in the duck–rabbit may not be conjectural at all. In the first-person present-tense case, when asked 'What do you see here?' we would expect someone simply to describe their perception: 'Now I am seeing it as a picture-rabbit' (see PI II, xi, pp. 194–5). Yet in the third-person context, another person might say 'He is seeing the figure as a picture-rabbit.' Clearly, in the latter case we have conjecture. But does it make sense to say I could be wrong when I say 'Now I'm seeing it as a rabbit?' Here we see a cross-current with numerous remarks about knowing and knowledge in both the *Investigations* and *On Certainty* (Wittgenstein, 1972). If it makes no sense to say I can be incorrect in my first-person present-tense verbal expression about seeing the duck–rabbit as a duck or rabbit, perhaps we have an angle to pursue against the interpretative view, in favor of the sense-and-cause view. This is why Wittgenstein says:

> It would have made as little sense for me to say 'Now I am seeing it as … ' as to say at the sight of a knife and fork 'Now I am seeing this as a knife and fork'. This expression would not be understood. – Any more than: 'Now it's a fork' or 'It can be a fork too'.
>
> (PI II, xi, p. 195)

Or, as another example:

> One doesn't '*take*' what one knows as the cutlery at a meal *for* cutlery; any more than one ordinarily tries to move one's mouth as one eats, or aims at moving it.
>
> (Ibid.)

In these and surrounding passages, Wittgenstein is indicating that although interpretative statements on the part of persons looking at the duck–rabbit may be cloaked in the appearance of conjectures, which could be correct or incorrect (and thus would be 'empirical'), the expressions have an element of what might be called 'direct-experience expressions' similar to 'I am in pain.' Here we think again of PI §244. When I see a rabbit while out walking, I might exclaim: 'Look! There's a rabbit!' It would not make much sense for me to say: 'Look! That thing! Now I'm seeing it as a rabbit!' Of course, this pertains to Wittgenstein's cutlery example. So really, we can think of someone saying 'Now I see it as a rabbit!' not as a report, but *as an exclamation*.

Remember that in the case of PI §244, when someone lets out a natural expression of pain or complains of being in pain, they are, in a sense, *doing something* or *trying* to get something done, for example, trying to get help or to get off work! Because of the similarities in grammar we are pointing out here, it might benefit us to look upon the report 'Now it's a rabbit' in the same light. Rather than thinking of a change in aspect so expressed as simply being a description of a shift from one aspect to another, we might think of it as a question of what one *does with the picture*. So 'Now it's a rabbit' serves, perhaps, as acknowledgment that the shapes on the page can be viewed in two ways, as two different animals. Or, we can imagine a contest where children are issued the duck–rabbit and told that the 'winner' will be able to say how many animals are in the picture. In this case, we have a direct relation to doing something with the picture toward achievement. Or, as another example, we might use the duck–rabbit picture to show someone what to look for in a marsh on a duck hunt. In *doing something with* the picture, one draws attention to the feature of the picture that brings to the fore its duckishness (PI §201).

We should pause here to discuss some other implications of the duck–rabbit – or other figures for that matter, ambiguous or otherwise – as mental pictures (or 'mental representations' in contemporary parlance). Richard Gregory proposed what we might term a 'storage objection' in the sense that it would be uneconomical to store such pictures of objects (or information about the pictures) in our heads so that they might be 'looked up' on some occasion. Perhaps we store only typical characteristics of objects and, using current sensory information, make adjustments to the current model 'in the head' to fit the situation at hand. This is, no doubt, an empirical matter. But it makes sense to discuss the relative quantities of information in a picture only if we have already moved away from the 'inner representation' story.

What is the diagnosis? How might we characterize the mistakes in thinking that lead us to turn the duck–rabbit into a mental picture as expressing an interpretation or conjecture, or into a visual sensation that is in no need of interpretation? It is, Wittgenstein says, the result of putting the organization of an experience *along with* its color and shape that tempts one to treat the visual impression of a duck as no more than a sensation. The argument has shown us that the achievement of now seeing it as a duck, now a rabbit, can be explained in terms of a family of likenesses, more so than as a sensation. We are tempted to think of experiences of a change in aspect on a par with those very attributes of the object seen. Thus we are tempted to introduce an 'inner picture' that is the location of the change in aspect itself, since the 'outer picture' has not changed.

'Seeing as ... '

What shall we say of 'seeing as ... '? Perhaps it is an amalgam of seeing and thinking. In one sense it is not part of perception because we can see the arrangement of lines and draw them without attempting to portray either a duck or a rabbit. Sometimes when we recognize an old friend after a moment we might say 'So it's you!' An expression of this sort serves both as a description and an expression of recognition. 'Recognizing something *as* something' is to be classified under the phenomena of 'seeing as ... ' Wittgenstein draws our attention to techniques by which we can focus on one or the other aspect of an ambiguous picture at will.

We describe these experiences as 'seeing something' because they are visual. However, as we have pointed out repeatedly, the retinal patterns caused by the arrangement of lines in a drawing are the same for both the duck-experience and the rabbit-experience. To do justice to this feature of visual (and tactile) experience, we need to supplement our vocabularies with such expressions as 'see as.'

Wittgenstein sets out a number of contexts and uses for the word verb 'to see' and its various grammatical parts as a field of family resemblances.

> The concept of 'seeing' makes a tangled impression. Well, it is tangled. – I look at the landscape, my gaze ranges over it, I see all sorts of distinct and indistinct movement; *this* impresses itself sharply on me, *that* is quite hazy. After all, how completely ragged what we see can appear! And now look at all that can be meant by 'description of what is seen'. – But this just is what is called description of what is seen. There is no *one genuine* proper case of such description – the rest being just vague, something which awaits clarification, or which must just be swept aside as rubbish.
>
> (PI II, xi, p. 200)

There is no essence to seeing. 'Seeing as' is neither an impression nor a thought. Nor is this a report of an observation of another visual property alongside color and shape.

Perhaps the most enlightening remark comes in PI II, xi, p. 201. Here Wittgenstein's interlocutor asks: "'What I can see something *as*, is what it can be a picture of'"?' The answer is: ' … the aspects in a change of aspects are those ones which the figure might sometimes have *permanently* in a picture.' We do not express our way of seeing what the picture 'is of' by using 'aspect-seeing' language. The reason perhaps lies in the way all the surroundings make one aspect seem paramount. We have done some experiments to test this. If some children who have never seen the duck–rabbit are shown lots of rabbits, then they are inclined to see a rabbit, but if they have seen lots of ducks around the figure, then they are inclined to see a duck. Wittgenstein, too, remarks that custom and upbringing also have a hand in this.

This kind of aspect – and no doubt there are others – we call 'aspects of organization.' 'When the aspect changes parts of the picture go together which before did not' (PI II, xi, p. 208). Wittgenstein goes on to say that "'Now he's seeing it like *this*," "now like *that*" would only be said of someone *capable* of making certain applications of the figure quite freely. The substratum of this experience is the mastery of a technique.' And indeed this is so. Concentrate on the 'ear tips' and 'eye' and you are likely to see it as a duck. Concentrate on the rightward dimple and 'eye' and you are likely to see it as a rabbit. With the Necker Cube (shown at PI II, xi, p. 193), attending to the lowermost corner tilts the box upwards, while attending to the uppermost tilts it downwards.

Learning point: seeing aspects

1. *Organization of the structure of visual experiences*

    (a)   'See … ' takes things and so on as grammatical objects. 'See … as … ' takes aspects of material things.
    (b)   Aspects cannot be displayed in drawings since the arrangement of lines is the same for seeing a duck as for seeing a rabbit.
    (c)   'See an aspect' makes sense when there is an alternative aspect, for example, seeing a face and seeing it as that of a friend.
    (d)   Not to be explained by two different 'inner objects' – duck image and rabbit image. Like the drawings, they would be the same in the mind and the problem reappears.

2. *What is 'seeing as … '?*

    (a)   The error is to put organization of structure along with color and shape as simple visual properties.
    (b)   'Seeing as … ' is like perception and yet not like it, in so far as 'seeing something as something' displays possibilities for what one might do with the object thus seen. In the ambiguous figures there are several uses to which they might be put. It is also like interpreting and yet not like it, though techniques for producing this or that aspect can be learned.

(c)   'Seeing as ... ' partakes of seeing *and* of thinking.

3.   *'Seeing'*

(a)   The concept of 'seeing' covers a field of family resemblances.
(b)   There is no 'one genuine proper case.'

Further reading

Gibson, J.J. (1965). *The Senses Considered as Perceptual Systems*. Boston: Houghton Mifflin.

Gillies, D. (1993). *Philosophy of Science in the Twentieth Century: Four central themes.* Oxford: Blackwell. (Specifically Chapter 7.)

Glock, H.-G. (1996). *A Wittgenstein Dictionary*. Oxford: Blackwell. (Specifically pp. 81–4.)

Gregory, R.L. (1970). *The Intelligent Eye*. London: Weidenfeld and Nicolson.

MacIntyre, A. (1992). Colors, cultures, and practices. In French, P.A., Uehling, T.E. and Wettstein, H.K. (eds), *The Wittgenstein Legacy: Midwest studies in philosophy* (Vol. 17) (pp. 1–23). Notre Dame, IN: University of Notre Dame Press.

Glossary

Action
Philosophers distinguish bodily movements from actions on the basis that the latter are intended. Rapidly withdrawing one's hand from a hot stove is not an action. Reaching for something in order to use it for brushing your teeth is an action. Many psychologists use 'action' to describe both intended and unintended bodily movements.

Agreement
A metaphor in Wittgenstein's remarks on rules and rule-following that serves to warn us against distinguishing too rigidly between agreement in (1) language, customs and so on and (2) what is true or false. Some agreement is necessary even to begin discussing matters of truth and falsity. In so far as discussing matters of fact is a normative practice, there must be some agreement on matters of fact for there to be normative practices in the first place. However, agreement does not *determine* what is true or false.

Ambiguity of exemplars
An ostensive definition will always be ambiguous to some degree. A particular dog will be an exemplar of 'dog,' ostensively defined, say, to a child by her father. However, the child may attend to one of many attributes of the exemplar (e.g. its tail). Or 'dog' might be taken as the name of *that* particular exemplar. This shows that pointing to an exemplar does not necessarily help someone to grasp the full meaning or significance of a word.

Artificial intelligence (AI)
A branch of cognitive science concerned with producing computer programs that model cognitive processes in order to test theories of how humans perform cognitive operations.

Aspect
Wittgenstein distinguishes between the 'dawning' of an aspect of something seen and the 'continuous seeing' of an aspect. The dawning of an aspect occurs when Jastrow's 'duck–rabbit,' which is now seen as a duck, and now as a rabbit. Seeing the figure as a duck only would be the continuous seeing of an aspect. An apparent

paradox arises as to just what occurs when lines of the figure, which remain unchanged, can be seen now as a duck, now as a rabbit. Perhaps the change in aspect is due to a different interpretation, an inner experience that accompanies perception. However, the grammars employed in such cases show that expressions like 'Now I see it as a rabbit!' are not descriptive reports, but exclamations (or avowals) similar to 'I'm in pain!'

Asymmetry principle

First-person statements about bodily feelings (or emotions) differ from third-person statements in that the former are expressive and the latter are descriptive. There is no question of correctness in a first-person expression of pain, for example, although there can be a question of sincerity. Furthermore, with their origins in primary language-games, words used to express bodily feelings in secondary language-games are *part of what it is* to experience and express bodily feelings. Third-person descriptions of pain, on the other hand, can be incorrect. To evaluate their accuracy we might defer to empirical evidence. The grammar of first-person expressive talk and third-person descriptive talk points, respectively, to asymmetry in expression versus description, their being or not being part of experience, and to deferring to evidence or otherwise.

Augustinian picture of language

This 'particular picture of the essence of human' of language is introduced at PI §1. The Augustinian picture of language carries with it numerous implicit claims about language-learning, communication, private experience and so on. As presented by Wittgenstein, its three basic claims are that words name objects, that the meaning of a word is the object (or event) for which it stands, and that sentences are combinations of names.

Autonomy of grammar

Features of the world do not determine grammar, or the possibilities of word use. Although we use words according to rules, we do not justify these rules by pointing to a matter of fact or state of affairs in the world. Grammatical rules are to be justified through reference to community practices in which the language-user participates. The implication is that the proposition 'red is a color' does not express some super-fact about a particular hue that dictates how the word 'red' is to be used. Rather, 'red is a color' expresses a *grammatical* rule.

Behaviorism

Its main presupposition is that subjective experience and reference to inner states and processes cannot be topics for *scientific* psychology. Thus scientific psychology is the study of statistical correlations between observable stimuli and observable responses. These responses are 'set up' through conditioning of various kinds.

Beetle in the box

A simile presented by Wittgenstein at PI §293 that shows the grammar of the language of bodily feelings cannot be based on the model of object and designation.

The 'beetle' is a bodily feeling (or sensation) and the box is one's conscious experience. Others have beetles in their boxes but no one can compare their beetle with that of another person, just as each person's bodily sensations are personal and private. Still, 'beetle' (like 'tickle') has a use in the language. In using 'beetle' correctly, the precise nature of each person's putative beetle is irrelevant to using correctly and understanding 'beetle.' The simile has ramifications for the learning of words to express and discuss bodily feelings, as humans must be able to learn such words without comparing their feelings, in part because the feelings are not 'thing-like.'

Cartesianism
A principal thesis of this perspective is that each person is a doublet, composed of two substances. In the writings of Descartes (1596–1650), a material body is associated with an immaterial mind.

Causation and causal explanation
In psychology, many uses of 'cause,' 'caused,' 'causes' and so on imply three basic characteristics of causal explanations. First, one event is said to cause another when there is a regular correlation between the purported cause and its effect. Second, the relation of causality is always asymmetrical, running from cause to effect. Third, there is a necessary relationship between the cause and effect, such that the effect must follow the cause unless something interferes. The 'necessity' is a reflection of the presumption that a causal mechanism *must* exist, linking cause and effect. Many traditional patterns of explanation in psychology employ a mixture of Humean and Aristotelian causation, borrowing regular correlation from Hume and the categories of material and efficient cause from Aristotle.

Cognitivism and cognitive psychology
Its main presupposition is that behind the exercise of cognitive skills and various kinds of thinking there are unobserved mental processes. There are cognitive (mental) processes of which we are unaware that explain those of which we aware.

Color exclusion
Color exclusion is exemplified in such statements as: '"A is red" necessarily excludes "A is green".' Simultaneous ascriptions of different colors to a point in the visual field are *logically inconsistent*. The 'color exclusion problem' played an important role in Wittgenstein's change in philosophical outlook after the *Tractatus*. The statement above seems inconsistent with the Tractarian supposition that all meaningful words (names) are independent in the sense that they point to particular things or states of affairs. This inconsistency led Wittgenstein to consider that color terms such as 'red' and 'green' are related and that color concepts form a system.

Computational model
To construct a computational model is to represent, through calculations, a mental process (such as making an inference or classifying into categories). Such models are assumed to specify the steps in cognition taken to carry out cognitive tasks. Computational modeling is a branch of cognitive science inspired by Alan Turing's

(1950) claim that computing machines can exhibit some of the same thinking behavior as living organisms.

Criteria

In Wittgenstein's later writings and in abbreviated form, they are reasons or grounds for applying a concept. For example, on what basis do we say a person has the ability 'to read'? In cases like this, Wittgenstein appeals to criteria to show that attribution of the ability to another person – or even to oneself – is not based on anything 'outside' the internal (grammatical) relationship between the concept's use and its criteria for application (e.g. good comprehension of a text). We might, for example, think that specific brain processes must be at work when someone reads and that these processes must obtain in order to say 'He can read.' But the meanings and correct use of psychological concepts like reading are not based on confirmation that such processes cause, accompany and so on display of the skill.

Denotational theory of meaning

The view that the meaning of a word is that to which it refers or which it names. Words denote things.

Descriptive language

In the *Tractatus*, words (or 'names') stand in one-to-one correspondence with objects in the world and meaning is born, so to speak, when this correspondence obtains. Factual (or 'true') sentences are collections of names that describe factual states of affairs in the world. This serves to summarize Wittgenstein's account of descriptive (or representational) language in the *Tractatus*. However, in his later philosophy, Wittgenstein distinguishes between descriptive and expressive language, in part to show that sentences such as 'I'm in pain' are not descriptions of one's bodily state. Grammatically, they are expressions.

Discursive psychology

An approach to psychological theorizing and research based on the twin principles that the core psychological phenomena are (1) the meanings of symbolic systems in daily use for the performance of all sorts of tasks and (2) the implicit and explicit rules that express standards and conventions of correct and proper performances in various contexts. As a response to the mainstream cause–effect model of explaining psychological phenomena, the discursive paradigm opens up the phenomena of psychology to include costumes and uniforms, household artifacts, words and other written and spoken symbols and so on.

Disposition

A characteristic or property that is manifested indefinitely under certain conditions. 'Expecting,' for example, might be manifested in a person's pacing back and forth before the arrival of a friend, setting out tea cups, or just saying 'I'm expecting him to arrive at any moment.' The implication is that because expecting can be manifested in so many ways, it cannot be a particular mental process. However, as a disposition, expecting can be thought of as a persisting state of mind.

Eliminative materialism
The thesis that neurophysiological terms will be substituted for everyday words used to describe and express psychological phenomena. It is based on the assumption that our everyday psychological vocabulary is defective and reflects a 'false theory' of the workings of psychological phenomena. Its proponents want to *eliminate* our everyday vocabulary and beliefs about psychological phenomena by substituting scientifically informed words referring to *material* processes.

Empiricism
The philosophical perspective that holds our knowledge claims may go no further than what we can observe with our senses. It thus restricts knowledge claims of mental states and processes to observed behavior.

Essentialism
Addressed to a wide range of phenomena, it is the general claim that the characteristics of something are essential to its being *that* thing. Pertaining to word use and meaning, it is the claim that there must be something in common to every situation in which we use a word that gives the word its meaning. There is a common essence to each instance of a word's use.

Ethology
A theoretical orientation and approach to research that investigates the relationships between biology and behavior. Certain of Wittgenstein's post-*Tractatus* remarks acknowledge *ethological foundations* of language-learning in primary language-games.

Expressionism
The movement for 'truthful literary and artistic expression,' also known as 'Austrian Expressionism,' that came into its own during the first two decades of the twentieth century. Its proponents were responding to the excesses of Austrian Impressionism. They sought more 'truthful' expression primarily by (1) stripping ornamentation from their various artistic and literary creations and (2) using words economically and truthfully.

Expressive language
Language-use that expresses rather than describes. 'I'm in pain' is not a description of one's bodily state. It is an expression of how one feels that finds its origin in primary language-games which themselves are based on natural *expressions* of pain. The appeal to expressive language is integral to Wittgenstein's attack on mentalistic and reductive accounts of psychological phenomena.

Fact
For Wittgenstein in the *Tractatus*, an object with properties it shares with other things. Everything in the world is given in the form of a fact. This perspective on 'fact' avoids the problem of contrasting between unique objects and general properties of objects.

Family resemblance
As a perspective on semantics, there is no 'essential' meaning to a word that is evident in all cases of its use. Thus definitions of words that are important in an inquiry will be misleadingly simplistic. A grammatical investigation will reveal that the word can be used in a variety of ways and have multiple meanings or shades of meaning. In PI §66 Wittgenstein offers the word 'game' as an example of a word with no single essential meaning, but as having a pattern of uses that are related by similarities and differences.

Form and function of words
Words and sentences that have similar form might serve very different functions. Also, a single sentence might serve more than one purpose. Our example is 'Why don't you eat your spinach?' A child can take this as a request or an order. Form and function is related to Wittgenstein's notion of surface and depth grammar.

Form of life
A controversial technical term Wittgenstein employs sparingly in PI, albeit for important purposes. For our purposes, 'form of life' implies a distinction between (1) the human form of life, or what is necessary to live as a human being, and (2) forms of human life, or variations on human living practices. In many cases, deference to form of life is necessitated when questions arise about why people do things (justification). Sleeping, for example, is a necessary ingredient to the human form of life (as with most members of the animal kingdom). However, the sort of bedding one uses, sleeping patterns influenced by work schedules and so on are justified through reference to forms of human life. If asked, 'Why do your people sleep on the hard floor with a brick as pillow?' one will eventually say something like 'That's just how we sleep!'

Framework statements
Propositions that express the framework of our ways of thinking are not subject to doubt. 'Human beings can see' is not to exclude non-sighted persons from being human, but to ground concepts related to seeing (e.g. colors) in 'what it is to be human.' Such statements are to be contrasted with statements geared toward expressing experiences that are subject to doubt (e.g. saying 'that's purple' in a poorly lit room).

Grammar, grammatical analysis and grammatical remark
In Wittgenstein's post-*Tractatus* writings, grammar pertains to all that is implicated in language-use as a normative practice. It has been described as the 'ledger of our linguistic practices.' A grammatical analysis of a word will explore its possible uses, impossible uses, borderline/problematic uses and connections with other words. Such analyses aim, in part, to uncover sources of philosophical confusion. Grammatical remarks are different from empirical generalizations in that they show logical connections between words and the phenomena to which they refer or express. That is, they point out rules of use. 'There is no bluish yellow' is not an empirical observation, but a statement about a particular facet of our color vocabulary and how it 'works.'

Grammar (surface and depth)

A distinction introduced by Wittgenstein at PI §664. The surface grammar of a sentence is the way it is constructed and 'taken in by the ear.' Its depth grammar relates to the combinatorial possibilities of words that make up the sentence. Glock (1996, p. 154) asks us to compare the sentences 'I have a pain' and 'I have a pin.' Their surface grammar (or sentence structure) is the same. But by not attending to their depth grammar, we might assume having a pain is like having a pin. So now a pain is like an object, and from there we will be inclined to think that 'I'm in pain' is a description, rather than an expression (or avowal). Many philosophical problems in psychology find their source in lack of attention to depth grammar.

Homogeneous and heterogeneous explanation regresses

A homogeneous explanation regress uses the same concept (or concepts of like kind) over and over again. So in the case of abilities, abilities in one sort of task are explained through reference to abilities in another sort of task, mastery of which is relevant to the first ability. The explanation of an ability to use color words by reference to an ability to use mental pictures as samples would be such a regress. A homogeneous regress in psychology and other human domains terminates in something like a habit, acquired skill, or natural ability. Such regresses are *closed*. A heterogenous regress shifts from one set of similar concepts to a different set of concepts, for example from norms and habits to neurophysiological states and processes. But in making this shift, psychological concepts are not being used.

Introspection

The process of finding out things about oneself by 'looking inward.' The era of modern experimental psychology was founded on the method of introspection. For various reasons, however, the introspecting person can be mistaken or untruthful about their 'observations.' Hence the birth of behaviorism, whose proponents believed that a scientifically 'objective' psychology could not be established through this method. Introspection is 'subjective.'

Language-game

A technical term introduced by Wittgenstein at PI §7. Its full meaning and import are controversial, but for our purposes a language-game is both a methodological tool and refers to practical activities where words are used.

Language of thought

A thesis advanced by Fodor (1975) which asserts that computation and a medium in which to compute are necessary for cognition. By Fodor's account, the 'medium' is a kind of 'representational system' that has the characteristics of a language.

Logical form

The study of relations between names in propositions and between elementary and complex propositions is the study of logical form. For Wittgenstein in the *Tractatus*, the study of logical form constitutes the domain of logic; logical form is to be found in the structure of states of affairs in the world.

Meaning
In Wittgenstein's sense, in the vast majority of cases if we want to know the meaning of a word we should look to its uses in the language. By the Augustinian (denotational) account, the meaning of a word is the object or event it denotes.

Mechanism
A general explanatory approach that emphasizes the workings of physical (material- and efficient-causal) processes and avoids reference to intentions, purposes, goals and so on. In the *Investigations* Wittgenstein devotes 22 remarks on the topic of reading as a skilled cognitive performance (§§156–78). The remarks not only extend his attack on mentalism, but target mechanism. Mechanistic explanations of human skills and abilities reject reference to purposes, aims and desires. In other words, they are a kind of causal explanation in which we find no reference to agency.

Mentalism
Any doctrine that insists upon the reality of inner mental states and processes. Often, mentalists explain cognition in terms of such processes.

Methodological behaviorism
In psychology, it is the suggestion that overt and observable behaviors should be the primary focus of research. The observable behaviors can be used to make inferences about unobserved (e.g. mental) processes. Originally, methodological behaviorism was a philosophical stance that evolved from John B. Watson's behaviorist principles.

Mind behind the mind fallacy
The mistake of projecting a half-hidden realm of thought behind the common uses of symbolic systems to perform cognitive tasks. Citing a covert mental process behind the overt performance (or results) of a cognitive task begs the question of what is behind the covert processes. So we enter into a regress. The 'brain behind the mind' fallacy is similar, in that explaining a cognitive task through deference to processes of the brain begs the question of what processes are behind the processes.

Mind–body problem
The problem that arises when we consider how the mind, which is immaterial and unseen, can cause or influence the material body to move. The problem is evident in such questions as: 'How can a mental process move my arm to reach for the light switch?'

Modus tollens
A logical deduction in the form: 'If p then q. It is not the case that q. Therefore it is not the case that p.' Sometimes a series of remarks by Wittgenstein take the form of a *modus tollens* argument.

Natural expression
An expression that is not learned and partly foundational for the development of more refined forms of linguistic expression. Natural expressions are the bases upon which primary language-games occur.

Nonsense
A technical term used by Wittgenstein primarily in the *Tractatus*, although it is found in his later writings as well. 'Nonsense' does not mean foolish, absurd, or not useful. It more closely resembles 'meaningless.' For example, we slide into nonsense if we try to use fact-stating language to describe and/or explain mystical experience.

Normative, normative explanation and normative constraints
Pertaining to behavior, 'normative' refers to right or wrong, what is accepted and not accepted, and standards of correctness. From a Wittgensteinian perspective, normative explanations require reference to local rules and customs in which the prevailing standards of correctness can be expressed. It is clear that in the domain of psychological phenomena, normative explanations far outweigh causal explanations in both number and force. Normative constraints are logically connected with standards of correctness. Standards of correctness and constraints on what is acceptable behavior are internally (grammatically) related. When the correct way is learned, to a certain extent the incorrect way is learned.

Ontology
In philosophy, a type of investigation concerned with being, or 'what is.' The ontology of a science is spelled out in the kinds of 'things' practitioners of that science presume to exist (e.g. 'electrons'). Everyday people can be said to have personal ontologies as well (e.g. the belief in spirits of the deceased).

Operational definition
In experimental research, it specifies variables in terms of the operations needed to bring them about. Operational definitions basically tell other researchers: 'If you want to replicate my research, do precisely what I did, namely *this*.' In psychology, an operational definition of 'reward' might consist in specification of a particular brand of food pellet, made by a specific company and having specific properties.

Ostension and ostensive definition
Pointing to something. We learn some words by having our attention drawn to the objects or events they signify; that is, by ostensive definition, or the pointing out of the relevant referent. A mother with child points to a dog: 'Look, honey, *that's* a dog!'

Paradox of interpretation
A paradox rooted in the question of whether there is only one way to interpret and follow a rule correctly. Such questions suggest that rules get their meanings through interpretation; that they do not 'speak for themselves.' Wittgenstein's analysis of

following the rule of a sign-post seems to suggest that a 'sign-post rule' can be interpreted and followed in many ways. Thus, whatever one does as a result of the sign-post can be seen to accord with its rule. The paradox ends when we acknowledge that there is a regular, customary use of sign-posts. That is, rule-following is not based on interpretation, but customary use.

Performative(s)

According to Austin (1975), in many cases words are used as means to bring about social acts and actions. They are not descriptions. A judge saying 'I sentence you to life' performs a legal act. The utterance is not a description of anything. The idea of performatives links up with language-games presented by Wittgenstein, for example at PI §§23 and 27. The distinction between performatives and descriptions has import for many topics in psychology, including the various forms of emotion expression and description.

Perspicuous representation

One aim of Wittgenstein's later philosophical method is to display the grammar of word use perspicuously (clearly or lucidly). He thought that lack of perspicuity in our use of words is a 'main source' of philosophical confusion (see PI §122).

Phase space

A phase space in physics is constructed to represent all possible states of a system, as represented by a certain set of variables. It is constructed through use of differential equations. Wittgenstein took this idea from the German physicists Hertz and Boltzmann and applied it to the idea that all combinatorial possibilities of propositions could be represented in the form of a truth-table.

Phenomenology

A school of philosophy that emphasizes direct awareness of experience as the foundation for truth. One of its methodological tenets is to eliminate presuppositions as part of philosophical analysis and to focus on how things appear to us.

Philosophy

In Wittgenstein's early and later philosophies, it is 'critique of language' for the purposes of revealing the sources of philosophical problems and thereby dissolving them. The goal of solving the problems through critique of language (as perspicuous representation) would amount to assuming the problems are legitimate, like empirical problems that require more scientific research for their resolution. But philosophical problems are not legitimate in that way. Thus they are not solved, but rather 'dissolved.'

Philosophical therapy

Philosophical problems cause confusion and take an emotional toll. Wittgenstein's later philosophical method aims, in part, to reduce or eliminate the latter. Philosophical therapy is successful when the source of our philosophical problem is revealed through grammatical analysis.

Physiognomic language-game
A term introduced by Hintikka and Hintikka (1986) referring to the context(s) in which the vocabulary and uses of words expressing bodily feelings are established. For example, in primary language-games we learn to substitute expressions like 'My knee hurts' for natural expressions of knee-pain. Physiognomic language-games are a kind of primary language-game, specific to the learning of more refined (linguistic) expressions of bodily feeling.

Picture theory of meaning
The principal thesis of the *Tractatus* is that sentences, or their mental counterparts, are 'pictures' of facts. Propositions form pictures, the elementary components of which correspond to states in the world they depict. The structure of any factual (true) picture-sentence must be the same as the structure of the situation depicted in the factual world.

Polysemous meaning
As a methodological aim of Karl Kraus's '*Sprachkritik*,' it is the demonstration of the multiplicity of meanings of words. Such demonstrations, according to Kraus, would reveal possible reasons for word-use, the hypocrisy of the speaker, and so on. In his later philosophy in particular, Wittgenstein applied the same idea to the domain of philosophy in order to reveal the sources of philosophical problems.

Positivism
A cluster of philosophical claims about the scope and possibilities of obtaining knowledge and an attitude toward the place of human beings in the world. Positivists argue for the restriction of claims to knowledge to what can be observed. The 'positivistic attitude' still can be found in psychology.

Powers (natural and acquired)
A power is what some stuff (an object, compound and so on) can do. For example, a falling meteor can cause an impact crater. Natural powers are innate abilities for people and animals to do things. For example, human children are born with a rooting reflex that facilitates finding the breast, whereupon the sucking reflex takes over. Acquired powers are abilities gained through development and training. At least to a significant extent, language use in humans is an example.

Primary and secondary qualities
Primary qualities of sensation, for example, are sensations of shape that resemble the 'real' qualities of material things. Secondary qualities (e.g. taste and color) do not resemble the states of material things that cause people to experience them.

Primary language-game
A language-game in which one participant (a child) is trained to acquire a certain vocabulary and means of linguistic expression to take part in more complex (secondary) language-games. Certain vocabularies are acquired in primary language-games

and, in the case of the vocabularies of bodily feeling, these games are based on natural expressions.

Private-language argument (PLA)

A collection of remarks (or 'arguments') running from §§234 to 315 in PI that challenge prevailing views about the relationship between putative mental states and processes, on one hand, and behavior on the other hand. Much of the PLA focuses on bodily feelings, although at points Wittgenstein considers visual experience. A private language would be used to name private events. But naming private events (e.g. 'pain') requires rule-following and standards of correctness in order for names to be meaningful and useful in communication. A private language of the sort described by Wittgenstein would make it impossible for the private-language user to be sure s/he has accurately identified a bodily feeling correctly or incorrectly. The words of such a language would be unintelligible to anyone and everyone. Wittgenstein suggests that meaningful communication about bodily feelings is possible as a result of primary language-games, which are based on the substitution of natural expressions with words, and along with words rules for word use and standards of correctness. Among other topics in psychology, the PLA has ramifications for language-learning and the very idea of cognitive representations.

Proposition

For the purposes of this text, a proposition is a putative fact-stating sentence. It is a sentence 'about' something. The term has been used in many ways by philosophers, and Wittgenstein, in the *Tractatus*, was at pains to articulate his own idea of 'proposition.'

Reductionism and reductive explanation

Phenomena explained at one level of analysis are explained in terms of purported phenomena at a more fundamental level of analysis. So, for example, a mental state is explained in terms of material brain states. This would be a reductive explanation of what is necessary and sufficient for the mental state to occur. Another example is Wittgenstein's denial that social regularities can be explained by reducing those regularities to causal mechanisms.

Reification

It involves thinking of an abstract notion as if it were a real thing. We might think of 'anxiety,' for example, as a mental entity of sorts. From a Wittgensteinian perspective, this move makes 'anxiety' appear as if it is a noun. However, there are only anxious people and with caution we might describe certain animals as being anxious. (See also 'Grammar (surface and depth).')

Request formats

In Jerome Bruner's work, they are ways of intentionally expressing wants or needs. Bruner's account of the development of such expressions shows there are three types of requests (for objects, role relationships, and to achieve goals). (See 'Primary language-game.')

Rule-following and acting in accordance with a rule
Rule-following involves acting on an explicit instruction, a rule-expression. Acting in accordance with a rule involves behaving in an orderly way while carrying on some practice. Both are normative actions because they involve standards of correctness.

Secondary language-game
More complex language-games that are not based on natural expressions, but on primary language-games. 'Putting on a brave face' while in pain is an example. One could never put on a brave face without already having mastered the primary language-games that involve learning to use the word 'pain' or related words.

Sense
Compare the structures 'Dog bites man' and 'Man bites dog.' Here, 'bites' denotes an action and is one of the attributes of the dog or the man. But it also serves to link the biting dog and the bitten man to a specific relationship. Thus the structural significance of 'bites' expresses the direction, or *sense*, of the relation between a biting being and a bitten being. Like language-game in Wittgenstein's later philosophy, the specific meaning of 'sense' in his early philosophy is still debated. But for our purposes, 'sense' is a kind of directionality.

Showing
The doctrine of showing in the *Tractatus* emerges from the question of how the truth of a proposition can be known. Since propositions consist of words in certain relational structures and since facts consist of objects in certain relational structures, Wittgenstein proposed that the 'match' between propositions and facts must be shown. Otherwise, illustrating the match between proposition and fact would take him to another level of analysis.

Sraffa's gesture
The gesture made to Wittgenstein by the Italian economist Pierro Sraffa in 1929. It consisted in Sraffa brushing the back of his fingers on one hand upward and across the underpart of his chin while saying 'What is the logical form of *that*?' The gesture called into question Wittgenstein's Tractarian assertion that true and meaningful propositions have a logical form that mirrors the form of things in the world to which they refer. Although Sraffa's gesture had no logical form and was neither true nor false, it was meaningful.

Stage-setting
Not to be equated with context, it is one form of context that makes meaning and understanding possible. A single action can be interpreted in more than one way. A definition, for example the name of a piece in the game of chess, can be understood only if the person to whom the definition is directed already understands the concept of 'game.' In other words, having already witnessed and/or participated in games provides the stage-setting for understanding a definition such as 'this is the king.'

Substitution principle
A term we derive from PI §244, where Wittgenstein suggests that a verbal expression of pain 'replaces crying and does not describe it.' The principle begins with the observation that human beings are born with a repertoire of natural expressions of feeling (or emotion) that are understood by others. This repertoire is replaced (substituted) by linguistic expressions through training. However, this substitution does not result in expressions that are descriptive. The linguistic utterance is expressive.

Surveyable representation
A way of characterizing a goal of Wittgenstein's later philosophical method. 'Surveyable,' which calls to mind Wittgenstein's engineering background, is similar to his use of 'overview' (*Übersicht*). A survey, or surview, involves examining or inspecting in a comprehensive way the grammar of our language and implies determining the boundaries, area and so on of a landscape of word use. The 'representation' so produced will be complete in so far as it reveals the source of philosophical problems of interest. Surveyable representation is connected with Wittgenstein's methodological goal of 'perspicuous representation' (PI §122).

Tautology
A proposition that is necessarily true due to its logical structure; for example, p or not-p ('It is sunny or it is not sunny'). In the *Tractatus*, Wittgenstein thought tautologies express the rules for use of the logical symbols with which complex propositions are constructed. Thus, the tautology 'p or not-p' expresses a rule for the correct use of 'not.' In his later philosophy, Wittgenstein generalized this insight to ordinary language.

Threshold fallacy
When faced with an apparently intractable philosophical problem in the form of a question or set of questions, we take for granted the legitimacy of the question. This is crossing the threshold, and doing so unknowingly constitutes the fallacy. According to Wittgenstein, we must retrace our thinking back across the threshold to consider our unthinking acceptance of the question's intelligibility. Usually, we will find the source of our unthinking acceptance in our use of language.

Truth-table
A formal device that displays, in schematic form, the way the true or falsity of a proposition depends on the truth or falsity of is components (e.g. conjunctions such as 'and' in 'The roses are blooming and the delphiniums are blooming.').

Understanding
The 'Augustinian picture' of language implies that understanding consists in connecting words with objects signified by words. A private essence links words and objects to attain meaning. Mentalists suppose that meaning is an idea or picture in the mind. Understanding a word, then, consists in matching its written (material) form or spoken sound with a mental picture or idea. For Wittgenstein, in his later

philosophy, meaning is revealed in word use, and meaning and understanding are linked inextricably. Understanding is not a 'match' between word and object or word and idea. By extension, understanding is not an experience. Rather, it is an *ability* that is exhibited in what we do in exercising skills and abilities, such as using words. Thus understanding has clear connections with rule-following.

Verificationism and verifiability criterion

The philosophical position asserting that, in order for propositions to be considered 'meaningful,' methods must be available to test their truth through observation. As stated by Carnap, the verifiability criterion holds that if a meaningful proposition is true, its truth can be verified by observation. The *Tractatus* was one example of verificationism because it proposed that that all meaningful propositions are truth-functions of simple observation statements.

Bibliography

Ackerman, R.J. (1988). *Wittgenstein's City*. Amherst, MA: University of Massachusetts Press.

Ajzen, I. (1991). The theory of planned behavior. *Organizational Behavior and Human Decision Processes*, **50**, 179–211.

Anderson, J.R. (1993). *Rules of the Mind*. Hillsdale, NJ: Lawrence Erlbaum.

Anscombe, G.E.M. (1957). *Intention*. Ithaca, NY: Cornell University Press.

Aristotle (1960). *Metaphysics* (R. Hope, trans.). Ann Arbor: The University of Michigan Press.

Arregui, J.V. (1996). Descartes and Wittgenstein on emotions. *International Philosophical Quarterly*, **36**, 319–34.

Saint Augustine (1961). *Confessions* (R.S. Pine-Coffin, trans.). New York: Penguin.

Austin, J.L. (1975). *How to do things with words* (2nd edn). Cambridge, MA: Harvard University Press.

Averill, J.R. (1974). An analysis of psychophysiological symbolism and its influence on theories of emotion. *Journal for the Theory of Social Behaviour*, **4**, 147–90.

Baddeley, A. (1998). *Human Memory: Theory and practice*. Boston and London: Allyn and Bacon.

Baker, G.P. (1991). *Philosophical investigations* section 122: Neglected aspects. In R.L. Arrington and H.-J. Glock (eds), *Wittgenstein's Philosophical Investigations: Text and context* (pp. 35–68). London: Routledge.

Baker, G.P. and Hacker, P.M.S. (1980). *Wittgenstein: Understanding and meaning. An analytical commentary on the Philosophical Investigations* (Vol. 1). Oxford: Blackwell.

Baker, G.P. and Hacker, P.M.S. (1982). The grammar of psychology: Wittgenstein's Bemerkungen Über die Philosophie der Psychologie. *Language & Communication*, **2**, 227–44.

Baker, G.P. and Hacker, P.M. (1984). *Scepticism, Rules, and Language*. Oxford: Blackwell.

Baker, G.P. and Hacker, P.M.S. (1985). *Wittgenstein: Rules, grammar and necessity. An analytical commentary on the Philosophical Investigations* (Vol. 2). Oxford: Blackwell.

Barsalou, L.W. (1995). ACT-R: Cognitive theory's simple, elegant tool. Review of J.R. Anderson's (1993) *Rules of the Mind*. *American Scientist*, **83**, 185–6.

Barnett, W.E. (1990). The rhetoric of grammar: Understanding Wittgenstein's method. *Metaphilosophy*, **21**, 43–66.

Bartley, W.W. (1985), *Wittgenstein*, 2nd edn. LaSalle, IL: Open Court.

Bedford, E. (1986). Emotions and statements about them. In R. Harré (ed.), *The Social Construction of Emotions* (pp. 15–31). Oxford: Blackwell.

Billig, M. (1987). *Arguing and Thinking*. Cambridge: Cambridge University Press.

Black, M. (1964). *A Companion to Wittgenstein's Tractatus*. Ithaca, NY: Cornell University Press.

Bodine, J.F. (1981). Paradigms of truthful literary and artistic expressivity. Karl Kraus and Vienna at the turn of the century. *The Germanic Review*, **56**(2), 41–50.

Bodine, J.F. (1989). Karl Kraus, Ludwig Wittgenstein and 'poststructural' paradigms of textual understanding. *Modern Austrian Literature*, **22**(3/4), 143–85.

Boltzmann, L. (1974). On the development of the methods of theoretical physics in recent times. In B. McGuinness (ed.), *Ludwig Boltzmann: Theoretical physics and philosophical problems* (pp. 77–100). Dordrecht, Holland: D. Reidel. (Original work published 1899)

Brenner, W.H. (1999). *Wittgenstein's Philosophical Investigations*. Albany: SUNY Press.

Brown, R. and Gilman, A. (1960). The pronouns of power and solidarity. In T.A. Sebeok (ed.), *Style and Language* (pp. 253–77). Cambridge, MA: MIT Press.

Bruner, J.S. (1983a). *Child's Talk: Learning to use language*. New York: Norton.

Bruner, J.S. (1983b). *In Search of Mind*. New York: Harper and Row.

Bruner, J.S. and Goodman, C.C. (1947). Value and need as organizing factors in perception. *Journal of Abnormal and Social Psychology*, **42**, 33–44.

Bruner, J.S. and Postman, L. (1947). Emotional selectivity in perception and reaction. *Journal of Personality*, **16**, 69–77.

Bruner, J.S. and Postman, L. (1949). On the perception of incongruity: A paradigm. *Journal of Personality*, **18**, 206–23.

Bruner, J.S. and Sherwood, V. (1976). Early rule structure: The case of 'peekaboo.' In R. Harré (ed.), *Life Sentences* (pp. 55–62). London: John Wiley & Sons.

Budd, M. (1989). *Wittgenstein's Philosophy of Psychology*. London: Routledge.

Burr, V. (2003). *Social Constructionism*. Milton Keynes: Open University Press.

Carnap, R. (1959). Überwindung der Metaphysik durch Logische Analyse der Sprache [The elimination of metaphysics through logical analysis of language]. In A.J. Ayer (ed.), *Logical Positivism* (pp. 41–52). Free Press of Glencoe. (Original work published in *Erkenntnis*, Vol. II, 1932.)

Chapman, M. and Dixon, R.A. (eds) (1987). *Meaning and the Growth of Understanding: Wittgenstein's significance for developmental psychology*. Heidelberg: Springer- Verlag.

Chomsky, N. (1969). Some empirical assumptions in modern philosophy of language. In S. Morgenbesser, P. Suppes and M. White (eds), *Philosophy, Science, and Method: Essays in honor of Ernest Nagel* (pp. 260–85). New York: St Martin's Press.

Churchland, P.M. (1981). Eliminative materialism and the prepositional attitudes. *Journal of Philosophy*, **78**, 67–90.

Cole, M. (1996). *Cultural Psychology: A once and future discipline*. Cambridge, MA: Harvard University Press.

Comte, A. (1835). *Cours de philosophie positive* [Course in positive philosophy]. Paris: Borrani et Droz.

Coulter, J. (1979). *The Social Construction of Mind*. London and Basingstoke: Macmillan.

Coulter, J. (1997). Neural Cartesianism: Comments on the epistemology of the cognitive sciences. In D.M. Johnson and C.E. Erneling (eds), *The Future of the Cognitive Revolution* (pp. 293–301). Oxford: Oxford University Press.

Coulter, J. (1983), *Rethinking Cognitive Theory*. New York: St Martin's Press.

Danziger, K. (1990). *Constructing the Subject: Historical origins of psychological research*. Cambridge: Cambridge University Press.

Darwin, C. (1872). *The Expression of the Emotions in Man and Animals*. London: Murray.

Davidson, D. (2001). *Essays on Actions and Events*. Oxford: Clarendon Press.

Descartes, R. (1958). *The Passions of the Soul* (S. Voss, trans.). Indianapolis, IN: Hackett. (Original work published 1649.)

Dewey, J. (1971). The theory of emotion. In J.A. Boydston (ed.), *John Dewey: The early works, 1882–1898* (pp. 152–88). Carbondale, IL: Southern Illinois University Press. (Original work published 1894.)

Dixon, R.A. and Bäckman, L. (1995). *Compensating for Psychological Deficits and Declines*. Mahwah, NJ: Erlbaum.

Dreyfus, H. and Dreyfus, S. (1986). *Mind over Machine: The power of human expertise in the era of the computer*. New York: Free Press.

Ebbinghaus, H. (1864). *Memory: A contribution to experimental psychology* (H.A. Ruger and C.E. Bussenius, trans.). New York: Dover. (Original work published 1885.)

Erneling, C.E. (1993). *Understanding Language Acquisition: The framework of learning*. Albany, NY: State University of New York Press.

Fehr, B. and Russell, J.A. (1984). Concept of emotion viewed from a prototype perspective. *Journal of Experimental Psychology*, **113**, 464–86.

Feyerabend, P. (1978). Wittgenstein's Philosophical Investigations. In K.T. Fann (ed.), *Ludwig Wittgenstein: The man and his philosophy* (pp. 214–50). Sussex: Harvester Press.

Finch, H.L. (1995). *Wittgenstein*. Rockport, MA: Element Books.

Fodor, J.G. (1975). *The Language of Thought*. Cambridge, MA: Harvard University Press.

Fogelin, R.J. (1987). *Wittgenstein* (2nd edn). London: Routledge.

Frijda, N. (1988). The laws of emotion. *American Psychologist*, **43**, 349–58.

Frijda, N. (1992). The empirical status of the laws of emotion. *Cognition and Emotion*, **6**, 467–77.

Gardner, H. (1985). *The Mind's New Science: A history of the cognitive revolution*. New York: Basic Books.

Garfinkel, H. (1967). *Studies in Ethnomethodology*. Englewood Cliffs, NJ: Prentice-Hall.

Gibson, J.J. (1965). *The Senses Considered as Perceptual Systems*. Boston: Houghton Mifflin.

Gillies, D. (1993). *Philosophy of Science in the Twentieth Century: Four central themes*. Oxford: Blackwell.

Glock, H.-G. (1996). *A Wittgenstein Dictionary*. Oxford: Blackwell.

Gregory, R.L. (1970). *The Intelligent Eye*. London: Weidenfeld and Nicolson.

Gregory, R.L. (1998). *The Eye and the Brain*. Oxford: Oxford University Press.

Greve, W. (2001). Traps and gaps in the psychological explanation of action. *Psychological Review*, **108**, 435–51.

Hacker, P.M.S. (1993a). *Wittgenstein: Meaning and mind. An analytical commentary on the Philosophical Investigations* (Vol. 3, Part I, Essays). Oxford: Blackwell.

Hacker, P.M.S. (1993b). *Wittgenstein: Meaning and mind. An analytical commentary on the Philosophical Investigations* (Vol. 3, Part II, Exegesis). Oxford: Blackwell.

Hacker, P.M.S. (1996). *Wittgenstein: Mind and will. An analytical commentary on the Philosophical Investigations* (Vol. 4). Oxford: Blackwell.

Harris, P.L. (1989). *Children and Emotion*. Oxford: Basil Blackwell.

Hertz, H. (1956). *The Principles of Mechanics* (D.E. Jones and J.T. Walley, trans.). London: Macmillan. (Original work published 1899.)

Hilmy, S.S. (1987). *The Later Wittgenstein: The emergence of a new philosophical method*. Oxford: Blackwell.

Hintikka, M.B. and Hintikka, J. (1986). *Investigating Wittgenstein*. Oxford: Blackwell.

Holiday, A. (1988). *Moral Powers: Normative necessity in language and history*. London: Routledge.

Hume, D. (1978). *A Treatise of Human Nature* (2nd edn). Oxford: Clarendon Press (Original work published 1739.)

Jacobs, W.W. (1902). *The Lady and the Barge*. London and New York: Harpers.

James, W. (1983). *The Principles of Psychology*. Cambridge, MA: Harvard University Press. (Original work published 1890.)

Janik, A. and Toulmin, S. (1973). *Wittgenstein's Vienna*. New York: Simon & Schuster.

Johnson, D.M. (1997). Good old-fashioned cognitive science: Does it have a future? In D.M. Johnson and C.E. Erneling (eds), *The Future of the Cognitive Revolution* (pp. 13–14). Oxford: Oxford University Press.

Just, M.A. and Carpenter, P.A. (1980). *The Psychology of Reading and Language Comprehension*. Boston: Allyn and Bacon.

Kenny, A. (1963). *Action, Emotion and Will: Studies in philosophical psychology*. London: Routledge & Kegan Paul.

Kenny, A. (1989). *The Metaphysics of Mind*. Oxford: Clarendon Press.

Köhler, W. (1947). *Gestalt Psychology*. New York: Liveright Publishing. (Original work published 1929.)

Laird, J.D. and Bresler, C. (1992). The process of emotional experience: A self-perception theory. In M.S. Clark (ed.), *Emotion: Review of personality and social psychology, Vol. 13* (pp. 213–34). Newbury Park, CA: SAGE.

Lapierre, R.T. (1934). Attitudes versus action. *Social Forces*, **13**, 230–37.

Lazarus, R.S. (1984). On the primacy of cognition. *American Psychologist*, **39**, 124–9.

Locke, J. (1972). *An Essay Concerning Human Understanding*. London: Dent. (Original work published 1690.)

MacIntyre, A. (1992). Colors, cultures and practices. In P.A. French, T.E. Vehling, and H.K. Wettstein (eds), *The Wittgenstein Legacy: Midwest studies in philosophy* (Vol. 17) (pp. 1–23). Notre Dame, IN: University of Notre Dame Press.

Mach, E. (1959). *The Analysis of Sensations and the Relation of the Physical to the Psychical* (trans. From the 1st German edn by C.M. Williams, revised and supplemented from the 5th German edn by Sydney Waterlow). New York: Dover. (Original work published 1886.)

Malcolm, N. (1958). *Wittgenstein: A memoir with a biographical sketch by G.H. von Wright*. London: Oxford University Press.

Malcolm, N. (1995). *Wittgensteinian Themes: Essays 1978–1989*. Ithaca, NY: Cornell University Press.

McDonough, R. (1989). Towards a non-mechanistic theory of meaning. *Mind*, **98**, 1–21.

McGinn, M. (1997). *Wittgenstein and the Philosophical Investigations*. London: Routledge.

McGuinness, B. (1982), *Wittgenstein and his Times*. Oxford: Blackwell.

McGuinness, B. (1988). *Wittgenstein: A life. Young Ludwig 1889–1921*. Berkeley, CA: The University of California Press.

McIntosh, D.N. (1996). Facial feedback hypothesis: Evidence, implications, and directions. *Motivation and Emotion*, **20**, 121–47.

Meltzoff, A.N. and Moore, M.K. (1983). Newborn infants imitate adult facial features. *Child Development*, **54**, 702–9.

Middleton, D. and Edwards, D. (1990). *Collective Remembering*. London: SAGE.

Moghaddam, F. (2004), *Great Ideas in Psychology*. New York: Worth.

Monk, R. (1990). *Wittgenstein: The duty of genius*. New York: Penguin Books.

Mühlhäusler, P. and Harré, R. (1990). *Pronouns and People*. Oxford: Blackwell.

O'Shaughnessy, B. (1980). *The Will: A dual aspect theory*. Cambridge: Cambridge University Press.

Parrott, W.G. and Harré, R. (1991). Smedslundian suburbs in the city of language: The case of embarrassment. *Psychological Inquiry*, **2**, 358–61.

Parrott, W.G. and Harré, R. (1996). *The Emotions*. Thousand Oaks, CA: SAGE.

Perloff, M. (1996). *Wittgenstein's Ladder: Poetic language and the strangeness of the ordinary*. Chicago: University of Chicago Press.

Peters, R.S. (1962). Emotions and the category of passivity. *Aristotelian Society Proceedings*, **62**, 117–34.

Peters, R.S. (1969). *The Concept of Motivation*. London: Routledge & Kegan Paul.

Peterson, D. (1990). *Wittgenstein's Early Philosophy: Three sides of the mirror*. Toronto: University of Toronto Press.

Pitcher, G. (1964). *The Philosophy of Wittgenstein*. Englewood Cliffs, NJ: Prentice-Hall.

Pittenger, D.J. (2003). *Behavioral Research: Design and analysis*. New York: McGraw-Hill.

Rachlin, H. (1992). Teleological behaviorism. *American Psychologist*, **47**, 1371–82.

Russell, B. (1918). The philosophy of logical atomism. *The Monist*, **28**, 495–527.

Ryle, G. (1949). *The Concept of Mind*. New York: Barnes and Noble.

Schachter, S. and Singer, J.E. (1962). Cognitive, social, and physiological determinants of emotional state. *Psychological Review*, **69**, 379–99.

Schönberg, A. (1950). *Style and Idea*. New York: Philosophical Library.

Schulte, J. (1992). *Wittgenstein: An introduction*. Albany, NY: State University of New York Press.

Schulte, J. (1993). *Experience and Expression: Wittgenstein's philosophy of psychology*. Oxford: Clarendon Press.

Schopenhauer, A. (1995). *The World as Will and Idea* (J. Berman, trans.). London: Dent. (Original work published 1818.)

Siegler, R.S. (1998). *Children's Thinking* (3rd edn). Upper Saddle River, NJ: Prentice-Hall.

Skinner, B.F. (1974). *About Behaviorism*. New York: Knopf.

Skinner, B.F. (1986). Why I am not a cognitive psychologist. In T.J. Knapp and L.C. Robertson (eds), *Approaches to Cognition: Contrasts and controversies* (pp. 79–90). Hillsdale, NJ: Lawrence Erlbaum.

Smedslund, J. (1988). *Psycho-logic*. Berlin: Springer-Verlag.

Stern, C. and Stern, W. (1999). *Recollection, Testimony, and Lying in Early Childhood* (J.T. Lamiell, trans.). Washington, DC: American Psychological Association. (Original work published 1909.)

Stern, D.G. (1991). Models of memory: Wittgenstein and cognitive science. *Philosophical Psychology*, **4**, 203–18.

Stern, D.G. (1995). *Wittgenstein on Mind and Language*. Oxford: Oxford University Press.

Stern, D.G. (1996). The availability of Wittgenstein's philosophy. In H. Sluga and D.G. Stern (eds), *The Cambridge Companion to Wittgenstein* (pp. 442–76). Cambridge: Cambridge University Press.

Stern, W. (1939). *General Psychology from a Personalistic Standpoint* (H.D. Spoerl, trans.). New York: Macmillan.

Thorndike, E.L. (1911). *Animal Intelligence: Experimental studies*. New York: Macmillan.

Tolman, E.C. (1932). *Purposive Behavior in Animals and Men*. New York: Century.

Tomkins, S.S. (1982). Affect theory. In P. Ekman (ed.), *Emotion in the Human Face* (2nd edn). Cambridge: Cambridge University Press.

Turing, A. (1950). Computing machinery and intelligence, *Mind*, **49**, 433–60.

Vygotsky, L.S. (1962). *Thought and Language*. Cambridge, MA: MIT Press.

Watson, J.B. (1919). *Psychology from the Standpoint of a Behaviorist*. Philadelphia: J.B. Lippincott.

Watson, J.B. (1925). *Behaviorism*. New York: People's Institute.

Wegener, A.L. (1912). Die Entstehung der Kontinente. *Geologische Rundschau*, **3**, 276–92.

Werhane, P.H. (1992). *Skepticism, Rules and Private Languages*. New Jersey and London: Humanities Press.

Wierzbicka, A. (1992). *Semantics, Culture and Cognition*. New York and Oxford: Oxford University Press.

Wierzbicka, A. (1999). *Emotions Across Languages and Cultures: Diversity and universals*. Cambridge: Cambridge University Press.

Wild, J. (1969). *The Radical Empiricism of William James*. Garden City, NY: Anchor Books.

Wilson, A.D. (1989). Hertz, Boltzmann and Wittgenstein reconsidered. *Studies in History and Philosophy of Science*, **20**, 245–63.

Winograd, T. and Flores, F. (1986). *Understanding Computers and Cognition: A foundation for design*. Norwood, NJ: Ablex.

Wittgenstein, L. (1961). *Tractatus Logico-philosophicus* (D.R. Pears and B.F. McGuinness, trans.). London: Routledge & Kegan Paul. (Original work published 1921.)

Wittgenstein, L. (1953). *Philosophical Investigations* (G.E.M. Anscombe, trans.). Oxford: Blackwell.

Wittgenstein, L. (1958). *The Blue and Brown Books*. Oxford: Blackwell.

Wittgenstein, L. (1967). *Zettel* (G.H. von Wright and G.E.M. Anscombe, eds; G.E.M. Anscombe, trans.). Oxford: Blackwell.

Wittgenstein, L. (1972). *On Certainty* (D. Paul and G.E.M. Anscombe, trans.). New York: Harper & Row.

Wittgenstein, L. (1977). *Remarks on Colour* (G.E.M. Anscombe, ed.; L.L. McAlister and M. Schättle, trans.). Berkeley and Los Angeles, CA: University of California Press.

Wittgenstein, L. (1979). *Notebooks 1914–1916* (2nd edn) (G.H. von Wright and G.E.M. Anscombe, eds; G.E.M. Anscombe, trans.). Oxford: Blackwell.

Wittgenstein, L. (1980). *Culture and Value* (G.H. von Wright, ed.; P. Winch, trans.). Chicago: University of Chicago Press.

Wittgenstein, L. (1980a). *Remarks on the Philosophy of Psychology* (Vol. 1) (C.G. Luckhardt and M.A.E. Aue, trans.). Oxford: Blackwell.

Wittgenstein, L. (1980b). *Remarks on the Philosophy of Psychology* (Vol. 2) (C.G. Luckhardt and M.A.E. Aue, trans.). Oxford: Blackwell.

Wittgenstein, L. (1982). *Last Writings on the Philosophy of Psychology: Preliminary studies for Part II of Philosophical Investigations* (Vol. 1) (G.H. von Wright and H. Nyman, eds; C.G. Luckhardt and M.A.E. Aue, trans.). Oxford: Blackwell.

Wittgenstein, L. (1993). 'Philosophie': Sections 86–93 (pp. 405–35) of the so-called 'Big Typescript' (H. Nyman, ed.; C.G. Luckhardt and M.A.E. Aue, trans.). In L. Wittgenstein, *Philosophical Occasions: 1912–1951* (J.C. Klagge and A. Nordmann, eds) (pp. 160–99). Indianapolis, IN: Hackett.

Wolpe, J. (1978). Cognition and causation in human behavior and its therapy. *American Psychologist*, **33**, 437–46.

Wundt, W. (1912). *Elements of the Völkerpsychologie*. Leipzig: Alfred Kröner Verlag.

Index

Note: Only those authors whose work is described explicitly are recorded in the index. Citations only are referenced in the bibliography

causality? 118
mental states? 119–20, 123
paradox of interpretation 124–7
propositional model 114
training 120
rules
ACT system 112
acting in accordance with 118
action, no gap 127
action-correctness 130, 136
causes 129, 131
contingencies 129–30, 131
conventions 9
expressed in practices 115
for the use of a word 113
grammatical 135–6
guided by 117
in cultures 116
knowledge displayed in correct
performance 117
multiple interpretations 125
not coercive 121
obeyed blindly 132
skills 113
social embedment 131
training 125–7, 130, 132
use in AI 112
Russell, B.A.O. 22–3, 43, 46, 73

Schachter, S. 154, 247
Schönberg, A. 33, 41
science
as classification and model-making 8
seeing 266
a likeness 274
as 278
aspects 275–8
aspects, interpretations 276–7
self, uses of 202
self-perception theory 246
sensations
identity criteria 194
mental entities 264
naming? 193
sense 293
Sherwood, V. 204
showing 46–7, 293
sign to word
deriving 96–8
no intermediary 98, 101
not causation 99–100
simple objects, necessity for 35
Singer, J.E. 154, 247
skills and abilities
brain process 128

mental processes 128
regressive explanations 85, 86
use signs 84
Skinner, B.F. 11, 56, 113
Smedslund J. 137
spectrum, Newton's additional color 135
Sprachkritik 27, 32
Sraffa, P. (and his 'gesture') 23, 293
stage-setting 70–71, 293
standards of correctness 113
stealing to order, 216
Stern, C. 224–6
Stern, W. 224–6, 239
structure, 44
substitution principle 188, 294
surveyable representation and 'surview' 5,
101–2, 177, 294
as philosophical method 168

tautologies 51, 294
temperature, concepts of 142
therapy, philosophical 151, 290
third-person descriptive talk 189–90,
271
and the emotions 247, 257–8, 260
and perceived changes 276
thought
and language 169–71
and feelings of others 183
as brain states 171–2
as mental entities 170–71
threshold fallacy 106–7, 294
Tolman, E.G. 55, 56
Tompkins, S.S. 245
Tractatus Logico-philosophicus Chapter 3
passim
transparent white 268–70
truth-table 47–50, 294
Turing, A. 59, 60
types and particulars 208, 210

understanding 86, 175–6, 294

values, ethical, religious etc. 47, 54
verificationism 34, 294
Vienna Circle 23, 34, 54, 56
visual room 274–5

Watson, J.B. 11, 55–6, 148
willing
development of 240–41
grammar of 234–9
psychic instrument 237
trying 234, 238
wishing 236

For Product Safety Concerns and Information please contact our EU
representative GPSR@taylorandfrancis.com
Taylor & Francis Verlag GmbH, Kaufingerstraße 24, 80331 München, Germany

www.ingramcontent.com/pod-product-compliance
Lightning Source LLC
Chambersburg PA
CBHW080230270326
41926CB00020B/4193

9 781138 358621